13⁹⁵

Sport and Society

Series Editors
Benjamin G. Rader
Randy Roberts

D1198664

Books in the Series Sport and Society

A Sporting Time: New York City and the Rise
of Modern Athletics, 1820–70
Melvin L. Adelman

Sandlot Seasons: Sport in Black Pittsburgh
Rob Ruck

West Ham United: The Making of a Football Club
Charles Korr

Beyond the Ring: The Role of Boxing in American Society
Jeffrey T. Sammons

John L. Sullivan and His America
Michael T. Isenberg

Television and National Sport:
The United States and Britain
Joan M. Chandler

The Creation of American Team Sports:
Baseball and Cricket, 1838–72
George B. Kirsch

City Games: The Evolution of American Urban Society
and the Rise of Sports
Steven A. Riess

Reprint Editions

The Nazi Olympics
Richard D. Mandell

Sports in the Western World
William J. Baker

City Games

STEVEN A. RIESS

City Games

The Evolution of American Urban Society and the Rise of Sports

University of Illinois Press
Urbana and Chicago

I am grateful to the Department of Special Collections, University Research Library, UCLA, for permission to quote from "Who Would Have Ever Dreamed," an oral interview with Norris Poulson; to Greenwood Press for permission to reproduce the maps from my book *Touching Base: Professional Baseball and American Culture in the Progressive Era* (1980), pp. 87, 89; to the University of Nebraska Press for permission to reproduce a map in *Detroit and the Problem of Order, 1830–1880* by John C. Schneider, copyright © 1980 by the University of Nebraska Press; and to the University of Chicago Press for permission to reproduce a map in Harold M. Mayer and Richard C. Wade, *Chicago: The Making of a Metropolis* (1969), p. 101. Permission to utilize material I previously published elsewhere was granted by Scholarly Resources, Inc., for "Sports and Machine Politics in New York City, 1870–1920," in *The Making of Urban America*, ed. Raymond A. Mohl (1988), and by the *International Journal of the History of Sport* for "Only the Ring was Square: Frankie Carbo and the Underworld Control of American Boxing," 5 (May 1988).

1 2 3 4 5 P C 5 4 3 2 1

This book is printed on acid-free paper.

Illini Books edition, 1991
© 1989 by the Board of Trustees of the University of Illinois
Manufactured in the United States of America

Library of Congress Cataloging-in-Publication Data

Riess, Steven A.

    City games : the evolution of American urban society and the rise of sports / Steven A. Riess.
      p.   cm. — (Sport and Society)
    ISBN 0-252-01573-8 (cloth : alk. paper)
    ISBN 0-252-06216-7 (paper : alk. paper)
    1. Sports—United States—History—19th century. 2. Sports—United States—History—20th century. 3. Labor and laboring classes—United States—Recreation—History. 4. Sports—Economic aspects—United States—History. 5. Sports—Social aspects—United States—History. 6. City and town life—United States—History.
I. Title. II. Series.
GV583.R54 1989
796'.0973—dc19

88–17346
CIP

To Tobi, for all the right reasons

Contents

Tables

Maps

Acknowledgments

This book is an outgrowth of my previous studies in American sport history and, in many ways, culminates nearly two decades of work in that field. I have accumulated many intellectual and other debts in the course of these years and am pleased to have the opportunity to publicly thank my benefactors. Richard Wade and Mark Haller first drew my attention to the relationship between sport and urban politics, crime and spatial relationships, while Neil Harris taught me that good writing is re-writing. Harvey Graff first encouraged me to assay an overview of American sport history, which in the course of time changed its focus into this analysis of urban sport. I have received invaluable assistance from Rudolph Haerle, Jr., who made available to me unpublished raw data from questionnaires he sent to former major league baseball players, from George Kirsch, who permitted me to read his recently published study of nineteenth-century team sports prior to publication, from Ted Vincent, who provided unpublished data on nineteenth-century baseball executives as well as an unpublished essay on sport and the labor movement, from Thomas Karnes, who shared his unpublished research on professional baseball parks, and from Horst Ueberhorst, David Q. Voigt, and John Cumming. Enormous assistance was provided by librarians and archivists at the New York Public Library; the National Baseball Library, Cooperstown, New York; the Museum of the City of New York; the Chicago Historical Society; Special Collections, Regenstein Library, University of Chicago; Special Collections, University Research Library, UCLA; and the Hebrew Union College. Special thanks must go to Lillian Matheson, the interlibrary librarian at Northeastern Illinois University, and Evangeline Mistaras, a remarkable reference librarian, also at Northeastern. Sections of the work encompassed in this study were read by Joseph Morton, Melvin Adelman, Mark Haller, and David Johnson, whose critiques were greatly appreciated. I am very indebted to Stephen Hardy, who read two entire drafts and provided unusually sage evaluations and suggestions which greatly enhanced this project. I am also grateful to Larry Malley, editor-in-chief of the University of Illinois Press, for his constant interest in the project and his guidance; to the series editors, Randy Roberts and Benjamin Rader; and to my editor, Cynthia Mitchell, who despite whatever failings remain in my prose, did a superb job in enhancing the clarity of the original manuscript. I am also indebted to the Graphics Department at Northeastern Illinois, principally to the late David Morror and Norbert Szczygiel, who drew the maps.

Writing and researching takes up a great deal of time, and I am grateful to the chairmen of my department at Northeastern for providing me with a schedule that facilitated my scholarly efforts. The Committee on Research at UNI provided funds for a research trip to Los Angeles to study the history of the Los Angeles Coliseum, and the UNI Foundation provided funds to devote a summer to studying working-class sport. The University subsequently provided a sabbatical to further that work. I also wish to thank the National Endowment for the Humanities for awarding me a fellowship to take a year off from my teaching duties to complete most of my writing.

Finally I want to thank my family for their unfailing support. My parents, Herman and Litzi Riess, helped in a most tangible way by translating German material for me. As far as my children go, Jodi was old enough to be unconcerned, and Jamie and Jennifer were both born towards the end of the project. Having now played Mr. Mom for about five years, I can truthfully say that without their help this book would have been completed a couple of years earlier, although I am very happy with the way things turned out. Besides, I did get a few ideas in the middle of the night, while walking one or the other to sleep. My greatest debt is to my wife, Tobi, to whom the book is dedicated. She has been a patient editor and listener, a gentle companion, and my best friend.

City Games

Introduction:
Sport and the City

The evolution of the city, more than any other single factor, influenced the development of organized sport and recreational athletic pastimes in America. Nearly all contemporary major sports evolved, or were invented, in the city. The city was the place where sport became rationalized, specialized, organized, commercialized, and professionalized. The urban area has long been the primary site of sports facilities—of billiard parlors and bowling alleys; of gymnasiums, ballparks, and racetracks; and of both amateur sports clubs and professional teams. Most first-class athletes grew up and trained in the city.[1] However, the city's role in the rise of sport was not merely that of a passive geographic unit with a large residential population that provided potential players and spectators. As cities underwent the process of urbanization and evolved into larger and more complex units that became parts of regional and national systems of cities, they played an active role in the rise of sports. Cities were organic entities comprised of spatial dimensions, governments and laws, neighborhoods, social classes, ethnic groups, voluntary organizations, communication and transportation networks, and value systems and public behavior that interacted over time to create changes in the cities. Urban development directly influenced the sporting culture and athletic institutions of their inhabitants, which impacted on certain aspects of city building, which in turn shaped American sport.[2]

American sport history is largely the product of the constant, continuous interaction of the elements of urbanization—physical structure, social organizations, and value systems—with each other and with sport.

The city's physical structure consisted of its space, demographics, economy, and technology, while its social organizations were comprised of class, ethnic and racial groups, social institutions, and legal and political institutions. The urban value system encompassed individual and group attitudes, ideology, and behavior. By considering the city in a dual perspective—as the site of sport and also as an organic environment whose changing elements shaped and were shaped by sport, we can achieve a comprehensive and sophisticated understanding of the social mechanisms through which the dynamic evolution of urban society and its component elements influenced the direction of American sport.[3]

The enormous urban influence on sport can be tracked back to the Colonial era and the early Republic, when 95 percent of the population lived in rural areas. Even though most sporting pleasures occurred outside the first urban clusters and were enjoyed by rural folk, urban sites were the locus of the rise of organized and commercialized sport. The concentration of relatively large numbers of men in close proximity provided a potential market for publicans—the first sports promoters—to exploit and facilitated the formation of voluntary sports associations, established in emulation of the English gentry and their well-to-do counterparts in London. Furthermore, relationships developed between sport and city government in early America foreshadowed future patterns established when the process of city building accelerated after the 1820s. Thus while weak colonial municipal governments were not expected to facilitate sports beyond setting aside public space like the Boston Common for vigorous activities associated with training days, they were called upon to protect community norms and morality, maintain order, and prevent the pleasures of a few from interfering with commerce and the rights of the majority.[4] The accelerated pace of urbanization that began in the 1830s resulted in huge population increases in established cities and the creation of dozens of new cities. Rapid city development had a pervasive and critical impact on sport and all other urban institutions that transcended site, which had been so fundamentally important in the colonial and early American towns.

The purpose of this study is to identify and analyze the impact of city building upon sport in three different periods of American urban history: the walking city (1820–70), the industrial radial city (1870–1960), and the suburbanized metropolis (1945–80). Walking cities were relatively small, compact units in which pedestrianism was the principal mode of locomotion. Settled areas were no more than two miles from the center of town, land uses were unspecialized, vacant lots and quiet streets were plentiful, and the countryside was close by. This pattern first began to change in a few large cities by the mid-nineteenth century and soon after the Civil

War was largely supplanted by the industrialized radial city. The undifferentiated spatial arrangements of the walking city were dramatically altered by the annexation of outlying communities, accelerated population growth, rapidly rising property values, and the development of public transportation that facilitated access to the newly distant city limits. The result was a highly specialized use of urban space for commercial, industrial, and residential purposes. Housing was not only separated from work sites but divided itself into slums, zones of emergence, and well-to-do urban fringes. After World War II the radial city did not disappear but was greatly modified by the next stage in the on-going process of urbanization—suburbanization, characterized by middle-class white migration to suburbs (which since 1970 have had a larger population than the central cities), the expansion of racial ghettos in the inner city, the decline of the rustbelt, and the boom in the urban sunbelt.

Although the dynamics of the process differed over time and space, in those three time periods urbanization played a crucial role in shaping sport. In the walking city growing populations provided a greater pool of potential spectators and athletes, which encouraged profit-minded entrepreneurs to establish sports businesses to cater to sportsmen. Although spatial considerations were significant (but less than they would be in the future because most cities were still relatively compact and underdeveloped), far more crucial at this time was the creation of a positive sports ideology, a reaction to such features of urban growth as overcrowding, crime, alienation, disease, and a perceived decline in the quality of life. This rhetoric sanctioned team sports and nonviolent, gambling-free sports as an alternative to the vile amusements of the male bachelor subculture. Clean sports would promote morality, build character, enhance public health, and serve as a substitute for the lost world of small-town America and its values. The new creed provided strong encouragement and powerful justification for Americans, especially the sedentary, hard-working middle classes, to get involved in sport. The elite and the upper middle class led the way, forming status-oriented sports clubs that promoted athletic competition by sponsoring contests and securing playing sites for their restricted membership. New immigrants, anxious to sustain their cultural heritage among like-minded people, established ethnic sports clubs in urban villages.

As the walking city expanded into the radial city, spatial considerations became crucial. Urban land use grew highly specialized, and traditional playing areas were lost to development, limiting space for outdoor or indoor sports in congested urban cores, especially in comparison to the more spacious periphery. One response was the rise of a nation-wide municipal park movement, which promoted the construction of large suburban parks right after the Civil War, and, a generation later, a small parks and playground movement, which secured the building of modest facilities in inner-city neighborhoods. A second response to the need for recreational space was the establishment of private sites for athletics. In the late nineteenth century elite voluntary sports organizations built extravagant gymnasiums in downtown sections and lavish country clubs in the suburbs. Ethnic sports clubs also established private facilities, albeit on a more modest level, where they could also enjoy privacy and convivial social relations, and escape the city, if only temporarily.

Along with the development of public and private space for athletics came a boom in semipublic sports facilities—privately owned places in which the general public was welcome, usually for a fee. The smaller, more numerous businesses had equipment and space for participatory sports, primarily billiards or bowling, and were usually located in urban slums or zones of emergence, where they catered to a working-class clientele. Far more prominent, however, were the edifices devoted to commercialized spectator sports. The large size of urban populations, the improved interurban transportation systems, the rise of intra-urban mass transit, the familiarity of urban folk with paid entertainment, and, of course, the popularity of sports, encouraged entrepreneurs to commercialize sports. Racetracks and baseball fields were enclosed at the urban periphery, ideally on cheap sites near public transportation. The best tracks were expensively constructed edifices, but early ballparks, cheaply fabricated and dangerous, were not built to last. After the turn of the century, when the national pastime enjoyed a popularity boom, major league owners responded by constructing large, relatively permanent structures at the most accessible sites they could afford. While these outdoor structures required lots of space, the requirements for indoor arenas, which promoted different kinds of sports, were far more modest and thus they could be more centrally located. Indoor facilities varied widely in their quality and ambiance, from modest boxing gymnasiums located in poor neighborhoods to elegant, tall, multifunctional downtown arenas where events ranged from professional pedestrianism, cycling, and pugilism to the elite horse show and amateur track championships.

In the postbellum era the sports creed developed in response to urbanization broadened its scope and, by the turn of the century, was accepted as the conventional wisdom. The widely held attitudes about the positive functions of sport had an important impact, promoting athletic participation among middle-class urbanites and encouraging youth workers to employ sports, especially team games, as a means of socializing inner-city boys into proper American behavior. The rhetoric was also a significant factor in justifying the municipal park and playground movements.

Changes in the urban social organization in the radial city had particularly important consequences for sport. Many of those changes were products of the city's altered physical structure and evolving patterns of values and behavior. The most important developments in the industrial city's organization involved its social structure, ethnic associations, and political institutions. The different residential patterns, standards of living, and values among social classes had important implications for their athletic pleasures. Impoverished inner-city residents had little free time, discretionary income, or accessible playing space. Consequently, they were for years limited to cheap sports available in their immediate neighborhood; they had difficulty achieving proficency in sports that required a lot of expensive equipment or space; and until mass transit became cheap they were underrepresented at legal spectator sports contests located on the urban periphery. On the other hand, in the late nineteenth century rich urbanites were encouraged to participate in sport as a means of escaping the crowded, unhealthy urban environment. The rich got richer during this era and could afford whatever sporting pleasures they desired, preferably those that were most exclusive and prestigious. In the post-Civil War era the middle classes enjoyed an enormous boom in sport, primarily because of their belief in the positive sports creed which justified recreation as time well spent away from the workplace. Middle-income people also had sufficient money and discretionary time to enjoy themselves and had ready access to parks located in their neighborhoods or ballparks an affordable streetcar ride away.

The different social classes intermingled as little as possible in their sporting pleasures. Until the 1920s, they often would not, or could not, attend the same spectator sports; if they did, they would sit in separate sections, determined by the price of tickets. Organized participatory sports were arranged by status-oriented voluntary sports associations that promoted competition by establishing eligibility rules, sponsoring contests, and securing playing sites. The middle- and upper-income clubs with restricted memberships, downtown athletic clubs, and distant country clubs organized their own competitions. Working-class sports clubs, usually based in a neighborhood in the zone of emergence or slum among people from the same ethnic background, could afford only modest clubhouses, competed at public sites, and relied on outside sponsorship (a political boss, union, or employer) to survive. The ethnic sports clubs of the old immigrants, which originated in the pre-Civil War period, survived in ethnic villages, where they were a prominent part of the community's culture. Although the first-generation immigrants were unfamiliar with American sports, these sports did become an important part of their sons' lives in the urban slums. Adult-directed ethnic sports clubs tried to involve the youngsters with their heritage and to slow down the pace of acculturation and structural assimilation, but the youth organized their own clubs so they could play American games and become Americanized, even if they were unwelcome in "American" sports clubs.

Finally, sport in the radial city was a product of local governmental and political leadership. The city actively served the recreational needs of its citizens, securing new public space for parks, schoolyards, and recreational piers; constructing civic arenas and stadiums; and sponsoring athletic programs at those sites. Civic boosters owned sports franchises and organized athletic competitions to advertise their town across the country. Political leaders were also the leading promoters of professional spectator sports, with machine bosses particularly prominent in gambling sports in conjunction with organized crime. Political connections provided protection for sports investments, inside information, and preferential treatment by the municipality, which was responsible for regulating behavior in public places, sustaining traditional standards of morality, and fighting illegal gambling. Once professional sports became well established and the gambling sports were legitimized, machine politicians became less prominent as entrepreneurs because their connections were less essential. By the 1920s gangsters were becoming the dominant force in boxing and a major factor in turf sports.

Since World War II urbanization has continued to be a crucial force in the evolution of American sport. The nature of life in the inner city still influences the sporting options of its residents; it is not by chance that black youth from the ghettoes dominate the sports of boxing and basketball and that the suburban boys and girls excel at swimming, fencing, and tennis. The decline of the industrial Northeast and the rise of the sunbelt has had major ramifications for professional sports leagues, which have expanded into the growing metropolises of the Southeast, Southwest, and Pacific Coast. As cities compete with each other to offer the most attractive inducements to secure teams or keep the ones they have, political involvement with professional athletics has increased. Older cities that have not lost sports franchises have built expensive stadiums and arenas for their teams to keep them in place. These projects are justified as efforts to boost the town's reputation and status and to promote commerce—a goal that has never been realized in any city.

Some recurring tensions or dynamics operated within the structural, organizational, and ideological dimensions of urbanization as it shaped the direction of sport history. The dynamic relationship between population change and urban spatial arrangements has always been central to the evolution of sport in the city. The walking city contained quiet streets with vacant lots available for sports; unpolluted rivers were close by for swimming and fishing; and even the woods were not too far away for hunting and other field sports. However, in the radial city spatial arrangements changed dramatically: close-in empty spaces were filled in, the countryside became less accessible to the masses, and the new outdoor spectatorial sports facilities were beyond walking distance, making sporting options unevenly available to urban populations because of their economic class. This change had the most negative impact upon slum dwellers, who lived in crowded, pathological neighborhoods and needed access to outdoor breathing space. They had to either rely upon city government to reshape its priorities and establish community parks or forego outdoor pleasures. Consequently, inner-city folk were drawn to local resources like settlement houses, boxing gyms, pool halls, or bowling alleys. Once mass transit became more affordable, inner-city folk had an easier time getting to outlying ballparks and racetracks, but as a general rule, children and young men still relied upon neighborhood facilities for participatory contests.

A second process at work was the effort of social reformers to ameliorate the quality of urban life through sports. First in the Jacksonian era, later in the Progressive era, and ever since then, athletics have been seen as a socially and individually useful activity which improves public health, character, and morality; provides an alternate vehicle for social mobility; and promotes community ties, acculturation, and structural assimilation. The reform impetus did a great deal to advance the cause of sport, starting out in the antebellum era with a convincing justification for the necessity for moral athletics to counter urban pathology and replace evil pleasures. Reformers played a leading role in articulating the need for public play space and led the fight to secure additional public parks. At the turn of the century they advocated adult-supervised team sport for inner-city youth to promote social order and the melting-pot concept— precepts that youth workers would continue to operate under for decades. The ideology had an enormous effect upon the behavior of the middle classes, who became convinced of the value of the strenuous life. Its powerful appeal led to efforts to bring together disparate groups through welfare capitalism, the popularization of the mobility myth, and the rationalized, articulate vision of saving children through team sports. However, in reality sport failed to serve as a social integrating mechanism because of the political, ideological, and spatial forces promoting separatism.

The quest for Americanization and community through the meritocratic and democratic world of athletics ran into major stumbling blocks with groups that did not necessarily disavow those goals but also had their own agendas. In theory athletics would bring disparate groups together and promote social harmony as they played with or against each other or simply sat together in the stands. While there was some truth to that belief, voluntary sports clubs in the nineteenth century were organized along class, ethnic, or racial lines. Their members either wanted to separate themselves from other (inferior or different) social groups or else were themselves cut off by others and thus could only associate with athletes of similar backgrounds. The result was the formation of status or ethnic subcommunities—self-selective associations based upon commonly shared values, a cultural heritage, socioeconomic standing, or racial appearance. The disaggregating influence of sports extended from private clubs to seating areas in semipublic audiences and even to public space, where hostile ethnic groups fought with each other for control of city parks.

The demographic, spatial, ideological, and organizational influence on sport were all tied to the rise of strong municipal governments and urban political machines. In the private city of the early 1800s local governments provided few public services like fire or police protection, which were left to voluntary organizations or private companies. However, increasing urban pathology and rapidly growing heterogeneous populations forced mid-nineteenth-century city halls to take a more active role. At the same time, the elite, old-guard political leaders gave way to new men—professional politicians for whom politics was a career, not a civic obligation. These politicos formed political organizations, or machines, to turn out the vote and stay in power. Through their control of public space and their obligation to protect the community's health, welfare, morality, and security, municipalities influenced the rise of sport. They served the public interest by building parks and stadiums, promoting better mass transit, and fighting sports gambling, thus boosting the reputation of their towns and the well-being of their citizens. However, the political bosses, concerned less with the commonweal than with their own interests, were among the first sports entrepreneurs, employing their power and connections just as they did for their other business ventures. Furthermore, sport provided a key nexus between the bosses and organized crime. In this symbiotic relationship, the machines provided protection for proscribed sports contests and illegal betting in return for payoffs and political support. These connections were bitterly fought by reformers, who demanded the enforcement of the penal codes and provided confirmation of the venality of the bosses, whose quest for private gain was often deleterious to the general community.

American urban communities come in a wide variety of shapes, sizes, and forms, ranging from towns with just a few thousand inhabitants to huge metropolitan districts with populations in the millions. This study will focus primarily on the bigger cities, because these main centers of organized sport established models for smaller cities to emulate and because these urban areas have been most exhaustively researched by historians and other scholars. In cities of all sizes organized sports are structured pretty much the same way, with the same latent and manifest functions. Important differences are more likely to occur in recreational sports because of spatial and demographic variables that we will try to point out in our discussion. For purposes of comparison the data for this study will be drawn, where possible, from cities in different regions, but since New York, the nation's largest city, has historically been the center of organized sport in America, the locus of the national media, and the urban area most intensively studied by sports historians, this essay will, of necessity, concentrate there.

SPORT IN THE WALKING CITY, 1820–70

[Cricket] afforded a convenient excuse for partially demolishing social barriers and for permitting a friendly reunion of Britons of every stripe—mechanics, small tradesmen and artisans—proving they could scientifically wield the will or deliver a true blow.

New York Clipper 16 (17 Oct. 1868): 220

I suppose you will admit that a man who does not pay his obligations, and has in his power to do so, is a knave and not fit to be trusted in a game of ball or anything else; and if he has not the money, his time would be better spent in earning the same than playing ball—business first, pleasure afterwards.

Francis Pidgeon, master shipbuilder, president of the Eckford Club, in *Porter's Spirit of the Times* 6 (26 Mar. 1858): 52.

When you start with a dog fight as a curtain raiser, continue with a cock fight, then rat baiting, next a prize fight, then a battle of billy goats, and then a boxing match between two ladies, with nothing but trunks on . . . I think you have a night's entertainment that has enough spice . . . to fill the most rapacious needs.

Frederick Van Wyck, *Recollections of an Old New Yorker* (New York, 1932), 113–14.

There was no place within the city limits in which it was pleasant to walk, or ride, or drive, or stroll; no place for skating, no water in which it was safe to row; no field for base-ball or cricket; no pleasant garden where one could sit and chat with a friend, or watch his children play . . .

Clarence C. Cook, *A Description of the New York Central Park* (New York, 1869), 13.

CHAPTER 1

Urbanization and Sport in the Walking City

American cities did not have much of a sporting culture in 1820, when just 5 percent of the national population lived in cities. The main sports then were traditional field and stream sports, blood sports, and contests of strength and skill; horse races were rare, team sports were virtually unknown, and many modern sports had not even been invented. But within a half century sport became one of the most popular entertainments for residents of the compact walking cities. Commercialized spectator sports like baseball, horse racing, and harness racing developed into highly organized and rationalized enterprises; competitive participatory sports like track and field were organized and specialized; and a wide variety of recreational sports, like croquet, skating, and cycling, gained widespread popularity, even if only as fads. The development of sport as an urban institution was heavily influenced by the urban revolution of the period from 1820 to 1870; during that time the percentage of the population living in cities quadrupled—the greatest proportionate growth in urban population in the nation's history. The boom was particularly impressive in the decades between 1830 and 1860, when the urban population appreciated by 63.7 percent, 92.1 percent, and 75.4 percent respectively. In 1860 there were 101 cities with over 10,000 residents, compared to just twenty-three in 1820, and nine cities exceeded 100,000.[1] Nevertheless, by today's standards these were geographically small cities, generally no more than two miles in radius, where people walked wherever they had to go.

In this dynamic era changing demographics, rising wealth (resulting from commercial and industrial capitalism), new spatial patterns, improved interurban transportation and communication networks, new voluntary class and ethnic organizations, the rise of modern political institutions, and traditional, transitional, and emerging modern values and behavior all interacted with each other and with sport to produce a variety of distinctive urban sporting subcultures.

This chapter focuses on the relationship between urbanization and sport in New York, the nation's largest city, whose population quadrupled between 1830 and 1860, when it reached 814,000. Because of its physical size, population density, and wealth, New York was hardly a typical urban site, but changes there often foreshadowed developments elsewhere. Urbanization created in antebellum New York conditions common to most cities—crowding, crime, extremes of poverty and wealth, and little sense of community. Urban anomie facilitated both the emergence of a sporting fraternity that sought to maintain a traditional life-style in the midst of rapid social change and the rise of a more mainstream sporting subculture that promoted moral athletics as a palliative for urban pathology. Communities of people who shared the same values and culture sought distance from men unlike themselves by organizing ethnic and class sport clubs. Spatial variables also influenced the spread of organized sport. The small size of walking cities facilitated access to sporting sites both within cities and beyond their boundaries. We will consider the private, public, or semipublic character of urban space utilized for organized or leisure sports by different groups and individuals and give particular attention to the growing needs for additional public space, the role of municipalities in dealing with spatial issues, and the commercialized use of semipublic space by entrepreneurs trying to cash in on the nearby presence of potential clients willing to pay to watch excellent athletic competition.

Sport and the Formation of Urban Subcommunities

Highly individualistic and transient urbanites needed to develop social and cultural ties to root themselves, especially in friendless cities where neighbors did not know, or even want to know, each other—circumstances far different than in close-knit rural villages. Thus, in their search for convivial, like-minded friends, urbanites became inveterate joiners of structured voluntary organizations. Some of the less-respected members of urban society were also joiners of unstructured informal subcommunities found at public places like street corners or semipublic sites like taverns. Although formal and informal subcommunities had existed in the colonial city, they were far fewer because the smaller size and greater homogeneity of the eighteenth-century city had obviated such a need. In the antebellum city sport became an important focal point for the formation of urban subcommunities that provided both ready-made associations of people who shared the same interests and values and facilities and organizations for the enjoyment of their common interest.

The Sporting Fraternity

The sporting fraternity was an informal brotherhood of pleasure seekers who sponsored, participated in, and attended traditional sporting contests. It was composed not only of certain members of the economic and social elites but also of urban machine politicians, artisans, butchers, seasonal workers, criminals, Irish immigrants, and various other lower-class men. All part of the male bachelor subculture, these sportsmen measured manliness by skill at wenching, drinking, gambling, and fighting. They found camaraderie and sociability in exclusively male environments in which they escaped "femininity, domesticity, and the demanding routines of the new economy."[2] In this democratic and anonymous environment, men of different backgrounds rubbed shoulders and entertained each other, forming a transient community in which sharing jokes and paying for drinks made for temporary acquaintanceships but not necessarily life-long friendships.

Elite participants in the bachelor subculture were usually young rakes looking for excitement by escaping familial supervision in the faceless taverns, gambling halls, and fashionable brothels. As Melvin Adelman notes, these slumming dandies, along with low-life urban floaters, comprised the crowds at illegal boxing matches, baiting contests, and cock-fights. Whether or not young men of breeding joined the sporting fraternity depended on local norms and traditions. Proper Bostonians or Philadelphians could deter their sons from the bachelor subculture with threats of social ostracism, but this threat did not work in New York, where old-line families were less prominent. In New Orleans continental traditions and an unbalanced sex ratio (men outnumbered women by 2 to 1 in 1840) discouraged the usual social constraints. At mid-century New York's elite sportsmen were known to frequent various well-known sporting sites like Harry Hill's Dance Hall, a favorite drinking spa for machine politicians, boxers, and other members of the sporting fraternity. Slumming elite youth who attended a blood sport contest like a cock main found it a *rite de passage* into adulthood. The bloody bird fights ranged from matches in dark alleys to expensive contests like that between birds belonging to aldermanic president Genet and boxing champion John Morrissey, reported by the press as "Amusements of the Ruling Class."[3]

The Working Class

Working-class men comprised the majority of the sporting fraternity. They were epitomized by butchers—tough and strong men who maintained a traditional life-style that included drinking on the job, taking extra days off from work, like St. Monday, and gambling at pedestrian contests, horse races, cockfights, billiards, dice, and cards. Labor historian Herbert Gutman attributed the casual work habits of English artisans and former farm workers to their prior work experiences. These newcomers, unaccustomed to the rhythms of the industrial system based on time-work discipline and the factory whistle, did not readily adjust to the industrialized world, in which they had less control over the workplace and their nonwork time.[4]

The "boys of pleasure," not only made ample time for sport; until cities became overcrowded and began encroaching upon the nearby countryside, they also had enough space for athletic amusements. Handloom weavers in antebellum Philadelphia took time off from work to turn their neighborhood into afternoon playgrounds or escaped the city to fish in the Schuylkill or hunt in nearby forests. Traditional recreations were also a way of life in the industrial city of Lynn, Massachusetts. Historian Paul Faler found that shoemakers had no qualms about taking time off for holidays, birthdays, or any time they wanted a break. Working-class members of the sporting fraternity often belonged to volunteer fire companies, which provided many opportunities for sporting pleasures. By the 1850s, fire companies, originally drawn from all social strata, were made up mainly of journeymen workers. Membership gave them a sense of status, stability, and affirmation of their worth in increasingly anonymous cities. Companies were often dominated by a rowdy element, renowned for fighting skills that had been useful when rival companies had raced each other to the scene of a fire and then brawled for the honor and profit of putting out the blaze. These voluntary societies also engaged in public competitions to demonstrate their speed, strength, and skill in such challenges as accuracy in throwing water. Such fire companies were described by one historian as "frat club-cum-athletic teams" because they were centers of recreation and camaraderie.[5]

A major segment of the sporting fraternity were Irishmen, the largest immigrant group at mid-century. Mainly illiterate Roman Catholic peasants from traditional backgrounds, they were inadequately prepared for urban life, encountered a lot of discrimination, and had a hard time adjusting. Because they were unskilled and lacked the funds to move beyond the ports of entry, they settled in cities like New York and Boston, took the jobs no one else wanted, and lived in the worst slums. These Celtic newcomers brought with them their tradition of a male bachelor subculture that glorified such manly activities as drinking, betting, and athletics, particularly violent sports like boxing. As Benjamin Rader has noted, "A high percentage of bachelors, delayed marriages, rigorous norms of premarital chastity, and traditions of segregation of the sexes made all-male groups far more important to the Irish-Americans than to any other ethnic group. Whether married or unmarried, a male's status within the larger Irish community tended to rest on his membership and active participation in the bachelor subculture. . . . The subculture furnished a refuge against loneliness, a substitute for the conjugal family, and served as an agency of social cohesion.''[6] Irish newcomers readily gravitated into the male bachelor subculture and became habitués of the working-men's tavern, where they alleviated their alienation and loneliness by making friends with other men of similar backgrounds who shared their values and needs and where Irishmen could improve their self-image and gain social status.

The tavern was the principal locus of the sporting fraternity, and as in the past publicans were important promoters and facilitators of sport, recognizing its value in attracting thirsty crowds. As late as the 1820s taverns located on distant roads might have sufficient space for marksmanship contests or horse races; however, most taverns were situated in such accessible locations as working-class residential neighborhoods, workplaces, and vice districts—areas without public space available for sport. Consequently, most activities were indoors. The neighborhood taverns usually featured the same kind of cushion-edged billiard tables found in the public pool halls and the homes of the rich. In the early 1820s New York boasted over a dozen public poolrooms, which at first catered to a respectable clientele. However, Adelman argues, by the late 1840s the solid citizens began to drift away in response to public criticism that decried these male bastions as centers for gambling and as the breeding grounds for even worse vices. Thereafter, the well-to-do billiardist played at home or in his prestigious metropolitan men's club, leaving the public billiard rooms to a lower-middle- and lower-class clientele that divided the cheap twenty-five-cents-a-game table fees among all the players.[7]

Few sports were as accessible to working-class urbanites as billiards. In addition to tables at taverns located near the workplace or the home, billiard parlors were located in the central parts of town, within walking distance of most people's homes or jobs. In Detroit, a major billiard center that was the site of the first American championship in 1859, billiard halls were situated mainly in and around the downtown area in close proximity to the city's saloons and brothels. Many unattached, transient males resided in that neighborhood, and these members of the bachelor subculture were an important segment of billiard players. The sport provided talented and experienced participants with a source of self-expression and a means to earn money through gambling.[8]

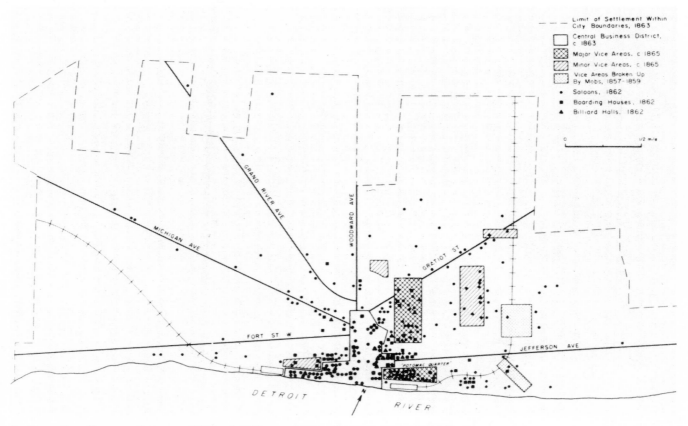

1. Boarding Houses, Saloons, Billiard Halls, and Vice Areas in Detroit 1862.

SOURCE: John C. Schneider, *Detroit and the Problems of Order, 1830–1880, A Geography of Crime, Riot and Policing* (Lincoln, Neb., 1980), 42.

Besides encouraging participatory sport, the urban tavern keepers also arranged many spectacular events—boxing matches, pedestrian races, endurance contests like walking the plank, and animal baiting—which all generated a lot of fervent betting.[9] Blood sports were particularly popular among the sporting fraternity, and publicans often arranged cockfights in an adjacent shed or a small amphitheater. The most notorious dive was Kit Burns's Sportsman's Hall, a New York tavern with space for 400 of the city's roughest and toughest rogues, which featured rat baiting, dog fighting, and the inimitable Jack the Rat, who bit off mouse heads for a dime and rat heads for a quarter. Such resorts were detested by the respectable members of urban society for the sinful behavior they encouraged. The large, impassioned crowds at sporting taverns had a great potential for violence and riotous behavior that far exceeded the ability of the constabulary or even the new police departments to control.[10]

The spectator sport most admired by the male urban counterculture in the antebellum period was pugilism, a violent and bloody sport that demanded great courage, physical strength, and athletic prowess. Boxing differed in significant ways from the sport of gouging, a product of the dangerous and uncivilized frontier. Boxing was too genteel for the backwoodsmen, who preferred rough-and-tumble, no-holds-barred matches in which the object was to protect one's honor through bravery and to deface the opponent by gouging out an eye, biting off a nose, etc. On the other hand, boxers fought under recognized rules, which forbade gouging and striking a downed opponent, and under the supervision of a referee and seconds. Though still barred everywhere, boxing was relatively more civilized and more acceptable to comparatively sophisticated urban sensibilities. Boxing matches were far less likely to be impromptu, even when they were motivated by personal, ethnic, or political animosities. Especially after the 1840s, matches were fought by professionals for sidebets and, though equally illegal, had far greater commercial potential than gouging.[11]

Pugilism thrived in New York, Philadelphia, Boston, Baltimore, and New Orleans, which all had large communities of traditionally oriented, lower-class immigrants who provided most of the fighters and the spectators. Between 1840 and 1860 over half (56.3 percent) of New York pugilists were Irish-born, 15.6 percent were second-generation Irish, and 18.8 percent were English-born. Many of the foreign-born fighters had competed professionally in the old country; the American-born had previously held unskilled or semiskilled jobs. The latter were usually the product of either street gangs or fire companies, which provided unattached young men with an all-male peer group based on common ethnicity, religion, occupation, or political loyalty. Intergroup rivalries often ended up in street fights or small-scale riots when they contested for control of territory (saloon, poolroom, engine house, or burning building). The toughest youths were recruited into notorious adult gangs like the Bowery Boys, which was comprised of native-born Americans. The Boys were mainly butchers and apprentice mechanics active in various volunteer fire companies. Unskilled or semiskilled second-generation Irish street fighters were drawn to other outfits, like Isaiah Rynders's Empire Club, established in 1843 as an Irish adjunct to Tammany Hall.[12]

Members of street gangs were regularly recruited by political parties and factions to work during elections as "shoulder hitters" to intimidate voters. The urban politicians who hired intimidators were among the principal patrons of boxing, often owning or being closely associated with the proprietors of leading sporting saloons where bouts were arranged and fought. Before the 1840s few formal bouts were actually prearranged, but in that decade weekly Sunday matches were held in New York, usually at groggeries, organized by politicians, saloonkeepers, gamblers, or other leading members of the sporting fraternity. In the 1850s the bare-knuckle bouts were drawing large enough crowds that they were moved to more commodious facilities like theaters, where admission cost fifty cents. However, most boxers still couldn't make a living boxing, and they depended on their political sponsors to help them out by securing patronage jobs, often in the police department, or work as emigrant runners, saloon managers, or bouncers.[13]

The social and political dimensions of boxing were epitomized by the career of John Morrissey, the son of Irish immigrant parents. Morrissey gained fighting fame as a street brawler and shoulder hitter with the Empire Club. Without much formal experience, he was matched with Yankee Sullivan in 1853 for the vacant American boxing championship. Morrissey's knock-out victory in the thirty-seventh round made him a great hero to his fellow Irishmen and many other members of the sporting fraternity. During the mid-1850s he and his followers won renown defending the Irish community against nativists; they fought several street fights with Butcher Bill Poole and the nativist Bowery Boys. "Old Smoke" retired as champion in 1858, after defeating James Carmel Heenan, and went on to use his fame and charisma among fellow Irishmen to become a power in Tammany Hall. He enriched himself in the gambling business, developing his betting parlor into a leading role in the development of Saratoga into an elite resort by establishing a casino and racetrack there. He was able to do business with the rich and well-born but never achieved their social prestige. However, he was enormously popular with the masses and in 1866 was elected to the first of two consecutive terms in the U.S. Congress. He subsequently broke with Boss Tweed, joined the Mozart Hall wing of the Democratic party, and was not incriminated in the investigation of the Tweed Ring. In 1875 Morrissey was elected to the state senate; he died in office three years later.[14]

Ethnic Communities

Just as the Irish immigrants came to America with a sporting tradition that firmly placed them in the sporting fraternity, other immigrants also brought athletic heritages that became focal points for the formation of ethnic communities in crowded American cities. However, English, Scottish, and German newcomers all brought sporting pasts that were far more acceptable than Irish blood sport to Victorian moral leaders.

English immigrants encountered relatively little cultural shock in American cities, and because they spoke English and were literate and skilled, they fared well financially and faced little discrimination in comparison to other newcomers. Nevertheless, English sportsmen quickly formed ethnic sports organizations, along with other ethnic societies, to sustain their culture and to promote their own sense of community. The most important English sports clubs sponsored cricket—a uniquely English sport that was manly, complex, competitive, and required considerable skill. By the 1830s English knitters and weavers in Philadelphia textile mills were already organizing teams and playing alongside mill proprietors, very much as English tenant farmers and servants bowled with the local gentry. During the next twenty years English merchants and workingmen organized cricket teams throughout the Northeast in cities like Boston, Brooklyn, Lawrence, Lowell, New York, and Newark. As in England, most games were scheduled for Saturdays, decades before the Saturday half-holiday became the norm for blue-collar Americans.[15]

The first and foremost English cricket organization was the St. George Cricket Club (SGCC), established in New York in 1840. Most members were businessmen. One-fourth belonged to the prestigious St. George's Society, the leading English voluntary association in the metropolis. The club enabled members to maintain their ethnic identity, make valuable business and social contacts, and enjoy their favorite sport. The SGCC scheduled high-level competition for its best players, who competed for sidebets, and even arranged for out-of-town matches.[16]

Cricket expanded beyond the Anglo community to become the most important ball sport, complete with considerable intercity and even international competition. By the 1850s native-born Americans in Albany,

Brooklyn, Yonkers, and especially Philadelphia were playing the English game, making it less of an ethnic sport. In Newark there were an equal number of English and American cricketers (45.3 percent apiece), and the rest were Irish, though Englishmen were well overrepresented in comparison to their share of the city's population. However, in New York, English dominance was so great that it had "almost utterly squelched the rising spirit of cricket amongst Americans in New York and driven it into base ball [sic]."[17]

Scottish immigrants also used their sporting tradition as a cornerstone around which to establish ethnic associations. In 1836 the New York Highland Society met for the first time to "renew the Sport of their Native Land." Various Highland organizations—most notably the Caledonian clubs, the first of which was founded in 1853 in Boston—periodically sponsored track and field games. There were eventually over 100 such clubs, located wherever there were large Scottish communities. The Caledonians sponsored professional competition in such traditional Scottish sports as throwing the caber and putting the heavy stone, and their picnics also included dinners, dances, and bagpipe performances. Their goal was to provide a sense of community by sustaining "the manners and customs, literature, the Highland costume and the athletic games of Scotland." As the contests' popularity and profitability outgrew the Scottish community, with crowds reaching 20,000 by 1870, the Caledonians became the first sporting organizations other than jockey clubs to make spectator sports a business. Their New York Games became the preeminent American track and field contests.[18]

While English and Scottish immigrants adjusted relatively easily to life in American cities, German newcomers had to make a far greater cultural transition. They were generally well prepared for economic success in the United States because they had education, skills, and some capital. Most Germans settled in cities; in the 1850s they comprised one-third of the population of Louisville and large segments of cities like Chicago, Milwaukee, and New York. In order to lessen the cultural shock of immigration and alleviate the need to adapt to New World customs and behavior, Germans chose to settle in neighborhoods that had a high concentration of other Germans. In Milwaukee, for instance, 83 percent of German homes were situated in German localities where the newcomers created a totally German environment and maintained their proud cultural heritage. Since business in the ethnic village was conducted in German, newspapers were printed in German, and schools, theaters, and voluntary associations were all German, the immigrants felt little need to become structurally or culturally assimilated into what they regarded as an inferior culture.[19]

The *turnverein* or gymnastic society, a vital part of the cultural baggage brought by German immigrants, flourished in German neighborhoods, just like the German theater and choral societies. American athletic reformers were already familiar with the romantic and nationalistic organization since in the 1820s some of the early students of Friedrich Jahn, the founder of the movement, had introduced gymnastics programs at a few American colleges and had received a lot of favorable publicity. The first turner societies in the U.S. were established in 1848 in Louisville and Cincinnati—two cities with large German populations—and others were soon organized in Baltimore, Brooklyn, Chicago, Milwaukee, New Orleans, New York, Newark, Philadelphia, St. Louis, and other cities with growing German communities. The leaders of the new societies were often former turners, including many political refugees, and they sought to promote gymnastics, free thought, liberal politics, the interests of workingmen, and the German culture and to provide a community center for German neighborhoods. The turners, highly regarded among sports-minded people, were described in the *American Journal of Education* in 1860 as "virtuous and accomplished, pure and active, chaste and bold, truthful and warlike." To stress their ethnic identity they built their *turnhalles* in German localities and held all meetings and kept all records in the mother tongue. Thus the *turnverein* unquestionably helped alleviate the alienation German migrants felt in cities thousands of miles from their beloved homeland.[20]

Most turners were artisans earning good livings; virtually none were semiskilled or unskilled. Blue-collar workers outnumbered white-collar members by two to one, which reflected the occupational pattern for German urbanites. The strong working-class character of the turner movement in America was reflected in the creation of overtly socialist societies—organizations that emphasized politics rather than gymnastics—in Philadelphia in 1849 (*Socialer Turnverein, Sociale Turngemeinde*) and a few years later in Baltimore, Brooklyn, and New York. In the booming cities of Milwaukee and Chicago the bourgeoisie played a more vital role in the turner movement. Milwaukee's first *turnverein* was established by prominent business leaders, and the great majority of its members were white-collar. Chicago's *Turngemeinde* began in 1852 with a mixed membership that was predominantly white-collar (56.7 percent) but included gunsmiths, blacksmiths, and other artisans who presumably all got along. Membership patterns indicate that the *turnverein* were not status communities within German neighborhoods but relatively democratic bastions of a "respectable" German male subculture whose halls served as community centers and political forums as much as gymnasiums to learn and practice traditional exercises and stunts.[21]

The Rich and Well Born

Urbanization had a limited impact on the sporting pastimes of the richest 5 percent of city populations. Their wealth, discretionary time, and accessibility to sports facilities enabled them to enjoy whichever pastimes they preferred. Seventeen-year-old Edward Tailer, Jr., son of a wealthy New York merchant who traveled in the highest social circles, partook of the kinds of pleasures typical of his peers. In the fall and winter of 1847–48 he took leisurely walks, fished at Kingsbridge or Greenpoint, picnicked in Hoboken, took dancing lessons, sleighed and ice skated. He devoted evenings to the theater, parties, and even to temperance meetings. Two years later, working as a clerk and concerned about his safety, he began taking boxing lessons along with other men who helped him advance in his chosen career.[22]

Urbanization encouraged the rich and well-born to use athletics as a mechanism to help define class boundaries, especially in cities too large to allow prestigious individuals to know each other personally. The new men of wealth who made their fortunes through real estate, banking, transportation, and the old fashioned way, in commerce (all aided by the rise of the city), sought entrance to metropolitan men's clubs that certified their high social standing. Thoroughbred racing and yachting, strongly identified in the public mind as elite sports because of the exorbitant cost of participation and the restricted memberships of jockey and yacht clubs, served as status-defining communities.

The turf, the most prestigious colonial sport, was widely banned in the Revolutionary era out of Republican opposition to its aristocratic status and connections to gambling. Barred in New York between 1803 and 1821, the sport was revitalized by the local elite who owned the racing thoroughbreds and formed the jockey clubs that operated the semipublic race courses. They justified the sport as the only means of developing superior horses for such uses as national defense (the cavalry) and transportation. The big impetus to the sport in New York came in 1823, when sportsman John Cox Stevens, the son of a rich Hoboken inventor-merchant, organized a local syndicate to back Eclipse, regarded as the finest thoroughbred in America, against a $20,000 wager by William Johnson of Virginia, who claimed he could find a superior southern horse. Stevens's confidence was well-placed: Eclipse ably defended the honor of the North against the southern steed, Sir Henry, at Long Island's Union Race Course in front of a crowd estimated at 60,000, which reputedly included 20,000 out-of-towners. This big match not only enriched local merchants and hotel keepers but, more importantly, rejuvenated the turf in New York and helped make racing a national sport.[23]

Over the next few years racing enjoyed some success in New York but declined after the 1837 depression ruined many rich horsemen and then virtually collapsed in 1845, when the breeding industry shifted westward. The gambling sport's demise was hardly lamented by Congregationalist and pietistic members of the elite who had long frowned on the turf's association with betting. The center of the sport shifted to the wide-open cosmopolitan city of New Orleans, which dominated racing until the coming of the Civil War. Its residents had few qualms about gambling, and the city's tracks became a haven for rich cotton and sugar planters who raced their thoroughbreds there for fame, status, and profit.[24]

After the war horse racing resumed in New York City under the auspices of the American Jockey Club (AJC), founded in 1865 by capitalists Leonard Jerome, August Belmont, William R. Travers, and James R. Hunter. Impressed by the success of thoroughbred racing at both Paterson, New Jersey, and Saratoga since 1863, the latter under John Morrissey, they decided to bring the turf back to New York. In 1866 the AJC built Jerome Park on a 230-acre estate north of the city. Opening Day was the social event of the year, and for the next several years, Jerome Park would draw a select crowd free of ''the masses.''[25]

Membership in the AJC carried some social status, but far less than membership in the New York Yacht Club or older men's clubs like the Union Club (1836) or the Century Club (1847). More an integrating organization of horse fanciers and bettors than a voluntary association differentiating among social elites, the AJC admitted nearly anyone willing to pay dues and gate admissions to support the track. Thus in 1866–67 its rolls included such politicians as Boss William M. Tweed and Peter Sweeney. The 862 members, mostly middle-aged residents of New York and vicinity, were mainly men of new wealth in commerce or finance: most (83.3 percent) had incomes in the top 1 percent of all New Yorkers and the great majority (80 percent) lived in the city's three wealthiest wards, including one-sixth who lived on Fifth Avenue.[26]

If membership in the AJC did not certify an individual as a member of the social elite, selection to the board of governors did. Its fifty life members came from the finest families, were far richer than regular members (a mean income of $59,700 compared to $25,500), and were more likely to own thoroughbreds (which were good only for racing and conspicuous display). They usually also held memberships in the most prestigious men's clubs, like the Union Club (61.1 percent) and the New York Yacht Club (56 percent).[27]

Yachting provided more social cachet than any other sport. John C. Stevens was the first preeminent yachtsman. In 1835 his sloop *Wave* competed in the first recorded American yacht race, and nine years later he organized and presided over the New York Yacht Club (NYYC). The original members, drawn from the old elite, sought pleasure, camaraderie, good health, and the advancement of American naval architecture. Interest in the sport skyrocketed in 1851 after the victory of Stevens's *America* in a race against seventeen British boats held in conjunction with the Crystal Palace Fair. The upset generated a lot of national pride and symbolized the maturity of the American shipping industry. Between 1850 and 1860 the size of the NYYC tripled from 157; many men of new money sought membership to confirm their gentlemanly status and to gain acceptance from the old elites. The NYYC became *the* preeminent American sports club, establishing a model for other yacht clubs to copy. Among New York's metropolitan clubs, the NYYC was just a cut below the Union and Century Clubs.[28]

Sport as Rational Recreation: The Ideological Foundations of Respectable Urban Sport

In the antebellum era social reformers developed a positive sports creed as a partial solution to the urban pathology that accompanied the growth of cities. While some observers, like poet and journalist Walt Whitman, were excited by the pace and excitement of urban life and its potential for the good life, most commentators were appalled by the materialism, artificiality, loss of pastoral values, and dangers of urban life. They feared that overcrowded, impoverished industrial cities like Manchester would develop, threatening traditional moral values and the national character.[29]

American cities were indeed becoming increasingly unhealthy, immoral, and dangerous. Urban populations were very heterogeneous (half of the heads of households in Boston in 1850 were foreign-born), and residents in the faceless cities lacked the shared culture and other social bonds common in small towns and villages. As both wealth and poverty increased, class divisions grew wider. The poorest urbanites lived in shanties and basements in overcrowded neighborhoods that had inadequate sanitation and impure water, causing frequent epidemics. A large pool of unsupervised, poor, young males contributed to a big rise in crime.[30]

Jacksonians believed that urban pathology could best be alleviated through greater municipal control over local water supply, waste disposal, and policing, through such civic ventures as the park movement, and through voluntary social movements organized to fight for temperance, compulsory education, and health reform. The Rev. William Ellery Channing, scientist Dr. Lemuel Shattuck, health faddist Sylvester Graham, and other reformers all believed that city folk were unhealthy because they had sedentary jobs that required little physical exertion, and because they were too tied to the discipline of the clock, compared to freer and more exuberant rural Americans. The largest cities already lacked space for walking, riding, boating, or playing games which might have provided urban residents with the vigorous exercise rural people took for granted. The physical culture movement hoped to bring many of the finest qualities of rural society to cities and thereby sustain traditional moral values.[31]

Sport and Urban Health Reform

Led by physicians, social critics, and sports journalists, health reformers strongly advocated participation by all urbanites in moral sports, which they believed benefitted individuals of both genders and all social classes and, hence, the general community. As early as 1829 the Philadelphia *Journal of Health* recommended the construction of public gymnasiums for blue-collar workers. The main argument in favor of public expenditures for manual workers maintained that employees who were physically and mentally fit would be more productive. One sports weekly, estimating the annual loss due to absenteeism and shoddy work due to ill health at $240 million, recommended physical exercise as the antidote. Labor leaders seeking the ten-hour day agreed on the value of sport. While their members got plenty of physical exercise on the job, they needed sport to refresh their minds. As the *Spirit of the Times* noted, "Heaving coal may be as good exercise as pitching quoits, or sowing wood or rowing in a regatta, but they are infinitely less inspiring, and therefore infinitely less healthful."[32]

Most of the published discussion regarding sport and individual health focused on white-collar workers engaged in sedentary activities. As late as the mid-1850s Dr. Oliver Wendell Holmes, Sr., found it necessary to chastise "the vegetative life of the American," in comparison to the robust life of the English gentry. He anticipated the impending decline of the race, certain that "such a set of black-coated, stiff-jointed, soft-muscled, paste-complexioned youth as we can boast in our Atlantic cities never before sprang from loins of Anglo-Saxon lineage." The most important spokesmen for middle-class fitness was Holmes's fellow Boston Brahmin, Thomas Wentworth Higginson, son of a successful merchant, graduate of Harvard, noted social reformer, and Unitarian minister. In a series of articles in the new *Atlantic Monthly* (1858) Higginson argued that the high rate of illness among white-collar workers indicated the need for outdoor exercise. He encouraged businessmen to worry less about making money and more about their physical and mental well-being, suggesting they leave the woes of the office behind and join him at the gymnasium. Higginson sought to assuage public fears of the immorality of sport as practiced by the sporting fraternity by denying that "physical vigor and spiritual sanctity are incompatible."[33]

The promotion of sports as an antidote to urban pathology was an integral part of the public health movement of the 1840s. The movement had started in England in the previous decade, following parliamentary investigations of factory conditions. The major problems in American cities were products of congestion and poor sanitation that resulted in physical and moral degeneracy and even death. The single biggest concern was epidemics, particularly cholera, which had severe outbreaks in 1832–33 and 1849. In order to prevent future catastrophes, physicians recommended that cities improve their water supplies, instruct residents in sound dietary habits, provide greater access to fresh air, especially for slum residents, and encourage moderate daily exercise to build up resistance to disease. The publicity generated by the public health movement greatly increased citizen awareness of the need for governmental intervention in this problem area and was directly responsible for the growing outcry at mid-century for municipal parks that would provide breathing spaces and sporting sites for all urbanites.[34]

Sport and the Promotion of Order

The widely perceived need for new agencies of social control in the burgeoning urban centers provided a second justification for the encouragement of rational urban sport. Public health reformers like Dr. John H. Griscom believed that depraved physical conditions led to immorality and that if urbanites participated in moral amusements, they would be healthier. In addition, sportsmen who played clean sports would learn good moral values that would improve their character. Thus all would be happy, contented, and righteous citizens who would avoid vile pleasures and become solid pillars of the community.[35]

Social commentators recognized that amusements were an integral part of urban life: young men needed outlets for their energies and were not too particular about the quality of pleasures they selected. Social critics warned that good wholesome farm youths who had moved to cities and were unsupervised and free of the traditional social-control mechanisms that had regulated village pleasures also needed protection. The new urban environment provided many new opportunities for people to misspend their discretionary time in such popular commercial entertainments as theaters, music halls, dance halls, brothels, saloons, gambling houses, and spectator sports. Such vile and immoral diversions, favored by the bachelor subculture, were not uplifting and in no way "re-created" participants.[36]

Americans had historically made a clear distinction between idle amusements and wholesome recreation. As Stephen Hardy has explained, recreation restored the individual and prepared him for greater usefulness, while idle amusement simply provided for immediate, personal gratification. Advocates of the new sports creed also strongly opposed traditional blood and animal sports, because of the gambling involved, the bad examples of behavior they provided, and their negative impact on men's souls. For Unitarian minister William Ellery Channing and other reformers, the answer to the problem of vile amusements was the promotion of moral sports and entertainments as a positive alternative. Channing set the stage for the rational recreation movement in the 1830s by urging the promotion of the legitimate theater and physical culture as a substitute for immoral pleasures. In 1847 an optimistic Frederick Sawyer argued in *A Plea for Amusements* that if wholesome athletic institutions were "established in all our towns and cities for the free use of people, we shall see to it that we have enough healthy sources of recreation to employ the gambling rooms, the tippling shops and the brothels." The New York press strongly seconded such views and even approved of rational recreation on Sundays, although that violated the spirit of the Sabbath. But since bosses would not grant workingmen who needed recreation a half-holiday on Saturday, as was becoming the custom in England, moral Sunday amusement seemed the next best thing to help draw the lower classes away from vice dens that were open daily.[37]

The leading advocate of rational recreation, the noted urban reformer and Boston Unitarian minister Edward Everett Hale, recognized the great need of urbanites, especially manual workers who labored long hours, for leisure. Hale knew that city folk had different amusement problems than ruralites, who could readily go fishing or hunting and enjoy traditional rustic pleasures, and he sought new alternative entertainments that would be popular and wholesome. The clergyman had no confidence in commercial amusements that often catered to the basest tastes in search of the largest possible audiences. Believing that the church and state should cooperate to promote wholesome recreation, Hale urged clerics to promote moral sports like cricket and football, which improved health, developed character, and promoted courage.[38]

With Higginson and Holmes, Hale was a leading advocate of the muscular Christianity movement, an English-based philosophy that sought to harmonize the mental, physical, and spiritual dimensions of man. Hale and the other reformers saw the amusement problem as a part of their broader concern with the pathological features of urban life. Along with other mid-Victorians, they saw sport as both a sexual substitute and a check on effeminency. Their goal was to create a manly Christian gentleman who "was the athlete of continence, not coitus, continuously testing his manliness in the fires of self-denial." The muscular Christians encouraged athletics to counter the growing feminization of American culture by directing young men into "God's open air, where health, strength [and] manhood may be earned." The ideas of the muscular Christians about the social functions of sport were not new; they simply repackaged familiar concepts in a novel fashion aimed at alleviating urban problems. The Young Men's Christian Association (YMCA), imported from England in 1851 to assist farm youth to adjust to urban life in a moral environment, embodied the principles of the new sports creed. [39]

The sports creed had an enormous impact on the legitimating of sport among respectable middle-income urbanites. Developed before the Civil War and eventually blossoming in the sporting boom of the late nineteenth century, the ideology criticized the antisocial character of much of the surviving premodern urban sports tradition and encouraged participation in moral sports that could help alleviate some of the problems caused by industrial capitalism and urbanization. Colonial sports like hunting and fishing had been functional because of their connection to food gathering and defense; clean antebellum sports offered a rational substitute for the rugged life in rural society, which taught individualism; promoted manliness (i.e., self-discipline, courage, and self-denial); got people into the fresh air; and provided an alternative for vile amusements. Such ideas justified the time hard-working Christians spent at sport instead of at work earning money. The ideology also supported construction of public parks in which men from all social classes could enjoy sport. However, when most of the new parks were built in the late nineteenth century, the principal beneficiary was the middle class.

The Bourgeoisie and the Labor Aristocracy

Until the middle of the nineteenth century, hard-working, forward-looking, religious, middle-income urban men had little interest in sport or physical culture. The bourgeoisie—shopkeepers, professionals, agents, and clerks—had precious little discretionary time to spend at idle pleasures and lacked the wealth necessary to participate in prestigious elite sports. With the exception of clerks, who were generally young men learning the business with aspirations of gaining a future partnership or establishing their own firm, middle-class men were competitive workers who were their own bosses. They abhorred the popular mass sports of the day, regarding them as time-wasting, immoral, illegal, and debilitating—to be avoided at all costs. The social ethic expressed by the premodern life style and values of the sporting fraternity were totally antithetical to the bourgeois ethos of the early Victorian, who gained his manly identity through work, not leisure; earned his money by hard work, not gambling; and was a good provider. He did not shun domesticity for the firehouse or poolroom but rather made family and home the centerpiece of his life. However, the development of a sports creed that justified and encouraged participation in clean outdoor sport that was not merely pleasurable but also built character, improved morals, and enhanced personal and community health dramatically changed middle-class attitudes and behavior. The positive role models of English, Scottish, and German sporting cultures proved athletics could provide the stoop-shouldered office worker with a moral equivalent of the healthful work habits of the yeoman farmer, a real man who earned his keep by the sweat of his brow. Respectable young urbanites enthusiastically participated in many newly developing sports—especially team games, because they enjoyed the camaraderie, excitement, and competition of group contests which, although not yet congruent with the independent nature of middle-class work in the antebellum era, seemed to superbly embody the spirit of the new sporting ideology.[40]

Many blue-collar workers who historians have described as "loyalists" and "radicals" were also influenced by the new sports creed. They were future-oriented men influenced by the course of industrial capitalism to recognize a need for self-discipline in their personal lives. These workers accepted the Victorian morality of sexual continence, work before pleasure, temperance, hard work, and punctuality. Men who supported capitalism believed such conduct was required to get ahead in the counting house, to keep one's job at the workshop, and to become an independent master (in trades that were not dying out). Radical workingmen believed that Victorian behavior would help them fight the system by revitalizing their own producers' culture through an emphasis on brotherhood and mutual cooperation. The culture and behavior of all of these sportsmen was distinctly different from the "traditionalist" blue-collar workers, who maintained a premodern lifestyle that rejected piety, sobriety, sexual abstinence, and steady work. They were part of the bachelor subculture that favored blood and gambling sports.[41]

If the type of sport selected by urban workers reflected their cultural preferences, their opportunities to participate depended upon their free time, discretionary income, and accessibility to sporting facilities. In general this meant the labor aristocracy, who were relatively well paid and exercised control over the workplace, or employees with unusual shifts, like men in the food trades, who were active participants in both moral sports and the sporting counterculture. In most cities except New Orleans, which observed a Continental Sabbath, sabbatarianism deterred working-class amusements. The slow encroachment of the factory system had a negative impact on working-class leisure, displacing artisans like shoemakers with semiskilled machine operators who worked at the machine's rapid pace for sixty hours. The loss of the casual work day had its greatest impact in northeastern mill towns like Lynn and Fall River, Massachusetts, but until full-scale industrialization occurred, the consequences on leisure time were less drastic in cities with more diversified economies. [42]

The Sporting Life of Middle-Income Groups

Historians have generally identified the rise of middle-class sport as a late-nineteenth-century phenomenon, but recent revisionist studies demonstrate that growing acceptance of the sport creed stimulated considerable bourgeois participation in wholesome physical culture before the Civil War. [43] Participation was enjoyable and uplifting, provided a means of gaining recognition, and served as a focal point around which urbanites, many of whom were newcomers from rural areas, could find a community of like-minded fellows in sports clubs that supplied members with friendships, identity, and stability in the alienating and anomic antebellum city.

Ironically, given the strong pietistic bent of much of the urban middle class, their first major sport was harness racing, a sport whose popularity depended on the element of gambling. Harness racing originated on city roads and subsequently developed its modern characteristics in urban communities. Trotting gained popularity in the 1820s because trotters were relatively cheap to purchase, cost little to maintain, and most importantly to the middle-class mind set, were useful, unlike the aristocratic thoroughbreds. The trotter was the "democratic American horse," bred in America and used by its owner for locomotion or to pull a freight wagon. The great trotter Lady Suffolk, winner of over $35,000 in purses, was discovered pulling a butcher's cart! [44]

Trotting was an exciting diversion that enabled owners to exhibit their property, make wagers, and display individual prowess, since they originally drove their own horses. Most New York races were originally spontaneous contests (brushes) arranged at one of the road houses along macadamized Third Avenue, which provided a straight and level five-mile route outside of the city's residential sections where racers would not interfere with families in buggies. Eventually, the coming of cobblestone pavement, the introduction of the omnibus, and other more permanent forms of mass transit that accompanied the northward expansion of the city's population made racing impossible on Third Avenue, and in the

1860s roadsters were forced to move to Harlem Lane in Upper Manhattan. By the early 1870s even Harlem Lane had to be relinquished because of the city's inexorable development and the need to use the avenue for more public purposes.[45]

In 1825 middle- and upper-middle-class horsemen formed the New York Trotting Association (NYTA), with many of the same goals as jockey clubs. The NYTA organized regular semi-annual meets to replace the brushes. It built a course in 1826 at Centerville, Long Island, for club meets and also used a privately owned half-mile track built in 1831 near the Red House Tavern in Harlem. The matches were originally five miles or longer, but in the 1840s one-mile heats were initiated because they were less wearing on the horses and permitted time for more contests. Like the more elite jockey clubs, the NYTA promoted a sense of community among men of the same social class who shared an interest in the turf.[46]

In the 1850s the nouveaux riches like Cornelius Vanderbilt and Robert Bonner became interested in the sport and quickly became the dominant breeders. Bonner and Vanderbilt wanted to gain acceptance among the social elite through such self-publicizing activities as success in sports. They began buying up the best trotters and rationalizing the breeding industry, making it difficult for less wealthy men to compete at the big trotting races. Bonner spent about $150,000 for trotters, even though he was opposed to gambling and racing for stakes and therefore never raced his horses in public. Bonner brought a certain dignity to the sport that some other owners like Vanderbilt could not. Bonner's example helped make the owning of trotters a respectable and prestigious amusement for the upper crust and brought elite dimensions to what had previously been a middle-class sport.[47]

Many middle-class antebellum Victorian sportsmen found team ball sports—the old English sport of cricket and the newly evolving American game of baseball—provided good vehicles for social interaction with other men of similar backgrounds and occupations in a healthful and pleasant outdoor setting. Outside of the Indian game of lacrosse, cricket was the first major team sport and the first organized team sport in America. It was played informally in cities during the colonial era, but few contests were actually organized until the 1840s, when a cricket fad developed; by 1860 there were reportedly about 400 cricket clubs with 10,000 players.[48]

In such large cities as New York, Boston, and Philadelphia, which all had mixed economies, major antebellum teams were predominantly middle class—mainly merchants, managers, and professionals. The St. George Cricket Club (SGCC), for example, was 77.1 percent nonmanual in 1848 and 94.3 percent in 1865. It was becoming less an ethnic and more a status organization. The well-to-do men of commerce and finance who joined cricket clubs used them to unite the business leadership, demonstrate their social status, and confirm their growing importance in the Anglo-American community. Yet at the same time, working-class English immigrants had been among the first cricketers and, in industrial cities like Newark, dominated the sport. In the late 1850s nearly 85 percent of Newark's players were manual workers; most (77.4 percent) were artisans, primarily metal or clothing workers. Working-class cricket players in Newark were far more prosperous than the city's average residents, and many could afford to live in its inner-and outer-ring middle-class neighborhoods. They did not have the time to play the standard two innings that could go on for days and instead played for a fixed time limit. Sometimes they played weekday pickup games in the street during lunchbreak or after work. To promote loyalty to the firm, some bosses gave employees time off to practice, especially if the company sponsored the team. Practice was usually twice a week, and matches were held on Saturdays, which was a workday for most Americans.[49]

Cricket was supplanted in the 1850s as the leading team sport by baseball, a game that had evolved from a simple, informal children's pastime into an organized team sport of considerable sophistication. From the start baseball was very much an urban game. Of the different forms of ball games played in the antebellum era, the one that eventually triumphed was known as the New York Game, which is essentially what we play today. It was developed by the Knickerbocker Club, an upper-middle-class social club organized in 1845 to play ball games in a convivial atmosphere. Its social prestige was less than that of the SGCC and well below that of the city's Yacht Club and various jockey clubs. Some of the club members had played a bat-and-ball game as early as 1842, in the Murray Hill section of New York at Twenty-seventh Street and Fourth Avenue; but once the club was established, developed rules of play, and drew up a constitution, it moved to the Elysian Fields in Hoboken, where Alexander J. Cartwright laid out a diamond-shaped field with bases at the corners ninety feet apart.[50]

The Knickerbockers were not themselves ardent proselytizers for baseball, but the game they developed gained quick acceptance among urban sportsmen who formed their own clubs based on the model of the Knickerbockers. Young men took to the sport because it was an exciting, American game similar to, yet simpler than, cricket, took less time to play, and did not require the perfect pitches of cricket fields, which were hard to find. Furthermore, since baseball's characteristics fit in well with the new sports creed, it became widely perceived as a valuable source of recreation that promoted sound moral values and good health as well as manliness (once the fly rule was adopted in 1864 to make the game more difficult). Baseball seemingly provided both an escape from and a remedy for some of the worst aspects of mid-nineteenth century urban life. [51]

About a dozen baseball clubs were in operation in New York and Brooklyn in 1855, ten years after the Knickerbockers had been formed. Three years later the number zoomed to ninety-six, with many more in the metropolitan area. Their members were predominantly, but not exclusively, middle-class white-collar workers. Adelman found that three-fourths of the Brooklyn and New York ballplayers active in the early 1850s were white-collar, almost evenly divided between high (37.2 percent) and low (39.4 percent) white-collar men, and the rest were skilled craftsmen (23.4 percent). After 1855, as the sport became more popular, the status of club members declined. Only two-thirds of the members were white-collar workers; low-level nonmanual workers outnumbered high-level players by two to one. The ratio of white-collar to blue-collar worker ballplayers remained approximately the same for at least the next fifteen years. Among the blue-collar players, virtually none in Brooklyn, New York, or Chicago (where 30.1 percent of ballplayers in the late 1860s were blue-collar) were semiskilled or unskilled workers. Only in industrial Newark, where 44.5 percent of its ballplayers were manual workers, was a noticeable proportion (6.5 percent) employed at the lowest status jobs. Their absence reflected a lack of time, money, interest, access to ball fields, or the social prestige necessary to join many of the early baseball teams. [52]

The first baseball teams were often organized by occupations, companies, political parties, or neighborhoods (the latter were mainly junior teams comprised of a mix of students, apprentices, and clerks). Teams organized by job included the Æsculapians (Brooklyn physicians), the Metropolitans (teachers), and the Manhattans (policemen). Far more prominent were the teams affiliated with political parties. In New York, Tammany Hall sponsored the renowned Mutuals, who started out as a volunteer fire company, along with several working-class ward teams. Across the river in Brooklyn the local Democratic organization was tied to the Atlantics, who held the mythical national championship in 1864 and 1865. The aid came from politicians—members of the sporting fraternity who wanted to use baseball to enhance their image and gain votes. The most prominent teams became vehicles of urban boosterism, and inter-urban rivalries arose. As the *Brooklyn Eagle* boasted in 1860, "If we are ahead of the big city in nothing else, we can beat her in baseball." After the Civil War, urban boosters formed professional nines like the famous Cincinnati Red Stockings with the expressed purpose of advertising the progressive character of their towns. [53]

Many of these ball clubs served as status communities, and at first white-collar nines would not play blue-collar clubs. Professional men and businessmen would not play firemen, who played mainly other firemen, policemen, or kindred workers. Factory teams usually played other industrial clubs. The first working-class team, the Brooklyn Eckfords, founded in 1855, had a hard time getting matches with top clubs who were reluctant to play them, partly due to snobbery, but also because of their unproven ability. The Eckfords were mainly shipwrights and mechanics, who only had enough time to practice once a week. However, the players were economically middle class and had an average wealth in excess of $3,000—double that of contemporary clerks. The team was named for the richest shipbuilder in the United States, and it has been argued that this symbolized their faith in hard work and other bourgeois values. The team's president was a well-to-do dock builder who advocated "business first, pleasure afterwards." Once this team got a chance to prove itself, it was regularly able to schedule other top teams and won the metropolitan championship in 1862 and 1863.[54]

Compared to cricket and especially to elite sports, the mixing of classes was relatively common in baseball. The sport was democratic enough to make room for non-Victorian artisans, especially from the food trades. While the Eckfords were popularly identified as a working-class team, one-fifth of the players, including a doctor, were nonmanual workers. A study of five Newark teams found that three were evenly divided between white-and blue-collar workers. The other two teams were mainly manual or nonmanual but included nearly a 30 percent share of the other category. Historian George Kirsch believes that for these Newark players, "Common economic status and residence outweighed their vocational differences." By the late 1850s baseball teams were less exclusive status communities than communities of respectable hard-working men seeking to get ahead, save money, lead righteous moral lives, avoid dissipation, and gain middle-class status. For the great majority of players, the game provided a focal point around which to develop an associational life which improved their health and character. Their voluntary associations were run by serious-minded officers who expected their players to be highly disciplined and to practice diligently.[55]

Sport and Urban Space

Urbanization affected sport most directly through its impact on urban space. Although this influence was far less dramatic in the walking city than it would become later on, when cities outgrew their pedestrian dimensions, it was still very important. Most sporting activity took place in outdoor public places—streets, vacant lots, parks, lakes, and rivers. However, by the 1850s, as cities became more densely populated and as laws were passed regulating behavior in public places (no nude swimming, no cycling or ballplaying in the streets or sidewalks, etc.) finding space for sporting pleasures grew increasingly difficult, particularly for working-class sportsmen in cities like New York. New York ball players depended on nearby Hoboken's Elysian Fields, just a fifteen-minute ferry ride from the southern part of the city, which became a popular resort in the 1830s and 1840s. In 1840, when the fledgling New York Cricket Club could not secure grounds in Manhattan, they first practiced at the Elysian Fields and then used part of a vacant racetrack behind John C. Stevens's home at Castle Point adjacent to the field. Five years later when the growth of the city pushed them out of their old space, the Knickerbockers moved to the Elysian Fields, where they rented a playing site and a dressing room for seventy-five dollars. Similarly, the elite SGCC had to move—first from its original location near Bloomingdale Road (Broadway) and Fifth Avenue north to the Red House Tavern in Harlem and then again in 1854 to the more accessible Elysian Fields—purportedly because the residential sections of the city were moving northward and using up the open spaces. In 1858 just two of the eight most popular playing fields in the metropolitan area were in the city. Even in New Jersey teams that had appropriated vacant lots for playing sites frequently lost their fields as cities expanded. Jersey City's teams "lost their first grounds in the 4th ward in consequence of the march of improvement, such as filling in streets" and lost a second location when railroad tracks were laid through it. Because top-flight cricket competition required a well-manicured surface, working-class cricket teams had an even harder time finding suitable fields. The Newark Cricket Club made repeated moves to find decent playing areas but never did secure a quality site. This problem was much less of a concern for upper-middle-class New York cricketers, who played at the Elysian Fields, or for elite Philadelphians, who played in Camden, New Jersey, or on club members' suburban estates.[56]

In the long run loss of public space for sport led to the construction of municipal parks with space set aside for active pleasures. However, before the Civil War the efforts of the municipal park movement achieved little. The most notable accomplishment, Central Park in New York City, was originally used primarily for receptive recreation. A second, and relatively modest, alternative was the establishment of private space for sports by voluntary organizations, particularly status and ethnic organizations which wanted to establish space between themselves and other urbanites. In Chicago the German turners built their own indoor gymnasiums, and in 1867 a German marksmanship society (*Jaeger* Corps) opened Sharp-shooters Park, northwest of the city, as a rifle range.[57] A third, and crucial, alternative was utilization of indoor and outdoor semipublic space, privately owned but open for a fee to the general public. A variety of semipublic places catered to every taste in the walking city: sporting taverns for the bachelor subculture, cycling schools for respectable sportswomen, racetracks for the gambling crowd, and ballparks for baseball fans. Semipublic space was used for both participatory sports (roller skating, ice skating, billiards, cricket), and spectator sports (horse racing, boxing, baseball).

Spectator Sport at Semipublic Sites

The large numbers of male sports fans concentrated in cities provided an enormous potential market for entrepreneurs in the business of spectator sports. During most of the antebellum period prosperity provided a large number of urbanites with discretionary income to spend for entertainment, and they became accustomed to paying for their amusement. Mass audiences, drawn to specialized semipublic sites of entertainment like Barnum's American Museum, the Astor Theater, the Union Race Course, and the Union Grounds, were often free to indulge in the kind of exuberant behavior that mid-Victorians normally frowned upon. Indoor spectator sports included animal sports, boxing, and billiards; the main outdoor events were horse racing, cricket, and baseball. Blood sports attracted mainly lower- and lower-middle-class crowds to shows staged in the seedier parts of town or outside the city's limits. Boxing matches inside sports taverns would draw several hundred fans at fifty cents a head, while fights at neighborhood theaters cost twice as much. One dollar was the normal admission price to billiard contests, though all 500 seats at the sold-out Michael Phelan–John Seereiter championship match in 1859 went for five dollars. High prices not only brought in more profits but kept out the riffraff.[58]

Far larger crowds turned out for outdoor sports, particularly the turf. In the antebellum era all of New York's race tracks, including the famous Union Course opened in 1821, were on Long Island, where there was a long racing tradition and land was cheap. Jockey clubs, the earliest organizations to try to run spectator sports on sound business principles, enclosed tracks and sold admissions, originally to pay for the cost of their meets. In 1829 Cadwallader R. Colden, scion of an old New York family, attempted to run the Union Course as a profit-making business. The track had a capacity of 5,000 seated and standing fans. But gate receipts proved inadequate and Colden failed. The course was about six miles from New York, which required either a very long walk or an expensive trip, by ferry and railroad, that in the 1830s cost one dollar each way. Furthermore, the cost of admission was at least twenty-five cents and usually double that.

An average ticket cost more than one dollar and went as high as three dollars for carriages. Thus attendance, which averaged 2,000 to 3,000 at most races, was largely restricted to the sporting fraternity and elite horse fanciers. But the sport did have some potential as a business venture. Motley crowds estimated by the press to be well in excess of 50,000 attended the five "Great Intersectional Races" staged in New York between 1821 and 1845. These events brought a lot of prestige to the city and also an income of twenty dollars a day from every tourist in town to see the races. The matches, held at the Union Race Course, drew spectators from all social classes ranging from the social elite to workingmen who saved up for the big event. Most spectators reached the site by a forty-minute train ride from Brooklyn which cost forty cents each way. They enjoyed a carnival-like atmosphere and purchased food and drink from vendors who had set up booths and tents. The enclosed section of the site, a mile in circumference, held not only carriages and horsemen but also the grandstand, to which a season's admission cost ten dollars. At the 1845 match between Fashion and Peytona, the grandstand supposedly held 30,000 spectators. Large, impatient crowds created some problems in maintaining order (overcrowded trains, people running onto the course, spectators sneaking into the stands), and consequently twenty to thirty constables, as well as shoulder hitters like Captain Rynders, Yankee Sullivan, and Butcher Bill Harrington, were employed for crowd control. The popularity of the intersectional races encouraged the owners of the Union Course to invest $60,000 to build the Beacon Race Course in nearby Hoboken, a cheap six-cent ferry ride from New York. But the onset of the Depression that year, high ticket prices, and the overall decline of thoroughbred racing in the North caused the track to discontinue thoroughbred racing.[59]

The first successful efforts to put racing on a profit-making basis occurred in New Orleans. In 1846, after the fall of New York racing, a local politician built the Bingaman Track at a suburban site expressly to make money. Track manager Richard Ten Broeck made it into a "people's track," cutting admission in half to fifty cents, admitting women free, and promoting other popular pastimes like bull baiting to cover expenses. In 1851 Ten Broeck, on his own, took over the ten-year-old Metairie Track, where he sought a high-class clientele. He raised purses to attract the best stables, renovated the grandstand, and created a ladies' section with parlors and restrooms. Races scheduled mainly for weekdays and a one-dollar ticket price kept down working-class attendance. As at other high-class tracks, social divisions were maintained by relegating masses to the infield or the public stand while jockey club members and their guests were isolated in the members' stand.[60]

The popularity of trotting racing on streets and tracks encouraged entrepreneurs in the 1830s to commercialize that sport. Within a decade it had supplanted thoroughbred racing as the preeminent spectator sport outside of New Orleans. By the 1850s suburban trotting courses were located all over the country. The New York metropolitan area had seven tracks—one-tenth the national total—some of which had been converted from thoroughbred racing. The New York meets offered the biggest purses, attracted the finest horses, and drew the largest gates, normally 6,000 to 8,000 spectators for important races but double when horses like the fabled Flora Temple raced in the late 1850s.[61]

The large suburban racetracks were used not only for saddleback and harness racing (introduced in the 1840s) but also for other popular spectator sports like pedestrianism and baseball. In 1835 John C. Stevens organized a contest at the Union course to win a wager that a runner could cover ten miles in an hour. His offer of $1,000, to be shared by the men achieving this feat, plus a bonus to the winner brought nine competitors, mostly artisans, to the starting line and about 20,000 spectators to see if it could be done. Henry Stannard, a Connecticut farmer, made it with twelve seconds to spare. Stevens won his bet and also profited from the sale of tickets to the event. He was a great sportsman, but no fool, and always tried to at least break even, if not make money, from his promotions.[62]

The "Great Footrace" helped make pedestrianism the second leading spectator sport after harness racing. The Beacon Race Course, mainly used for trotting contests, became a major site for pedestrianism. Promotions at the Hoboken track were highlighted by a series of international matches between the leading British and American professionals. Pedestrianism peaked in 1844, when one of these contests attracted 30,000 spectators. However, fan interest soon paled amid rumors of fixed races, and in 1845 the elite promoters turned their attention to more respectable sports and closed the Beacon Course.[63]

At baseball games the size of crowds depended on the population of the site, the quality of competition, and the cost of attending. Typical crowds at cities like Newark and Jersey City would be a few hundred; regular matches in Brooklyn drew a few thousand; and championship games attracted from 5,000 to 15,000. Attendance at major contests staged at distant locations was mainly middle and upper-middle class because of the cost of travel; working-class fans were primarily seen at local neighborhood fields in walking distance of their homes. Blue-collar spectatorship was also influenced by the introduction of admission fees, which became commonplace for important matches after the Civil War. The first time that onlookers were charged an admission fee to a baseball game was in 1858, when Brooklyn and New York all-star teams played a three-game series at the neutral Fashion Race Course in Long Island. The spectators each paid ten cents to watch (plus an additional twenty cents for their one-horse vehicle; forty cents for a two-horse vehicle), which paid the expense of preparing the grounds. Four years later William H. Cammeyer commercialized the sport. He converted his ice-skating rink in Brooklyn's Eastern District, located some three to four miles from the center of the city, into an enclosed baseball field at a cost of $1,200, and then offered it free to three prominent teams in return for the right to charge spectators ten cents each for admission. The example of the Union Grounds encouraged other local entrepreneurs to convert a skating area in the city's western section into a ballfield known as the Capitoline Grounds. By then leading teams like the Atlantics were demanding and getting a share of the gate. Admission prices increased to twenty-five cents in 1867, and doubled three years later for such big games as the Atlantics versus the Cincinnati Reds. The fees not only benefited promoters and players but also paid for improved accommodations for ladies, whose presence indicated the respectability of the sport, and other paying customers and sought to discourage rowdy lower-class spectators.[64]

Crowd behavior was a problem by the late 1850s. The carnival-like atmosphere at big games attracted con men, pickpockets, and "overgrown boys" who were a disruptive influence at games held in open fields with only ropes to restrain the audience and also at games held in enclosed fields. Interference with play was more likely at the open grounds, especially at games involving nines whose highly partisan fans viewed the teams as representative of their class and ethnicity. The 1860 championship game between the Atlantics and Excelsiors had to be halted because of the verbal abuse heaped on the umpire and the Excelsiors by the Atlantics' working-class fans. Unfortunately, building enclosed stands and charging admission did not eliminate rowdy behavior. Ticket holders were hassled outside the stands, and lower-class hooligans were also disruptive inside the grounds after purchasing a ticket or sneaking in. There were still fights, interference with play, verbal abuse, drinking, and gambling, despite the presence of police and an overwhelming majority of well-behaved spectators.[65]

Preservation of Public Space: *The Park Movement and Central Park*

The problem of declining public space suitable for healthful outdoor pleasures accelerated together with the pace of urbanization in the antebellum city. The dilemma was most severe in older cities, particularly the rapidly growing northeastern cities, which had crowded, unhealthy slums, but was also apparent by the 1860s in newer big cities like Chicago. In the South the need to preserve public space was less crucial: urbanization occurred at a slower pace and major cities like Charleston, New Orleans, and Savannah had long ago laid out public squares, small parks, and private gardens to alleviate the harsh summer heat and periodic epidemics. The best municipal park in the North was the Boston Common, described in 1841 by Lydia Maria Child as "a blessing unrivalled by any other city." The Common maintained a rustic atmosphere, formal gardens, and space for children's games and youthful athletics in the heart of the city. However, the population of Boston and its suburbs quadrupled between 1830 and 1870, and even the Common became inadequate to meet public demands for space. [66]

In the 1830s, to provide fresh air and a moral environment for urbanites, particularly the masses who could not escape to the countryside, several eastern cities began to construct rural cemeteries like Mt. Auburn in Cambridge (1831), Laurel Hill in Philadelphia (1836), and Greenwood in Brooklyn (1838). They were designed in a romantic style—landscaped gardens, meandering tree-lined walks, lakes, and sculptured tombstones and monuments—which provided a marked contrast to the hustle and bustle of urban life. The cemeteries were open all day and were visited by large numbers of city folk in search of fresh air, a peaceful and lovely place to rest, or a spot for a picnic. Mt. Auburn's popularity actually resulted in considerable overcrowding and rowdiness. [67]

In the 1840s public health reformers introduced another approach to meet the health, social, and recreational needs of urban folk—the municipal park movement. Such public facilities could provide space for both fresh air and exercise for people of all social backgrounds—an ideal use of public space for rational recreation. As public health leader Dr. Lemuel Shattuck noted in his *Plan for the Promotion of Public and Personal Health* (1850), "Intellectual culture has received too much and physical training too little attention." He recommended the appropriation of public funds to pay for "open space [which] would afford to the artizan [sic] and the poorer classes the advantages of fresh air and exercise." City governments had traditionally regulated such public places as docks, wharves, markets, and streets, which were essential for commerce. Hence municipalities had banned various lower-class street games and sports like quoits on city streets. In the 1840s and 1850s, as local governments extended their scope of activities to provide such essential services as fire and police protection, the development of new public parks seemed a natural extension of municipal responsibilities. [68]

The center of the municipal park movement was New York, where the need for such public space was greatest. As early as 1785 a citizen had petitioned the mayor seeking improvement of the inadequate facilities for outdoor exercise: "It is a very general complaint that there is not in this great city, nor its environs, any one proper spot where its numerous inhabitants can enjoy, with convenience, the exercise that is necessary for health and amusement.'' A survey in 1849 found that the city owned just 170 acres of open space, divided up among several small parks that were inadequate for popular sports like cricket. As one antebellum New Yorker reminisced, ''There was no place within the city limits in which it was pleasant to walk, or ride, or drive, or stroll; no place for skating, no water in which it was safe to row; no field for base-ball or cricket.''[69]

The municipal park movement in New York was led by William Cullen Bryant, poet and editor of the *Evening Post*, and Andrew Jackson Downing, the prominent landscape architect. As early as 1836 Bryant had recommended that the city reserve a section of its forest for a future park for the masses who could not afford expensive suburban excursions. Downing advocated the construction of a public park based on European models because it would promote social order by enabling people of different backgrounds to meet in a convivial setting. The public park would be a republican institution that ''would soften and humanize the rude, educate and enlighten the ignorant, and give continual enjoyment to the educated.''[70]

The publicity generated by Bryant and Downing helped create a broad-based coalition that included social reformers, physicians, labor leaders, businessmen, urban boosters, and politicians. Advocates argued that a city park would improve public health, alleviate class conflict, improve the economy, and enhance the city's prestige. Health would be improved by providing a place for sedentary workers to exercise and for slum residents to breathe fresh air, play, and temporarily escape their disease-riddled neighborhoods. A park would promote the social order by facilitating the mingling of classes and thereby giving the masses an opportunity to learn from their betters. Park goers would develop a sense of community with each other. They would feel as if they had a stake in a society that cared enough about them to build magnificent parks for them. Promoters hoped such sentiments would counter social pressures that promoted violence and disorder among the city's least fortunate residents. A park would contribute indirectly to the economy by providing a place for workers to re-create themselves so that absenteeism would decline and bosses could get the most out of their labor, saving money on police and jails because crime rates would drop, and boosting the city's reputation through cultural development which would attract additional residents and businesses. Its direct economic benefit would be to raise property values in the surrounding neighborhood.[71]

The concept of a municipal park for New York first became an important political issue in 1850, when it received strong support from Mayor Caleb S. Woodhull, who advocated a city park for the purposes of beautification and improving the health of the toiling masses. A year later the common council began considering a site known as Jones' Wood on the East River from 68th to 77th Streets, first suggested by Bryant in 1844. The debate over possible sites, costs, and land uses went on for five years until Tammany Mayor Fernando Wood successfully shepherded a bill through the common council that resulted in the selection of a much larger and more expensive 780-acre central park site in mid-Manhattan. This location, originally proposed by Downing in 1851, was geologically un- suited for private development and was inhabited only by squatters, while the other major site had important commercial and residential potential. Of course, Mayor Wood's support was hardly selfless; he anticipated huge opportunities for graft and patronage in the construction of Central Park.[72]

Construction of the new park was supervised by Frederick L. Olmsted, who with partner Calvert Vaux had designed the prize-winning landscape plan for Central Park. Work on the $1.5 million city-funded project began in 1857, but only after the Republican-dominated state government had taken away the municipality's power to manage construction and substi- tuted a state-appointed board of park commissioners. The purpose of this move, at the same time the state took over the city's police department, was to prevent city Democrats from using these agencies for patronage. Nonetheless, Superintendent Olmsted was constantly besieged with job requests from aldermen and other politicians, especially during the De- pression of 1857–58. Olmsted refused to buckle under and was later applauded by the *Times*: "[Olmsted] proved the possibility, in which hardly anyone previously believed, of conducting a great public work . . . in absolute disregard of political influence. . . . Workmen found . . . that they could earn money in the public service without having to throw in their votes with their labor, and the people found it was possible to spend enormous sums for public purposes without jobbery, corruption, or leakage."[73]

In 1870 the Democrats regained control of the state government and rushed through a new city charter that replaced the park board with a department subordinate to City Hall. The parks department under Peter Sweeney quickly became a center for spoilsmanship and Olmsted was forced out. Thousands of good Democrats were hired for make-work projects that destroyed much of the beauty of the park. Fortunately for the future of Central Park, the Tweed Ring was broken a year later and, with it, the most blatant corruption in the parks department.[74]

Olmsted's vision for the municipal park reflected his awareness that urbanization created terrible problems. Urbanites suffered from loosened social ties, lost opportunities for reflection and repose, and desensitization. The close bonds that had characterized his hometown of Hartford could not be maintained in the large modern city. Olmsted believed that direct action was needed to protect the city, that men of his social class should intervene to make urbanization socially beneficial rather than destructive, and that through nature the moral and social life of a city could be elevated. His ideal park would glorify nature and serve as a complete contrast to the "restraining and confined conditions of town." Olmsted's grounds, designed to be centers of receptive recreation in which the park goer received pleasure without conscious exertion by looking at tranquil scenes, gentle streams, and grassy meadows, would promote morality, self-control, temperance, a sense of community, and a decline in class conflict. Olmsted hoped that Central Park would be a working-class refuge, a diversion from "unwholesome, vicious, destructive methods and habits of seeking recreation." However, since the lack of cheap public transportation from lower Manhattan, three to four miles away, made the park relatively inaccessible to the masses, especially during the week, it became mainly a middle-class resort. [75]

Olmsted's design for Central Park included, as required by the park commissioners, play grounds and a fifty-acre parade ground for athletic and cricket fields. Certain park advocates felt that cricket grounds were essential, since there were none in the city. Anticipating the cricket field, an 1858 convention of baseball players organized a committee to lobby the park board for equal treatment. Over the next few years dozens of cricket and baseball teams petitioned to use the public space for sports, but it was not until 1865 that a cricket club was finally permitted to use the park to practice for a game. As long as Olmsted was superintendent, adult ball sports were almost never allowed in Central Park; they created financial problems, attracted gamblers and rowdy crowds, and ruined grassy meadows. Olmsted would not countenance any sports "which must be enjoyed by a single class . . . to the diminution of the enjoyment of others." He was not opposed to exertive recreation but believed it had no place in Central Park. He purposely designed curved roadways to prevent trotting matches that could disturb the repose of the park (although impromptu races were held), and the curved roads permitted "quiet drives, rides and strolls" through the park. Carriage driving and horseback riding were enjoyed by fashionable ladies and gentlemen. [76]

Ice skating was the most important sport in Central Park. Since the frozen pond simply replenished itself during the winter, skaters would not damage the natural beauty of the park. The same space was used for boating in spring after the ice melted. A pond in Central Park opened for skating in the winter of 1858–59 and skating quickly became a popular fad among middle-class men and women. Women comprised one-tenth of the skaters. They originally skated on a separate pond, but in 1860 a daring woman left the ladies' pond for the men's ice. Other women followed, and coed skating became the rage. It gave women a chance to exercise, exhibit athletic skills, and socialize with men in a proper setting. Skating and horseback riding were the only physically exertive sports regarded as appropriate for mid-Victorian women. By 1866 the daily average attendance at the skating pond reached 20,000, with evening skating under gas lamps especially popular.[77]

The success of Central Park had an enormous impact on the municipal park movement. It provided a model for other cities to emulate, often under the guidance or design of Olmsted, who subsequently planned large suburban parks or park systems—all emphasizing receptive recreation—in Boston, Brooklyn, Chicago, Philadelphia, San Francisco, and other cities. Furthermore, Central Park's example motivated municipal governments to get more involved in urban planning to protect valuable natural resources for future generations and taught the value of using efficient and independent single-purpose agencies to administer urban development projects.[78]

Conclusion: Sport, Urbanization, and the Walking City

Urbanization had a strong and multifaceted impact upon the development of sport in the mid-nineteenth century, when American cities were undergoing a highly accelerated rate of growth. The social, demographic, economic, and cultural conditions engendered by the fast pace of change led to the evolution of several distinctive sporting cultures that catered to the needs and interests of social elites, ethnic groups, the male bachelor subculture, and the bourgeoisie. Sports provided elites and the old immigrants with a focal point for the development of an associational life that enabled them to separate themselves from the rest of society. The growth of the sporting fraternity and its unsavory subculture generally occurred away from public scrutiny in anonymous dives located in the roughest, unpoliced sections of town, where men enjoyed blood and gambling sports organized by sports entrepreneurs. Their sporting pleasures were very much a part of their traditional life-styles. The middle-class sporting culture developed in response to the growing urban pathology, exemplified by the lowlife behavior of the male bachelor subculture. Social reformers developed a sports creed that recommended physical culture as a remedy for many of the problems of crowded, anomic urban life. Clean sport provided sedentary workers a substitute for the idealized rustic way of life by improving health, morals, and character. Men who subscribed to this ideology were sporting gentlemen—respectable forward-looking individuals who believed in hard work, planning for the future, and leading Christian lives. Their favorite sports, such as baseball, were moral, personally uplifting, and socially functional.

The growing middle-class interest in sport was also justified by the ideology of rational recreation but was also a product of the growing wealth of cities, booming urban populations, sufficient discretionary income and leisure time among nonfactory workers, the positive example of English, Scottish, and German sportsmen, the rise of middle-class voluntary associations, the development of sports entrepreneurship, and various technological innovations that improved interurban transportation and communication networks. Municipal governments did not as yet contribute much to alleviate the recreational needs of residents, although things were beginning to change as cities started to emulate the example of New York City's well-planned Central Park. [79] For the most part, cities were more concerned with regulating public space rather than with adding to it.

The growth of cities themselves played a crucial role in mid-nineteenth-century sporting developments. The increased urban populations provided sufficient numbers of people with similar interests to facilitate the formation of sports clubs based on ethnic and class backgrounds. These voluntary associations secured the needed athletic facilities, organized competition, and provided a source of community so important to residents of dynamic urban centers undergoing unprecedented change. The large numbers also encouraged entrepeneurs to enter the sports business or related ventures. Taverns continued to use sports to encourage trade, while new semipublic enterprises were initiated, such as roller rinks, billiard parlors, baseball parks, and race tracks.

The growing physical size of cities and the rapid development of former open space within cities had a negative effect upon sporting opportunities. The countryside, an important venue for field and stream sports, became more distant and expensive to reach. In the meantime, the intensive use of land within towns resulted in a significant loss of old public playing sites, which made it increasingly difficult for working-class sportsmen to find suitable playing areas, particularly out-of-doors. They became more dependent on indoor semipublic facilities like taverns and billiard parlors. At the same time, the intensive use of land and a desire to escape urban blight and people who were different from themselves encouraged sports clubs and individuals to seek out new sports facilities that were either private or distant and well beyond the walking range of the urban masses. The pressure of development left New York, which was in the forefront of urbanization, with virtually no baseball fields or public lanes for trotters.

Turf and baseball fans had to travel long distances to attend their favorite sports at sites where land was cheap, and while public transportation was available, its cost was beyond the means of most urbanites unless they had saved for that special occasion. These early semipublic sites came into their own in the late nineteenth century, which enjoyed a great boom in sports and a revolution in urban mass transit that significantly increased access to distant semipublic sports areas.

"Grounds of the Chicago Sharpshooters Association . . . June 1866." Courtesy of the Chicago Historical Society (ICHi-03968).

"Central-Park Winter. The Skating Pond," from a drawing by Charles Parsons for Currier & Ives. In the 1860s ice skating was a popular social activity.

"The American National Game of Baseball. The Grand Match for the Championship at the Elysian Fields, Hoboken, N.J.," from a drawing by Currier & Ives, 1866. In this contest between the Brooklyn Atlantics and the New York Mutuals, 3 August 1865, shortstop Dickey Pearce of the Atlantics is at bat, prepared to bunt the runner on third base home. This is the only Currier & Ives baseball print. Courtesy of the Library of Congress.

First tournament for the American billiard championship, held in New York in June 1863. Dudley Kavanaugh defeated seven rivals in four-ball. *Frank Leslie's Illustrated Weekly* 16 (27 June 1863): 221.

"The [New York] Caledonian Club at Randall's Island." *Harper's Weekly* 11 (2 November 1867): 692.

"Fast Trotters on Harlem Lane, New York," 1870, drawn by J. Cameron for Currier & Ives.

"Peytona and Fashion in Their Great Match for $20,000 over the Union Course, Long Island, May 13, 1845," from a drawing by Charles Severin for Currier & Ives. The southern horse Peytona won two straight closely contested four-mile heats in 7:39¾ and 7:45¼ before a crowd estimated at from 70,000 to 100,000.

SPORT IN THE INDUSTRIALIZED
RADIAL CITY, 1870–1960

The Quest for Identity and the Separatist Dynamics of Urban Sport

Why there should be such constant strife to bring together in sport the two divergent elements of society that never by any chance meet elsewhere on even terms is quite incomprehensible, and it is altogether the sole cause of all our athletic woe. . . . The laboring class are all right in their way; let them go their way in peace, and have their athletics in whatsoever manner best suits their inclination. . . . Let us have our own sport among the more refined elements, and allow no discordant spirits to enter into it.

> Caspar A. Whitney, *A Sporting Pilgrimage*
> (New York, 1895), 164, 167.

If a gentleman and a chimney sweep rub against each other, the sweep will be no cleaner, while the gentleman will be dirtier. If you take down the fence and allow amateurs and professionals to graze in the same field all day, it will be hard to separate them at night. Some will be sure to be driven into the wrong stable.

> William B. Curtis, in *Spirit of the Times*
> 104 (28 Oct. 1882): 367.

To the pious people of the ghetto a baseball player was the king of loafers.

> Eddie Cantor, *My Life Is in Your Hands*
> (New York, 1928), 50.

CHAPTER 2

Sport and the Urban Social Structure

The development of the industrial radial city had a crucial impact upon the sporting pleasures of all urban social classes. The greatest impact was economic: the rise of industrial capitalism enriched a small number of people, improved the standard of living for the nonmanual middle class, weakened the position of the artisan class, and gave rise to a huge pool of poorly paid, semiskilled and unskilled industrial workers who worked long hours at a backbreaking pace. As widening income levels, substantial differences in discretionary time, and diverse social values resulted in different leisure options for different social classes, sport came to mark social boundaries and to define status communities. Spatial and demographic changes in the radial city also influenced the development of urban sport along class lines. The enormous physical growth of cities, accompanied by extraordinary increases in population, had major impacts on historic patterns of land use, which in turn influenced each class's sporting opportunities. In the era of the walking city, the countryside had been relatively accessible to most urbanites, who could enjoy there a wide variety of outdoor sports, but after the 1870s, empty lots, the woods, and unpolluted streams were harder to reach, especially for lower-class men who could not afford costly transportation fees. Furthermore, traditional playing fields and sports centers in the old urban core were displaced to make way for more valuable development, and consequently workingmen lost many traditional recreational sites. But the changing spatial patterns were far less of a problem for middle-and upper-income groups, who were more likely to live near sports facilities and could afford the cost of transportation to their favorite athletic sites.

Sport and the Urban Upper Class

In the Gilded Age a segment of the urban elite constituted a community of conspicuous consumers who built costly mansions and estates, held extravagant balls, belonged to prestigious men's clubs, and enjoyed costly sports. As Thorstein Veblen recognized, the elite watched and participated in sports not merely for the sake of having fun but also to be trend setters and to acquire the prestige associated with such exclusive sports as racing, yachting, and polo. The nouveaux riches were particularly prominent in elite sports through which they could certify their acceptance by the social elite whose lifestyles they admired and sought to emulate.[1]

The elite found sport at a wide variety of athletic venues. They enjoyed spectator sports like horse racing and football at semipublic places and leisurely participatory sports like croquet and ice skating at public parks. Elite hunters indulged in manly field sports at distant public locations under the auspices of voluntary associations like the Boone and Crockett Club. Its 100 members, including Theodore Roosevelt, could afford expensive trips led by professional guides who helped them commune with nature in an urbane style.[2] But the sporting venues most characteristic of this class were private sites like athletic clubs and country clubs, which fostered a heightened awareness of social exclusivity.

The "sport of kings" was dominated by the social elite, who raced expensive thoroughbreds, organized high-status jockey clubs, operated prestigious tracks, and governed the turf. The best breeding farms and stables were owned by very rich sportsmen, mainly members of the elite, although some wealthy men of less standing, like Tammany boss Richard Croker, also raced thoroughbreds in an effort to secure social status. Although his horse won the Epsom Derby in England in 1907, Croker's quest for respectability was a failure. More typical of the leading horsemen were members of such families as the Belmonts, the Keenes, and the Whitneys, who at the turn of the century were paying as much as $40,000 for a top thoroughbred. Their horses dominated the prestigious stakes races and their stables were invariably among the top money winners.[3]

Elite jockey clubs that had a restricted membership organized the major racing meets and operated the preeminent racetracks like Monmouth Park, Jerome Park, Pimlico, Churchill Downs, and Washington Park. Chicago's Washington Park, established in 1884 by an elite organization whose president was General Philip Sheridan, was the leading track in the west. Its goals were to improve the breed and to "promote good fellowship among its members by providing a club-house [sic] and pleasure grounds for their entertainment, where at all times they may meet for social intercourse." Opening Day at Washington Park became one of the most important dates in the spring social calendar, attracting the fashionable elite in handsome carriages. The spectacle of the opulent men and women riding down the city's wide boulevards to the South Side track was repeated for major races like the American Derby. Once inside the track they were carefully segregated from the crowds in the exclusive clubhouse, where they enjoyed a convivial afternoon with others of their social set. Similar scenes occurred at other major tracks throughout the country. For instance, New York's Jerome Park was for years a meeting place for the elite. Then when the track was closed in 1889 in anticipation of the site being utilized for a reservoir to satisfy the city's growing needs for pure water, it was replaced by the opulent Morris Park Racetrack, a palatial facility with the longest track and largest grandstand in the United States, built by the new Westchester Racing Association (WRA). The new track immediately became a popular recreational center for the metropolitan elite.[4]

The elite not only joined jockey clubs, operated the prestigious tracks, and raced expensive thoroughbreds but also governed the "sport of kings." In 1894 a number of leading New York horsemen and track owners, including financier August Belmont II, traction magnate William Whitney, and brewer Jacob Ruppert, Jr., created the Jockey Club (TJC), a voluntary association whose purpose was to regulate the turf in the United States. It assumed quasi-governmental powers including licensing jockeys and trainers, appointing judges and stewards, establishing rules and regulations for contests, and dividing up the dates for meets in the East. Horsemen who wanted to race at the prestigious tracks that adopted TJC rules were forbidden from competing at tracks that did not accept its jurisdiction. A year after its founding, TJC was granted semiofficial status as an adjunct to the new New York State Racing Commission, which was created to supervise the turf in New York. This helped institutionalize TJC as the ruling body of American thoroughbred racing.[5]

Besides racing, another spectator sport that drew elite interest was college football. Intercollegiate sport had originated at elite eastern universities, and the sons of the elite were among the most prominent amateur athletes of the late nineteenth century. Collegians enjoyed sport because it was exciting, promoted community among the student body, and operated independently of adult supervision. Furthermore, they anticipated that athletic training in combination with fraternity life and the study of modern subjects would prepare graduates for the modern business world.[6]

Football, more than any other intercollegiate sport, fit in with the needs of upper- and upper-middle-class urban youth at a time when America was ripe for a violent and virile sport that stood for honorable values in stark contrast to the corruption, greed, and materialism of the Gilded

Age. A manly game played by gentlemen, it represented the highest ideals of Theodore Roosevelt's Strenuous Life philosophy. Young men worried about their masculinity, threatened by their lack of physical fitness because of a sedentary life style, fearful of the overcivilizing effects of the feminization of culture, uncertain of their sexual potency, and concerned about their ability to measure up to their courageous fathers, uncles, and older brothers who had been tested in combat, turned to football to recover and reassert their own manhood. Football players proved their masculinity by displaying the virtues of a martial life (endurance, bravery, and strength of character) in what was a "moral equivalent of war." Most elite opinion makers in the late nineteenth century, like Theodore Roosevelt, Woodrow Wilson, and Casper Whitney, had great respect for the game, which epitomized social Darwinism and inculcated, in the words of Brahmin Charles K. Adams, president of the University of Wisconsin, "those characteristics that have made the Anglo-Saxon race pre-eminent in history."[7]

The first off-campus football game occurred in 1878: Yale played Princeton for the Intercollegiate Football Association (IFA) championship in front of 2,000 spectators at Hoboken's St. George Cricket Grounds. The growing popularity of the title game encouraged a move to New York, where the match was held on Thanksgiving Day so more people could attend and the sponsoring student athletic clubs could make more money. In 1881, 10,000 spectators saw Yale defeat Princeton at the old Polo Grounds. The Thanksgiving Day contest became an important part of the holiday season. The social set was very disappointed when the IFA championship match was moved to New Haven in 1885, but it was back in New York two years later when the Harvard-Yale game attracted 23,000 spectators at a dollar or two a head.[8]

In the 1890s the Thanksgiving Day contest was played in various metropolitan sites, but mainly at Manhattan Field at 155th Street, adjacent to the new Polo Grounds. The IFA championship game, along with the Horse Show, marked the beginning of the winter social season. Two weeks before the game boxes were sold at auctions for up to $100, and on game day scalpers could get $40 for a single ticket. Yale, Harvard, or Princeton banners ribboned Fifth Avenue, and carriages conveying the sons and daughters of the elite paraded up the avenue to the playing field. The upper-class spectators came as much for the conviviality and the spectacle of the day as for the football, enjoying lavish champagne lunches before the game, and returning downtown afterwards for extravagant parties and dances.[9]

While the elite did not totally avoid public and semipublic sporting facilities, at least as long as they could enjoy themselves in privacy, most elite sport did occur at private sites and facilities owned and operated by status communities. At a time of declining urban space and rising property values, voluntary athletic associations constructed gymnasiums, boathouses, running tracks, and other facilities. Sports clubs arranged competition, including championships; formulated playing rules; and guaranteed the character of competitors. Membership criterion was strict and candidates could be blackballed for no reason. High initiation fees and annual dues also discouraged undesirables from joining. Acceptance into such a restricted club proved certification of a candidate's high social standing. [10]

Athletic clubs were among the first restricted sports societies to be formed after the Civil War. They emphasized participation in track and field contests which had been previously dominated by professional pedestrians and Caledonians. The first athletic club to gain widespread recognition was the New York Athletic Club (NYAC), incorporated in 1868 by three upper-middle-class sportsmen who modeled it after the London AC. They wanted to be able to compete in athletics with other men from the same social class. The NYAC facilitated the rise of track and field as an amateur sport by building the first cinder running track and by sponsoring the first American amateur championships in 1876. The NYAC provided an attractive model for other well-to-do sportsmen in New York and elsewhere, and by the 1880s, all major cities had at least one upper-middle-class track and field club. [11]

In 1882 the NYAC was taken over by a new leadership who sought to make the club more an elite metropolitan men's club than a sports society and initiated a new recruitment policy to attract rich and well-known New Yorkers regardless of their athletic prowess. They brought in members listed in the Social Register like William R. Travers, who belonged to the Union Club and the NYYC and was a founder of the prestigious Racquet Club in 1875. The NYAC reached its self-imposed limit of 1,500 well-screened members in 1885, when it raised the initiation fee to $100 and dues to $50. The club had drastically changed from one originally dominated by young athletes to one with an older membership more interested in its social functions. However, at least two other athletic clubs in New York, the University AC, which required a college degree, and the Manhattan AC, were more restrictive than the NYAC. [12]

The 1880s and early 1890s were the glory years of the athletic clubs, when "membership . . . became an important link in a web of associations that constituted an exclusive community." They spent enormous sums of money to provide luxurious facilities for the members. In 1885 the NYAC built a clubhouse that cost $150,000 and included a gymnasium, swimming pool, bowling alley, billiard tables, dining rooms, a wine cellar, and sleeping quarters. It was an elegant recreational center that got a lot of use: during the extensive social calendar it hosted extravagant parties for members and their wives. Three years later the NYAC secured a country place, where it constructed a boathouse, running track, tennis courts, and a clubhouse. In 1892, when the membership was increased to 2,500, the NYAC built a new and more lavish midtown clubhouse. However, other clubs in New York were more elaborate, as were some out-of-town organizations like the Chicago AC. [13]

While the athletic clubs emphasized their social functions, they also gave a lot of attention to competitive athletics. Winning was highly valued because it reflected well on a club's prestige; consequently, clubs like the NYAC and Manhattan AC (MAC) recruited top athletes even if their social backgrounds did not measure up. Top athletes were offered free initiation, room and board, jobs, and even cash to sign up, even if that violated the spirit of the amateur codes. For example, the MAC recruited Lon Myers, a Jew who was the greatest middle distance runner of the nineteenth century, by hiring him as club secretary. The demands for victory led to covert professionalism—one of the reasons the NYAC led the movement to form the Amateur Athletic Union (AAU) in 1888 to maintain strict amateur rules and thereby preserve the athletic clubs as viable status communities. But many prestigious clubs went under because of overbuilding and the Depression of 1893. [14]

In addition to athletic clubs, elite sportsmen formed other participatory sports organizations that utilized private space. Cricket was an important elite sport in Philadelphia, where five major clubs, each with memberships of 500 to 1,300, had elaborate clubhouses located on large lots in prestigious Mainline neighborhoods. The new polo clubs used private sites like the original Polo Grounds located just north of Central Park. When the Westchester Polo Club was founded in 1876, its matches were at Jerome Park, which in this case would have to be considered a private field, not the semiprivate space it was during the racing season. [15]

The most important sports organizations that utilized private space were country clubs, located in suburban areas where they provided members with a taste of English country life. The first was The Country Club, established in Brookline, Massachusetts, in 1882, and it became a model for future clubs. Its membership list constituted a veritable Who's Who of Boston, with names like Cabot, Forbes, Lowell, and Saltonstall. Half of the original 403 members were Harvard men; 30.5 percent were also in the Union Club and 67.2 percent in the Somerset, the city's most prestigious men's clubs. Boston historian Stephen Hardy argues that the club was "part of an interlocking constellation of financial, cultural and industrial institutions." Membership clearly signified one as a proper Bostonian. [16]

The best country clubs had sumptuous clubhouses and lavish grounds. For instance, Tuxedo Park, built by Pierre Lorillard in 1885 in a fashionable New York suburb, had a huge clubhouse with glass-enclosed verandas and a ballroom, and enormous property used for golf, steeplechasing, pigeon shooting, and tobogganing. At the turn of the century golf was the most important country club sport, even though the first American course in Yonkers was just thirteen years old. It was not an exertive sport, but did require concentration and eye-hand coordination, and was suitable both for older men seeking an excuse to escape the city for the out-of-doors and for their daughters as well. Although a golf course was an expensive use of private land because it could not be used for anything else, in 1900 Chicago alone had six golf courses. All of these courses were on the urban periphery or in suburbs where they were accessible only to the well-to-do. The other major club sport was tennis, which required expensive courts but far less space than golf. The first courts were often built expressly for country club wives and daughters who played leisurely doubles matches while garbed in full-length skirts. However, women did play on a competitive basis, and their first national championship was held in 1887, or eight years before the premier ladies' golf tournament. Male championships were annual affairs at the fashionable Newport Casino from 1881 until 1915, when they switched to the prestigious West Side Tennis Club in Forest Hills.[17]

The country club's promotion of sport was secondary to its promotion of sociability and status. It brought together people of similar means and tastes and provided them with a place to escape the problems of running large corporations and the anxieties of urban life. The club was located in a beautiful, tranquil site, far from the turmoil of cities, near a train station or within easy driving distance along a pleasant parkway. Late-nineteenth-century sportswriter Casper Whitney regarded the country club as an institution that promoted a sense of community for the elite, an oasis of rustic life for urbanites, a place to preserve traditional values, and a setting to teach social skills that would protect and insulate wealthy children from social change or contact with parvenues. The rusticity and serenity of these lovely resorts contrasted dramatically with crowded, noisy, and chaotic cities. Members got not only peace of mind but also a strong sense of identity, of belonging, and of stability.[18]

The urban elites who used sport and athletic institutions to escape or alleviate the worst aspects of city life and the social changes caused by urbanization were mainly members of voluntary sports organizations who controlled their own space and effectively excluded different people from their facilities. When semipublic places were utilized for sport, it was normally under highly controlled situations in which the elite had their own space in high-priced seating areas. Athletic participation occurred among social equals in a non-threatening situation, and thus provided a potential means for strengthening class bonds among the well-born and the new rich seeking social acceptance. Elite athletic organizations provided a means for upper-class young men to participate in appropriate sports in an environment that fit into a social world of prep schools, ivy league colleges, high fashion, and marriage.

In the period from 1870 to 1920 the enormous size of cities and their populations, the growth in the number of the elite, and a high degree of impersonalization meant that urban elites could no longer know everyone of their class on a face-to-face basis. They relied on club membership to provide a comfortable and safe haven spatially segregated from the problems of the industrial city and to help them distinguish the proper people with whom to socialize and do business. It became important to men of new money to join sports clubs to certify their level of status and to further advance into more restricted metropolitan clubs. Prestige hierarchies existed, not only between different sports, but also among clubs in the same sport, and clubs in the same sport in different cities (New York clubs were usually more prestigious than those in Buffalo). While membership in sports societies carried less status than membership in those urban clubs that emphasized wealth, ancestry, culture, or even politics, they were status communities which enabled a segment of the elite to withdraw and close ranks against social inferiors, to promote an exclusive life-style, and to integrate their families into an elite subculture.[19]

The Urban Middle Class

In the antebellum era the development of a positive sports ideology that justified and encouraged participation in respectable sports, and the increased middle-class participation in those sports paved the way for the great postwar boom in bourgeois athletics. The Victorian bourgeoisie continued to oppose gambling and plebeian blood sports, joining organizations like the ASPCA (1866) and Anthony Comstock's Society for the Suppression of Vice (1874), but enjoyed other sports that were useful and either enabled them to personally escape the woes of business and urban pathology or else enhanced city life by improving individual character, public health, or social morality.[20] Middle-class sportsmen had sufficient discretionary income and free time, and were psychologically prepared to take advantage of the social changes wrought by urbanization to enhance their athletic prospects. By the late nineteenth century, office workers were down to a forty-four hour week, including a half-day on Saturday. Although they could not afford expensive elite sports staged at private resorts, they could utilize the new mass transit facilities to travel to respectable semipublic sporting sites and the new public parks located on the suburban fringe beyond the old boundaries of the walking city. This enabled them to physically separate themselves from the lower orders of society.

The rising middle-class interest in sport reflected a desire by workers in sedentary jobs to demonstrate physical prowess and manliness and to gain recognition which bureaucratic occupations did not always supply. The enormous changes underway with urbanization, industrialization, and the rise of big business and the corporate state were blamed for a loss of individuality. The expansion of governments after the Civil War and the rise of big business in the 1880s were accompanied by the bureaucratization of the workplace. These white-collar workers were now subordinates, no longer independent workers or entrepreneurs, and they did not enjoy the same sense of creativity and accomplishment previously enjoyed by the old middle class. Middle-class men were also concerned about their courage, about becoming "overcivilized," about losing their sexual identity, and about the feminization of culture. New terms like "sissy," "stuffed shirt," and "mollycoddle" entered the English language. Manliness became less the opposite of childishness and more the opposite of femininity. Vigorous physical activity was seen as one possible antidote to the loss of masculinity. A strenuous life and a return to nature would invigorate the body and revitalize the spirit of a young man. Many new middle- and upper-middle-class magazines devoted to field sports, like *Field and Stream*, *Sports Afield*, and *Outing*, lauded the outdoor life, and competitive athletic sport became a staple topic in all the major newspapers and periodicals that catered to the bourgeoisie.[21]

Middle-class participation in sports ranging from noncompetitive co-educational leisure sports to highly competitive team sports was facilitated by voluntary athletic organizations and by ready access to public space. Middle-class athletic associations performed many of the same functions as more elite sports clubs in securing private space, purchasing equipment, and organizing competition, as well as providing status and opportunities to communicate with other individuals with similar backgrounds and values. Members of these organizations and other middle-class folk living in the radial city did not have to go far from their homes to enjoy sports; their residential communities were the least developed and most likely to still have empty lots, and the new municipal parks were primarily established in the suburban fringe. After the invention of the bicycle even such basic public space as streets became a locus for middle-class athletic pleasure.[22]

Middle-class residents of the suburban fringe were among the first urbanites to use parks for sports. As public parks were built or purchased throughout the country, nearby residents used them for sports like sleigh riding and ice skating in winter and boating and croquet in summer. These were sociable sports, enjoyed by both men and women, which did not harm the beauty or serenity of the parks. In the 1880s municipalities began building tennis courts in suburban parks, making that relatively new elite sport available to the middle classes. Central Park had thirty courts by 1885, but demand was so great that the number tripled in seven years. Chicago's beautiful South Park system had 100 courts in 1905 and well over 300 a decade later.[23]

Public golf courses were not established until nearly the turn of the century because of the cost, spatial requirements, and golf's elitist image. The first was constructed in Boston's Franklin Park in 1898, and players were charged twenty-five cents a round. New York's first course opened two years later at distant Van Cortlandt Park, located at the northern extremity of the city. It was difficult to get there until the subway, completed in 1904, was extended to the park nine years later. Membership cost two dollars and there were no daily greens fees. As late as 1910 there were just twenty-four municipal courses in the entire country, but the number of public greens doubled in a decade. These municipal facilities mainly benefited the middle classes, who could afford to buy permits, which cost from five to ten dollars plus a daily fee of one dollar. Such high fees sought to keep out the casual players.[24]

Until the 1920s, middle-class golfers were limited to public courses or semipublic courses at which they paid a fee. In the twenties there was a big boom in the construction of private golf courses in suburban locations, and ambitious upper-middle and middle-class businessmen felt compelled to join the most prestigious club that would have them, even if it cost as much as $500 for initiation fees. They saw golf as a means of escaping from the cares of business and the rigors of city life, playing in a private, well-controlled, carefully manicured environment, where they could enjoy the exercise and fresh air. But the real purpose of joining the country club set was to expand business contacts, entertain clients, certify their social advancement, and widen their family's social world.[25]

The Machine in the City:
The Bicycle and the Escape from Urban Reality

The middle-class sporting rage in the 1890s was the bicycle, which enabled millions of middle-class men and women to leave behind the problems of industrial cities for relaxing pastoral landscapes, momentarily fleeing progress on a vehicle that was itself a product of that technological progress. The cycling fad of the 1890s followed two earlier ones, the boneshaker of 1868–69 and the ordinary of 1876. The boneshaker was a clumsy and uncomfortable machine that was banned from the sidewalks of Fall River and Hartford and New York's Central Park because it interfered with pedestrian traffic. The ordinary—an English import that debuted at the 1876 Centennial Exposition in Philadelphia—was an odd looking contraption with a large front wheel whose diameter could reach sixty inches and a tiny rear wheel to lighten weight and increase speed. The ordinary was dangerous, uncomfortable to ride, and expensive, costing about $100 to purchase. Riders were mainly daring and athletic middle- and upper-middle-class young men who had mastered the difficult techniques of mounting, riding, and braking.[26]

Ordinary riders organized themselves into voluntary associations like the Boston Bicycle Club (1878) and the Chicago Cycling Club (1879). The Boston society, the first in the United States, grew from ten to one hundred members in just four years. These clubs sought to enhance the pleasure of riding by holding club meets, tours, excursions, and races; by acting as a pressure group to promote the sport and the rights of cyclists to share public roadways; and by giving one another "the emotional support so necessary for their deviant activities."[27]

In 1880 the League of American Wheelmen (LAW) was formed with local branches all over the country. The LAW promoted competitive racing and touring and fought for good roads and equal access with horses on municipal thoroughfares. Its *Bulletin*, one of eighty-five American cycling periodicals, had a printing of nearly 100,000 by the turn of the century. In 1883 the LAW achieved an important political victory when New York City opened Central Park and Riverside Drive for part of the day to bicyclists. Within the next few years few city streets and parkways were off limits to wheelmen.[28]

The bicycle craze of the 1890s followed the invention of the safety bicycle, which had equal-sized pneumatic tires, chain gear drive, a diamond-shaped frame, and more efficient coaster brakes. It was still primarily a middle-class vehicle which cost $50 for a cheap bicycle and nearly $100 for a medium quality one. The introduction of installment buying and the resale of second-hand bicycles brought the cost down to where clerks and artisans could afford it. However, it was too expensive for unskilled workers. Residents of poor neighborhoods resented middle-class folk using their streets for riding paths, interfering with street life and endangering children at play as well as other pedestrians. Wall Street workers in the late 1890s commonly rode to work through the Lower East Side, and as one businessman confessed, "The children in the streets are so numerous that it is impossible to avoid riding them down. I have run down these children while riding through the streets, but the accident was absolutely unavoidable." Historian Cary Goodman, a chronicler of street life in that neighborhood, claimed that ghetto denizens covered "streets with glass, garbage and sharp stones. They pelted the cyclists with eggs and vegetables and used pushcarts to block the riders' progress." In 1896 anarchists and socialists led community opposition to the asphalting of streets in the Jewish ghetto because that would make the community more vulnerable to speeding cyclists.[29]

In the 1890s cycling achieved considerable popularity as a spectator sport, with a number of important road races, most notably the fifteen-mile Chicago-to-Pullman Race held on Memorial Day that attracted from 200 to 400 competitors. Far more consequential were the professional indoor races, which were popular from the late 1870s through the 1920s and drew crowds of up to 10,000. But the key to the cycling fad was the enormous number of recreational cyclists. By 1893 there were over a million riders in the United States, and they quadrupled in three years.[30]

By 1895 there were over 500 cycling clubs in America. Each had its distinctive uniform worn by members on their outings, when they took scenic routes through their home town on the way to a park or nearby suburb, or on long-distance tours that exceeded 100 miles. Riders constituted an important subcommunity of sportsmen. LAW and local clubs were significant voting blocs who would turn out on behalf of politicians advocating better roads and equal access to streets and parks. In 1897, when Carter H. Harrison II ran for the first of his five terms as mayor of Chicago, he became an active cyclist and participated in 100-mile tours in order to gain the support of bicycle riders.[31]

Physicians and other health advocates strongly supported bicycle riding as an excellent exercise for sedentary urban workers and women. Middle-class urbanites influenced by the cult of masculinity and the strenuous life theory turned to cycling like Yuppies turned to jogging. Riding a bicycle provided exercise and fresh air, and could be enjoyed alone or with a few friends. It was one of the few exertive sports positively sanctioned for late Victorian women, who had traditionally avoided taxing exercises as unfeminine. The rational sports clothing female riders adopted and the independence and freedom cycling provided were important symbolic challenges to Victorian social standards of dependence and subservience to men.[32]

Cycling's greatest benefit may have been as a pleasurable vehicle of flight. While the safety bicycle epitomized the progress of civilization, symbolizing the victory of technology over environment, it paradoxically provided a means of escaping the impact of technology, industrialization, and urbanization. "It was no small achievement," noted cycling historian Richard Harmond, "for a machine to be the means by which people temporarily delivered themselves from the disruptions and stresses of a machine-based society." Riding supplied the psychic pleasures of motion and speed, and the exhilaration of riding down a hill with the wind blowing in one's face. The bicycle made nature more accessible by providing transportation to enable urban folk to get out of the city and into the countryside. Streetcar lines provided special cars for cyclists. It was the perfect leisure sport, especially for businessmen, who needed a respite from the office that would provide exercise, fresh air, visions of natural beauty, and peace of mind in the shortest amount of time. After an hour of riding the businessman would be ready for another day of mental work.[33]

Under the auspices of the LAW touring cyclists could be sure of enjoying a highly organized recreational experience. Urban tourists did not set out to find danger or discomfort on their trips, which could be either close to home or to distant national parks, but preferred riding on well-planned routes. While ostensibly escaping the city for the pristine countryside, cyclists expected to enjoy all the comforts of urban life on their travels. They secured detailed maps from the LAW, or cut them out from big-city newspapers and sports magazines, and generally stayed at inns and hotels that met the approved middle-class standards of the LAW. Cycling historian Gary Tobin concluded that "the traveller was able to combine a controlled contact with nature with a maximum of comfort. . . . The tourist was able to mingle with nature without suffering because of it." This ideal, sanitized rustic experience would minimize, if not eliminate, urban pathology.[34]

By the turn of the century there were ten million bicycles in the United States, but the bicycle fad had passed. The market was saturated and innovative manufacturers were turning to a more sophisticated vehicle, the automobile, which enabled the tourist "to see more, faster, with urban comfort and social isolation built into his machine." While in other parts of the world the bicycle remained an important mode of transportation and a major sporting device, Americans increasingly regarded it as a child's toy. The car replaced the bicycle in the hearts of Americans because it was more exciting and ownership conferred greater prestige.[35]

The National Pastime

Baseball was the most important sport played by the middle classes in the period from 1870 to 1920. Despite its pastoral mythology, baseball was very much an urban game, first played in cities, and the best players were mainly urbanites. The first fully modernized American team game, the sport was rationalized and bureaucratized in cities, where its spirit of nationalism, wholesomeness, excitement, and drama made it the national pastime. The character of the team game was congruent with the work experience of bureaucrats. But in one important way the sport did not fit in with industrialized urban society: baseball was not controlled by the clock. The length of games was determined not by a fixed time or distance but by innings, which in theory could be timeless. However, games normally took two hours or less, an important factor in a society where time was money.[36]

In the post-Civil War period baseball was a democratic sport which lacked social prestige, but the ideology of the sport fit in nicely with the bourgeoisie's prevailing value system as well as their social experiences. The baseball creed—an extension of the positive sports ideology developed in the antebellum era in response to modernization and urbanization—fully touched base with the beliefs, values, and social needs of middle America, reassuring old-stock folk that their traditional small-town values were still relevant to the increasingly impersonalized, bureaucratized, and urbanized society. As Stephen Freedman has pointed out, "It is no coincidence that the game of baseball became popular at a time when the Arcadian myth of the small town in the countryside and of the neighborhood bound together by primary associations was becoming increasingly difficult to realize within the confines of the city. . . . The game's associations with a rural setting and American rural values underscored the reluctance of the city dweller to part with the best elements of the staid and known world of the small town."[37]

While there is little evidence that baseball actually built character or provided a social catharsis, the baseball creed had a strong influence on contemporary thought and behavior because people perceived the ideology to be accurate. They regarded baseball as a rural game played on large verdant lots and through it identified with the values of a simple, pristine world. They believed that baseball provided the means to prevent or at least alleviate many urban social problems, particularly those that affected the indigent children of recent immigrants living in slums, as well as youngsters living in more affluent neighborhoods. The creed convinced middle-class Americans, regardless of where they lived, that playing and watching the game made better citizens, but in the Gilded Age and the Progressive era, it seemed that primarily urban folk needed such socialization. Sportswriters and other journalists writing in mainstream middle-class periodicals like American Magazine, Collier's, Harper's Weekly, The Independent, and Scribner's all accepted the cultural fiction that baseball was a useful sport that promoted social integration by instilling hometown pride, providing a setting where people from all walks of life could come together, and enabling hard-working urbanites to release their pent-up emotions in such socially sanctioned rituals as booing opponents and cursing umpires. Playing baseball was regarded as a good exercise that also improved the mental health of participants; just attending games was even said to help urbanites improve their fitness by getting them out into fresh air, where they could wave their hands and exercise their vocal chords. The baseball creed further asserted that the sport was an educational game that taught modern values such as teamwork and certified traditional values like rugged individualism, honesty, hard work, temperence, and respect for authority—qualities that would make urbanites better citizens and disciplined workers. Ballplayers might gain individual glory by their personal accomplishments, but they learned that in the end it was the team effort, the sum of all individual parts, that counted. [38]

Baseball received early and widespread support from business executives, a group initially very critical of baseball. Before the Civil War they had chastised employees who played baseball for neglecting their duties, but after the war they began to see baseball as a useful activity that improved morals, physical fitness, and productivity. Chicago department store magnates J. V. Farwell and Marshall Field adopted the conventional wisdom that baseball was a rational recreation that would keep young men away from vile amusements and instead teach proper values like thrift, sobriety, virtue, and hard work—all essential qualities needed to maintain stability at a time when their city was undergoing incredibly rapid changes. Chicago business leaders organized more than fifty teams by 1870, often granting white-collar employees time off for practice and games because it helped their staffs become more reliable, cooperative, and healthy, improved morale and loyalty to the firm, and secured good advertisement through local press coverage. Interest in baseball among Chicago's office workers was so great that in the 1870s a commercial league was established which provided a model for similar leagues a decade later in Baltimore, Boston, and New York. [39]

White-collar workers not only played baseball, but had the time, money, access, and interest to attend professional games and appreciate the high quality of play on the field. They could afford the cost of public transportation to ballparks located on the suburban fringe as well as the cost of admission, which was as low as twenty-five cents, but normally fifty cents for major league games. Big-league teams in the National League catered to a middle-class fandom by establishing different priced sections to separate respectable people from the rabble, hiring police to keep order, promoting Ladies' Days to encourage decorum, and starting games at times convenient to the schedules of local office workers. In Chicago the Board of Trade closed early, so White Stockings games began at 2:30, but in New York games commenced an hour later, to give the Wall Street crowd time to make the long trip north to the Polo Grounds after the market closed at 3 P.M. The latest starting time was in Washington, D.C., where games began at 4:30 P.M. to conform to the work day of government clerks.[40]

Fans became part of a community of like-minded spectators who rooted for the local club in a collective demonstration of hometown pride and boosterism. Baseball competition became a metaphor for interurban rivalries, and a victory over other towns in the league symbolized the superiority of your city. The presence of a person at a ball game, particularly on Opening Day, became a means of publicly displaying civic-mindedness. In the early 1900s residents of Atlanta made a major effort to attend the first game of the season so the Crackers could outdraw the New Orleans Pelicans and show the South that Atlanta, though smaller, was far more progressive than New Orleans. Since players on professional nines were mercenaries recruited from out-of-town, the local pride exhibited in sports teams was hardly rational: a victory by the Braves over the Giants did not prove Boston's superiority over New York any more than an East German sprinter defeating an American in the Olympics would demonstrate the ascendancy of communism over capitalism. Nevertheless, journalists believed that if a city deficient in self-pride developed a positive spirit because of baseball, then localism was good and proper.[41]

Blue-Collar Sportsmen

In the late nineteenth century, when middle-class white-collar men living in the industrialized radial cities were becoming avid sportsmen, a major segment of the manual work force was constrained in their leisure opportunities by the social impact of industrialization and urbanization. Until the 1920s working-class sportsmen were primarily drawn from the labor aristocracy or municipal service workers—groups that earned about twice as much as laborers, worked shorter hours, and had a tradition of participating in sports and physical culture. Most workingmen could afford only the simplest, cheapest pleasures. These employees—mainly the unskilled, new immigrant factory workers—had long working hours, few holidays, and little discretionary income. They were unfamiliar with sporting institutions, their crowded slum neighborhoods offered little outdoor space for athletics, and they could not afford the cost of frequent trips to outdoor facilities located at the increasingly distant urban periphery. As Peter Shergold has pointed out, unskilled laborers were impoverished workers "to whom leisure was sleep, to whom recreation was a half hour at the nickelodeon, or a drink in the saloon after work, to whom contentment was a full pipe of tobacco or a Sunday afternoon spent gambling at cards."[42]

Industrial workers at the turn of the century worked long hours (60 for laborers, 54 for artisans), and while the workday declined by one hour by 1907, it was still a long day and a six-day week. Low wages (under ten dollars a week for unskilled workers as late as 1915), underemployment, and unemployment meant that approximately 40 percent of the work force in the early 1900s lived below the poverty line ($500 a year), unless supplemented by a wife or children. Low wages made it hard for married unskilled workers to afford the cost of carfare to sporting sites and the price of admission to a spectator event, and the length of the working period made it difficult for regularly employed blue-collar workers to attend afternoon sporting events unless they worked unusual hours, skipped work, or were artisans, who by the turn of the century were enjoying half-holidays on Saturday.[43]

Leisure options of working-class urbanites were further limited by prevailing Sabbatarian customs which varied by geographic region. In the late nineteenth century, in cosmopolitan port cities, like Memphis, Mobile, and especially New Orleans, with large Catholic minorities and in Texas cities with substantial Mexican and German populations, a Continental Sabbath was the norm. However, in the Old South, cities adhered strictly to the American Sabbath because of common consent and social pressure from pietistic residents. Sabbatarianism was also very strong in the East, where rural-dominated state legislatures passed a variety of Sunday blue laws to maintain a traditional American Sabbath in order to exercise social control over the immigrant-dominated cities. Enforcement of proscriptive laws fell on local police and jurists, who generally tried to conform to community norms and to avoid interfering with children and amateur sportsmen who were not creating a public nuisance, if that was the community will. In New York, for instance, progressive leaders of the Social Gospel movement believed that workers should have an opportunity to enjoy rational recreation even if their day off was Sunday. These liberal clergymen hoped that their advocacy of participatory sport and the construction of gymnasiums at their churches would bring alienated workers back to their flock. But the Social Gospelers and many community leaders usually regarded professional sport as inappropriate Sabbath entertainment.[44]

Working-Class Spectator Sport

Working-class attendance at spectator sports was limited by time, discretionary income, and access. In the days before cheap mass transit the easiest sites to reach were indoor gymnasiums located in slums or arenas in the Central Business District. Boxing matches that attracted a working-class clientele were usually held in neighborhood gymnasiums, often known as "athletic clubs"—firetraps that were "nothing more than a loft, with tiers of wooden benches to the ceiling." Occasionally a higher-priced match was staged at an armory or multipurpose arena like Madison Square Garden. These semipublic facilities also attracted working-class fans who could afford the modest twenty-five cent admission to a six-day marathon race in the 1880s or six-day bicycle races a decade later. Promoters learned to clear their halls at 5A.M., ostensibly to clean up but actually to keep spectators from staying too long on one ticket.[45]

Outdoor sporting events like thoroughbred racing or baseball were more difficult to attend because of the cost and time. These events were held at distant sites that required public transportation. Professional baseball did not gear itself as much for the poor urban masses as for the middle classes, who paid higher admission fees and lent the sport an aura of respectability. Games were scheduled for times when most employed blue-collar men were on the job, the general admission ticket to a National League game was set at fifty cents in 1876, and the fields were far from the inner city. Thus lower-class urbanites were underrepresented in the stands in most large cities until the 1920s. Manual workers who attended were mainly artisans who worked half-days on Saturday or city workers and other employees like butchers and bakers who worked unusual shifts and had free time in mid-afternoon.[46]

Unlike the NL, the American Association, the second major league, did try to cater to working-class fans. Founded in 1882, the AA charged just twenty-five cents for admission, sold alcoholic beverages, and scheduled Sunday games wherever possible. When the two leagues merged in 1892, the new NL adopted the AA policy of Sunday ball and gave each team the option to sell bleacher seats for a quarter to build up attendance, a pricing policy later adopted for one season by the new American League (AL) in 1901. In the early 1900s major league teams usually set aside about 2,000 cheap seats in distant bleachers, and in 1910 one-fourth of all admissions were in those sections. The franchise with the greatest number of working-class spectators was probably the Chicago White Sox, who had 7,000 quarter seats, played on Sunday, and was the only team located in a working-class neighborhood. By contrast there were only 200 quarter seats in the new Polo Grounds, and in Pittsburgh the Pirates deliberately doubled the price of cheap seats for holidays when large crowds were anticipated.[47] After the new ballparks were built, the cheap seats were largely a thing of the past.

Team owners were strong supporters of blue-law reform because they believed, correctly, that Sunday games would attract large numbers of fans unable to attend during the week, and they utilized their political connections to secure that goal. In the early 1900s New York magnates tried to circumvent the state's penal codes by selling programs or requesting "donations," instead of selling tickets for Sunday games, which was against the law. Local police and magistrates supported the ball clubs, but these machinations were turned down by superior courts. Sabbatarians fought hard in New York to maintain the status quo because of the symbolic importance of defending traditional values in the nation's largest city, which was 76.9 percent foreign origin in 1900—mainly Jews and Catholics opposed to a strict Sabbath. Sunday ball was not allowed in New York until 1919, when a broad-based coalition of organized labor, machine politicians, progressives, veterans' associations, and women's groups got the state legislature to approve Sunday ball on a local option basis. They argued that doughboys who had fought for freedom overseas were entitled to the freedom to enjoy wholesome recreation any day of the week. The introduction of Sunday baseball was a great success, especially for blue-collar fans who had never before attended a game. After the bill was passed, every Sunday there were crowds in excess of 20,000 at either the Polo Grounds or Ebbets Field. But despite this victory in New York, Boston did not get Sunday ball until 1929, Philadelphia and Pittsburgh, until 1934.[48]

The Sabbatarian tradition was weakest in western and midwestern cities where there was a strong tradition of home rule and social democracy. Sunday blue laws were particularly ineffective in such cosmopolitan cities as Cincinnati, Chicago, Milwaukee, and St. Louis, where politically powerful German communities had sufficient clout in the late nineteenth century to prevent enforcement of local blue laws. However, in its quest for middle-class respectability, the NL banned Sunday games, and when Cincinnati's club refused to abide by this rule, the franchise was forfeited in 1880. Two years later, when the AA was established, its midwestern teams scheduled Sunday games whenever possible, even if the clubs had to play in the suburbs to evade the long arm of the law. By the time the AA merged with the NL in 1892, Sunday ball was pretty widespread in the region; even Muncie, Indiana, enjoyed Sunday ball—preceded by a concert of sacred music. A year later, despite some strong public opposition, Chicago got Sunday ball after the World's Fair promoters had decided to keep the exposition open on Sundays. Yet reform took longer in some major cities, notably Detroit and Cleveland, which, because of various local political problems did not get Sunday ball until the early 1910s.[49]

Working-class sports fans unable to attend their favorite sporting events kept abreast of developments and read about their heroes through the media, which was very accessible. Even before the Civil War innovations in production had made newspapers affordable, and improvements in distribution made the penny papers widely available. Newspapers began to build up enormous circulations, topped by the morning and evening editions of the *New York World*, which reached 374,000 in 1892. These papers featured yellow journalism, which emphasized sports, crime, and sex, providing next-day reportage of even the most distant events. In addition specialized weekly sporting periodicals appealed to a primarily urban audience—the *New York Clipper*, one of the first popularizers of baseball and a leading defender of pugilism, and the *National Police Gazette*, which focused mainly on boxing. The *Gazette* dated back to 1845 but became a big success only after Richard Kyle Fox had become publisher in 1877. Printed on garish red-tinted paper, the weekly was full of salacious stories and illustrations of scantily clad young women. Fox made the *Gazette* the national bible of boxing. The average weekly circulation was 150,000 copies in the late nineteenth century, peaking in 1880 with sales of 400,000 when it reported the results of the Paddy Ryan-Joe Goss championship fight. Fox did an excellent job of merchandising his product, selling reduced-rate subscriptions to saloons, barber shops, hotels, and fire companies, the major centers of the male bachelor subculture that comprised the periodical's core readership, where each issue passed through dozens of hands.[50]

Working-Class Participatory Sport

The athletic options of low-paid blue-collar workers in the late nineteenth century were further limited by the declining accessibility of outdoor play space. The growth of cities reduced the number of open lots available for ball games in the vicinity of the inner city and pushed far away the once accessible woods and polluted the old streams that had been used for field sports. As Francis Couvares points out, until the 1880s inner-city Pittsburghers "still had easy access by foot or by short train or boat ride to numerous sites for swimming, sledding, fishing, pigeon-trapping, picnicking, and other forms of informal play," but growing demands for residential and industrial property made traditional pleasures less and less possible. For example, as late as 1887 there were still working-class boat clubs in Pittsburgh, but then they disappeared because of the commercial demand for riverfront property, along with the economic decline of local artisans.[51]

Inner-city sportsmen used whatever space was available in their own neighborhoods. Young men who lived near rivers or lakes swam there, often in the nude, which resulted in considerable public outrage. Respectable citizens petitioned the city council to restrict the location and hours of such public bathing and to require clothing; spokesmen for the plebes demanded public swimming baths for recreational and health reasons. In the 1880s certain cities began to establish public swimming sites for their poorer residents. Urban youth also used city streets for their playing areas.

Young boys played stickball, football, handball, and other games in the street. Local businessmen demanded the police keep the streets and sidewalks clear because they needed the roads to transport freight and feared that youths hanging around would scare away customers. The boys of pleasure interfered with commerce and had to be stopped.[52]

To escape urban crowding and middle-class outcries, most slum residents had to rely on semipublic neighborhood sites like taverns and billiard parlors for their sporting pleasures. The saloons, or "workingmen's clubs," described by their leading historian as game rooms and quasi-gymnasiums, provided many sporting services, including some spectator sports such as boxing matches and cockfights. Saloons were also gambling centers where by the 1880s one could find neighborhood bookmakers who took wagers from men who could not afford, or did not have the time, to go to the racetracks.[53]

Saloons provided the equipment for various participatory sports which kept up the interest of customers in slack hours and provided additional sources of revenue. Some large saloons had full-size handball courts, and nearly all had various table games, particularly pool. At the end of the nineteenth century 140 Chicago taverns had billiard tables and by 1909 nearly half of the city's 7,600 saloons provided a place to play. As historian Perry Duis concludes, "the pool table was almost as much a necessity as the bar itself."[54]

Billiard table games were enormously popular among urban males; they provided a cheap opportunity to display skill, kibbitz, gamble, and meet friends in a warm and accessible location. Since a game cost only about five cents per player, everyone could afford to play. Of course a consistent loser, who by custom paid for his opponent, might run up a sixty-cent bill in a day's play plus lost wagers. At the turn of the century nearly 30,000 establishments had pool tables; in the mid-1920s the sport reached its peak, with about 42,000 poolrooms, 90 percent of which were semipublic places. In New York alone, the number of poolrooms went from sixty in 1850 (when they were known as billiard saloons) to 300 in 1900 and to over 4,000 in the 1920s.[55]

Poolrooms had a very bad public image even though the sport of pool was not inherently evil. A 1913 survey in Toledo found that over half of high school pool players had learned the game at home or at the YMCA. With the endorsement of Denver's renowned juvenile court judge Ben Lindsey, the leading pool-table manufacturer encouraged middle-class fathers to purchase tables for their families to promote family unity. However, the conventional wisdom held that pool halls were hangouts for loafing inner-city boys and men of immigrant stock who gambled, plotted crimes, drank heavily, and corrupted minors, and thus these gathering places should be stamped out. As one former Brownsville resident recalled, his favorite haunt, Label's Poolroom, was not only a surrogate home in which to meet friends but also a place to find "someone to break a head, beat up a guy, break a strike, buy junk, set a fire, plan a robbery, or muscle a peddlar." Municipal surveys and sociological investigations generally estimated that from 15 to 25 percent of urban poolrooms—one Kansas City study set the figure at over half the rooms—were public menaces.[56]

A survey of 806 New York workingmen completed in 1913 found that the men who frequented billiard parlors were overwhelmingly seventeen to twenty-four years old, single, and born in the United States or Great Britain. They were mainly transportation workers, clerks, or in domestic and personal services. Men with short workdays were the most likely to visit pool halls, but it took up a larger proportion of the discretionary time of those who worked eleven or more hours a day. There was also a very strong correlation between income and use of the poolroom. People earning under thirty-five dollars a week.[57]

The poolroom business was very unstable; smaller facilities came and went with great regularity. In Chicago in the late nineteenth century, an exceptional room—a big downtown room with the best facilities—might stay in business for a decade. The city had 1,169 licensed rooms in 1910, but only 900 in 1918. Then one year later there were 2,156. The number of rooms rose to 2,244 in 1920 but fell to just 861 two years later. The big postwar increase resulted mainly from the coming of Prohibition; saloonkeepers went into the business in order to stay afloat. A license was still relatively easy to get, even with a criminal record, and the expenses of operating billiards tables was low. While a high quality new table cost about $500, three used ones cost $700. However, the billiard market was quickly oversaturated, and in the early 1920s it became harder to secure a license because of strict new regulations that were enforced by the new Billiard Commission, established in 1920 to regulate and clean up the sport.[58]

The character and quality of the billiard facilities in the early twentieth century city varied substantially. The finest rooms—professional billiard halls located in the CBD—were either resorts for downtown businessmen or centers of that city's male bachelor subculture. They had as many as fifty or more tables, were located above street level, and were relatively well maintained. Their busiest hours were around lunch time and early evening when white-collar players were off work. The largest billiard parlor in the country was Graney's in San Francisco, owned by a prominent boxing promoter with important connections at City Hall. In the most famous was the Recreation Room in Detroit with 142 tables,

1910s Graney's was a well-known hangout for the sporting crowd, particularly local politicians, and its clientele ranged from pool hustlers to the carriage trade.[59]

The large, well-appointed billiard parlors with six or more tables were a small minority of a city's pool room facilities (13.8 percent in Cincinnati in 1913), although they had a disproportionate number of tables (25.0 percent in Cincinnati). Far more common were rooms with one, two, or three tables, located in residential slum neighborhoods, usually in or adjacent to a saloon. Rooms with so few tables were not profitable unless operated in conjunction with another business that catered to the male bachelor subculture or unless the owner permitted criminal activities in his store. Pool tables were most commonly found in cigar stores, candy stores, barbershops, and coffee houses, as well as saloons. In the nineteenth century they were mainly located in Irish and German working-class neighborhoods, and later on they became very popular among Poles, Greeks, Italians, Jews, and blacks. WASP urban reformers were frightened by the ethnic poolrooms because they were bastions of old world culture, and in 1913 a law was passed in Cincinnati banning foreigners from owning billiard parlors.[60]

The poolrooms regarded as the greatest danger to the public welfare were the small rooms, located in slum neighborhoods, frequented by a "rough" element. These rooms were screened off from the street to hide what was going on inside. A 1919 study sponsored by Chicago's Juvenile Protective Association found that about one-fourth of a sample of approximately 400 rooms fit this picture. Repeated instances of minors being present and episodes of immoral or disorderly conduct and gambling were uncovered in these rooms. As in all poolrooms, about 80 percent of the patrons were spectators, but the general feeling was that at the rough rooms they were up to no good. Often these pool halls were operated by individuals with police records who were seldom interfered with by the police though everyone in the neighborhood knew what was going on inside.[61]

Billiard parlors were probably more widely distributed than any other commercialized entertainment except perhaps the movies. In the nineteenth century, when pool tables were less likely to be found outside billiard rooms and in cigar stores and saloons than in the future, a greater proportion of facilities were in the CBD. During the mid-1880s in Chicago, two-fifths (41.6 percent) of billiard halls listed in the city directory were in the CBD. The proportion declined to nearly one-third in 1900 and then dropped drastically over the next decade to 9.1 percent. In 1936, 5.3 percent were in the CBD. The CBD had far more tables than any of Chicago's seventy-five community areas, and the rooms were the biggest and most lavish in the city. Together with two adjacent inner city areas, the downtown zone was the site of over one-fourth of all Chicago poolrooms (27.1 percent). There were poolrooms in sixty-five of seventy-five community areas. Only four residential sections—all in the inner city—had over 100 tables: Near North, Near West Side (both Italian), West Town (Polish), and Grand Boulevard (black). [62]

Billiard parlors were concentrated not only in downtown neighborhoods but also on just a handful of heavily travelled commercial streets where they could attract a walk-in clientele. At the turn of the century, one-fourth of Chicago's billiard rooms were on either Madison or State streets, which together with Clark and Halsted streets were the addresses for over one-third of the city's pool halls. Subsequently, as the concentration of facilities in the CBD declined, so did the proportion of rooms on those streets (23.5 percent in 1910 and 15.3 percent in 1936), but it was still quite high and very significant. [63]

During the Depression the poolroom business struggled, along with other small businesses, but provided many poor inner-city youth with a place to congregate and amuse themselves very cheaply. The seeds of its future decline as an urban institution were laid in 1933 by the repeal of Prohibition. When the taverns reopened, often with pool tables for their patrons, they drew off an enormous share of the poolrooms' potential clientele. By 1936 there were just 580 licensed establishments, averaging 4.7 tables per room, in Chicago. The turnover rate was still quite high: one out of every five rooms (21 percent) was brand new. More than one out of eight rooms had either liquor licenses or bowling alleys in order to compete, but that was not enough. The waning of the downtown and neighborhood poolrooms was epitomized by the situation in New York, which once had over 4,000 billiard facilities, but had just 257 in 1961—a consequence of the sport's low status, a decline in the male bachelor subculture, the rise of suburbia after World War II, and the availability of alternate sites for inner-city young men to hang out, particularly taverns and bowling alleys which provided coin-operated down-sized pool tables (that are easier to play on and have shorter games) along with the camaraderie of the old-time billiard hall. [64]

As a popular commercialized urban entertainment bowling was similar to billiards—cheap and readily accessible to the working classes and historically heavily associated with saloons, gambling, and the male bachelor subculture. The sport, actually banned in cities like New York for several years because of the gambling nexus, was revived in the 1880s among members of German-American voluntary associations like the Turners and the *Schützengesellschaft* (shooting clubs), who enjoyed Sunday bowling in outdoor parks and laid out lanes in their clubhouse basements. At the turn of the century alleys were usually located in restaurants or saloon basements, where they were the scene of considerable betting, and thus bowling was not regarded as a respectable sport for women. Most bowling alley owners (80 percent) in Chicago in the early 1900s had white-collar jobs before they took over bowling facilities, but over one-third (37.5 percent) of the proprietors had been involved in an occupation associated with the male bachelor subculture, ranging from the liquor or saloon business to professional sports to barbering. Nevertheless, the sport certainly had a public standing superior to that of billiards, and many local leagues were comprised of teams representing local professional and business firms. [65]

The number of bowling alleys in cities was far smaller than the number of billiard parlors, which were less expensive to open and operate and required less space. A small cigar store which might have space for a pool table or two was too small for a bowling lane. In Chicago in 1910 there were 230 licensed alleys compared to 1,179 poolrooms. Bowling alleys had a high turnover rate in the early 1900s: none of the fifteen alleys listed in the *Chicago City Directory* in 1901 were listed nine years later. By 1918 there were just 139 licensed alleys, a decline of 39.6 percent in just eight years. [66]

The coming of Prohibition had an important impact on the bowling business. Saloon alleys either went out of business or emphasized the game instead of the potables, and many ex-tavern keepers went into the bowling business. In anticipation of Prohibition, the number of Chicago's alleys increased in 1919 by 41 percent. Bowling began to lose its connection with the low-life sporting fraternity and came to be regarded as a source of good clean fun that required a lot of hand-eye coordination and provided sociability and camaraderie. The new alleys built in the 1920s were usually large facilities designed specifically for bowling and featured sound proofing, good lighting, air conditioning, and seats for spectators. A single alley cost as much as $1,500—triple the cost of a top-flight billiard table. The construction of superior new lanes drove many small operators out of business. In 1926 Chicago had 168 alleys with an average of 6.5 lanes (six was the minimum needed for profitability), but a decade later, when there were just 123 alleys, the average number of lanes had increased to 10.6. Only two-fifths (39.8 percent) had been in business as long as ten years. [67]

The drop-off in the number of bowling alleys in the 1930s was proportionately far less than that for pool halls. During the Depression bowling was enormously popular for both men and women because it was cheap, clean fun. Two-thirds of Chicago's bowling alleys had bars and billiard tables, but the main attractions were the bowling and the socializing. By the late 1930s Chicago had about 500,000 bowlers, many of whom belonged to one of the more than 900 leagues sponsored by church organizations, ethnic societies, civic groups, industries, and companies. And although just one generation earlier alleys had not been regarded as proper places for women, bowling was now the most popular women's sport in the city. Over 10,000 women participated in the annual *Evening-American* tournament.[68]

The geographic distribution of bowling alleys was less widespread than that of poolrooms, which were more numerous. In Chicago, where just ten community areas had no billiard parlors in 1931, thirty-one were without bowling alleys. Bowling alleys—far more expensive to build and maintain—needed to be located in busy sections of town where large numbers of possible players congregated. They were also kept out of middle-class peripheral neighborhoods by zoning laws. In 1900 Chicago's alleys were more likely to be in the CBD (20 percent) than in any other community, but after a quick decline (to 5 percent in 1910) some blue-collar areas overtook it. Yet in 1936 the most *lanes* were still in the CBD's superior facilities. Elsewhere, as in Cincinnati, alleys were at first mostly in the CBD (38.1 percent in 1913). Bowling alleys were more likely to be in the CBD than pool halls (in Cincinnati alleys were three times as likely to be downtown compared to billiard rooms), but in Chicago alleys were only about half as likely to be located in the large downtown community area (perhaps because it encompassed the old vice districts, where amusements like pool were very popular). Bowling alleys were not just disproportionately located in central areas but were also highly concentrated on certain busy streets where they would be accessible to the greatest number of potential patrons who might choose to bowl a few games on the spur of the moment. In 1936 nearly half of Chicago's alleys were found on just four major commercial thoroughfares (Milwaukee, Clark, Halsted, or Broadway), considerably more than the still substantial one out of seven for pool halls.[69]

Bowling had a strong appeal among working-class ethnic sportsmen. In the early 1900s, for example, one-third of Chicago's alley owners were foreign-born, primarily German, and they catered to a large ethnic clientele. Later on, in the interwar period, all of the city's poor and modest white neighborhoods had bowling lanes, and this was typical of all the major industrial cities along the Great Lakes. In Chicago, the residential communities with the greatest number of bowling alleys were German Lakeview (N.S.), the Italian Near West Side, and the Czech-Polish South Lawndale (W.S.). The Polish interest in bowling was particularly well known. As early as 1906 there was a Polish-owned alley in Polish Downtown (West Town), and twenty years later there were fourteen bowling alleys in South Lawndale and eight in West Town. Bowling leagues there

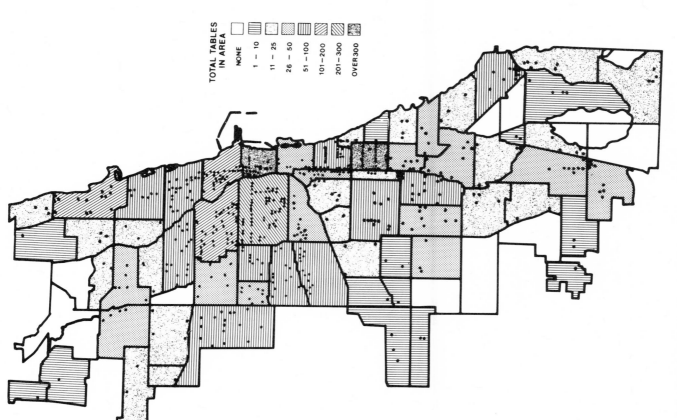

TOTAL TABLES
IN AREA

NONE
1 – 10
11 – 25
26 – 50
51 – 100
101 – 200
201 – 300
OVER 300

2. Distribution of Licensed Billiard Halls in Chicago, 1936.

SOURCE: Chicago Recreation Commission, *The Chicago Recreation Survey, 1937*, vol. 2, *Commercial Recreation* (Chicago; 1938), 58f.

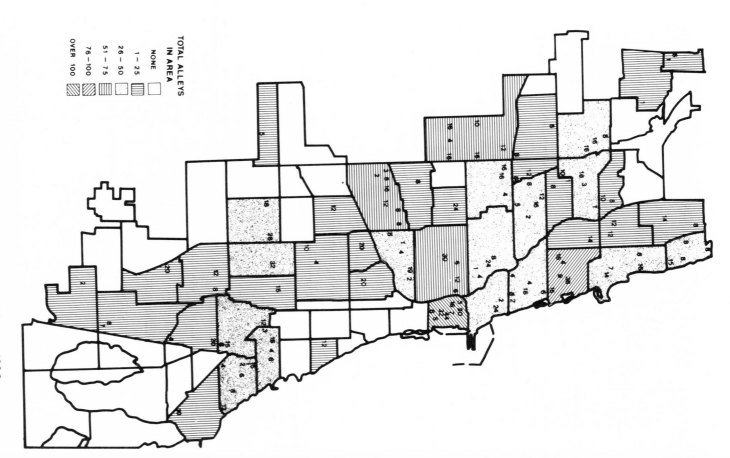

TOTAL ALLEYS
IN AREA

NONE	
1 — 25	
26 — 50	
51 — 75	
76 — 100	
OVER 100	

3. Distribution of Licensed Bowling Lanes in Chicago, 1936

SOURCE: Chicago Recreation Commission, *The Chicago Recreation Survey, 1937,* vol. 2, *Commercial Recreation* (Chicago, 1938), 56f.

were sponsored by fraternal societies like the Polish National Alliance. The sport provided a source of cheap fun, self-display, and sociability in an all-Polish environment that helped sustain a sense of peoplehood. Furthermore, Polish success in national championships provided recognition in the broader American community. However, the situation was far different in black Chicago. Only a few black neighborhoods had alleys in the 1920s, and none in the 1930s. The cost of a line, usually twenty cents during the day and a quarter at night, may have put the sport beyond the budget of black Chicagoans, especially during the Depression, when their unemployment rate exceeded 50 percent. Even in the flush 1920s it was difficult for black entrepreneurs to buy a bowling alley or construct a new one, and the lack of disposable funds in the community in the 1930s put established operators out of business.[70]

The bowling alley, like the poolroom, was an important adjunct for street-corner life in the interwar era. It provided young men with a hangout where they could socialize and demonstrate individual skills, but it was far more respectable than the poolrooms. Young Italian South Bostonians studied by William F. Whyte in the late 1930s talked about bowling more than virtually any other topic. Each fellow's status in the group was correlated with his bowling prowess. Their principal social activity in the winter was Saturday night bowling. Bowling also facilitated sociability with the opposite sex. Alleys provided a public, non-threatening environment where street-corner boys could meet groups of young women and enjoy their companionship without the awkwardness that often accompanied blind dates.[71]

At the end of the Depression, there were twelve million bowlers in the United States, and unlike pool, the sport became more popular over the next decade. By 1948, there were twenty million bowlers. Bowling adapted well to urbanization and suburbanization. Between 1945 and 1955, the number of alleys rose by 62 percent, much of that coming in suburbs following the advent of automatic pinspotters. Entrepreneurs invested heavily in large, multipurpose bowling alleys located in shopping centers, where they particularly appealed to housewives who had a lot of free time during the day. They comprised as much as 40 percent of the suburban patronage. In two generations the bowling alley had been transformed from a neighborhood working-class sport of dubious respectability into a family recreation (still predominantly working class) enjoyed at shopping centers on the urban periphery or in suburbia.[72]

Sponsored Organized Athletics in the Blue-Collar Community
Despite a tradition of working-class professional track and field athletes who participated in long-distance races, sprints, and the Caledonian

Games, few leading amateurs were manual workers. While training reg-
imens were less rigorous than today's, and athletes might not have to take
too much time off from work, they still lacked regularly established free
time to practice, suitable equipment, proper coaching, and sponsorship.
Only the most gifted athlete might be recruited for a major athletic club,
and there were few workingmen's clubs to organize competition for other
blue-collar sportsmen. Some of this need was filled by private companies,
trade unions, benevolent societies, or political parties, who all had their
own reasons for sponsoring working-class sports.

In the late nineteenth century the most important sources for amateur
working-class competition were the annual picnics arranged by businesses, unions, and ward heelers. The public picnic started in the mid-
1850s, mainly as a middle-class entertainment to raise money for philanthropic purposes, and as late as 1891, 78 percent of the events in Montreal
were sponsored by non-working-class groups. They were usually held on
Sundays or holidays in the late spring or summer at a private park rented
by the organizers. The typical company picnic in the 1880s was staged by
a retail or commercial firm for its clerical staff, although other enterprises, like traction companies, ran outings for their blue-collar employees. The main features of the day would be track and field competitions,
other sports like bowling and marksmanship, and an evening dance. Most
events were open contests that attracted professional athletes if the prizes
were valuable enough, but a few events were restricted to athletes affiliated with the sponsor. The presence of well-known pros brought out
larger crowds and gained additional publicity for the picnic's organizers. [73]

While companies sponsored outings to improve employee-management
relations, political machines sponsored picnics as a service to their constituents and to raise money. Tammany sponsored baseball leagues and
tournaments, and precinct captains organized teams which often became
sources of future political workers. Tammany-sponsored outings attracted
primarily Irish crowds who played and watched competition in track,
baseball, football, bowling, and Gaelic football. The most famous outings
at the turn of the century were sponsored by Tim Sullivan's machine on
the Lower East Side. His picnic in 1900, for instance, was attended by
about 6,000 people whose five-dollar tickets were paid by local saloonkeepers and other businessmen who wanted to stay on good terms with
Tammany's number-two man. The revelers enjoyed a boat ride to Long
Island, where they played baseball, watched a boxing match, and gambled, and then returned home to the Bowery for the customary post-picnic
parade. [74]

Artisan fraternal organizations and unions sponsored sport to encourage a sense of community among men who shared the same work expe-

rience and the same social and economic problems. As John Cumbler has noted, unions sought to establish "a network of institutions upon which the individual workers depended, not only for higher wages and job security, but also for the job itself, for social life, and even for family security." Union halls were the workers' private space that doubled as centers of sociability and camaraderie where men could enjoy pool matches with their peers. During the 1880s New York's typographers, plumbers, stonecutters, and bricklayers were all sponsoring annual picnics. A decade later the biggest outings would be on Labor Day in conjunction with marches and other demonstrations. Unions and other labor groups also sponsored baseball teams that, at least by the 1880s and 1890s, were playing in local amateur leagues. The purpose was to raise money, increase the size of crowds at rallies, and attract positive attention. [75] Labor historian Bryan Palmer regards these teams as vehicles for artisans to develop their own culture independent of the values and financial backing of their bosses. But these players were not revolting against the dominant core values like sobriety, hard work, and self-reliance that were congruent with their jobs. These teams played for fun, but also to win, and thus would not permit the unpredictable behavior characteristic of the boys of pleasure. [76]

After the turn of the century, industrial corporations played an important role in sponsoring working-class sport through welfare capitalism, which sought to promote company loyalty, retain skilled workers, forestall unionization by promoting a sense of community at the workplace, increase profits, and improve the firm's public image. Athletic facilities, club rooms, and picnics were financed under the supervision of an industrial relations department. Many of the first tentative efforts were carried out by company-financed YMCAs, first called into the railroad industry in the aftermath of the 1877 strikes to improve workers' living conditions. However, urban working men—especially recent immigrants—found the YMCA too expensive, too Protestant, and too middle class, and resented having a value system imposed upon them. In 1902 the YMCA underwent a major reorientation when it established an industrial department, and by 1910 one-fifth of its members were industrial workers. The YMCA provided health lectures and recreational programs which included bowling and baseball right inside factories. However, it still had a long way to go: 75 percent of the male work force in major urban centers at this time were industrial workers and few were being reached by the YMCA. [77]

The first major American company to promote athletics for its blue-collar workers was the Pullman Palace Sleeping Car Company. In 1881 George Pullman built a carefully planned model town twelve miles south of Chicago. There he could exercise social control over his skilled workforce and insure himself a hardworking, stable, and sober corps of loyal workers. Right from the start public space was set aside for athletics, including a lake for aquatic sports and an athletic island for outdoor competition. Pullman believed that these facilities, plus a gymnasium, would attract workers to his shops, provide a rational substitute for vile amusements in Chicago, and bring fame to his company. The available resources encouraged both recreational sports among residents of the town, competitive intershop contests in sports like rowing and baseball between factory hands, and championship competition by top-level athletes. Pullman sponsored amateur national championships, professional regattas that drew over 15,000 spectators, and the annual Pullman Road Race, a cycling tour from Chicago. The cornerstone of the sports program was the Pullman Athletic Association (PAA), established in 1881 to engage in high-level competitive sport. Its leaders were company executives, but members were drawn from all branches of the company. Over half (54 percent) were blue-collar workers, predominantly craftsmen, and the rest were white-collar staff, foremen, and local businessmen. A number of the finest soccer players and oarsmen were actually recruited by the promise of a job because they were excellent athletes. The crew, coached by professional rower Hank Ward, was good enough to compete in national championships, while the largely English cricket club was one of the finest in the Midwest.[78]

Welfare capitalism reached its height in the 1910s and 1920s. Big city firms did not stress athletic and other recreational aspects of the program as much as was done in isolated mill towns, where workers had less access to uplifting sports and other entertainments. Nevertheless, sports programs were an important part of welfare capitalism among industrial firms with over 500 workers. In metropolitan areas where workers could not readily go home for dinner and then return to the plant to participate in sports, companies like NCR in Dayton and Heinz in Pittsburgh organized lunch-hour sports programs. Most athletic programs emphasized mass participation and provided such indoor facilities as gymnasiums, swimming pools, and game rooms and outdoor space for baseball diamonds. About one-third of all indoor industrial sports programs had gymnasiums, bowling alleys, or poolrooms, and nearly seven in ten had ball fields. Baseball was the most popular outdoor industrial sport in the 1920s; participation was viewed as a means to promote ''Americanism,'' meaning good character and company loyalty.[79]

During the 1920s, municipal governments in heavily industrialized cities often assisted local factories and community service organizations in promoting workers' sports. Industrial city leagues were established in such manufacturing centers as Paterson, New Jersey, Oakland, and

Baltimore. Paterson's Industrial Athletic Association, which comprised about 125 major factories, was an outgrowth of the Board of Recreation's work in adult recreation. The PIAA utilized city outdoor facilities and public-school gymnasiums. The Baltimore industrial leagues were organized differently; they emphasized non-industrial ties, relying on neighborhoods, churches, or lodges as the basis for establishing teams. In Newark, which had the smallest per capita park system in the U.S., forty companies in the Ironbound Community, a three-square-mile district in the heart of the industrial area, took the lead by establishing extensive recreational facilities that included a clubhouse, gymnasium, game rooms, and bowling alleys. The complex was later taken over and operated by the city.[80]

While most athletic programs emphasized mass participation, a lot of companies also sponsored high-quality baseball, soccer, and football teams that played before hundreds and sometimes thousands of spectators. The purpose was to exercise social control beyond the factory gates, to deflect labor unrest by providing a source of moral entertainment, and to advertise the name of the company. Many early professional football teams like the Columbus Panhandles were stocked by blue-collar workers recruited to work for the company. These men were boilermakers who worked a six-day week and played football on Sundays. Players on company baseball teams might include former professionals who got easy jobs, paid time off to practice, and travel allowances. Several of the original NFL franchises, like the Decatur Staleys (Chicago Bears), were the products of industrial relations departments which secured the necessary playing fields, scheduled the games, hired the coaches, and paid the players.[81]

Company reports and governmental surveys indicated that the industrial sports programs were a big success. A 1919 federal investigation found that industrial athletics encouraged a ''closer welding of the heterogeneous groups of employees, together with a closer and more friendly relationship between workers, foremen and superintendents.'' Sports programs were said to stimulate interest and good morale among younger workers. A 1926 report from the Bureau of Labor Standards encouraged expanding programs as an answer to the overspecialization and boredom of industrial work because competitive sports provided for workers' needs for self-expression. However, the athletic services had little impact on older, foreign-born employees, who were less interested in American sports and had familial obligations to take care of.[82]

The Depression had a debilitating impact on welfare capitalism. One-fourth of all industrial sports programs were eliminated to save money, and the rest were run on a bare-bones level. In Chicago in 1937, nearly half of the plants surveyed by the Recreation Commission still had recreation programs, primarily in athletics (85 percent), with at least a baseball or bowling team. Three years later a nationwide study of 639 firms reported that two-fifths (38.3 percent) had recreation programs. The most popular men's sports were bowling (87 percent), softball (74 percent), and basketball (54 percent). Just one-third had baseball, which required more space and greater skill than softball. The most popular women's sports were also bowling (35 percent) and softball (11 percent), with tennis (10 percent) close behind.[83]

There was a big revival in industrial sports during World War II. Tensions ran high in large industrial cities like Detroit and Los Angeles, which were terribly overcrowded by newcomers employed in defense plants and living in substandard housing. Both cities had race riots in 1943. Corporate officials turned to sport to calm tempers, attract workers, and demonstrate their concern and that of the community for its new workers and neighbors. Defense contractors like General Electric and Lockheed were particularly renowned for their high-quality athletic programs. Lockheed's eight plants sponsored over 300 bowling teams and eighty-two softball clubs, along with facilities for golfers and tennis players.[84]

Sport and Social Mobility: Baseball as a Case Study

The glamor, fame, and earnings of top professional athletes encouraged athletically gifted lower-class urban youth who lacked traditional alternate avenues to success to become professional sportsmen. In 1879 the winner of the final Astley Belt race earned $19,500 plus sweepstakes money; top jockeys at the turn of the century earned over $10,000; and Jack Johnson's share of the purse for his heavyweight championship fight with Jim Jeffries was $75,000. However, these earnings were made by just a select few; most competitors earned far more modest incomes during brief careers before they faded away.[85]

Participation and success in professional sport were functions of class, ethnicity, size, and urban space. Prizefighters, for example, were nearly always the products of urban slums, where they had learned to fight to protect themselves and their turf from rival ethnic groups. Boxing could be readily learned in the streets or in neighborhood gymnasiums. Pugilists were rarely young men who had alternate possibilities for success, for they would have surely chosen those paths rather than getting into a ring where they could get their heads bashed in. Baseball, on the other hand, was more appropriate for youths living in more prosperous communities where there was sufficient outdoor space to play regularly and achieve a high level of proficiency.

American-born players in the National Association (NA), the first major league (1871–75), were predominantly urban in origin (83 percent). Two-fifths came from Philadelphia, Brooklyn, Baltimore, and New York—among the most important sites of franchises. Adelman found that three-fifths (61.8 percent) of the Brooklyn and New York amateurs active in the 1860s who later played in the NA were artisans and the rest were white-collar workers. They were attracted by high salaries, which averaged from $1,300 to $1,600, or triple an average worker's wages. Despite the good pay, the occupation then had little social prestige—baseball players were placed on the same unfavorable social level as actors and prize fighters—and because of that and a lack of education, marketable skills, or savings, many players found it difficult to secure good positions after leaving the diamond.[86]

Most major leaguers in the late nineteenth century were from blue-collar backgrounds, but that changed after the turn of the century when the status of the sport—especially the prestige and wages of ballplayers—improved considerably. The standing of the national pastime was never higher as it touched base with prevailing middle-class attitudes, beliefs, and values, was applauded for its character-building qualities, and drew large middle-class audiences. At the same time, players' unions and management both encouraged greater decorum and proper attire on and off the field to secure respectability and acceptance for the athletes. From 1901 through 1903 salaries rose significantly because of competition between the NL and the upstart AL to fill the 240 positions on major league rosters. By 1910 salaries had risen to an average of about $3,000, which lured young men whose social and educational backgrounds were well above the national norm. One-fourth of all major leaguers active between 1900 and 1919 had attended college, compared to one out of twenty in their age group. Over two-fifths of the ballplayers (44.6 percent) had white-collar fathers, more than double the national proportion of white-collar workers in 1910 (20.2 percent); one-third (34.4 percent) had blue-collar fathers, approximately three-quarters of the national percentage (45.9 percent); and the remaining one-fifth (20.9 percent) were sons of farmers, who were still a major segment of the American workforce (33.9 percent). Particularly significant was the near total absence of players from the poorest sectors of urban society; just 3.3 percent of the big leaguers had unskilled fathers.[87]

Once baseball expanded nationally, beyond its urban origins in the northeast, fewer players (58.4 percent in 1900–19) came from cities. But this number still far exceeded the national urban proportion, which did not reach 50 percent until the 1920 census. Players continued to come in disproportionate numbers from large cities; one-fourth (24.4 percent) of big leaguers active between 1900 and 1919 came from cities with over 100,000 residents. Because of spatial variables the big cities were unevenly represented. Densely populated New York (Manhattan) and Boston, severely underrepresented, contributed just one-half their proportionate share compared to Cincinnati, Cleveland, and St. Louis, which overproduced by 300 percent, and Chicago, by 150 percent. Chicago had done even better in the past, but as it became more crowded in the late nineteenth century, there was less space than before for diamonds. As the *St. Louis Post-Dispatch* noted, "The passing of Chicago from recruiting fields was due wholly to the activity of the builders. Only a few years ago great spaces, even in the thickest settled parts of Chicago, lay vacant, and on these lots myriads of youngsters pitched, caught, and batted. As the city grew, these lots were covered one by one. Today [1905] the boy who would play ball in Chicago has to travel long distances to find a diamond, and the ambitions of the Chicago juveniles seem to have shrunk in inverse ratio to the length of these journeys." Close-in suburbs were potentially good sources for recruitment (Boston was outproduced by Cambridge by 250 percent) because of the available space, their acculturated populations, and community support for sport in the schools and at public spaces.[88]

The proportion of urban-born American players declined over the next forty years. Between 1920 and 1939, 53.7 percent came from cities— below the American urban population in 1940 (56.5 percent). Between 1940 and 1959 the number of active players of urban origin rose to 62.4 percent, but that was still below the country as a whole (70.6 percent in 1960). These trends further reflected the nationalization of baseball and the continued importance of space as a condition for the preparation of future top-flight ballplayers. Still, the proportion of recruits from large cities was about the same between the wars as in the early 1900s, and the fifty-two largest cities produced 19 percent more players than their share of the white population. Productivity improved markedly in warm-weather cities that had a lot of space and a longer playing season and declined in colder eastern and midwestern cities. Newark failed to produce a single major leaguer between 1920 and 1939, while Oakland produced 6.2 times more players than its share of the population, followed by San Francisco (4.5) and Los Angeles (3.9). This trend continued over the next twenty years, when one-third of major leaguers (32.8 percent) came from big cities, where competition to make high school teams was especially fierce.[89]

In the 1920s and 1930s, when there were 400 spots available on major league rosters, just a minority came from impoverished inner-city backgrounds. Nearly half (48 percent) of the players active in the 1920s and

Table 1. Occupation of Major League Baseball Players' Fathers, Active 1900–1958

Occupation	1900–1919 n = 117	1920–1940 n = 100	1941–1950 n = 90	1941–1958 n = 170	1951–1958 n = 80
White collar	44.6%	48.0%	35.5%	40.6%	46.25%
Blue collar	34.4	30.0	38.9	38.8	38.75
Farmer	20.9	22.0	25.6	20.6	15.00
Total	99.9[a]	100.0	100.0	100.0	100.00

SOURCE: Steven A. Riess, *Touching Base: Professional Baseball and American Culture in the Progressive Era* (Westport, Conn., 1980), 172; and computed from unpublished questionnaire data collected by Rudolph Haerle, Jr., and used with permission.

[a] Error due to rounding off.

1930s had white-collar fathers; just three out of ten (30 percent) had blue-collar fathers. However, this pattern changed in the 1940s, when white-collar players (35.5 percent) were outnumbered by their blue-collar peers (38.9 percent), a result of the Depression drying up alternate routes of mobility and the increased presence of acculturated inner-city ethnic youths in professional baseball. In the 1950s most players were again coming from white-collar backgrounds, although a survey of star players born between 1920 and 1939 found them to be overwhelmingly blue collar in origin (62.5 percent), which was probably a result of the integration of baseball.[90]

Even if a lower-class athlete made the majors, his tenure was short—four years is generally accepted as the average—and consequently he had to secure other employment at a time when most men were well into their lifelong occupations. The first professionals, active in the period from 1871 to 1882, had a difficult time obtaining white-collar positions after baseball; over one-third (35.6 percent) skidded down into a blue-collar occupation, an unusually sharp intergenerational decline that reflected their low status and lack of education, savings, or marketable skills. Nearly half (48.4 percent) ended up in low-level white-collar jobs as clerks, salesmen, petty shopkeepers, or managers of baseball teams—jobs in which they hoped to utilize their fame or expertise. One out of eight worked at a position tied to saloons, billiard parlors, or bookmaking—low-status enterprises intimately involved with local politics and the male bachelor subculture. There were a few instances of rags-to-riches tales like store clerk A. G. Spalding, who utilized his pitching talents to become owner of the Chicago White Stockings and head of the nation's leading sporting goods company. Spalding got in at the ground floor of the sports boom, but few players ever duplicated his success.[91]

Ballplayers active after the turn of the century fared considerably better. While one-third of the retirees who played in the early days of major

Table 2. Subsequent Jobs of Retired Major League Baseball Players, Active 1871–1959

Occupation	1871–1882 n=219	1900–1919 n=478	1920–1939 n=321	1940–1949 n=216	1950–1959 n=790
High white collar					
Professionals	1.8%	5.9%	10.3%	7.4%	7.8%
Mgrs., high offs., and major props.	12.8	19.0	10.0	8.8	14.1
Total	14.6	24.9	20.3	16.2	21.9
Low white collar					
Clerks, sales, & kindred workers	18.3	10.0	20.2	28.0	24.5
Semi professionals,	13.2	33.5	24.3	26.9	29.9
Petty props., mgrs., & low offs.	16.9	14.0	12.1	11.6	10.9
Total	48.4	57.5	56.6	66.7	65.3
Total white collar	63.0	82.4	76.9	82.9	87.3ᵃ
Farmers	1.4	3.6	4.5	1.9	0.9
Blue collar					
Skilled	11.9	3.8	4.7	7.4	4.7
Semiskilled & service	21.0	8.8	13.1	6.9	6.5
Unskilled	2.7	1.5	0.9	0.9	0.6
Total	35.6	14.0ᵃ	18.6ᵃ	15.2	11.8
Grand Total	100.0	100.0	100.0	100.0	100.0

ᵃ Error due to rounding off.

SOURCE: Adapted from Steven A. Riess, *Touching Base: Professional Baseball and American Culture in the Progressive Era* (Westport, Conn., 1980), 159, 201; study data of 353 men active between 1920 and 1939 and 243 active from 1940 to 1959; data computed from Rich Marazzi and Len Fiorito, *Aaron to Zuverink: A Nostalgic Look at the Baseball Players of the Fifties* (Briarcliff, N.J., 1982)

league baseball ended up with blue-collar jobs, the ratio was one out of seven (14.0 percent) for men active between 1900 and 1919, one out of five (18.3 percent) for those active in the interwar decades, and one out of nine (11.8 percent) for those in the 1950s. They ended up mainly in low white-collar jobs, particularly in sports (24.6 percent for players active in the 1950s) or positions which required a lot of direct contact with clients, such as sales, real estate, and insurance, which presumably enabled them to utilize their fame.[92]

In the long run retirees succeeded largely because of their educational and social backgrounds. Fame was crucial in determining a player's initial retirement occupation, but thereafter receded into the background. Among players active in the early 1900s, for example, nearly all college attendees became white-collar workers (93 percent) compared to two-thirds (67.5 percent) of the noncollege men. In that era the overwhelming majority of players with nonmanual fathers secured white-collar work (85 percent), but barely a majority of manual fathers' sons did (58 percent). Social background was important because of its correlation to educational and cultural values. Middle-class sons were encouraged to have a strong self-image, high expectations, and such traditional bourgeois values as thrift and deferred gratification. Players from blue-collar families did not get the same kind of positive reinforcement as youths and were not so-cialized to plan for the future. Lower-class players who were insecure and lacked experience in saving money often engaged in conspicuous con-sumption to demonstrate their success to friends, teammates, and them-selves. When the time for retirement arrived, they had no skills, no connections, and no money in the bank. [93]

Conclusion: Sport and the Urban Social Structure

The nature of the urban social structure and its dynamic interaction with such elements of urbanization as space, demography, economic develop-ment, social institutions, political structures, and ideology had an impor-tant bearing on the development of sport and sporting institutions in the industrialized radial city. Because of different economic situations, social and cultural environments, neighborhoods, and value systems, members of different social classes did not have the same opportunities or options to partake of sports. However, over time sporting choices did become more democratic, especially by the 1920s and 1930s as the standard of living improved and municipal and private institutions increased their sponsorship of mass sport.

In the late nineteenth century, capitalists enriched by industrialization, commerce, and booming urban land values, together with scions of the old social and economic elites, utilized sports to separate themselves from the latest parvenus and maintain the same privacy away from home that they enjoyed in such prestigious neighborhoods as Fifth Avenue, Beacon Hill, and Nob Hill. They readily escaped the worst pathological features of the industrial city by withdrawing to their own private spaces in lavish urban athletic clubs and sumptuous suburban country clubs. These elite sports clubs were established to encourage and facilitate high-level ama-teur athletics while also segregating men of high status from the negative features of city life and from lower status individuals.

Urbanization had a much more direct impact on the leisure activities of other social classes, who could not afford to escape so easily the growth of cities. There was an enormous boom in middle-class athletics, fostered at first by the ideology of sport which extolled the ameliorative influences of moral sport for the health and character of sedentary urbanites. Middle-class urban males, who had sufficient free time and discretionary income to enjoy sports, became ardent spectators at outdoor semipublic fields, especially baseball parks, which were accessible by affordable mass transit. The middle classes also became active participants in sports in public spaces like the streets, where they rode their bicycles, or city parks located near their homes, where they skated, rowed, golfed, and played tennis and baseball. By the turn of the century they began emulating the elite by establishing their own private spaces for play—at first modest athletic clubs, and even country clubs by the 1920s. There they could gain certification of their status (and possibly move on to more prestigious clubs), make business connections, and separate themselves and their families from their self-perceived social inferiors.

Urbanization had a negative effect upon working-class sport, particularly for poor inner-city residents living in crowded neighborhoods. The growth and development of cities resulted in the loss of traditional playing and swimming sites, which could not be replaced. Residents of zones of emergence had some access to the new, large suburban parks. However the slum dwellers, most in need of fresh air, could not afford the cost of carfare to the large parks located well beyond walking distance on the urban periphery. Limited in discretionary time, restricted by Sunday blue laws, and short of extra money, these people had few pleasures other than a beer. Sport was, nonetheless, a vital part of the popular culture of acculturated working-class men, who for the most part depended primarily on accessible neighborhood institutions for their sporting entertainment—primarily the tavern and, after the turn of the century, the billiard hall and the bowling alley where they could have a little privacy. Local political machines, labor unions, and industrialists vying for the loyalties of the urban blue-collar men sponsored some picnics and other athletic opportunities. By the 1920s, those who were Americanized participated in or attended nearly all forms of sport. Nonetheless, spatial and economic constraints effectively restricted most inner-city residents to those sports that fit in best with their environment, such as pool, bowling, basketball, and boxing—sports widely identified with ethnic groups that dominated the urban slums.

CHAPTER 3

Sport, Race, and Ethnicity

In addition to social class, urban sport was also strongly influenced by ethnic demographics and culture as these variables interacted with such elements of urbanization as spatial patterns, racism, and prejudice. The sporting experiences of non-WASP urbanites differed significantly from those of members of the core culture which reflected their immigrant heritage (norms, customs, values), income levels, degree of assimilation, and concentration in large, crowded cities. The disproportionate presence of newcomers in major cities posed a serious threat to old-stock Americans and their culture. At the turn of the century over three-fourths of New Yorkers and Chicagoans were of foreign origin, a ratio that was even exceeded in such eastern industrial towns as Fall River. In 1920, when just half of the national population lived in cities, over 80 percent of the new immigrants, 84 percent of the Irish, and 67 percent of German newcomers resided in cities, mainly in major cities. Blacks comprised the least urban ethnic group in 1900, but when they migrated north, 70 percent settled in cities, crowding into ghetto communities.[1]

This chapter examines how the athletic participation of white ethnic and black urbanites was influenced by the cultural baggage they brought from their points of origin, the timing of their arrival, their social class, their degree of acculturation, and the spatial relationships in their slums or zones of emergence which influenced access to sports facilities. We shall also examine the voluntary institutions developed to sustain traditional pleasures or introduce newcomers to American games and give particular attention to the sporting interests of second-generation immigrants whose parents had little interest in or experience with sports but who themselves became ardent fans as they sought Americanization.

Sport and the Ethnic Voluntary Association

Since sport was one part of the constellation of recreational activities, along with the ethnic theater, music societies, saloons, and religious festivals, that helped immigrants and their children adjust to urban American life, it needs to be addressed as part of the subculture of ethnic villages.[2] One of the important features of ethnic voluntary associations, particularly among the old immigrants and others who brought a sporting tradition with them, was the maintenance of historic old-world sporting organizations or the creation of new ones which emphasized the "ancient and honorable games" of the homeland. In addition, these old sports associations and new ones established in America by both the old and new immigrants fostered athletic participation by the second generation in American sports, under the supervision and direction of ethnic recreation leaders, in hopes of maintaining an ethnic identity for the American-born and reared.

The Old Immigrants

The Irish-American Community. The Irish prominence in urban sport, established in the antebellum era, continued after the Civil War. In Irish neighborhoods the traditional male bachelor subculture continued to provide a focal point for their association life. But besides promoting manliness and solidarity, as in the past, sport also provided both a means to encourage and express Irish nationalism and a vehicle for social mobility.

In the 1870s and 1880s independence leaders in Ireland revived long-forgotten Irish sports like hurling and Gaelic football as a means to promote Irish nationalism. To show solidarity with the revolutionaries and to encourage ethnic pride, Irishmen living in the United States quickly adopted these sports, forming an ethnic subcommunity that gave members dignity and a heightened sense of nationalism. Among the first organized groups to play these sports was the Irish Athletic Club in Boston in 1879. The club's inaugural meet featured such traditional sports as goaling, trapball, and stone throwing. Five years later, the Gaelic Athletic Association (GAA) was formed in Ireland to promote traditional Hibernian sports, and through them greater self-esteem and national pride. Branches of the GAA were soon established in American cities, where it became best known for its Sunday track and field meets at sites like Gaelic Park in the heart of Chicago's South Side Irish community. Political clout in that neighborhood protected the games in the face of Sabbatarian opposition. Irish sport was also promoted by overtly political organizations, most notably the Clan-Na-Gael (United Brotherhood), a secret revolutionary society that arranged athletic meets to gain favorable publicity, attract new adherents, and promote Irish nationalism.[3]

Traditional Irish games received a lot of coverage in the Irish press in the late nineteenth century and got considerable community support. Hurling was a particularly popular sport among second- and third-generation Irish-Bostonians, who played for teams like the Irish Athletic Club, the South Boston A.C., and the Shamrock Hurling Club. In New York, Irish football games were well attended by local Irishmen, who cheered for teams named for Irish nationalist leaders like Wolfe Tone. However, since the matches were played at Celtic Park in Long Island City, fans had to take public transportation from the poor, downtown, Irish neighborhoods.[4]

While traditional Irish pastimes continue to be played in Irish neighborhoods to the present day, they were far less important in the community than American sports. Sports like baseball, boxing, and basketball provided a major focal point around which Irishmen living in the slums or the zones of emergence organized their social life and secured self-esteem. Most young Irish-American athletes played in their own neighborhoods on teams they organized, often by block, to compete against boys from across the street or from different neighborhoods. These aggregates were commonly based on a youth gang that formalized as the members got older into a "social and athletic club" (SAC), which gave members, generally at least sixteen to eighteen years old, a greater sense of belonging and status than just "hanging out" on the corner with their peers. SACs first gained popularity around the turn of the century in predominantly Irish sections of cities like Chicago and were later copied by other ethnic groups. The initiative in organizing a club was usually taken by an outside agent, like a politician, saloonkeeper, or youth worker. A typical SAC had a spartanly furnished clubhouse, usually in a store-front or back room of a store, where members spent their free time shooting pool, tossing dice, or playing cards. They generally had about one hundred members who enjoyed the camaraderie of the clubs, along with SAC-sponsored stags, dances, and athletics. SACs sponsored baseball, football, and other team sports; obtained uniforms; and scheduled matches with other SACs. SACs had the potential to be destructive asocial agencies or positive integrative forces that replaced the uncontrolled, pugnacious behavior of street punks with the cooperative values taught through team sports.[5]

One of the most prominent aspects of the SACs was their political character. They depended heavily on political assistance to get organized, secure a charter, become well-known, and succeed. As sociologist Frederick Thrasher, the leading student of the SACs, pointed out in 1926,

The tendency of the gangs to become athletic clubs has been greatly stimulated by the politicians of the city. It has become a tradition among gangs throughout Chicago that the first source of possible financial aid is the local alderman or other politician. . . . The ward "heeler" often corrals a gang like a beeman does his swarm in the hive he has prepared for it. The boss pays the rent and is generous in his donations for all gang enterprises. He is the "patron saint" of the gang and often leads the grand march or makes a speech at gang dances and in return his protegés work for him in innumerable ways and every gang boy in the hive is expected to gather honey on election day. It is doubtful if this sort of athletic club could long survive if it had to depend solely upon the financial backing of its own members.

Former SAC members commonly ended up as Democratic machine aldermen, police captains, or gamblers. The most famous politician to come out of the SACs was Richard Daley, who got his start as head of the Hamburg A.C.[6]

The preeminent Chicago SAC was the Ragen Colts, whose territory was the impoverished "Back of the Yards" district on the South Side, though in time it also terrorized neighborhoods west of that area. Founded in 1908 by politico Frank Ragen, a future county commissioner who rented them a clubhouse and bought uniforms and sporting equipment, the Colts rapidly gained fame for their athletic prowess and notoriety for their slugging and political intimidation. In the words of one member, "when we dropped into a polling place, everyone else dropped out." The gang became infamous as a lawless group that terrorized the Southwest Side, better Irish neighborhoods, and the nearby black community on the east side of Washington Park. During the Chicago Race Riot in July 1919, the Colts played a prominent role in attacking black Chicagoans. One historian of the riots blamed their violence on the Colts' antipathy to the growing number of black workers at the stockyards, Republican Mayor William H. Thompson's support of black civil rights, and the increased presence of black ballplayers and picnickers in Washington Park. By this time the Colts were accurately described as "athletic only with their fists and brass knuckles and guns." SACs were becoming less social and athletic and more a hangout for rough young men who had graduated from youth gangs.[7]

The German-American Turnverein. Ethnic athletics in German-American neighborhoods revolved around the turnverein, important community centers as integral a part of German culture as the beer garden, German-language theaters, and German choral societies. Membership nationally reached 13,387 in 1880, up from about 5,000 in 1859, and then nearly tripled a decade later to 35,912 in 1890. The members were mainly lower-middle and middle-class first- and second-generation Germans. A majority of senior members in the 1880s were blue-collar workers (55.5 percent) and virtually all the rest (44.2 percent) were white-collar workers, predominantly petty bourgeois. Virtually all of the manual working members were craftsmen, mainly printers, brewers, and cigarmakers—all typically German occupations (see table 3). In all, the membership constituted a hard-working, respectable element who resided in heavily German urban villages.[8]

Table 3. Occupations of German-American Turner Pioneers (1848–62)

Occupation	Active in the 1880s	
	Number	Percent
High White Collar	114	14.6
Low White Collar	231	29.6
Total White Collar	345	44.2
Farmers	3	0.4
Skilled	408	52.4
Semiskilled	21	2.7
Unskilled	3	0.4
Total Blue Collar	432	55.5
Total	780	100.1[a]

SOURCE: Computed from data in Hugo Gollmer, *Namensliste der Pioniere des Nord-Amerik Turnerbundes der Jahre 1848–62* (St. Louis, 1885).

[a] Error due to rounding off

The social backgrounds of members in the oldest, and what were presumably the most prestigious, societies varied substantially from city to city. The Boston and Williamsburg (Brooklyn) turnvereins were nearly 90 percent blue-collar, as were over two-thirds of the membership in Cincinnati and Philadelphia. Yet in Milwaukee and Chicago, newer midwestern cities with large and prosperous German communities, the proportions were markedly different. Four-fifths of the Milwaukee turnverein was white-collar. One-third of its senior members (34.6 percent) had high-level white-collar jobs. The Chicago turngemeinde, the city's oldest and most prestigious society, was 70.6 percent white-collar, and increased to 82 percent by the turn of the century. Chicago's large and vital German community could support several separate turner units with a combined membership of about 5,000 in 1890, the most of any city. At least one of the other units, the Aurora turnverein, was distinctly working class. Still, the turners were probably less class based than any other major sport organization. Certain units in New York and St. Louis were evenly divided between white-collar and blue-collar workers at a time when most German-Americans were blue-collar workers. Respectable, hardworking German immigrants from different social classes could exercise and socialize together in a gemütlich atmosphere because they shared the same culture and values. Unlike the antebellum cricket clubs, the turnvereines did not, as a matter of course, evolve into purely status communities. The turnhalles, located in the heart of German neighborhoods, were social centers that provided far more than places for physical exercise. A major turnhalle like that of the Chicago turngemeinde, located in the center of the city's North Side German community, had a well-equipped gymnasium, of course, but also a billiard room, library, club room, dining room, and one of the largest dance halls in the city. German-language theatrical productions were staged there, and it was a forum for public debates.[10]

The goals of the turners were to maintain the German character of their communities, encourage physical fitness, and improve conditions of working-class folk. They were politically active as a pressure group on ethnocultural issues like the preservation of the Continental Sabbath and the use of German as the primary language of instruction in neighborhood public schools. They tried to improve the quality of urban life by advocating better health through construction of gymnasiums in all schools, physical education and gymnastics for public school students under the supervision of trained instructors, and development of municipal parks. The turners were strong advocates of trade unionism and socialism. During the 1870s their national organizations supported such traditional socialist demands as worker control over the means of production as well as general social reforms like compulsory school attendance, regulation of monopolies, government inspection of factories, restrictions on child labor, and the eight-hour day. Turner halls were frequently utilized by unions for meetings and public debates. By the 1880s an influential minority in the overtly socialist turnvereins, like August Spies in Chicago, began to openly avow anarchism and in 1891 briefly took control over parts of the turnverein movement in the United States.[11]

By the turn of the century, the movement had become increasingly embourgeoised, reflecting the general economic well-being of the German-American urban community. Middle-class members preferred divorcing politics from athletics and focusing their efforts on the promotion of physical education rather than left-wing politics. Yet while the turnverein was no longer identifiable as a German workingmen's institution, the turners at the national level still maintained a socialist perspective, regularly supporting Eugene V. Debs for president. The socialist impulse was strongest in Milwaukee, ironically a city where the old German elite had dominated the early turner movement, and local members there helped elect a socialist mayor and congressman. During World War I the turner movement languished because of anti-German sentiments and afterwards failed to reestablish itself as a major German-American institution because of declining interest in gymnastics and the widespread assimilation of potential members. [12]

The New Immigrants

While ethnic sports facilitated the adjustment of old immigrants in their urban villages, they were far less important among the new immigrants from eastern and southern Europe, who had little if any sporting tradition and would not become ardent sportsmen in America. In general, they regarded sport as a childish pursuit and ridiculed their peers who were interested in sports. Those who ventured into athletic institutions like the YMCA were quickly put off by Americans who made fun of them. Instead, hardworking male newcomers, exhausted by backbreaking jobs, preferred relaxation to physically exertive pleasures and enjoyed themselves at ethnic saloons, clubs, or coffeehouses or at family gatherings and religious festivals. [13]

The Bohemians. One of the few new immigrant groups who came to America with any sporting heritage at all, the Bohemians established themselves in heavily Czech neighborhoods like Pilsen on the Near Southwest Side of Chicago and other industrial areas in the midwest. In 1862, as part of a romantic resistance movement against the ruling Austrians, Bohemian nationalists organized the sokol movement. Its philosophy, modeled after the turnverein, sought to develop nationalism and strong bodies and minds for the future revolution. The sokol tradition in America goes almost as far back as in Bohemia; a unit was established in St. Louis in 1865. The primary goals of American sokol units were to promote physical culture and to encourage newcomers to identify with their fellow Bohemians and their language and culture. By 1900 there were 184 units in the United States. The members were mainly working class or small merchants who were freethinkers. Hostility between freethinkers and devout Catholics eventually caused the latter to organize their own sokols. The example of the sokol encouraged other slavic peoples to organize their own athletic associations for similar purposes, like the Polish Falcons, organized in 1867 and first imported to America twenty years later, when the first nest was established in Chicago. [14]

The sokol hall was normally one of the largest buildings in a Bohemian neighborhood, and the center of its cultural and social life. It often housed the community's major recreational institutions like the Czech theater and choral societies. Sokols sponsored annual gymnastic exhibitions and family holiday outings that would include sokol drills and folk dancing. The physical culture programs emphasized calisthenics, which did not appeal to the second generation. In Pilsen the sokol leaders met the challenge of attracting the interest of the American-born by organizing Sunday Bohemian baseball leagues for them. This got the youth involved in the sokol and encouraged them to sustain their ethnic identity. The quality of play was quite high: by 1910 several Chicago Bohemians had made the major leagues. Their achievement was a source of great pride in the community, even among non-baseball fans. [15]

The Jews. The brief athletic tradition of the Bohemians completely surpassed that of the two million eastern European Jews who migrated to the United States between 1880 and 1914 to escape pogroms and antisemitism. They were stereotyped as weak, unhealthy, physically unfit, and unaccustomed to respectable "manly" labor. Noted sociologist E. A. Ross described them as "the polar opposite of our pioneer breed. Not only are they undersized and weak-muscled, but they shun bodily activity and are extremely sensitive to pain." The presence of these strangely garbed, bearded, Yiddish-speaking Orthodox Jews embarrassed German-American Jews and unleashed a wave of antisemitism that resulted in restricted admission into colleges, prestigious men's clubs, and well-known athletic clubs. Until then, the prosperous German Jews had been hardly distinguishable from other German-Americans in their social and athletic activities, having served as leaders of turnvereins and gained prominence in mainstream sports ranging from thoroughbred racing to professional baseball as participants and entrepreneurs. The result was that German Jews like Bernard Baruch had to organize their own exclusive athletic organizations like the City Club in New York, formed in 1906. [16]

In 1854 in imitation of the YMCA, German-Jews organized the Young Men's Hebrew Association. The YMHA promoted sociability, physical fitness, and spirituality, substituting "muscular Judaism" for muscular Christianity. While facilities were at first modest, by the turn of the century, German Jewish communities were building substantial structures with gymnasiums, swimming pools, and other features that became important community centers in middle-class German-Jewish neighborhoods. The best known was the multistory 92nd Street Y on the Upper East Side near Yorkville, which became nationally renowned for its sports and cultural programs. [17]

Philanthropic German-Jews accepted the responsibility of assisting the new Jewish immigrants to adjust to life in the new world by establishing settlement houses and other social agencies which helped the newcomers find jobs, secure housing, and acculturate. Settlement houses established in inner-city slums, like the Educational Alliance (1893) in New York's Lower East Side and the Jewish People's Institute (1908) in Chicago's West Side ghetto, sought to sustain a Jewish identity among their clients while helping them to become good citizens. Youth workers emphasized athletics to attract Jewish youth and to encourage good health habits, improve morality, and build character, while disproving negative stereotypes about Jewish manliness. After the turn of the century, once YMHAs were constructed in Brownsville and other crowded Jewish slums, the YMHA movement also began to respond to the needs of Russian Jews. By the 1910s Russian Jews had begun moving to better neighborhoods like Harlem, which was close enough for their sons to walk to the 92nd Street Y, where they could participate in such urban sports as boxing and basketball under expert instructors. What had originally been an exclusively German-Jewish facility was fast becoming a Jewish community center.[18]

The Catholics. The most important Catholic group to utilize athletics to uplift inner-city youth was the Catholic Youth Organization (CYO), established in Chicago in 1930 by Auxiliary Bishop Bernard J. Sheil. Sheil recognized that young Catholics like Studs Lonigan and his ilk were being drawn away from the church by the competition of such exhilarating pleasures as drinking, fighting, and womanizing. The church, along with family and schools, apparently had lost its historic function as agent of socialization and had little relevance to the needs of young Catholic males in the 1920s and 1930s. Sheil wanted to find a way to bring the young men back into the fold.[19]

The Catholic church's concern over the protection of its young in America dated back to the early nineteenth century, when it created parochial schools to counter Protestant influence in the public schools. In the early 1900s, when most Catholics were unassimilated urbanites of new immigrant stock, bishops worried that adult-directed boys' organizations like the YMCA and the Boy Scouts would undermine the faith of good Catholics by promoting the values of the Protestant core culture to the detriment of their own religious heritage. Two decades later, the church was still on the defensive, despite the efforts of Chicago's Cardinal Mundelein and others in the hierarchy to Americanize their communicants.[20]

The emphasis on education and socialization continued in the 1930s. Pope Pius XI's 1929 encyclical, ''Christian Education of Youth,'' urged that full attention be given to the complete supervision of all aspects of Catholic education. The problem of coping with a perceived hostile environment was exacerbated by the onset of the Depression, which created high levels of unemployment and left a lot of young men with free time but nothing constructive to do. These concerns struck home in Chicago, which had the largest parochial school system in the country, and prompted Bishop Sheil to devise a program of supervised recreation for older boys as a partial solution to some of the church's problems. He believed that athletics would help Americanize the second generation, promote citizenship, and enable young men to direct their antisocial energies in a positive direction. Sport would fill up idle time and promote sexual and moral continence. Sheil publicized the CYO to the non-Catholic community as an organization that would prevent juvenile delinquency and premarital sex and sold the program to the church by emphasizing that it would bring boys closer to their religious heritage and save those who had fallen away.[21]

The CYO began operations in 1931 with a huge boxing tournament and a ten-team basketball league. Sheil originally relied on local parishes to train and instruct members, but since their facilities were inadequate, he set up a training center in the Loop. By 1938, three-fifths of the city's parishes had CYO units serving over 10,000 boys in recreational, educational, religious, and social programs. But the CYO became best known for teaching boxing, which provided a lot of favorable publicity. Sheil emphasized boxing because it appealed to poor working-class youth, the people he wanted to bring into the CYO. Boxing did just that, and the CYO became an important training ground for talented boxers, three of whom made the 1936 Olympic team.[22]

CYO branches were soon established all over the country and by 1940 were reaching 150,000 Catholic youth. Besides boxing, the CYO sponsored a baseball league and the biggest basketball association in the United States. Its philosophy, which differed significantly from the Protestant-inspired athletic associations founded in the late nineteenth century, reflected a Catholic perspective which did not fear the influence of women as teachers for older boys, as the late Victorians had. The CYO used sport, not to build manly, healthy, and physically muscular Christians, but rather to save souls. In addition, the CYO always served a heterogeneous lower-class Catholic clientele, while Protestant boys' workers started out with a homogeneous middle-class WASP population.[23]

Urban Space and Ethnic Sports

The choice of sports among athletically inclined ethnic youth was heavily influenced not only by their social class and ethnic heritage but also by the spatial and social patterns of the neighborhoods where they lived. Second- and third-generation youth living in the more well-to-do communities in the suburban fringe, or even the moderate income zone of emergence, had many different opportunities available to them than did slum dwellers. Residents of the inner city, who had high drop-out rates and less free time, if employed, had less exposure to sports in school. But, in addition, they had virtually no access to distant suburban parks with space for outdoor sports like baseball and, until the turn of the century, did not even have small parks within walking distance. Therefore, a lot of their outdoor play was relegated to the streets. Between 1870 and 1935, new immigrant youth seldom achieved great success in baseball but instead turned to indoor sports, more congruent with the living conditions of urban slums. Consequently, the sports at which the new immigrants became most successful were basketball, track, weightlifting, and boxing, which required little space or expensive equipment and could be learned in neighborhood athletic centers.

Baseball

As we have already noted, the best baseball players were mainly recruited from upper-lower- and lower-middle-class urban families, the kinds of people who lived in the zone of emergence or even the suburban fringe. Major league rosters before 1920 were dominated by American, Irish, and German players who lived in localities with sufficient space to play baseball. The Irish lived in urban sections of the country where the sport had been popular from an early date, so they had a head start on other ethnic groups. In Irish neighborhoods, everyone followed the sport, and many communities like the southwest side of Chicago, the locale of James T. Farrell's novels, had plenty of space to play ball in the nearby parks. Furthermore, neighborhood teams were often sponsored by SACs, local politicians, or saloonkeepers. The nicknames given certain sections of ballparks, like the "Kerry Patch" in St. Louis or the section of the Polo Grounds bleachers called "Burkeville," reflected the well-known presence of Irishmen at games. White Sox Park drew well with the South Side Irish in Chicago—not just because the owner was Irish but also because the park was just a few blocks from Bridgeport, a heavily Irish community. Irish attendance was also facilitated by Sunday ball, a work schedule for many Irish workers in construction or in city employment that permitted afternoon recreation, and the cheap cost of tickets, since Comiskey operated the largest quarter section in the major leagues. A dramatic sport whose frequent lapses in action gave spectators a chance to talk over the game and drink beer, baseball fit in well with the norms of the Irish bachelor subculture. It was a manly sport, rarely attended by Irish womenfolk, and provided Irishmen with a rare topic for conversation with their sons, whom they would take along to the games.[24]

The Irish familiarity with the sport and their opportunities to play the game proficiently enabled them to achieve great success in baseball. By the 1880s and 1890s they had many role models to emulate, like "King" Kelly, John J. McGraw, and Ed Delehanty, and parents encouraged talented youth to practice so they could become professional ballplayers and earn high wages. By the early 1890s, one-third of all major leaguers were believed to be Irish, and they soon comprised a large proportion of managers. In 1915, for instance, eleven of sixteen major league managers were sons of Erin.[25]

By comparison, the new immigrant groups had very little success in breaking into the major leagues during this period. There was not a single rookie of new immigrant stock in 1910 and just two Italians and one Bohemian out of 133 first-year men in 1920. Baseball was enormously popular with the second-generation newcomers, who ardently followed the exploits of their heroes and favorite teams in the local press but seldom attended games because of the expense. Boys liked to play baseball, which was fun and demonstrated that they were not greenhorns but "real Yankees." However, the lack of playing space in the crowded inner city was the key factor which made it difficult for second-generation youth to secure the skills and experience necessary to become professionals. Because of spatial limitations that consigned slum youth to the streets, their ballplaying was often constricted to cognate games like stickball, and they had to develop special rules to conform to the idiosyncrasies of their playing area ("anything hit to left field is out"). Other factors also constrained them—limited discretionary time for working youth, afternoon attendance at Hebrew School, low rates of attendance at secondary school (where they could play on interscholastic teams with other talented players under the supervision of trained coaches), parental opposition, and limited community support. Before the 1920s, Yiddish, Italian, and Polish language newspapers almost never covered baseball, although it did become a staple of the Czech and French-Canadian press. Immigrant parents, especially eastern European Jews, saw baseball as a silly sport played by men in short pants, a waste of time that introduced their sons to some of the worst features of the host society. In 1903 a Jewish father wrote to the Yiddish *Forward* (New York): "What is the point of this crazy game? It makes sense to teach a child to play dominoes or chess . . . but not baseball. . . . I want my boy to grow up to be a *mensch*, not a wild American runner." Jewish parents felt that baseball was a dangerous game that required too much physical exertion![26] As late as the 1920s parents still opposed baseball as a waste of time, a threat to their authority, and an entering wedge for total assimilation and loss of one's traditional culture. As "Jim," a Jewish boy in Los Angeles, told an interviewer: "My father won't allow us to play ball on the lot. He says it's a waste of time and a disgrace to make such a lot of noise over nothing. He was raised in Poland. . . . I hate to stick around here with no friends and nothing to do. My mother reported me to the judge of the Juvenile Court. He told me to stay off Augusta Street, and I did for a couple of days, but I wasn't going to be lonesome all by myself, and when I started to long for the boys, I ditched school and went out there to join them. They sure are a slick bunch, and we have a lot of fun together." Jim felt his parents did not understand his needs: "They expect me to be old-fashioned and go to *schuhl*."[27]

A similar story of intergenerational conflict concerned an Italian youth named Nick and his immigrant mother. When the son was brought before the Chicago Juvenile Court on charges of misconduct, his mother told the judge: "Nick no wanna work. He big man, 14, and wanta to play ball all day. Father say, 'You go-to-day and work in restaurant with your uncle. . . .' He makes faces, cusses, laughs, and runs out to play ball. . . . He very bad boy. . . . He no wanta work. . . . He get up at noon and go out to play. That not right. I go out to the ball game and say, 'Nick, come home with me from these bad boys and work.' He laugh at me, make a face, tell me to go home and to mind own business. He like nothing but ball. . . . The father work hard. Have heart trouble. Nick ought to help."[28]

Since youths often played on teams sponsored by church groups, fraternal organizations like the Polish National Alliance, or even in all-Polish leagues that dated back in Chicago's Polonia to 1913, simply playing baseball did not structurally assimilate a boy. When French-Canadians in the predominantly Francophone industrial town of Woonsocket, Rhode Island, became baseball fans in the 1890s, they did not lose their ethnic identification. They read box scores in a French-language newspaper and followed the exploits of local hero Napoleon Lajoie, the premier second baseman of his day. French-Canadians playing Anglo teams often gave signals in French, which was still their primary language. Playing baseball under these circumstances promoted ethnic pride and cultural pluralism as much as Americanization.[29]

A generation later a similar situation existed on "The Hill," an Italian ghetto in St. Louis. Older residents in that poor working-class community had little to do with the outside world (the Hill did not get public transportation until the 1920s), and barely supported the local public school, which was perceived as a threat to parental authority. In the 1920s an athletic program was organized through the local parish by a YMCA worker who convinced the immigrant generation that sports would make their sons into "good Americans" by promoting clean living and sound morals. The church emphasized baseball—popular with the second-generation who idolized ethnic heroes like Tony Lazzeri, the great Yankee second baseman—and soccer—very popular with German and Irish St. Louisians, who played in ethnic and industrial leagues. The immigrant generation was not familiar with soccer and thus it did not bear the burden of being an "Italian sport." The program was a great success, producing several major leaguers like Yogi Berra and a number of champion soccer teams. These achievements helped alter the stereotype townsfolk had of Hill residents, and they became accepted as part of the broader community. Local youth became more assimilated through the experience of playing outside the neighborhood. But while sport promoted individual assimilation, historian Gary Mormino argues that, for the community as a whole, "sport channeled forces that had historically divided Italian immigrants in St. Louis and harnessed these divisive energies into creative participation." Local support and pride in the neighborhood athletic federation accented the Italian character of the Hill, serving as an important ethnic symbol. Rather than Americanizing the neighborhood, Mormino found, "Sport encouraged not only the preservation of an ethnic subculture, but the preservation of the community itself."[30]

In the 1920s, if not before, several major league teams made a concerted effort to recruit ethnic ballplayers to build up fan interest. The Giants, for example, signed Moses Solomon, the "Rabbi of Swat," to a brief trial in 1923 and three years later brought up Andy Cohen, who was widely publicized as a ghetto boy making good. Born in Baltimore, Cohen had actually grown up in Waco, Texas, and was educated at the University of Alabama—hardly the typical Jewish inner-city youth. Even though New York contained half of the American Jewish population in 1920, New York produced less than its proportionate share of major leaguers. Only one-third of the Jewish major leaguers active between 1920 and 1964 were New Yorkers, and most of them came from the outlying boroughs that had more space to play, such as the Parade Grounds in Brooklyn. Its major leaguers did not come from the poorest, most crowded neighborhoods. Jewish superstar Hank Greenberg, for instance, was not a product of the inner city, but grew up in the 1920s in a middle-class household in the relatively prosperous and spacious Bronx.[31]

The other new immigrant groups achieved greater success in baseball, though until 1935 Slavs and Italians together comprised just 7 percent of all major leaguers. In the next few years, second-generation new immigrants began flocking into the major leagues, attracted by the pay and the prestige. In 1941, 8 percent of big leaguers were Italians and 9.3 percent Slavic—more than double their share of the national white population. These groups were more geographically dispersed, were less urban or concentrated in ethnic neighborhoods, and had greater parental support than Jewish boys, whose elders stressed education rather than obtaining a well-paid manly job. The first Italians and Slavs were less likely to come from cities like New York or Boston, which had limited open space and inadequate baseball facilities, than from smaller cities or metropolises like Chicago, and San Francisco, where there was more space to play baseball and where the sport was strongly emphasized and supported by active amateur programs.[32]

Basketball

One of the most popular indoor sports was basketball, a team game invented by Dr. James Naismith to provide football players with wintertime exercise. Because it did not require much space or costly equipment—a rag ball and an ashcan could suffice—it fit in well with the inner-city environment. The spatial factor was a clear advantage for basketball over baseball, for as Basketball Hall of Famer Barney Sedran remembered, "It was difficult for an East Side youngster like myself to play baseball because there were no diamonds nearby." However, basketball was played in school yards, settlement houses, and churches, and that was why, he felt, his neighbors became so proficient in basketball. The sport spread like wildfire through eastern and midwestern cities. By the mid-1890s, it was being played in YMCAs, settlement houses, institutional churches, schools, and even on outdoor courts. In 1898 there was already a professional league in Philadelphia.[33]

Inner-city settlement houses became the breeding grounds for future interscholastic, collegiate, and professional stars, almost all drawn from inner-city ethnic groups. In New York Jewish players at Clark House and the University Settlement dominated the intersettlement tournaments. Even though basketball was a bruising sport that required padding to play, it gained adult approval. Basketball, *The American Hebrew* noted, "requires a good deal of quick thinking, lightning-like rapidity of movement and endurance; it does not call for brutality and brute strength." The sport also attracted Irish youth who lived in the heavily Irish section of Manhattan serviced by the Hudson Guild. In 1912 a club called the Celtics was formed there, and it went on to become the most prominent professional quintet of the 1920s.[34]

During the 1920s and 1930s urban basketball maintained a very strong ethnic character. Ethnic fraternal groups organized athletic clubs for basketball and other sports to facilitate sporting competition and social events among the second generation, who were unwelcome in prestigious WASP voluntary athletic organizations. In the 1930s there were Serbian, Lithuanian, and Polish national championships. Ethnic championship games in Chicago could draw in excess of 10,000 spectators. Interethnic competition also purportedly provided a broadening experience, though one might argue it encouraged as much ethnic hostility as friendship and understanding. In Chicago one of the most popular events was an annual exhibition game between the CYO and B'nai Brith All-Stars.[35]

The ethnic dimension was also very strong, if not stronger, at the professional level. Before World War II, professional basketball in major urban areas was very much an ethnic community entertainment. The best known teams, like the Celtics, often started out as ethnic clubs and maintained that identity when they recruited new talent. In the 1920s the Celtics, fortified with some Jewish athletes, was the best team in professional basketball, and stars earned up to $12,000 a year. The Celtics toured the nation, playing hundreds of games against professional and semiprofessional quintets, and rarely lost; in 1923 they won 204 out of 211 games. The next best teams were the Harlem Renaissance Five, a barnstorming black team organized in 1922, and the South Philadelphia Hebrew All-Stars (SPHAS), originally sponsored by the South Philadelphia Hebrew Association. These teams, along with others like the Irish Brooklyn Visitations and the Polish Detroit Pulaskis, were important community institutions that instilled ethnic pride in their fans and gained respect from other ethnic groups. Games were often played at dance halls, where they preceded an evening of dancing, all for fifty cents a couple. Many Jewish Philadelphians met their future spouses at SPHA Saturday-night "Basketball and Dance" parties at the Hotel Braidwood, which provided a respectable environment for meeting members of the opposite sex.[36]

Professional basketball players active before 1940 were nearly 90 percent urban, and almost one-third of them came from New York City. Three-fourths of a selected sample of prominent players were either German, Jewish, or Irish. While they were presumably from lower-class backgrounds, an exceptionally large proportion (74.6 percent) had attended college even though entrance into the professional sport before the 1930s did not require college experience. Salaries were generally modest, and during the Depression players active in weekend leagues, like the midwestern National Basketball League, all held full-time jobs. Nevertheless, basketball offered some social mobility, helping indigent urban youths obtain college scholarships, because nearly all of the early professionals (95.1 percent) ended up with white-collar jobs. They became not only coaches but also teachers, attorneys, and other high-level nonmanual professionals, which suggests their success came more from their education than from whatever fame they derived from basketball.[37]

Track and Field

One of the sports that best fit in with the social conditions of slums and zones of emergence was track and field. While the prestigious athletic clubs discriminated against many ethnic groups, especially sons of the new immigrants, a talented athlete could achieve a high level of success without sophisticated coaching or equipment or fancy private facilities. Competitions sponsored by settlement houses, ethnic organizations like YMHAs, and quasi-governmental associations like the Public Schools Athletic League (PSAL) provided poor urban youth many opportunities to develop their talent. The Yiddish press in New York strongly advocated the PSAL, which gave Jewish youth a chance to improve their health and gain the respect of Gentiles through meritocratic competition. In the 1910s the PSAL borough champions were invariably from predominantly Jewish grammar schools in the Lower East Side. Jewish youth emulated important role models like Meyer Prinstein of Syracuse University, world record holder in the long jump and Olympic gold medal winner in 1904 and 1906, and world record holder Abel Kiviat, silver medal winner at 1,500 meters at the 1912 Olympics. Both Prinstein and Kiviat, who grew up in Staten Island, ran for the democratic Greater New York Irish-American Athletic Club which, unlike the NYAC, admitted Jewish athletes. Organized in 1903, the IAAC quickly became one of the most successful track and field clubs in America, winning both the junior and senior AAU championships just one year later. It had strong backing from Tammany Hall, which provided government sinecures for some of the club's top performers.[38]

The Prize Ring

The sport that probably best fit in with the urban slum environment was pugilism. Because boys and young men from different ethnic backgrounds were constantly getting into fights to protect their honor or their turf, self-defense was a very useful skill to learn. Jewish boys coming home from school or walking to a swimming pool often had to cross neighborhood lines where Irish lads were waiting to beat them up to guard their territory, to extort money, or just to have fun at their expense. They learned to fight back, either to break the vicious cycle or to protect those weaker than themselves. Neighborhood settlement houses, YMHAs, and local boxing gymnasiums provided excellent coaching, which helped boys learn to defend themselves and built up their self-confidence. The ability to fight well in the streets and in the gym was a means for these youths to prove their manhood, to win respect from their peers, and, for some, to gain training for a possible future occupation.[39]

Inner-city youths who learned to discipline their street fighting in the ring might take advantage of their training to become professional pugilists. For boys who lacked more traditional means of advancement, boxing had long been an escape from the slums. However, only young men from the poorest neighborhoods chose to become prizefighters because it required intensive training and certain physical punishment. Novices who became sufficiently proficient might be recruited to fight at a Knights of Columbus smoker and develop a reputation leading to a paying bout at a local bar/boxing club. Between 1870 and 1920 the sport was totally dominated by Irish pugilists. In the 1890s, for instance, nine of the American world champions were of Irish descent, including John L. Sullivan, heavyweight champion from 1882 to 1892 and the most prominent sportsman of the nineteenth century. Sullivan, whose picture was displayed in virtually every saloon, was regarded with awe as the toughest man in the world. While lace-curtain Irish-Americans were embarrassed by Sullivan's profession and baudy life-style, most Irishmen regarded him as the champion of their race.[40]

Contemporary observers at the turn of the century believed that the hero worship and social solidarity that boxing engendered overcame Irish feelings of individual inferiority. The courageous boxer—a prominent member of the sporting fraternity who had fame, money, and women— was idolized by poor Irish boys growing up in impoverished neighborhoods in New York, like Hell's Kitchen or the Lower West Side, that provided an environment conducive to the development of prize fighters. From such humble origins sprang many hungry contenders and champions. Between 1900 and 1920 there were more Irish champions (thirteen out of forty-seven) and more contenders (40 percent in the late 1910s) than from any other ethnic group. However, their predominence was declining, partly because of improving opportunities for success for Irish youth, but mainly because of the growing competition from impoverished second-generation newcomers.[41]

The sons of eastern and southern European immigrants enjoyed considerable success in prize fighting, the sport with which they were most identified by the general public. Boxers were desperate, driven men at the bottom of the social ladder who lived in neighborhoods like New York's Lower East Side, Chicago's Near West Side, and San Francisco's Mission District. They were tough kids, usually ex-street fighters whose idols were either local boxers or hoodlums, the only well-paying occupations that many poor youth saw open to them as an escape from poverty. Jewish, Italian, and Polish youth highly esteemed the ability to fight: it was a sign of manliness and was a useful skill because of the frequency of interethnic gang fights at public parks and playgrounds and other border areas separating rival groups. In Chicago, for example, there was a lot of hostility in the early 1920s between the Jewish and Polish communities located along Roosevelt Road, the West Side's major commercial district, where Jewish businessmen and pedestrians were regularly attacked by Polish thugs, and also at Douglas Park, a "no-man's land" that divided the two ethnic communities. Hoodlums and other tough Jews organized gangs euphemistically called "social and basement clubs" to retaliate against Poles and other enemies. One day in 1921 the equilibrium at Douglas Park was upset when Jewish boys playing baseball were attacked by a gang of Polish lads. The news spread rapidly to the nearby poolrooms, and Jewish reinforcements quickly arrived, eager to "wallop the Polock." Such defenders of the community like the Miller brothers' gang, one-fourth of whom were boxers, and gangsters like "Nails" Morton became local heroes in such confrontations. Street fighters who acquitted themselves well in such confrontations might be encouraged by friends or interested observers to learn the formal art of boxing at neighborhood gyms or settlement houses.[42]

Second-generation newcomers achieved a lot of quick success in the prize ring. The first Jewish-American world champion was bantamweight Harry Harris, a Chicagoan of English extraction who won his crown in 1901, shortly followed by Abe Attell of San Francisco, a Russian Jew who was featherweight champion from 1901 to 1912. In the 1910s the number of Jewish champions was only exceeded by the Irish. The first Polish champion was middleweight Stanley Ketchell (1908–11), and the first Italian titlist was bantamweight Pete Herman (1917–20), a generation before either group would have a major league batting champion. Furthermore, Italian fighters in the mid-1910s were third in the number of contenders after the Irish and Germans. Most of the prize fighters of Italian and eastern European stock were small and slightly built, as were most of their fellow countrymen, and they found their niche in the lower weight classifications. During the 1920s and 1930s there were twenty-four Italian-American and fifteen Jewish-American champions. More contenders in the late 1920s were Jewish than any other group, but they were superseded by the Italians in the mid-1930s. However, neither group approached the prominence in the sport that the Irish had earlier achieved.[43]

Ethnic boxers became popular heroes among the second generation, and even the immigrants who normally frowned on boxing were proud when their youths won championships and proved the courage and manliness of their people. In the 1930s Jews in the West Side of Chicago and all across the country felt such pride for Barney Ross, just as Italians did for Tony Canzoneri. Ross, like many second-generation fighters, strongly identified himself with his ethnic heritage and wore a Star of David on his trunks. When Barney was a rising amateur, his neighbors followed him all over Chicago to cheer him on, and they glowed with pride when he turned professional and went on to win world championships in the lightweight (1932) and welterweight (1934) divisions. Ross and other Jewish pugilists usually drew opponents who were Irish or Italian whenever possible because promoters knew that such ethnic rivalries generated enormous excitement and helped attract large crowds.[44]

Boxing was an enormously popular sport during the Depression. Neighborhood gyms and small boxing clubs were kept busy as thousands of young men tried to become professional boxers. They were drawn by the glamour and the large purses won by champions like Barney Ross, who earned $500,000 in the ring, but also by the modest winnings of amateurs who sold the medals they won for five or ten dollars or professionals who fought preliminaries for fifty dollars. There were about 8,000 professional boxers in the 1930s, although only a fraction of them ever became contenders. Boxing was the most democratic American sport, open to talented athletes regardless of size or ethnicity, and presuming one had capable and well-connected management, success was based solely on merit.[45]

Former fighters fared worse than any other professional athletes after retirement, even though champions earned more than any other athlete. Titlists like Barney Ross and Joe Louis made huge amounts of money but ended up broke because of fast living, gambling debts, and crooked management. Boxers came from poor backgrounds, did not understand the need to save for the future, and indulged in some of the worst cases of conspicuous consumption when the money was rolling in. Most boxers, of course, did not make the big money. Between 1938 and 1951 just 7.1 percent of a sample of 127 fighters achieved national recognition and 8.7 percent became local headliners. The rest (84.2 percent) never advanced beyond semiwindup or preliminary matches. Boxers rarely left the ring prepared for retirement, having saved little of their earnings, having few marketable skills, little if any education, and more than likely, at least mildly punch-drunk (60 percent). A survey of 154 notable boxers active between 1900 and 1960 found that one-third (32 percent) ended up with blue-collar jobs; 17 percent remained in the sport in some capacity in which they could utilize their expertise. Sociologist Kirson Weinberg found similar results in his study of the retirement occupations of ninety-five former contenders and champions active in the 1940s who had earned at least $100,000 during their careers. One-fourth (25.3 percent) of those boxers ended up with blue-collar jobs, one-fifth (18.9 percent) became trainers or managers, one-tenth (11.6 percent) worked in the entertainment field, and one-fourth (27.3 percent) owned, "fronted," or worked in a tavern. Former fighters were probably more dependent on their fame and personality in their future occupations than any other athletes. As a result, many retired fighters, especially the club boxers who didn't have any substantial fame, ended up about where they had started out. In Chicago in the 1960s only three-fourths (77.1 percent) of ex-club fighters even held steady jobs after boxing, much less well-paying jobs, and they were in mainly semiskilled or unskilled positions.[46]

Sport in the Black Urban Community

The sporting options of black urban residents were influenced not only by such factors as class, culture, and space but also by their race. At the turn of the century most urban blacks lived in southern cities. They comprised the majority in Charleston and Savannah, nearly half of Memphis, and two-fifths of Atlanta, Birmingham, Charlotte, Nashville, and Richmond. Unlike the European immigrants, blacks were completely familiar with and actively involved in the American sporting culture. However, in the post-Reconstruction South their athletic experiences were totally segregated, by either law or custom. Black athletes could not compete with whites, and seating at commercialized spectator sports like horse racing and baseball was segregated. The black sporting life was, by necessity, centered within their own neighborhoods. Black communities in larger cities supported at least two black baseball clubs while fraternal organizations, churches, and politicians organized picnic games at black-owned fairgrounds or in black sections of municipal parks. By 1876 there were black YMCAs in Richmond and Nashville, described by historian Howard Rabinowitz as middle-class social centers which "gave [blacks] a chance to seek the reformation of their erring brethren," who enjoyed billiards and other pleasures of "the sporting life."[47]

The one exception to the pervasive segregation of southern urban sports facilities was in New Orleans, with its peculiar racial traditions. Dale Somers, in his extensive study of Delta City sports, found that although most sports were segregated, there was considerable interracial competition and that "until the mid-eighties, participants in racially mixed contests encountered little hostility." Until 1871 local racetracks had always permitted blacks into the general admission section, but that year the Metairie Course erected a separate stand for blacks. Black economic pressure promptly reversed that policy. But even in New Orleans, segregation existed at the various lakefront athletic facilities, and since white clubs would not admit them, blacks had to form their own athletic clubs. In the 1880s the color line was drawn tighter: game laws were passed to protect wildlife—aimed at curtailing black hunters who were blamed for depleting the woods (probably for food)—and also white baseball teams that played blacks were threatened with a boycott. Finally, in the 1890s local cyclists withdrew from the LAW because northern units had black members.[48]

The last sport in New Orleans to draw the color line was boxing. Since fighters were seen as merely entertainers rather than as the social equals of spectators, mixed bouts were traditionally accepted. However, blacks were not allowed to attend these fights until 6 September 1892, when black featherweight champion George Dixon defended his crown against Jack Skelly at the Olympic Arena; then, of course, they sat in a segregated section. Dixon won the fight with a brutal eighth-round knockout which citizens saw as a shocking blow to the prestige of the white race, and as a result, no more mixed matches were allowed in New Orleans.[49]

At the turn of the century black populations in northern cities were rather small—15,000 in Chicago, for example—but beginning in 1915 large numbers of blacks migrated north to escape racial violence, get better jobs, secure civil rights, and enjoy a more sophisticated life-style. Black populations in industrial cities like Chicago more than tripled in a decade, and by 1920 New York had over 150,000 black residents. Consequently, black ghettoes fostered an enormous development and expansion of black social and cultural institutions in segregated settings.

Although black amateurs were usually able to compete against whites, black athletes in northern cities encountered considerable discrimination. Like the Irish and the new immigrants, black athletes had to form many of their own sports clubs, which ranged from track and field and baseball to cycling, because white status and ethnic clubs would not admit them. Black athletic associations themselves sorted out individuals by class or origin, just as white clubs did. In Boston, for instance, Stephen Hardy found that long-time and upwardly mobile residents formed tennis clubs just like the white elite, while new arrivals from the South "found a common bond in social networks at neighborhood gymnasiums where the latest boxing news might be discussed." West Indian newcomers formed cricket clubs to facilitate competition and sustain their Caribbean heritage.[50]

Black access to semipublic and public sports facilities was limited by expense, discretionary time, accessibility, and discrimination. In the late nineteenth century separate black YMCAs were established in Boston, Brooklyn, New York, and Philadelphia; in Detroit, only the black elite could use the white Y. As early as 1889, black community leaders in Chicago considered establishing a separate black branch, but integrationist sentiment at the time defeated the proposal. After the turn of the century, white hostility to blacks in the Y movement became so sharp that they were virtually shut out. As a result, prominent black Chicagoans in 1910 initiated a campaign for a Y in their own neighborhood. The building was completed three years later at a cost of $190,000, with generous contributions from philanthropist Julius Rosenwald and various local meatpackers and industrialists who further demonstrated their concern by purchasing memberships for their black employees.[51]

Black or integrated teams that traveled outside the growing black neighborhoods to play white teams in white neighborhoods often encountered rough treatment on the playing field and even tougher situations off the field. In the 1910s, when an integrated Chicago basketball team went to play in a white section, trouble often followed: "On the way over here fellows on the outside bailed them out, but our fellows sure got them on the way home. There were three black fellows on the team and those three got just about laid out. Our team wouldn't play them, so there was a great old row. Then, when they went home some of our boys were waiting for them to come out of the building to give them a chase. The coons were afraid to come out, so policemen had to be called to take them to the car line. The white fellows weren't hurt any, but the coons got some bricks."[52]

Boxing

The most popular spectator sports in the black community were prize fighting and baseball. Although black fighters encountered less discrimination than other black athletes—which reflected the low status of the sport—they were subject to terribly abusive language from white fans. At a time when black professional athletes were being forced out of thoroughbred racing, cycling, and organized baseball, blacks were achieving considerable renown in the prize ring. Between 1890 and 1908 there were five black world champions, though many prominent contenders never even got title matches because champions like John L. Sullivan drew the color line.[53]

Top black fighters usually lived in northern black communities, where they would be treated with respect, could get more fights, found opportunities for investment in businesses like Jack Johnson's Café de Champion (a cabaret in Chicago's black belt), and enjoyed the pleasures of the demi-monde. In working-class black communities black pugilists were heroes and had such a wide following that an historian of black Boston discovered that "black attendance at boxing matches outdrew the Sunday sermon." Black fans preferred to see mixed bouts in which their idols could win symbolic racial victories, but local customs or city and state laws often restricted inter-racial contests for fear of fomenting racial antagonisms. Immediately after Jack Johnson successfully defended his heavyweight crown on 4 July 1910 against former champion Jim Jeffries, "The Great White Hope," there were racial conflicts in cities across the country. Many communities subsequently barred exhibitors from showing the film of the fight for fear of generating more incidents.[54]

Over the next several decades boxing continued to attract black interest because it was the only democratic professional sport. One expert estimated there were as many as 1,800 black pros during the 1930s. Like their white peers, they were attracted by the opportunity to make a name for themselves, earn a living, escape the ghetto, and maybe get rich. At a time when no other major professional sport was open to blacks, Afro-American pugilists were achieving great success. The 1930s produced five black champions, including Henry Armstrong, who won three different titles, and Joe Louis, the first black to fight for the heavyweight championship since Jack Johnson. Champion from 1937 to 1949, Louis represented to white America what the ideal negro should be, but for his own community, Louis symbolized black power, racial pride, and an insistence that blacks be accepted in American society. He was a role model for ghetto youth like Malcolm Little (Malcolm X), who became an amateur fighter. His victories were received with great glee in northern black communities, where thousands took to the streets to celebrate, deriving, as Lena Horne remembered, "all the joy possible from this collective victory of the race."[55]

Blacks quickly achieved dominance in the ring. By 1948, nearly half of all contenders were black—a reflection of widespread black poverty and the success of role models like Joe Louis. Italians were second in the number of contenders and Mexican-Americans, a new group to achieve prominence in boxing, third.[56] The ethnic succession in the ring reflected the changing racial and ethnic complexion of the inner city as older ethnic groups who were doing better economically moved out and were replaced by the new urban poor. This dynamic was epitomized by the absence of Jewish fighters from the lists of contenders. Jews had formerly dominated the sport, but as they became better educated or succeeded as entrepreneurs, they moved to the urban periphery or the suburbs. Jews no longer needed to get their brains knocked out to make a living.

Basketball: The Ghetto Game

Class and environment—the main reasons that blacks achieved ethnic succession in boxing—are also the primary factors behind current black dominance in professional basketball (75 percent of the NBA in 1980). Professional ballplayers had always been disproportionately urban, particularly from major cities, and that pattern still holds. In the 1960s and 1970s nearly all NBA players (91.3 percent) were urban; and nearly half, from large cities (49.5 percent)—usually from the inner city, where boys did not have much money or many constructive alternatives for their free time other than sports.[57] As Bob Gibson, a Hall of Famer and one-time Harlem Globetrotter, remembered from his youth in Omaha during the early 1950s: "It always seemed to me that the Negro kids in the project spent more time in sports and participating in things like this than the average white kid. The white kid had more things to do. He could go to the movies, but we could not. We never had the money. So we ran footraces and played ball because there was nothing else to do, unless you wanted to go out and get in trouble."[58] Over the past thirty years basketball has been the major athletic passion of black ghetto youth, as it had once been for Jewish, German, and Irish youth. As Pete Axthelm pointed out a few years ago, "Other young athletes may learn basketball, but (inner) city kids live it." The playground is their heaven, wrote journalist Rick Telander, where city youths study the moves of their heroes, develop their own, and try to make a reputation for themselves. They practice diligently for hours a day, all year long, motivated by the immediate gratification of prestige at neighborhood courts and the longer-term goals of starring in high school, getting a college scholarship, and ending up in the NBA. This of course is a pipe dream, since only 4 percent of high school players are good enough to play in college, much less the NBA. Unlike earlier cohorts of inner-city basketball players, the latest generation devoted *all* their attention to their game and little to their brain, with the result that even if they excelled in basketball and achieved a degree of fame, there was a strong chance they would end up right back in the ghetto where they had started.[59]

Baseball in the Urban Black Community

Baseball was the most important sport in the black communities. Unlike the immigrants from overseas, rural black migrants were very familiar with the national pastime. Until 1898, when blacks were barred from organized baseball by a common understanding among racist owners, there had been around fifty professional black ballplayers, including two in the majors in 1884. Blacks responded to being shunned by forming their own professional teams. By 1900 there were five salaried black teams, including two in Chicago despite the small size of its black community. Chicago teams played on Sundays, when black fans were off work; during the week they toured the Midwest playing local town teams. The preeminent black team then was Chicago's Leland Giants, owned by local black politicians. The club played at their own park four miles south of the

Black Belt, next door to their proprietors' amusement park. The Leland Giants played from 1907 to 1909 in the otherwise all-white City League, the finest semiprofessional league in the United States. The club was so good that in 1909 they played a postseason series with the Chicago Cubs. The Giants, a great draw at the box office, brought out to 15,000 fans of both races. Management problems led to the team's demise in 1910; a year later the club was succeeded by the American Giants, jointly owned by white tavern keeper John M. Schorling and former star pitcher Rube Foster. They played on the site of the old White Sox Park across the street from the growing Black Belt. The team became a symbol of pride in the community, and one black editor urged "all race loving and race building men and women" to support it. The American Giants were so popular that on one Sunday, when the local major league clubs were at home, the Giants outdrew both of them with a crowd of 11,000 black and white fans.[60]

The success of black baseball was strongly influenced by the great migration north that began in the mid-1910s and continued in subsequent decades. Between 1920 and 1950 the black populations of Chicago, Cleveland, Detroit, and New York all quadrupled, and other northern cities also had substantial increases. These newcomers could secure only low paying jobs and, because of their income and discrimination, had little choice over where to live. The resulting northern black ghettos—with inadequate housing, high rates of crime, and poor municipal services—created new opportunities for businesses that catered to a predominantly black clientele—particularly businesses in the entertainment field, like baseball.

Before 1920 most black teams had been owned by white entrepreneurs, who scheduled games and rented ballparks. Black journalists deplored these conditions, urging that profits "should be received by the Race to whom the patrons of the game belong." After World War I Rube Foster, sole owner of the Chicago American Giants since 1916, initiated a movement to wrest control of black baseball from white promoters and put it into the hands of black entrepreneurs. Foster believed that the growing black urban communities provided a potential market for a top-flight negro league, and he also argued that since all players and two-thirds of the spectators were black the profits should remain with the race.[61]

In 1920 Foster organized the Negro National League (NNL), with eight mainly midwestern franchises, all but one of which were owned and operated by black businessmen. NNL teams played from forty to eighty league contests and a total of about 200 games a year, including exhibitions. Tickets cost twenty-five cents. The leading expert on the negro leagues estimated weekend crowds exceeded 5,000, but the average attendance was only about one-third of that. Although the league was highly regarded by the black press and urban fans, it struggled financially, lasting through twelve shaky seasons. Of the original eight teams, only the American Giants lasted from start to finish. A crucial problem was lack of control over their playing area: only the American Giants had their own field; the others leased local parks, where they were usually secondary tenants and could not schedule choice dates. In 1926 Foster suffered a mental breakdown, and the subsequent absence of sustained leadership plus the impact of the Depression led to the death of the NNL in 1931.[62]

In 1933 a new NNL was organized by numbers bankers, one of the few lucrative, if illegal, occupations in the black neighborhoods during the Depression. The most prominent owner was Gus Greenlee, king of the Pittsburgh numbers racket, owner of the city's leading "black and tan" resort, and manager in the mid-1930s of light-heavyweight boxing champion John Henry Lewis. Greenlee first got involved in baseball in 1930, when he sponsored the Crawfords, a well-known independent black nine, and two years later he spent $100,000 for the first black-built ballpark. Greenlee and his fellow owners were well regarded by the black press, which saw them as strong race men who provided hundreds of jobs through their business ventures and supplied badly needed cheap entertainment.[63]

The NNL started out inauspiciously, playing its games at old minor league fields, former federal league parks, or second-rate semiprofessional fields. In the inaugural season Greenlee lost $50,000, but he justified it as an investment in the future. But within a few years business perked up, and the NNL and its rival—the Negro American League, founded in 1937—were on a "reasonably sound financial ground." Most teams at least broke even except for the star-ladden, high-salaried Crawfords. As the NNL became more successful, its teams began to rent major-league parks, where there was a better ambiance and more space for the large crowds coming out to see exciting and high-quality play. White landlords profited handsomely from fees that ranged from 10 to 20 percent of the gate. In the 1940s the Yankees were earning about $100,000 a year from their black tenants. The negro leagues reached their zenith during World War II, when urban black populations grew dramatically because of the opportunities for jobs in war-related industries.[64]

In the interwar era the negro league teams were prominent community institutions, and cities without NNL franchises were regarded as second rate. Opening-day games became important public rituals, embellished with such ceremonies as pregame parades or the throwing out of the first ball by celebrities like Lena Horne or politicians like Congressman William Dawson of Chicago. Fans dressed up for opening day, and according to historian W. Donn Rogosin, "society pages of the black newspapers gushed with baseball stories that suggested opening day's importance for a culture with limited opportunities to partake in American tradition." Games during the season were employed for community activities ranging from beauty contests to "Stop Lynching" campaigns. [65]

The biggest event in the black community, outside of Joe Louis's fights—was the annual East-West All-Star Game. In 1933 Gus Greenlee initiated the All-Star Game, which became so popular that by 1943 it was attracting 50,000 spectators. Most contests were held at Comiskey Park, located across the street from one of the most important black communities in the United States. Fans from all social backgrounds, including out-of-town tourists, flocked to the stadium. The game became one of the highlights in the social calendar of the black elite, who sat in expensive $1.50 seats where everybody could see them. [66]

Ironically, at the same time the negro leagues reached their height, a major movement developed to integrate organized baseball, which eventually meant the end of the negro leagues. Black sportswriters, civil-rights organizations, and left-wing political groups made the integration of baseball a political issue. In 1945 a Boston councilman threatened the city's teams with the loss of their Sunday permits unless they gave blacks tryouts, and New York's Fiorello LaGuardia formed the Mayor's Committee on Baseball to encourage local teams to sign black ballplayers. A Communist councilman running for reelection in New York distributed flyers captioned "Good enough to die for his country," but not good enough for organized baseball. [67]

The integration of baseball by Jackie Robinson, and his courage, perseverance, outstanding play, and "class," made him a great hero in black communities and his exploits front-page news in the black press. As Branch Rickey had hoped, Robinson's presence in the Brooklyn Dodgers lineup had a positive impact on black attendance, which had previously been limited. During his rookie season in 1947, black Kansas Citians took a five-hour-long train ride to St. Louis, traveling under Jim Crow conditions, to see Jackie play in segregated Sportsman's Park. When Robinson made his first appearance at Wrigley Field, he drew a record crowd of 46,000. Thousands of blacks attended, wearing their best Sunday clothes. At the time blacks were almost never seen on the North Side, and as journalist Mike Royko remembered, "It was probably the first time . . . (blacks and whites) had been so close to each other in such large numbers." [68]

The integration of baseball, a slow and torturous process, was not completed on the major-league level until 1959, when the Boston Red Sox signed their first black player. The process had a significant impact on black urban life, promoting racial pride, securing begrudging respect from white fans, and demonstrating a potential for future gains in race relations. However, during the 1950s, southern training camps remained segregated, and several teams moved to Arizona to escape Jim Crow. Modest advances did occur in the South; for example, the Dodgers scheduled integrated exhibition games in cities like Atlanta, Macon, and Miami, where inter-racial sport was previously forbidden. In addition, by 1953, every professional league except the Southern Association was integrated; blacks played in such Deep South cities as Jacksonville, Montgomery, New Orleans, and Savannah, albeit in front of segregated crowds.[69]

The worst abuses of black athletes and spectators did not end until the civil-rights demonstrations and economic boycotts of the 1960s and the implementation of federal civil-rights legislation that forbade discrimination in such public facilities as municipal parks, swimming pools, and golf courses, as well as restaurants, hotels, and common carriers. Organized baseball did not do everything in its power to eliminate Jim Crow, though Casy Stengel did insist that hotels in Chicago and Kansas City cease discriminating against his black players. Historian Jules Tygiel argues that professional baseball was one of the first American institutions to accept blacks on virtually equal terms, and because baseball is the national pastime, that was an important symbolic achievement.[70]

Conclusion: Sport, Race and Ethnicity in the American City

The sporting culture of urban ethnic groups was a product of their cultural heritage, social class, and discrimination. Yet while these variables affected all groups, some were more important for different categories of ethnic cohorts than others—the old-world heritage for the European immigrant, economics for second-generation white ethnics, and racism for blacks.

European immigrants who settled in cities alleviated their alienation and facilitated their adjustment to strange and hostile environments by developing ethnic subcommunities as much like the Old World as possible. In zones of emergence and slums the newcomers established ethnic villages to sustain their language, customs, and religion and a sense of peoplehood. These communities nurtured such old institutions as the Church and such new ones as mutual aid societies and foreign-language newspapers, which helped the newcomer cope with urban America. The old immigrants brought over a sporting heritage which remained a vital part of their cultural life in their new land. The turnverein's gymnasiums and community centers played a central role in German neighborhoods. Irish sports clubs promoted nationalism, and their traditional love of sport enabled them to readily fit into a male bachelor subculture, in which they could find friends and possible routes of social mobility. However, sporting traditions were far weaker among the new immigrants, and with the exception of slavic groups, who were beginning to develop an oppositional and revolutionary sporting subculture in eastern Europe, sport had no appeal to these newcomers.

Sport did play a prominent role among all second-generation immigrants. Success in sports was a step towards assimilation—a means of disproving negative ethnic stereotypes, gaining respect from the outside community, and cementing social relationships among street corner youth; a source of ethnic pride and feelings of community; and a possible vehicle for vertical mobility. The sons of the old immigrants had distinct advantages over the new immigrants; they had parental approval and often lived in the zone of emergence, where they had opportunities to participate in a wide variety of sports. But Italian, Jewish, and Polish youths faced parental opposition, needed to work, and lived in crowded slums that placed severe limitations on their athletic options. Since it was difficult to become proficient in baseball because of the lack of space for playing fields, inner-city youth mainly participated in sports within their own communities. Because of accessibility, cost, and fear for their security in strange neighborhoods, inner-city youth favored sports like basketball, boxing, billiards, and bowling, which did not require much space, could be played indoors at night, and provided status to good players. Boxing was especially appropriate for young men living in tough neighborhoods, where fighting was part of daily life. Park districts, social agencies fighting against juvenile delinquency, and ethnic voluntary organizations trying to maintain a sense of peoplehood among the American-born youth provided facilities for basketball and boxing. Once the white ethnics moved into better neighborhoods, the second and third generation had the time and the necessary space to enjoy whichever sports they preferred.

Black urbanites, completely familiar with the American sporting culture, still faced severe limitations because of class and racism. Black use of sports facilities was restricted in the South by social custom and laws and in the North by discrimination and ghettoization. Their neighborhoods, always underfunded, were the last to get public parks and other facilities. Nonetheless, sport was very important in black localities for recreational and other purposes. Urban blacks, less successful at building their own community institutions than the European immigrants, used sport, along with the church, press, and politics, to develop a sense of community in their neighborhoods. Blacks established their own voluntary sports associations, their own teams, and even their own heroes. Success in sports raised black pride, provided fans with a sense of self-worth by vicarious identification with athletic heroes, and gained some begrudging respect from the broader community. Sport also provided hopes of social mobility—less from college scholarships, which were very rare for blacks, than through professional sports, either segregated baseball or integrated boxing, a meritocratic sport that was a natural outlet for impoverished, tough ghetto youth. As white ethnics moved out of the inner city, they were replaced by blacks, who also succeeded in boxing and basketball, the two major sports most congruent with the physical and cultural character of inner-city life. But unlike the white groups, blacks have not been able to escape urban poverty and the ghetto, and one result has been the unfortunate over-reliance on athletics as a means of getting ahead.

Rationalized Visions of Social Integration and Urban Sport

Ballplaying and "tip cat" on the sidewalks are a danger as well as an annoyance to every passer-by, and the fact that the city does not possess adequate public playgrounds is no excuse for allowing children to monopolize the sidewalk and crossings with games which are dangerous and annoying to pedestrians.

"Civis" in *New York Times*,
16 June 1902.

The great congestion . . . has resulted in depriving the children of New York of opportunities to exercise, . . . so that their development tends to drop below the normal. The energies they should work off in wholesome exercise, in vigorous play, finds vent in the worst feats of the gangs which create so much that is vicious in our city life. It is a great disadvantage to a boy to be unable to play games, and every boy who knows how to play baseball or football, to box or wrestle, has . . . fitted himself to be a better citizen.

General George Wingate in *New York Times*,
29 Nov. 1905.

We consider baseball one of the best means of teaching our boys American ideas and ideals.

West Side Chicago settlement house workers to Huge Fullerton, syndicated baseball writer, in *Atlanta Constitution*,
18 July 1919.

CHAPTER 4

Sport and Public Space

The process of urbanization had a very deleterious impact upon sport in the radial city in the late nineteenth century. After the Civil War cities outgrew their walking limits as surrounding woods formerly used for hunting were subdivided for residential use. On the urban periphery empty lots were quickly taken up for residential or commercial use, and as the value of property in the central business districts reached astronomical proportions, intensive utilization of all available space overran traditional athletic sites in the center of town and in the surrounding slums. And the pressures of commerce made it difficult and dangerous to use old wharves, crowded city streets, or busy sidewalks for play.[1]

City boys tried as best they could to maintain control of their traditional playing areas. At the turn of the century boys continued to swim off public or private docks despite the danger of polluted water, drowning, or arrest. Most swimming was without suits; one old New York swimmer remembered that swimming was legal in the East River "provided one wore one's underwear." Young athletes mainly relied on the streets in front of their homes, where there were always lots of children, for their sporting entertainment. As George Burns reminisced, "Our playground was in the middle of Rivington Street. We only played games that needed very little equipment, games like kick-the-can, hopscotch, hide-and-go seek, follow-the-leader. When we played baseball we used a broom handle and a rubber ball. A manhole cover was home plate, a fire hydrant was first base, second base was a lamp post, and Mr. Gitletz, who used to bring a kitchen chair down to sit and watch us play, was third base. One time I slid into Mr. Gitletz he caught the ball and tagged me out."[2]

This chapter analyzes the response of urbanites to the loss of accessible public spaces that could be used for sports, emphasizing outdoor facilities that provided badly needed breathing spaces. In the post–Civil War era a nation-wide municipal park movement organized to secure and maintain large public parks for immediate and future use. In the late nineteenth century the failure of the suburban parks to meet the crying need for breathing and recreational space in urban slums led to the rise of the small park and playground movement, regarded as the work of do-gooders (with sometimes questionable motives) who wanted to make city life more bearable, promote order, and alleviate pathological and chaotic living conditions. Historians now acknowledge the contributions of groups, including inner-city residents, in shaping the direction of spatial reform and recognize the complexity of reform motivations among park advocates.[3] The third era of park development occurred after World War I, when cheap mass transit and the end of blue laws made city parks widely accessible. Municipalities stressed the improvement and increased utilization of existing space and further catered to public interest by constructing public stadiums for spectator sports.

The Era of the Suburban Park

Frederick Law Olmsted's Central Park was a beautifully landscaped horticultural delight widely admired by urbanites for the restful pleasures it provided New Yorkers. In the decades following the Civil War cities across the country hired landscape architects like Olmsted and Horace Cleveland to design large attractive suburban parks based on the model of Central Park. These substantial municipal projects, among the earliest and most important efforts at urban planning, were justified by the same rationales used in behalf of Central Park in the 1850s—improving public health, raising morals, increasing property values, bolstering the town's reputation, and protecting public lands for future generations.

One of the first major park systems established on the Central Park model was in Chicago, the American shock city, whose population tripled in the 1860s to about 300,000, and then more than tripled in the following decade. Local civic leaders realized that if they did nothing to protect land for future public use all open space in the vicinity of the city would fall into private hands. In 1869, when there were just a few small parks in the entire city, the local government organized an ambitious park system under separate agencies for each of Chicago's three divisions, each empowered to levy taxes to raise money. In only a decade, Chicago developed the second largest park system in the United States, consisting of 1,500 acres located on the outskirts of built-up areas, all designed as year-round pleasure grounds. Lincoln Park on the North Side and the Olmsted-designed South Park system across town both had frontage on Lake Michigan combining the natural beauty of the lake front with landscaped woods, gardens, and knolls. Lincoln Park was about 2.5 miles from the central business district, but the West Side and South Side parks ranged from 4.5 to 7 miles from downtown. The more distant sites were just twenty to thirty minutes from the CBD by commuter railroads, but the high cost of train travel discouraged poorer Chicagoans from going there. Olmsted believed that the southern parks were too far away for daily use and envisioned them as holiday suburban parks for day-long outings. However, anticipating future urban growth in the direction of Jackson and Washington parks, he planned facilities that could be used on a daily basis.[4]

In the nineteenth century riding to recreational facilities was one of the most popular uses of public transportation. New streetcar routes were usually laid out toward the periphery, terminating at a distant suburban park. In Philadelphia, one of the first cities to outgrow its walking size, one-fourth of all passengers in the period from 1850 to 1880 used mass transit for pleasure. Nearly every street railway in the city went past Fairmount Park, the largest park in the country. Though only four of the city's fifteen lines offered direct service to the heart of the financial district, eleven went past the park's two main entrances. In New York after the Civil War the construction of transit lines greatly facilitated the use of Central Park; the completion of the subway line in the early 1900s to Van Cortlandt Park enhanced its utility.[5]

The lofty plans and goals of the suburban park planners did not go unopposed. Fiscal conservatives opposed the concept of any public expenditures for parks; athletes opposed receptive recreation and favored active recreation; working-class residents and their political representatives demanded more accessible parks; and various business and social groups favored the commercial use of public space for boisterous amusements. Inner-city folk disapproved of appropriating public money to buy and improve land on the urban fringes that they and their children would almost never use because of its inaccessibility. They did not buy the arguments of municipal park advocates that park systems would benefit all urbanites regardless of specific location. As Stephen Hardy has pointed out in his study of the Boston park movement, neighborhood politicians and citizens' lobbies, far more parochial on this issue than the park reformers, demanded new parks that would best serve their own constituencies. The result was a political conflict which began in the mid-1870s and threatened the development of a park system for Boston. Appropriations bills in 1877 and 1881 nearly failed as countervailing

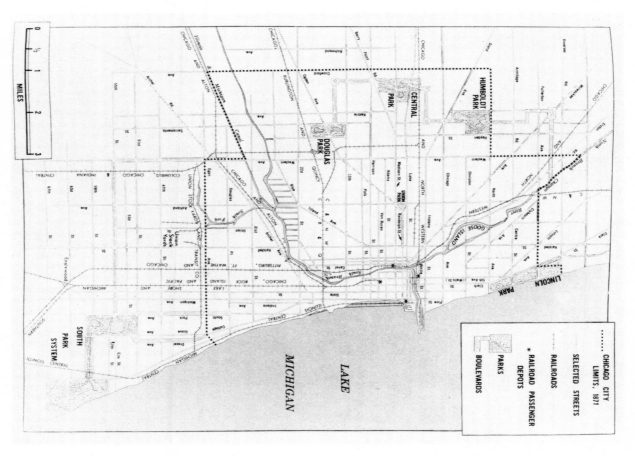

4. Chicago's Parks and Railroads in 1871.

SOURCE: Harold M. Mayer and Richard C. Wade, *Chicago: Growth of a Metropolis* (Chicago, 1969), 101.

groups fought for their own interests. Hardy argued that in the long run the provincialism may have ironically "*ensured* success, by forcing central planners to accommodate local interests." In 1881 the city council approve the Olmsted-planned park system because it provided a little something for everyone.[6]

Considerable conflict over the form of use of suburban park facilities followed the debates over park location. As greater numbers of people visited the parks and interest in competitive sports grew, park managers and park goers inevitably disagreed about the "appropriate" use of scenic parks. Urban planners, elite reformers, and other suburban park idealists ardently fought encroachments upon Olmsted's vision of beautiful, restful parks, opposing commercialized entertainment on park space, demanding police protection to forestall boisterous behavior (Chicago's parks had their own police force), and making "Keep Off the Grass" signs ubiquitous. Such restrictions were aimed mainly at the working classes, whose pleasures, relatively noisy, active, and raucous, included sports, drinking, and sexual promiscuity—activities that were either allowed or ignored in the few inner-city parks. During the 1880s, for example, people from all over Worcester, Massachusetts, used the middle-class Common and Lake Park, creating considerable conflict over what was appropriate use of the grounds and what constituted proper behavior. Industrialists who had lent their support to the park movement as a means of teaching workers respectable behavior were chagrined to find lower-class folk loafing and drinking at the parks. As Roy Rosenzweig points out, "Parks were providing a setting for precisely the sort of behavior they were supposed to inhibit."[7]

Friends of the parks were alert to all kinds of threats to their pastoral retreats. In 1892 politically well-connected New York horsemen tried to establish a two-mile speedway for trotters in Central Park with the support of Tammany Mayor Hugh Grant and the park commissioners. The infamous George Washington Plunkitt guided the necessary legislation through the state legislature and had it approved by the governor. However, taxpayers associations, good government groups like the City Reform Club, trade unionists, and reform-minded newspapers like the *Times* formed a coalition to protect the park from encroachment. The coalition organized large protest rallies in New York City and sent trainloads of track opponents to Albany to lobby for repeal. The strong public reaction to the proposed speedway persuaded Tammany Hall to back down, and the bill was quickly repealed. However, a year later public funding was secured for a Harlem Speedway which, when completed in 1898 at a cost of over $3 million, extended from 155th Street north nearly three miles along the Harlem River. Restricted to trotters and pacers, it became the preserve of the 1,500-member Gentlemen's Driving Club. Supporters claimed that the Speedway attracted huge crowds of spectators to watch free horse racing every Sunday—crowds that surpassed the attendance at Central Park's walks.[8]

Considerable conflict arose over the use of suburban parks—indeed, all city parks—for athletic games played on grass. Opponents feared games would damage park property and encourage the gathering of large and potentially rowdy crowds. Efforts to alter traditional practices could result in disorder or political crises, as occurred in Boston in 1869 when aldermen temporarily prohibited baseball on the Common. But ballplaying at the new suburban parks was usually proscribed fairly effectively, especially for organized teams. In 1884 Boston's park commissioners announced that all athletic contests were forbidden in its domain unless prior permission was granted. The only exception was a corner of Franklin Park set aside for children. Similar restrictions existed in Baltimore, Buffalo, Chicago, Hartford, New York, and Philadelphia. But the trend was in the opposite direction. In the 1880s major parks built tennis courts, and baseball diamonds and other accouterments soon followed. By the 1890s even Boston allowed baseball in the parks, along with cricket, football, and tennis. Franklin Park even had a golf course. By 1902 the city's parkways were opened to bicycles and automobiles. Suburban park athletic facilities in Boston and across the country were geared primarily to the middle classes, who lived in the vicinity of the parks. Working-class residents living in the zone of emergence also either walked to the parks or took public transportation. However, working people found their opportunities somewhat limited by Sunday blue laws that proscribed sport in the parks on the Sabbath. Even a relatively open city like Chicago had such laws on the books in the late nineteenth century, and events that drew large crowds might be stopped by the police unless arranged by men with political protection. In Boston, higher-status sports like cycling or rowing were allowed on Sundays, although the more plebeian games like baseball were forbidden until 1920. Despite this caveat, Hardy is correct in his assessment that special-interest groups such as athletic clubs and neighborhood organizations succeeded in using their political clout to radically alter the conventional conception of public parks from centers of receptive recreation to sites of exertive amusements.[9]

Inner-City Parks and Playgrounds

While middle-class youth from the urban periphery and working-class residents from the zone of emergence had opportunities to utilize the beautiful suburban parks for outdoor sports, slum dwellers derived much less benefit from them. As late as the turn of the century, the distance, travel time, and cost of carfare discouraged widespread use of suburban parks except for holidays or Sunday outings, and of course many popular sports were proscribed on Sundays. In addition inner-city youth were not welcomed in the big parks by the local dominant groups, particularly in parks or sections of parks controlled by young men living in the volatile and hostile zone of emergence. Jewish, black, or other youths who encroached on Irish turf were looking for trouble.[10]

In the late nineteenth century municipalities not only were slow in providing outdoor public space for inner-city youth but were actually falling behind because of the enormous rate of population growth in the urban core, where nearly every lot was needed for housing. For example, in Chicago, which reached a population of two million by 1900, the poorest neighborhoods were virtually untouched by the suburban park movement. Three South Side communities (Englewood, the Stockyards, and the Calumet Manufacturing region), with a combined population of 360,000 that suffered from overcrowding, poor health, and a high crime rate, did not have a single public recreational area. Conditions were even more dismal in sections of New York, particularly the Lower East Side, the most densely populated neighborhood in the world, whose residents had no nearby parks of any consequence and knew little of Central Park's pleasures. When journalist Jacob Riis interviewed forty-eight downtown schoolboys, he found only three who had ever been to Central Park.[11]

Efforts to address the needs of slum residents came from a variety of individuals and groups who agreed that small parks and playgrounds should be constructed in the inner city, where they would do the most good. Adults, youths, and children, who rarely ventured more than a quarter mile from their home to go to a park, would have an accessible place in which they could recreate and fill their lungs with fresh air. A lot of the original impetus for the movement in the 1880s came from elite reformers like New York Mayor Abram Hewitt, old charity organizations like the Children's Aid Society, settlement house workers, Social Gospel ministers, crusading journalists, and certain landscape designers like Horace W. S. Cleveland. Recent research also indicates that special-interest inner-city groups, such as athletic clubs, community organizations, and machine politicians, also contributed to the quest for reform.[12]

Social reformers believed they could protect city youth from the pathological defects of their neighborhoods by building parks, playgrounds, and public baths that would provide an uplifting and healthful environment and an alternative to gambling halls, poolrooms, saloons, and brothels. The "best people" hoped to use parks to raise the moral level of urban folk, improve their character, and Americanize them, or, if that did not work, to use playgrounds as a source of social control. The first "play grounds" were simply places where children could play safely. The youngsters were originally free of adult supervision, but research convinced playground advocates in the early 1900s that supervised play would be far more effective in educating children than their own independent, undirected play. Children playing under adult guidance would learn obedience, punctuality, self-sacrifice, and other traditional American values and would grow up to become adults "who combined individual initiative with the cooperative abilities demanded by modern commerce and industry."[13]

One city where mugwumps and, later, progressives seem to have played the leading role in the small park movement was New York, where Tammany representatives from the inner-city districts obstructed efforts to ameliorate the spatial needs of their constituents. Reform Mayor Abram S. Hewitt (1886–87), touched by the slum dwellers' outcry for recreational space, tried to help their children gain relief from an oppressive environment. He was convinced that small parks would improve the health and morals of the poor immigrant children and prevent the need for more radical solutions to their problems. In 1887 Hewitt's administration came out in support of municipally sponsored small parks that would combine in a congested space the best features of landscaped parks with playground facilities. For similar reasons, the municipality also advocated constructing libraries and baths next to the parks. Hewitt convinced the state legislation to empower the city to spend up to $1 million a year for small parks.[14]

Despite Hewitt's legacy, little was accomplished in the way of small parks over the next eight years. Tammany mayors were uninterested in small-scale projects that provided few jobs and limited profits. They preferred instead expensive developments like the construction of Van Cortlandt and Pelham Bay parks, which provided a lot of contracts and patronage. But these suburban parks, located in northern sections of the city, were totally inaccessible to its slum residents. Also, given New York's dismal financial position, especially during the Depression of 1893, city leaders could justifiably argue that there were more pressing problems than new small parks.[15]

The first concrete achievements came during the reform administration of Republican William L. Strong (1896–97), who pledged during his campaign to construct small parks in the slums. In 1897, after a ten-year-long wait, New York finally opened a much-anticipated park on the site of the notorious Mulberry Bend tenement, but it still had no play areas. Strong also initiated the construction of economical recreation piers on waterfronts located near impoverished neighborhoods. Recreation piers were large facilities (up to 720 feet by 60 feet) but only cost one-fourth as much as a comparable small park built on valuable New York real estate. Third, in response to the 1894 Tenement House investigation, which castigated the inadequate play space in the city's slums, the Board of Education required each new school to have an open-air playground for the use of its community. Schools economized on scarce inner-city space by building play areas on their roofs. [16]

When Tammany returned with the election of Frederick Van Wyck, the first mayor of Greater New York (1898–1901), it continued to do little for the sporting needs of inner-city residents. Even though the state had appropriated $4 million for five projects, only one park was completed under Van Wyck. The private sector then took up the initiative: in 1898 a broad-based coalition organized the Outdoor Recreation League (ORL) to secure small parks and slum playgrounds. Its leaders included social workers Mary Simkhovitch and Lillian Wald, Social Gospelers William S. Rainsford and Bishop Henry Potter, philanthropist Nathan Straus, Columbia University president Nicholas Murray Butler, and AFL president Samuel Gompers. They sought public recognition of the need for recreation and physical fitness for poor urbanites, donations of land and money to construct recreation centers, and the establishment of a model park for the municipality to emulate. In June 1898 the ORL opened the Hudsonbank, a model outdoor gymnasium on the Lower East Side, free to the public and open days and evenings. The first such facility in the city, Hudsonbank was set up to demonstrate the public demand for sand gardens, running tracks, and gymnastic apparatus. One year later the ORL built a playground, gymnasium, athletic field, and grandstand on the site of a long awaited, but uncompleted, municipal park that eventually became Seward Park. [17]

Residents of slums like the Lower East Side generally supported the WASP reformers' goal of building small parks and playgrounds for physical and moral uplift, although they might not have agreed with some of their other reasons that seemed to them like social control. In 1901 the city finally completed Seward Park, based on a design drawn up by the ORL and supported by Yiddish petitioners who wanted a large playground in the new park. Local citizens wrote letters to the press, and neighborhood clergymen, aldermen, and property owners petitioned the municipality and attended meetings of the Board of Street Openings to pressure for local parks. However, historian Jeffrey Gurock found that the Russian-Jewish community on the Lower East Side would not always support the park movement because they needed cheap housing even more than pleasant breathing spaces. A park developed in a crowded location displaced many people and the subsequent housing shortage encouraged landlords to raise rents. [18]

By 1905 New York's municipal government had finally fully acknowledged its responsibility for providing public recreational facilities for all its residents. The park commissioners managed the city's large suburban parks plus nine small parks (including three on the Lower East Side); the Board of Education ran over a hundred playgrounds and a wide-ranging summer program for children; and the Department of Docks operated nine recreation piers; and other city agencies managed the fifteen municipal swimming baths. While this was a large improvement compared to the situation before the small park movement had started, the needs of city youth, especially those living in the inner city, were still inadequately met. Park department programs reached only 6 percent of Manhattan's children; in 1912 the Lower East Side provided fewer than eighteen acres of play space for 237,222 children. [19]

While middle-class and elite social reformers led the small parks movement in New York, elsewhere the working classes took a more active role in securing public play space. Hardy and Rosenzweig argue that in Boston and Worcester residents of modest neighborhoods, allied with elite and middle-class reformers, played a prominent role in securing space for small parks and playground space. They believed that outdoor exercise would benefit their communities by promoting sound health and prevent- ing juvenile delinquency. Working-class folk, supported by elitist volun- tary societies such as the Massachusetts Emergency and Hygiene Asso- ciation, which had fancy theories about child development and adult- supervised play, worked with their political representatives for control over the public spaces. [20]

In 1870 residents of central Boston were probably better served by parks than citizens of other eastern cities, principally because of the Common. However, opposing ideas about how best to protect and utilize that great resource caused considerable conflict. When the city tried to close that space to baseball players in 1869, citizens formed the "Red Ball" coalition, which elected two-thirds of the aldermen that year. As a result a section was kept open for boys' sport. But this was insufficient, and four years later 2,000 people signed a petition, presented to the city council, speaking in behalf of an estimated 30,000 young men who needed play space but were "unable to afford expensive recreations, nor have the time to go to the outskirts of the city to obtain exercise." The petition was denied, but in 1877 the common council and the board of aldermen appropriated $2,000 for playgrounds, although they were not sure what a playground was. [21]

In the 1880s inner-city neighborhood groups began to lobby for playgrounds for their children. Lower-middle- and upper-lower-class Irish communities in zones of emergence like Dorchester, East Boston, and Brighton mobilized to fight for their old playing fields, which were rapidly being developed, leaving no space for youth to play. The situation was far worse in inner-city slums, where boys had to play in the streets. The Park Department responded slowly to public pressure, but in 1889, at the same time the Playstead was established for middle-class children in Franklin Park, the department also constructed a gymnasium on the banks of the Charles River, in walking distance of the West End slums. Designed by Olmsted and Dr. Dudley Sargent, director of the Hemenway Gymnasium at Harvard, the Charlesbank Gymnasium was the first American effort to provide active play space for slum residents. This combination park and playground, with scenic sections, play areas for children, and separate gymnasiums for men and women, proved a huge success. The women's gymnasium—the first to provide supervised free public amusement for women—was especially noteworthy. Most of the clientele were local residents seeking better health and an improved sense of well-being, but the fine facilities also drew middle-class and elite young women.[22]

Boston's playground appropriation, just $2,780 in 1892–93, skyrocketed a year later to $41,400 and to $180,000 in 1897–98. These expenditures included funds not only for "rich men's parks" but also for small parks in central city wards where land was expensive and hard to secure. By the early 1890s inner-city neighborhoods had enough political clout to have their demands respected. Inner-city politicos traded off votes for suburban parks in exchange for small parks and playgrounds for their wards. North End ward boss John F. Fitzgerald secured a park for his constituents, a park was constructed in Charlestown, and the West End got improvements for the Charlesbank Gymnasium. At the turn of the century Boston had a comprehensive playground system with facilities all over the city.[23]

In Worcester working-class Irishmen took the same active role in the small-parks movement as they did in nearby Boston. By 1879 letters in the city's only pro-labor paper, the Evening Star, complained about the unequal treatment given the Common compared to the less accessible middle-class Elm Park. In 1882, as housing and business development gobbled up in the crowded Irish East Side, East Siders began to demand play space in their own communities. Irish temperance and civic leader Richard O'Flynn held a meeting to arouse support for public playgrounds and got nearly 140 neighbors to petition the city council to set aside land for playlots and sport. Nearly 80 percent of the signers were blue-collar workers, and half of the rest were local small businessmen. When the petitioners failed to get their parks, Worcester's two Democratic aldermen joined the conservative bloc to defeat a reservoir addition proposed for fashionable Elm Park. The conflict was resolved in 1884 by legislation which funded the purchase of park land for both sections of town. Two years later the parks commission produced a comprehensive program—one of the first city-wide system plans developed in the United States—which solved local class and sectional differences by providing scenic parks for the middle-class West Side and two small parks (playgrounds) for the plebeian East Side. Subsequently, other working-class communities also used their political influence to secure neighborhood play space.[24]

The long-term results were less sanguine than anticipated. Neighborhood groups failed to get children off the streets and into parks. Ninety percent of boys' play remained in the streets—in part because slums still lacked enough accessible playgrounds but mainly because boys enjoyed the excitement of the streets, where they played traditional street games, adapted popular sports like baseball to their limited space, and amused themselves dodging streetcars and automobiles free from adult supervision and interference. Crowded inner-city neighborhoods became even more densely populated than in the past. As one Worcester sportsman pointed out in 1904, "If you want the use of a baseball diamond at Crompton Park, you must sleep on the ground the night before." Another problem was that city funds were unfairly divided. Labor leaders complained that "most of the park money has been expended upon parks where the wage workers and their children are least seen." By the turn of the century inner-city parks, inadequately funded and poorly maintained, were regarded as dumps. A system of "class parks" had been created, and each social class sought to exercise autonomy over the use of public space in their respective neighborhoods.[25]

Although Boston and Worcester were pioneers in the playground and small-park movements, the Chicago system became the national model. Once in the forefront of the suburban park movement, in 1880 Chicago was exceeded only by Philadelphia in its total park acreage. However, over the next twenty years, the Windy City added just a single thirty-six-acre park and became one of the lowest ranking cities in its ratio of park acreage to population. At the turn of the century nearly half the city's residents lived at least one mile away from suburban parks even though those sites were no longer on the outskirts of settlement. Annexation and the centrifugal diffusion of the middle classes and the better-off working classes because of improved mass transit made those parks even more accessible to an important segment of the city. However, suburban parks were of little benefit to impoverished slum dwellers who could not afford the twenty-cent round-trip ride by el or streetcar to the large parks. The Near West Side, for example, had just one small park within walking distance, and the need for breathing spaces encouraged Jane Addams and her Hull House colleagues to get involved in political reform, and later, the playground movement, in order to provide the neighborhood with an essential service that the municipality had failed to supply.[26]

The lobbying by settlement house workers, women's clubs, and community organizations and a series of newspaper articles on the park question convinced Mayor Carter H. Harrison II to appoint a special park commission in 1899 to investigate neighborhood needs and to propose solutions. The report reiterated the complaints of the reformers that the large parks were inadequately accessible, particularly for inner-city folk, and were still insufficiently adapted to public demands for active recreation. The commission recommended establishing and thereafter maintaining well-equipped play areas in the slums for year-round use. Despite their modest budget, between 1900 and 1904 the commission operated nine parks that ranged from one to five acres, either on city land or on sites leased from philanthropists. Over one million children used these small parks.[27]

All the attention given to the small park movement encouraged the Illinois legislature to empower the local park districts to raise money for small parks by the sale of bonds. The South Park District in 1901 floated a $7.7 million bond and constructed thirty-one small parks and playgrounds—ten- to sixteen-acre recreation centers equipped with outdoor gymnasiums, athletic fields, swimming pools, and spacious fieldhouses which became community centers, "distinctive additions to dreary industrial neighborhoods." These were expensive and beautiful parks, complete with grass, trees, and flowers, that cost from $220,000–$400,000 to develop. Annual maintenance ran as high as $50,000. The parks were kept open until early evening to accommodate people of all ages, especially teenagers, most of whom were out of school and working and badly needed centers of rational recreation to replace pool halls and the like.[28]

The small parks built on the South Side developed a national reputation. They were described by President Theodore Roosevelt as the greatest municipal accomplishment of the day. Chicagoans placed a lot of faith in small parks as excellent investments for the future. Mary McDowell of the University of Chicago Settlement House assured businessmen, "Muscle exercised on a punching bag, or a swinging club, or a turning pole or in a swimming pool, is not apt to be used to bully fellow workers and lead to struggles against law and order." The anticipated value of parks in promoting social order was apparently confirmed by a Russell Sage Foundation study which reported that when a new park had been constructed in the stockyards district, delinquency had declined by 44 percent compared to an 11 percent rise for the entire city. Of course, the same youths who would have been arrested for loitering on street corners might have simply moved to the park, where they were less likely to be arrested for the same behavior.[29]

Despite the acclaim given the South Side's new small parks, much less was done for the impoverished Near West Side. The West Side Park Board was run by machine Republicans who operated their parks dishonestly and uneconomically, using park jobs for patronage. The commissioners in the early 1900s opposed the small park movement because of the high cost of land in the congested neighborhoods and the expectation of securing few contracts and patronage jobs. Only in 1905, when a newly elected reform governor appointed non-politicians to the board, was serious attention given to community needs. A $1 million bond issue was approved to pay for West Side recreation centers, and over the next two years three small parks, no larger than eight acres, were built in imitation of the South Side model. Of course, this hardly satisfied the glaring public needs for breathing spaces.[30]

While working-class groups supported most of the special park commission recommendations, they did oppose regional planning of a comprehensive belt of forest parks outside the city. Urban planners argued it would benefit everyone by preserving pristine areas for future generations. However, labor leaders opposed the concept because the forest preserves would be accessible only by automobiles, which left out working-class Chicagoans. When a referendum was held in 1905, the Chicago Federation of Labor urged union members to oppose these picnic grounds for the rich. Although a wide majority of the ballots cast favored the proposal, it was defeated because of complex legal technicalities. Nine years later the same measure was passed under different election rules that required just a simple majority.[31]

The Park Movement in the 1920s and 1930s

The park movement had a positive effect throughout the nation: by the early 1930s every city with over 50,000 residents had a public park. Most of the 60 percent improvement in national acreage in proportion to urban population between 1907 and 1932 occurred in large cities (100,000 to 300,000), which quadrupled. However, relatively little was achieved in major cities, whose ratios increased by just 18 percent. The worst results were achieved in the densely populated industrial centers in the East and Midwest, which had little space for growth. Even though New York had the second greatest acreage of any city (after Los Angeles), it had a very poor ratio of 485 people per acre, placing it 33rd out of 37 cities with over 250,000 residents. Chicago was even worse in 35th place. Newark was last with a dismal ratio of 11,403. Chicago's poor showing was particularly noteworthy since it had long been, and continued to be, a leader in park planning, providing an important model for rationalizing recreational services when in 1930 it consolidated nineteen independent park districts into one to facilitate planning and development. All the best-rated cities were west of the Mississippi—Denver, Dallas, and Minneapolis, which were able to purchase a lot of land outside their city limits. However, these remote holdings, not readily accessible for inner-city residents, did little to resolve their needs for play space. Municipal parks in the largest cities were supplemented by county parks, like the 33,000-acre Cook County Forest Preserve. However, since the county parks were only accessible by car or bus, their value for inner-city folk was still seriously limited. Furthermore, even the middle classes only used distant parks on rare occasions, such as for family outings, and their sons preferred to play ball at sites within walking distance of their homes. [32]

Along with the increase in acreage, between 1915 and 1928 municipalities also doubled their per capita expenditures for operation and park maintenance. However, that was insufficient to meet growing public use—the result of growing urban populations and their improved standard of living, which gave city folk more leisure time. Greater use also resulted from the rescinding of old Sunday blue laws in former eastern and southern bastions of Sabbatarianism. City governments initiated a variety of schemes to cheaply and efficiently utilize existing resources, such as adopting Daylight Savings Time (major northern and midwestern industrial cities went to DST to give factory workers more outdoor time in the summer) and employing artificial illumination to lengthen playing time at playgrounds, baseball fields, and tennis courts. Such innovations were enormously welcomed and proved very useful during the Depression, which created unwanted leisure for millions of urbanites. [33]

Municipal parks offered an enormous variety of facilities for strenuous sports, ranging from baseball diamonds to swimming pools, as well as provisions for less exertive games like golf, croquet, and shuffleboard. But the demand for space often exceeded the supply, especially in major cities and their poorest neighborhoods. New York had 162 baseball diamonds, but that was insufficient for the number of teams seeking permits, which were invariably reserved for clubs with political clout. There was a marked improvement in municipal golf and tennis facilities, which mainly benefited the middle class. The number of courts increased by 81 percent across the country between 1924 and 1931; Chicago alone had nearly 750 courts. New York also had hundreds of courts but not enough; players had to wait hours to get a court. The development of municipal golf was even more impressive, growing from 24 courses in 1910 to 543 in 1931. Even this growth could not keep up with demand and in the late 1920s entrepreneurs established private daily fee courses, which soon exceeded the number of public golf courses. New York was particularly underserviced: at its single modern public course, "a player standing on line at dawn is lucky if he gets through his rounds by sunset."[34]

Local geographic and climatic variables influenced major aspects of the municipal park programs. Cities located on bodies of water historically made little effort to control waterfront development for noncommercial uses, such as safe beaches. This had largely been the case in Chicago until the implementation of Daniel Burnham's Chicago Plan of 1909, which called for the preservation of the lakefront as a series of attractive parks and beaches. The implementation of many of Burnham's ideas resulted in a six-fold increase in beach attendance between 1905 and 1930. During the 1920s, as many cities gave new attention to the preservation of their waterfronts, the number of cities with public beaches increased by 70 percent. Park departments improved the beaches by building changing areas and fieldhouses and hiring lifeguards to protect the swimmers.[35]

Warm-weather cities emphasized the use of nearby oceans, lakes, or rivers or built public swimming pools, while colder cities devoted special attention to winter sports. During the winter, park workers in the north flooded skating areas, constructed toboggan chutes and slides, and closed streets for coasting. By the late 1930s over sixty cities had ski jumps and over one hundred had toboggan slides. The finest winter sports facilities were in St. Paul, which had ten hockey and eighteen skating rinks and sponsored an annual winter carnival to promote tourism.[36]

A lot of these projects were completed under the work relief programs of the New Deal, first the Civilian Works Administration (CWA) in 1933, the Federal Emergency Relief Administration (FERA) a year later, and finally the Works Projects Administration (WPA) in 1935. New Deal agencies spent about $750 million for athletic facilities. Between 1936 and 1941 the WPA employed nearly one-fifth of the national labor force at one time or other and was alone responsible for building or improving nearly 3,300 stadiums, grandstands, and bleachers, 8,333 recreational buildings, 5,898 athletic fields and playgrounds, and 770 swimming pools. One-third to one-half of the cost was put up by the federal government to encourage hundreds of cities to plan new undertakings and repair old facilities.[37]

New York benefited most from New Deal programs, both because of its great needs and because park commissioner Robert Moses and his staff of planners were able to provide federal agencies with detailed proposals and then implement them. One-seventh of the entire WPA budget went to fund

New York projects. Not only was park space insufficient; it was also terribly maintained because jobs had gone to Tammany hacks and virtually no money had been appropriated for materials and equipment. Badly needed repairs were deferred or forgotten, lawns were rarely mowed, bathrooms seldom worked, and playgrounds did not get resurfaced. Politics even ruled the use of space: permits for athletic fields went to individuals or groups with political clout; park buildings were leased for nominal fees to politically connected commercial enterprises; and for just fifteen dollars politicians could lease choice frontage at Orchard Beach in the Bronx, build bungalows, and close the beach to the public. [38]

Residents of the city's poorest neighborhoods were still in dire need of play space. The crowded Lower East Side had just two small parks, and Harlem was no better off. Together they had a total of six playgrounds. Historian Robert Caro attributed these conditions to three factors: the difficulty of relocating families whose buildings were torn down for parks; the veto power exercised over city policies by local Tammany district leaders who did not want to lose good Democratic voters who would have to move to make way; and the lack of will or the fiscal conservatism of various mayors. [39]

Moses brought to his appointment as park commissioner in 1934 years of experience as a park builder in the metropolitan region. He was best known for establishing Jones Beach in 1929 and securing new highways to facilitate access. Jones Beach was an excellent alternative to Coney Island for New Yorkers with access to automobiles. Early in 1934 Moses employed CWA and FERA workers to reseed lawns, plant 11,000 trees, and repaint every park structure, to resurface tennis courts, remake golf courses, and resurface every playground with a new asphalt finish that prevented skinned knees. By Labor Day, 51 new baseball diamonds, 10 golf courses, and 240 tennis courts had been added to existing parks. Moses and his staff also secured sixty-nine new park and playground sites, many in slum areas, without any public expenditure; they rediscovered long-forgotten municipal lots, seized land from tax delinquents, and acquired donations from churches, philanthropists, and various benevolent organizations. He subsequently used WPA money to hire 6,000 men and women to supervise recreation in parks, playgrounds, and schools and also for various construction projects. [40] The New Deal building programs in New York, and elsewhere, probably had a greater positive impact on sport participation for the average urbanite than anything else in American history.

Municipal governments in the 1920s and 1930s did not limit their expenditures for public sport to beaches, parks, and playgrounds; for virtually the first time, they invested money in sports stadiums. Urban boosters encouraged the construction of expensive sports fields to enhance the prestige of their towns, to provide facilities for local pageants and sports events, and to encourage tourism. The San Diego Board of Park Commissioners built the first major field in 1914–15. It seated 30,000 and was paid for by a $150,000 bond issue. However, no important sporting events were held there. The first public stadium to become a sports fixture was Pasadena's Rose Bowl, built in 1922 at a cost of $325,000. It sat 52,150, later expanded to over 100,000, and was operated by the city in conjunction with the Tournament of Roses Association, primarily for the Rose Bowl football game. The 50,000 Los Angeles Coliseum was built a year later, followed in 1924 by Baltimore's 80,000 seat Municipal Stadium, which cost $500,000, and by Chicago's Soldier Field.[41]

While Soldier Field opened in 1924, it was not fully completed until five years later when it sat 125,000, which made it the largest sports stadium in America. The field was located in Grant Park on the city's lakefront, approximately where Burnham's 1909 Plan of Chicago had placed an "athletic grounds" and various major museums. Designed in a classical style to conform to the neighboring Field Museum, it was originally known as Grant Park Stadium—one of the first modern sports structures to recall the Greek *stadion*. The building cost $6.5 million, financed by bond issues, and was operated by the South Park Commission. Soldier Field became the site of some of the largest crowds ever to attend sporting events in North America, including the memorable Dempsey-Tunney rematch in 1927, seen by 104,000 people who paid a record $2,658,660 for their tickets. Ten years later the high school football championship drew 120,000 spectators.[42]

The most important public stadium was the L.A. Coliseum, built in anticipation of a future Summer Olympics. Its capacity was doubled in time for the 1932 Olympics, and the total construction cost came to $1.9 million. Both projects were largely conceived by the Community Development Association (CDA), a group of self-appointed boosters who wanted to encourage tourism, capital investment, and migration to Southern California. When a public bond issue to raise construction funds was defeated, the CDA secured on its own an $800,000 bank loan—using as collateral the good name of the city and county, which together promised to pay back the cost over five years in rents—and privately built the structure on public land at Exposition Park, across the street from USC, its first major tenant.[43]

Despite the Depression the 1932 Summer Olympics was a great success and brought international renown to the City of the Angels. The games promoted tourism, demonstrated the excellent managerial capabilities of

Angelenos, and turned a $27,000 profit that was divided between the city and county. Nine months later, control of the Coliseum was turned over to the local governments, which jointly operated it through the Coliseum Commission. Los Angeles was the first major metropolis to complete a municipal stadium—a testament not only to the foresight but also to the power and arrogance of the local power elite, who, because of their lack of confidence in the electorate and public officials, chose to go outside proper channels, often using devious means to secure their goal.[44]

Public stadiums in warm-weather cities were utilized during the Depression for college bowl games, on the model of the Rose Bowl, to promote tourism and outside investment to give a shot in the arm to their failing economies. In 1935 Miami inaugurated the Orange Bowl to help revive that resort city—a strategy soon emulated elsewhere. In 1936 El Paso established the Sun Bowl, followed a year later by New Orleans (Sugar Bowl) and Dallas (Cotton Bowl). The latter, built by the city in 1930 for $350,943.41, was the scene of many large football crowds even before the post-season classic was introduced.[45]

Ethnicity, Race, and the Control of Park Space in the Radial City

Despite the expectations of WASPish park reformers that the new inner-city parks would become vehicles for Americanization and places where good citizenship and moral order would be indoctrinated into second-generation immigrant children, the actual results were usually quite different. Parks and playgrounds did not automatically become sites for structural assimilation, even under trained recreation leaders, because they usually maintained a strong ethnic character and were upon occasion the scene of interethnic violence. The dominant ethnic group in the vicinity of a park usually controlled that public space and did not welcome other groups. In multi-ethnic neighborhoods, each community might carve out a niche in the park for itself but would rarely challenge the turf of its neighbors. As long as everyone recognized one group's prior claims, usage was largely restricted to it. Others could use the facilities as guests and would be treated with temporary courtesy, but not intruders, who had "taken the first step off the known path of orderly social relationships." Difficulties typically arose in neighborhoods undergoing a change in ethnic composition when the prior group was challenged by a newcomer. Problems also arose at parks that served as boundary lines between rival ethnic groups. In such instances, parks not only failed to promote good morality but became the battle grounds for interethnic hostility.[46]

Ethnic groups developed vested interests in neighborhood parks used by youngsters for play and by adult organizations for outings. In Worcester, for example, ethnic and church groups in the working-class Elm Park never mixed. Instead, in the 1910s each "took over" a section as its own, usually the parcel located closest to its community. Rosenzweig found that rather than facilitating acculturation, the "parks provided a leisure space in which workers expressed and preserved their distinct ethnic cultures." Three-fourths of the city's playgrounds were dominated by one particular ethnic group, usually the most prominent one in the surrounding area. The Irish and the other largest ethnic groups were generally the most frequent users of the public playgrounds, while smaller ethnic groups were generally underrepresented. Rosenzweig suggested that the larger and tougher groups succeeded in privatizing the public space by frightening away outnumbered children from other groups. Consequently, playgrounds, like parks, reinforced ethnic barriers instead of breaking them down.[47]

Violence often resulted when interlopers began invading a park that had historically "belonged" to another group. Fights were also common in parks located between two ethnic groups that both perceived themselves holding valid claims to the public space. Youth gangs would try to gain dominance over the site to enhance their prestige and that of their ethnic group. If neither was sufficiently powerful to eliminate rival claims, the park would become a dangerous "no-man's land," utilized only at great peril unless the boys came with a large enough contingent to insure their safety. One such site was Chicago's Douglas Park, which divided Jewish North Lawndale from the predominantly Polish Lower West Side. When Jewish youths playing in the park saw large numbers of Polish boys coming, they would leave, and vice-versa. In the summer of 1921 hostilities between these groups were particularly hot: "One Saturday a group of Jewish boys, who were playing baseball in Douglas Park, were attacked by a gang of about thirty Polish lads. Everything from rotten tomatoes to housebricks were used for ammunition in the onslaught. The news of the affray reached the poolroom hang-outs and brought the much needed reinforcement. Men like 'Nails' [Morton] . . . went into the fight for revenge. A good many others, including high-school boys, amateur prize fighters, and hangers-on of the poolrooms were eager for the fun of 'helping the Hebes lick the Polocks.' Their slogan was 'Wallop the Polack,' and they rushed fifty strong to the scene of the battle. Finally, policemen dispersed what was left of the Polish gang."[48]

As inadequate as municipal recreation facilities were in poor white ethnic neighborhoods, they were even worse for black urbanites. In the South there were few municipal parks until the 1880s, and custom and expense kept blacks out of the privately owned parks operated by streetcar companies to build up traffic on their routes. When new public parks were opened in the 1880s, blacks were not allowed to use many of the facilities, like swimming pools, were segregated at other sections, like zoos, or were simply barred by the police from even entering. In New Orleans, which had the most liberal racial climate in the South, black access to new parks, like the well-equipped Audubon Park, was limited by the long trolley ride to the park and by customs which proscribed their presence on weekends when most were likely to have free time. Once Jim Crow policies were institutionalized into law in the 1890s, a few separate and inferior parks were set aside for blacks. Southern cities, generally tight-fisted, did not spend much even for white parks and playgrounds, much less for blacks. The relatively prosperous city of Birmingham, Alabama, had no supervised playground program until 1908, when, influenced by local pressure and the work of the Playground Association of America, it undertook a playground construction project. Seventeen were built for white children before the first black playground was built in 1914. The small black facility operated on $300, just 2 percent of the city's total playground budget, and the community had to rely on volunteers to su-pervise the youngsters.[49]

Northern blacks were free of *de jure* discrimination, but their growing communities rarely received adequate municipal services. They lacked public recreational facilities because they lived in crowded slums with little open space, in ghettoes located far from the large suburban parks. In addition, since they had less political clout than any major ethnic group, they were discriminated against in the allocation of municipal resources. Theirs were the last inner-city neighborhoods to get new parks, play-grounds, and swimming pools and received the smallest maintenance budgets. Blacks were not welcomed outside of their neighborhoods, and white residents in the zone of emergence would use any means necessary to prevent black encroachment into their turf. Consequently, in 1920 black children were permitted into only 3 percent of all American playgrounds and had few alternatives to the streets.[50]

In the 1910s residents of Chicago's rapidly growing Black Belt encoun-tered a lot of racism when they tried to utilize public space outside of their neighborhood for sports. Children in the area were actually well served by playgrounds (17.1 percent of the city's playgrounds were in or near black areas), but none of Chicago's twenty-nine recreation centers were in black neighborhoods. No official discriminatory policies existed, but the atti-tudes of each park and playground director were heavily influenced by the surrounding community. Consequently the heads of recreation centers near the Black Belt rarely encouraged black patronage. The director of close-by Armour Square Park admitted that her community was hostile and that she could not guarantee the safety of black visitors. Blacks were afraid to go into white parks even when invited by recreation leaders because they knew what might happen. By 1913, even before the Great Migration, racial clashes had already occurred at public recreation centers, often on the street when black youths led by adult supervisors were blocked coming from or going to white parks or public beaches. Fighting was especially common at Washington Park, particularly on crowded Sunday afternoons. The park divided the Irish on its west side from the southern-most edge of the Black Belt on its east side. When blacks began using the baseball diamonds in 1919, it was perceived as an infringement into Irish turf and was challenged by Irish SACs with the full support of white residents who wanted to maintain the status quo.[51]

Racial conflict extended to the use of the South Side beaches. Three of the city's eight beaches were in black areas, but blacks could use only the Twenty-sixth Street Beach, a small site that was hard to walk to. Black bathers elsewhere were discouraged verbally by the police and violently by rock-throwing youths. The Twenty-sixth Street Beach was "officially" designated by the city as a black beach, with a black director and black lifeguards. On 27 July, Eugene Williams wandered too far south of the black area and ended up swimming in the waters of the Twenty-Ninth Street Beach. Whites on the beach threw stones at the interloper to chase him off, but the youth was struck on the head and drowned. The Williams murder precipitated the bloody Chicago Race Riot which resulted in the deaths of thirty-seven blacks and fifteen whites.[52]

Over the next several decades cities did relatively little to alleviate the need for public recreational space in the growing black ghettoes. During the Depression some new facilities were built in black neighborhoods, but hardly a fair share. In New York during the 1930s, just two out of 255 new playgrounds were built in black neighborhoods. The WPA did build a lovely park on Randall's Island, located less than a mile by bridge from the border of Harlem, but it was inaccessible to most of its residents because buses were forbidden from stopping on the island. Consequently the park was nearly always vacant, even on weekends. Robert Moses built a new swimming pool in Harlem, at an inconvenient site in Colonial Park (146th Street), mainly to keep blacks out of a more accessible pool in Italian Harlem. Moses feared interracial conflict if blacks mixed with whites.[53]

Moses was right to worry about interracial relations at public spaces. By the 1930s interethnic conflicts occurred rarely between different white groups, many of whom were moving or had moved to better neighborhoods, but between whites who had been left behind and blacks. Several major race riots, such as the Detroit Riot of 1943, were precipitated by racial conflict at public parks. Control over such a scarce resource as a city park continued to be very important, both instrumentally and symbolically, in the inner-city. The potential for violence in the 1940s and after was especially high at parks that divided black ghettoes from working-class white ethnics. The white residents living on the edge of the ghetto were afraid of losing their community and, since they could not afford to move elsewhere, were prepared to use any means necessary to protect "their park" against black inroads and symbolically to preserve the neighborhood. Consequently, if black ballplayers or civil rights workers appeared in the park, the result might be racial fighting, if not a riot. After World War II, as northern black ghettoes expanded to make room for newcomers from the South, blacks moved into adjacent white neighborhoods and certain old suburban parks, like Washington Park on the South Side of Chicago, were indeed "taken over" by black residents.[54]

Conclusion: Sport and Public Space

After the Civil War municipalities in the Northeast and Midwest responded to the declining availability of public play space caused by urban development by establishing large suburban public parks. These facilities were expected to provide space for recreation, improve health, and promote social cohesion. Before this time, due to the prevailing philosophy of self-reliance and limited governmental responsibilities and powers, very few cities had built public parks, but by the 1850s such antigovernment attitudes had been widely superseded. The new suburban parks were located in or near middle-class neighborhoods, accessible by expensive public transportation, and their use was mainly determined by bourgeoise values. Eventually the space that urban planners had saved from private development would be used for sport by inner-city residents, but that usually took at least another generation. Immediate needs for breathing space and play space in the inner city were left unfilled. Because of the high cost of land and the demand for housing space, slum residents had a difficult time securing outdoor public parks in their neighborhoods. Small park and playground movements organized in the late nineteenth century received support from local inhabitants, certain machine politicians, and progressive reformers, and a number of small parks were established with community input into their use.

By the 1920s municipalities, very involved in improving the quality of life of their residents, increased expenditures for parks and park improvements and for the construction of outdoor stadiums for spectator sports, all of which redounded to the prestige of the sponsoring cities. The bulk of the construction projects and other improvements occurred during the Depression, as local governments took advantage of WPA projects to build new parks, playgrounds, and swimming pools and fix up long-neglected facilities. Yet the new basketball and handball courts and other improvements failed to keep up with the great demand for playing space in the slums. Modest improvements in the standard of living and improved and cheap mass transit gave poorer urban residents access to suburban parks and beaches, but they were still not as convenient as neighborhood small parks and "invaders" were not made welcome. Parks in the zone of emergence and the slums were often less a force in promoting social cohesion than a focal point of violent interethnic conflict.

The park movement between 1870 and 1950 benefited black urbanites less than anyone else. Northern blacks had less access to public parks and beaches than other city folk because racist urban planners built few facilities in their neighborhoods, and racist whites wanted them out of their community space. Southern blacks were even more limited, by custom or law, either to inferior facilities or to none. The courts made some efforts to end legal discrimination. In 1954, within a week after the pathbreaking *Brown* decision, the Supreme Court ruled that Louisville blacks could not be excluded from an amphitheater in a "white-only" park and that Houston's public golf courses had to admit black patrons. By the end of the decade, the NAACP had secured equal access to public beaches in cities like Baltimore and St. Petersburg, though other cities frequently opted to close the beaches rather than integrate them. Additional efforts to secure equal access to public recreational facilities came in the Civil Rights Movement of the early 1960s through demonstrations and economic boycotts and in the mid-1960s by federal civil rights legislation.[55]

CHAPTER 5

Organized Youth Sport

Municipalities and voluntary reform associations responded to the problems urban pathology caused for youths in the inner city by organizing adult-directed youth sports programs. Formal educational institutions and private social agencies believed they could use athletics to promote better health, sound morality, and good character; give participants a feeling of accomplishment; and encourage a sense of community. Public institutions like the elementary and high schools, quasi-public agencies like the PSAL, and private agencies like the YMCA, settlement houses, and the Playground Association of America tried to direct boys and teenagers into approved social behavior and prepare them to become contributing members of society. Late-nineteenth-century social reformers, frightened about cities populated by new immigrants with different values, beliefs, and traditions, worried about the future of Anglo-Saxon America and its traditional values. They saw sport as a substitute for the social life of small towns in which families had functioned as social and economic units, community ties were strong, and religion had played a dominant role in teaching sound moral values. While the small town was being displaced by the metropolis, sport would supposedly provide the same training for urban youth, especially children of the new immigrants, that daily country life had taught previous generations of Americans.

While reformers had little hope of remaking the adult immigrants into solid citizens, they felt confident that the second generation could be acculturated in the classroom and on the sports field. Participation in team sports would in theory teach such basic American values as hard work, cooperation, and respect for authority. Boys' workers also believed that rational recreation would provide an attractive substitute for the degenerate street amusements popular in slum neighborhoods—playing with fire, gambling with dice, or simply idling on street corners or in pool halls—which taught bad values, encouraged youths to join street gangs, and led them into lives of crime. Youth workers hoped organized, adult-supervised sports would appeal to the sporting instincts of street urchins who enjoyed baseball and other competitive games. [1]

High School Sports

The high school was a middle class institution developed in mid-nineteenth-century commercial cities to train youth for white-collar occupations or to prepare them for college while at the same time regulating their social behavior to conform to traditional standards. At first the demand for high schools grew slowly; as late as 1890 there were only about 200,000 secondary school students in the entire country. However, over the next three decades an enormous period of growth resulted in a 711 percent gain in enrollments. By the end of World War I attendance reached 1.6 million, but since only one-third of the elementary school students attended high school, and just one-third of those graduated, it was still mainly a middle-class institution. Poorer boys and girls had to go to work. Over the next twenty years the high school became much more democratic. By 1930 one-half of Americans of high school age attended, usually a comprehensive high school; and a decade later attendance rose to 75 percent. Inner-city youth, (especially second-generation Catholics) were still less likely than middle-class youngsters to go to high school, but their increased presence in the 1920s reflected the conventional wisdom that more education would enable them to secure "respectable" jobs. During the Depression students stayed in school because there were few full-time jobs to be had even if they dropped out. [2]

Although during the Civil War Era health reformers like Dr. Dio Lewis advocated physical education for high school students as a substitute for hardy rural living, regularized systems of physical education were rarely introduced until the late 1880s. The early programs emphasized gymnastics, largely because of the proselytizing efforts of the turners; and before long gymnastics became commonplace in metropolitan schools. In Chicago male and female students at West Side High School learned gymnastics with turner instructors in 1871. Thirteen years later a regular program was adopted, taught by graduates of German-American gymnastics schools. The turner system of exercising, which stressed the use of apparatus, became very popular in the Midwest. In New England, most schools adopted the Swedish system, which emphasized calisthenics. Brooklyn, New York, and Washington educators used a mixed system. [3]

While administrators preferred exercising over team sports because it was cheaper, less time consuming, and fit better into the school curriculum, students preferred competitive team sports, which were a lot more fun. High school students organized and ran athletic associations independent of their institutions on the model of contemporary college sports organizations. Providence (Rhode Island) Central had an athletic association by 1876, and Ann Arbor, Detroit, and Flint high schools all established similar organizations between 1883 and 1886. Student leaders raised funds, scheduled matches, and secured playing fields. In large cities, they established leagues, like the Interscholastic Football Association founded in Boston in 1888, which fostered competition and even in some cases city championships in major sports.[4]

Athletic programs became an increasingly important part of high school extracurricular life. Students liked interscholastic sport because it functioned independently of adults, provided entertainment and conversation, facilitated a spirit of teamwork, released surplus energy, and promoted a sense of community between new students, upper classmen, and alumni. Loyalty to the school became a vital first step in the development of hometown pride. Stephen Hardy has pointed out that the use of sports for community building was crucial both for schools like Boston Latin, which drew students from the entire city, and for new schools like South Boston (1901), which lacked the heritage of older established schools and could use sports to encourage pride in the neighborhood school, demonstrate its progressive qualities, and make it a focal point for the entire community.[5]

In the 1890s, just as college officials and faculties began taking over their schools' sports programs, high school administrators also began to assume control of interscholastic athletics. Educators worried that their institutions' standing in the community could be harmed if teams engaged in unsportsmanlike behavior and that too many athletes gave little attention to their studies. Student leaders welcomed adult control over athletics because they "could not resolve the tension between the rules and winning." The creation of administration-controlled leagues seemed to guarantee fair competition and the prevention of various abuses, like using ringers. Students did not feel threatened by this loss of autonomy because the entire school community shared the same basic middle-class values and the same beliefs about the role of sport in society, particularly "the potential for character development inherent in well-regulated athletics."[6]

The change from student to administrative control did not alter the emphasis on competitive elite male athletics, highlighted by city, regional, and state championships. But physical educators also gave more attention to the health and well-being of all students, utilizing sports in their classes and developing intramural programs in the early 1900s. These instructors sought to use sport both to promote health and to help students prepare themselves to fit into the industrial urban society, which required teamwork, self-sacrifice, punctuality, and discipline. They expected the lessons taught in physical education classes to be easily transferrable to the commercial and industrial world their students would be entering. However, at least until the 1920s, working-class teenagers were not in school and thus could not benefit from these programs.[7]

After World War I public support for physical education increased because of the reported poor physical records of draftees and the stereotyped weak bodies of many second-generation immigrants, and by 1934 over half of all high school students were enrolled in physical education classes. However, funding was insufficient. Facilities were not of the best quality; only half of all urban high schools even had athletic fields or playgrounds; and those were not in the most crowded neighborhoods, which needed them most. Ironically, the Depression helped alleviate a lot of the inadequacies; building programs under the Public Works Administration and the WPA spent about $75 million for new and improved gymnasiums, swimming pools, tennis courts, and athletic fields.[8]

The big emphasis remained on high-level interschool competition. Educators still believed that playing and watching competitive sports helped socialize students into a system that demanded cooperation and discipline. In preparing students for their future occupations and roles in society, athletics taught respect for hard work, achievement, and recognition that life was a struggle for which everyone was not equally endowed and that rewards like social prestige and money went to those who were not only talented but worked hard. Since schools were enrolling youth from a wider variety of social backgrounds than ever before, these lessons were even more important than in the past.[9]

Competitive sports programs also encouraged the less academically oriented youths—particularly those in inner-city schools—to remain in school by providing them with an interesting and enjoyable extracurricular activity that earned them self-satisfaction and esteem. High school baseball players were motivated by the promise of a professional career; and basketball and football players, by the chance for a college scholarship. Recent studies have found that athletes from traditionally noncollege-bound families were four times as likely to aspire to college as their nonathletic peers.[10]

In the post-World War I era competitive sports continued to provide entertainment and community identification, particularly in small and mid-sized cities and suburbs. High school teams promoted hometown pride, encouraged school spirit and orderly relations among students, and advertised the town's name.[11] These reasons were less important in metropolitan centers, where residents had many alternate recreational options, community loyalties were divided amongst several city schools, and funds were often insufficient for expensive sports.

The most popular interscholastic sports were football and basketball. Basketball was most successful as a spectator sport in the Northeast and Midwest. Games in metropolitan areas generated a lot of local fervor, especially when teams represented schools in different ethnic neighborhoods, but they were relatively less prominent than contests in smaller cities, where there was not much else to do on Friday nights. During the late 1920s in Muncie, Indiana, for instance, the Central High School Bearcats totally monopolized the city's sports fans during the winter. The Bearcats became an important source of community identification that crossed class, ethnic, and religious lines. During the Depression, when the city was in dire financial straits, the city council approved a $100,000 appropriation for a new fieldhouse for the team. The state government blocked the measure, but a group of local boosters took the initiative and built a 9,000 seat arena anyhow at a cost of $347,000.[12]

Football was also popular throughout the country, but especially in the Southwest and in industrial and mining cities in the Ohio Valley. Towns there provided a lot of financial support for what was a very expensive game, secured quality coaching, and rewarded athletes with considerable social prestige. Like basketball, football controlled the tempo of life in the smaller urban areas where there was little else to do on Friday nights. Citizens in cities like Canton and Massillon, Ohio, regarded the football team as the community's most important representative to the outside world and strongly supported the local boys. The sport was also very popular, though less dominant, in the two regions' big cities. In the 1960s, the major cities that produced the highest per capita proportion of future college football players were Pittsburgh, Houston, and Dallas, all located in the football belt. However, New York, Baltimore, Philadelphia, and St. Louis were very underrepresented; their schools lacked the funds, the space to play, and the necessary community support. In those cities residents had many recreational options not available to people living in small Texas towns. Football was a big draw in large cities during the Depression, when it provided a much-needed source of cheap mass entertainment. For example, in Chicago, which was located just at the edge of the football belt and which had a strong football tradition, especially in the Catholic schools, the game was enormously popular in the late 1930s. The 1937 city championship game between the public and Catholic league champions at Soldier Field was attended by 120,000 spectators, the largest crowd for a team sports event in American history.[13]

In the big cities spectator sports contests were believed to promote mutual understanding and respect between the players and student bodies of schools from different neighborhoods. Given the symbolic weight of such matches, this was probably an overly optimistic perspective. In post-World War II America, as these divisions became racial rather than ethnic, the reverse was often the case. As sociologist Harry Edwards has noted, "far from generating a spirit of friendly intergroup or intercultural relations, athletic confrontations . . . may serve to precipitate violent outbreaks." Postgame fights between black and white spectators from rival schools was a serious problem in the racially turbulent sixties. The 1962 city championship football match in Washington D.C., between a predominantly black lower-class public school and a middle-class white private school, ended in a brawl involving thousands of spectators and leaving over 500 injured. But violence at urban interscholastic sports contests was hardly restricted to racial antagonisms; it occurred at basketball games between black schools, too, caused by gangs or hooligans. As a result, New York City championship games were moved from Madison Square Garden to smaller quarters, and in other cities they were often held at neutral courts in virtual isolation.[14]

The Y Movement

After the Civil War the YMCA movement, originally organized to give aid and spiritual comfort to rural youth who had flocked to cities in order to reach larger numbers of men and older boys, broadened its program. The Ys organized classes in physical culture to develop muscular Christians who were physically and spiritually strong and to attract new members who wanted to take advantage of the gymnasiums and thus might become interested in the movement's spiritual message. By the 1890s the YMCA was the principal institutionalized supporter of muscular Christianity, widely perceived as a valuable adjunct to nationalism and patriotism and an important element of the "Strenuous Life" philosophy. Through religious devotion and exercise at the YMCA, an individual could develop into a Christian gentleman who would abstain from sex (especially masturbation, which ("depleted the body of vital energy"), exercise self-control, and avoid sentimentality or giving in to pain. He would insist on justice and honor and, like Frank Merriwell, the idealized hero of juvenile literature, would use his strength to protect the rights of those weaker than himself. As Benjamin Rader aptly put it, "The Christian gentleman's spirit found its truest expression in the out-of-doors, the refreshing vigor of the countryside, and on the athletic field."[15]

The philosophy of muscular Christianity implied a new view of Jesus as athlete or warrior. At a moment in American history when the culture appeared increasingly feminized, Protestant leaders found this an exciting concept which could help them reach boys put off by such feminine virtues as humility, weakness, and submission. Virile Christianity might help bring young men into church pews mainly occupied by women and girls. This problem was particularly grave in inner-city parishes, where Protestant churches were trying to bring the Social Gospel of Christ to alienated working-class urbanites by providing needed social services, like building gymnasiums and organizing sports programs for local residents.[16]

YMCA buildings were usually located in better neighborhoods, where they aimed their efforts at youthful clerical workers, but so many boys drifted in to use the gymnasiums for physical training that some Y leaders decided to sign up middle-class boys who could afford the membership fees that ranged up to five dollars. Thus junior boys' departments were established in the 1880s. The lads were allowed to use the gyms during the afternoon—a means of preventing good boys from becoming idle and corrupted by commercial entertainments. The YMCAs were run by professional secretaries like Robert McBurney in New York, who applied business techniques to assure the efficient organization of boys' work but made no effort to maintain the occasional missions of the Civil War era that had sought to rescue street rowdies. Juniors ranged in age from ten to sixteen, when they were eligible for the adult departments. Ten was the age when boys started "to drift out upon the streets, to make up the knots of eager debaters on matters of games and sport, and to come within the outer circle of temptation to bad language and its cognate evils.'' Boys' workers wanted to keep their charges busy, supervised by male role models, to counter fears of growing effeminacy due to the influence of mothers and school teachers and also to prolong boyhood as long as possible, because once they became adolescents, then sexuality and emotionalism began to weaken self-control.[17]

By 1892 about 250,000 Y members had access to 348 gymnasiums staffed by 144 full-time physical culture leaders. The most influential executive was Dr. Luther H. Gulick, Jr., a son of missionaries and an ardent believer in muscular Christianity, who would become the preeminent individual in the adult-managed boys' sports movement. Gulick, an instructor at the YMCA Training School in Springfield, Massachusetts, created the Y emblem (an upside-down triangle), which represented the spirit supported by the mind and the body. Unlike earlier Y leaders, Gulick advocated sport in Y programs, although he opposed intense competition, specialization, and professionalism. Gulick played a key role in replacing gymnastics with sport as the cornerstone of YMCA athletic programs, and his students invented such new sports as basketball (1891) and volleyball (1895) that could be played in small indoor spaces.[18]

The YMCA sports program became very popular and highly competitive. In 1895 the Y organized the Athletic League of North America to regulate competition under the rules of the Amateur Athletic Union. Y teams competed against each other, against other athletic clubs, and against colleges in basketball, swimming, and track and field. In 1905 Y teams played over 2,000 contests against outside groups. The most famous YMCA aggregate was the Buffalo German Y basketball team, which won the 1901 Buffalo Exposition championship and the gold medal three years later at the St. Louis Olympics before turning professional. Local Y units gave their best athletes free membership, free room and board, and traveling allowances. The heavy emphasis on competitive sport lasted until 1911, when the newly appointed physical director, Henry F. Kallenberg, redirected the focus of the program. The Athletic League dropped out of the AAU, restricted competition by size and weight, and organized local amateur athletic associations. Instead of emphasizing competition and victory, the new YMCA philosophy encouraged a comprehensive program of athletics for the greatest number of participants.[19]

The Young Women's Christian Association (YWCA) lagged behind the male society in promoting athletic facilities. Its original purpose was to prevent respectable middle-class girls living on their own in cities from being contaminated by the vile forces present in the modern city by protecting, housing, and educating those young women. After the Civil War interest in promoting women's athletics increased, and in 1882, the Boston YWCA held its first athletic games. Two years later, its new building included a well-equipped gymnasium. By 1890, according to one sport historian, physical education had become a crucial aspect of the YWCA movement, although it was far less important than for the YMCA.[20]

In the early 1900s the justification for the Y movement underwent a significant change from muscular Christianity to Gulick's biological theory of play. He believed that man had acquired the fundamental impulses to play during human evolution and argued that the development of each individual (ontogeny) recapitulated all the stages of human evolution (phylogeny). The growing child repeated as instinctive drives many of the various traits that had been vital for mankind's psychological evolution. Thus children from ages seven to twelve played tag and various track and field sports that had all sprung from the hunting instinct acquired in the pre-savage period of evolution; adolescent boys participated in team sports that combined the old hunting instinct with a new instinct for cooperation that had emerged in the savage stage. Youth played those games for their physical, mental, and moral growth.[21]

Gulick believed that the team sports of the superior Anglo-Saxon race provided adults with a valuable means of encouraging sound moral and religious reflexes in youth, especially inner-city adolescents who were at a critical juncture when they could go either good or bad. Slum youngsters often joined juvenile gangs—vehicles for the expression of moral instincts, recapitulating their racial heritage of tribal hunting and warfare by such activities as thievery, vandalism, and violence. Ghetto boys were prey to the forces of evil that seemed inherent in urban settings. They lacked the protective influences of rural society—close family ties, a strong sense of community, ardent religious faith, and a belief in such traditional values as hard work. The remedy Gulick offered to reform urban youth was adult-supervised sports that stemmed from the instinct for cooperation and required the highest moral principles. Inner-city kids would learn teamwork, obedience, self-control, loyalty, and respect for authority.[22]

Rader argues that Gulick's biological theory of play was the key element justifying the endeavors of boys' workers. Gulick's ideas had a profound influence on the renowned psychologist G. Stanley Hall and such leaders of the Playground Movement as Joseph Lee and Henry S. Curtis and were popularized by advice manuals like Rev. William Forbush's *The Boy Problem* (1901). Hall's great study, *Adolescence* (1904), had an enormous impact among Protestant boys' workers, who believed their charges should be sheltered and converted to save them from the urban vices of crime and sexuality. Adolescent boys who quit school had a lot of free time, and even if employed, had dead-end jobs, making them prime candidates for immoral behavior. Hall's ideas encouraged boys' workers, parents, and educators to prolong boyhood and keep teenagers economically, emotionally, and psychologically dependent through such institutions as the public schools, the YMCA, and the Boy Scouts.[23]

Rader points out that the biological theory of play had four important implications for the use of sport as a socializing agency. Firstly, the theory justified the creation of special institutions for boys that would be closely supervised by adults. Spontaneous, unregulated, and unstructured boys' games, in which keeping score or gaining victory was not crucial, would be supplanted by highly organized team sport under adult supervision. Secondly, the philosophy encouraged boys' workers to deemphasize piety. The YMCA became increasingly secularized and available to non-members, partly because leaders recognized that few boys were heavily influenced by its evangelical programs. However, Rader did not recognize that at the same time many institutional churches were trying to use sports and other social programs to attract youth and raise their faith. A Sunday School Athletic League was organized in Brooklyn in 1904, and membership on its teams (usually supervised by a trained Y leader) required regular attendance at Sunday School. Thirdly, boys' workers were encouraged to deemphasize ethnocultural differences among their clients, who all shared the experience of maturity. The idea that all boys could be remade into good citizens encouraged a major effort by child savers to use sports to remake ghetto youth. Finally, the biological theory of play provided a justification to continue segregating play by sex. Because of the instincts acquired during evolution, boys and girls had different play preferences. Primitive man had needed to be skilled in fighting, running, and hunting, while prehistoric woman had required knowledge of household skills. As Gulick noted, "Athletics do not test womanliness as they test manliness." He recommended that girls' play be directed toward areas that would help them learn how to manage a home, but not towards competitive athletics.[24]

The Public Schools Athletic League and Organized Sport for Children

In 1900 Gulick left the Y training school for the principalship of Brooklyn's Pratt Institute; three years later he was appointed director of physical training for the New York City public school system. This new position gave him a great opportunity to put his theories of play into practice. Dissatisfied with the traditional physical fitness program of calisthenics and gymnastics, Gulick sought a new, more interesting system that would have the widest possible appeal since "*all* the boys in the city needed the physical benefits and moral and social lessons afforded by properly conducted games and sport." In the fall of 1903, in cooperation with school superintendent William H. Maxwell, board of education member General George W. Wingate, and James E. Sullivan, secretary of the AAU, Gulick organized the Public Schools Athletic League. Local high schools already engaged in interscholastic competition in baseball, football, and track and field, and a few elementary schools held athletic competitions. However, Gulick's proposals went much further and constituted the most sophisticated athletic program ever proposed for American schoolboys.[25]

The PSAL was justified as an answer to New York's terrible slum conditions. Gulick's own biological theory of play assumed that the evil influences of a bad environment could be remedied through the ameliorative functions of sport. Additional support came from the progressive education movement, which promoted a child-centered curriculum and presumed that play would facilitate learning. Gulick wanted a project that could benefit all city boys, particularly adolescents unreached by summer or evening programs. Gulick's PSAL emphasized team sports that taught the kinds of traditional qualities absent from the modern industrial city, channeled bad gang conduct into constructive behavior, encouraged the development of primary relationships, provided opportunities for altruistic experiences (putting the team above the individual), and promoted school spirit.[26]

General Wingate strongly supported a program of wide-scale athletics for urban youth so they would grow up to be as healthy as country boys, who seemed to dominate the business and professional world: ''Country boys develop hard, rugged, and muscular bodies because of the increasing round of chores upon the farm. That is the reason why the majority of the highest positions in commercial and professional life are occupied by men who spent their boyhood under conditions that gifted them physically to withstand the tremendous pressure of the strenuous times in which we live. Should the city boy be thus handicapped in the context of life? I think not, but the problem all along has been how to make it possible, and also interesting for the boys of our public schools to get the sort of exercise that could develop their bodies and bring them to sturdy manhood.''[27] Wingate emphasized a prorural (or anti-urban) perspective with which educator William Maxwell empathized. Maxwell agreed with Gulick's philosophy of mass sports and believed that athletics would encourage school spirit. Like the boys' workers, the superintendent also saw adult-directed sports as a vehicle for social control to deal with the problems of the city streets:

The substitution of controlled athletics for uncontrolled, erratic contests is different only in degree from substituting pure, clean, valuable exercises and sport for the undesirable amusements to which a city subjects a child. The city child has naturally little that encourages the healthy, young animal growth. The crowded conditions, the absence of convenient playing places, the inhibition of many games in the street because of their danger to pedestrians and to property, all make more alluring abnormal methods of passing the time, or rather wasting it. Lecturing a boy about cigar smoking may be effective but I doubt it will work half so quickly as the argument in practice that he who smokes cannot run so well, jump so high, or play ball so effectively as his more temperate comrade whose lungs breath air instead of smoke charged with noxious drugs. The dishonesty and brawling in play seen so constantly in the street wherever children gather may be corrected by ethical argument, but a much quicker teacher is that practice which gives the boy a taste of the other thing—an athletic contest won fairly and squarely by sheer, clean prowess of body and mind. The league is to encourage these things. [28]

The Board of Education supported the formation of the PSAL and agreed to implement its program in New York's 630 schools. However, since the PSAL was a private corporation and ineligible for public funding, it had to find its own revenue. Gulick and his colleagues appealed to the city's financial community for fiscal assistance and to the press for public moral support. Arguments that adult-managed after-school athletics would improve physical development, teach fair play, and provide a good site for boys to work off their potentially mischievous energies struck a responsive chord with philanthropists like Andrew Carnegie, John D. Rockefeller, and Solomon Guggenheim, who all contributed generously to the movement. The PSAL achieved instant visibility and recognition through its initial sports promotion on 26 December 1903 at Madison Square Garden, advertised as the largest athletic meet in the world. It attracted 1,040 competitors, mainly elementary school students, and was enthusiastically reported by the local newspapers, which became strong advocates of the PSAL. [29]

One of Gulick's major goals for the PSAL was to promote "sports for all" and to deemphasize competition for just the most talented boys. The PSAL instituted two important innovations to promote mass sports—class athletics and the athletic badge test. Class athletics encouraged good students with limited athletic abilities to participate since the entire class competed together and their score was based on the group's total average. Gulick established strict eligibility requirements: 80 percent of a class had to participate, and they all had to be well behaved and carry a B average. These rules not only promoted mass participation and better discipline but also encouraged poorer students to study harder. Boys in the fifth through the eighth grades could compete in pull-ups, dashes, the broad jump, and similar contests. In 1914, for instance, 63,901 boys participated in the broad jump tests. [30]

Athletic badge tests also stimulated athletics and schoolwork. Eligibility required a B average for elementary schoolboys and "satisfactory" progress for high school students. Standards were established in running, jumping, and chinning, and boys who reached the achievement level for their age group won a bronze or gold medal. In the first year of testing (1904) only 1,162, or 2 percent of the competitors, reached the standards, but by 1915 nearly 25,000 won badges. [31]

The third part of the PSAL program was interscholastic athletics for the most talented boys. A city-wide league was organized for the high schools, and there were twenty-two district leagues for elementary schools. Participation still required decent behavior and good grades. The first sports were baseball, basketball, track and field, and riflery, and by 1907 soccer, cross-country running, swimming, lacrosse, tennis, roller and ice skating, and rowing were added. Competitors were divided by weight classification to promote safety, and there were district, borough and city-wide championships. Baseball was particularly popular, and in 1907, 106 teams competed for the city title, making it the largest baseball tournament in the country. The final game was played at the Polo Grounds in front of 15,000 spectators.[32]

The PSAL also arranged special events, often sponsored by the *World*, and other newspapers. The *World* first held field days for elementary schoolboys in 1906 and eight years later organized 181 field days at 176 schools involving over 100,000 boys. The PSAL itself sponsored occasional public exhibitions to publicize their successes and vigorously supported such programs as Mayor William Gaynor's "Safe and Sane" July 4 Games. These games were first held in 1913 to promote social control over inner-city youth and give those youngsters an alternative to firecrackers and other dangerous incendiaries that killed and maimed many boys. "Safe and Sane" Games were mainly held at public parks and swimming pools throughout the city, where they drew in 1917 about 20,000 participants and 100,000 adult spectators. The victory stands were dominated by second-generation new immigrants, which seemed proof of their acculturation and the democratic character of sport.[33]

Although the PSAL was organized primarily to exercise social control over urban boys, it also sponsored a girls' branch starting in 1905, financed by wealthy New York matrons who wanted to provide exercise and activity programs for girls. Physical educator Elizabeth Burchenal was the influential director of the Girls' Branch, and her philosophy coincided with Gulick's theory of play and his view of the biological inferiority of girls. Burchenal thought that, while sport provided a necessary outlet for the fighting instincts of boys, girls needed athletics to secure health and happiness "of which convention and dress and resulting unnatural habits have deprived her." Burchenal believed that women physical educators should determine which exercises were best for girls based on the criterion of promoting fun, agility, and wit. Group participation was stressed and individual and interschool competition was prohibited. The Girls' Branch followed the philosophy of "athletics for all girls" and "sports for sport's sake" and consequently emphasized such activities as folk dancing along with basketball and track.[34]

PSAL workers were convinced their programs succeeded in improving the health, morality, and character of urban youth. The large numbers of active participants and the increasing number of medal winners was taken as evidence of improved athletic achievement. Teachers reported that students had become better behaved, "not because they want to be saints, but because they want to compete," and needed a letter from an instructor testifying to their good behavior. PSAL supporters felt that bad health habits like cigarette smoking stopped since students recognized that smoking curtailed their athletic performance. Open-air athletics became a means of building up lungs and preventing tuberculosis, a ravaging illness in the city's slums. Finally, advocates asserted that second-generation children were acculturated through participation in the PSAL. Yet while the PSAL's activities seemed to fill the free hours of thousands of city youth, keeping them busy and off the streets and providing a spark of joy and self-accomplishment in an otherwise dreary existence, it failed to reach a majority of adolescent city boys who were out of school and either working or hanging out on the streets, or both. They were the youngsters most vulnerable to the vile pleasures of the street. [35]

The PSAL organized athletics on the largest scale anywhere in the world, providing programs for about 100,000 children. It led in developing innovative athletic programs and establishing academic and behavioral standards of eligibility. Within a few years, cities such as Baltimore and Chicago organized similar programs. By 1910 seventeen cities had organized athletic leagues patterned after the PSAL in an effort to promote social control, good health, and traditional values among their inner city youth. [36]

Settlement House Workers and the Playground Movement

The men and women actively involved in private, nonsectarian, voluntary associations that focused on youth were deeply influenced by the recapitulation theory, environmentalism, and the prevailing ideology of sport. Kind-hearted settlement house workers who lived in the worst urban slums knew first-hand the dismal conditions there and sought to help the impoverished make their lives more bearable. Settlement workers like Jane Addams and Lillian Wald ardently supported athletics as a means of attracting local youth into their institutions, where they could be saved from urban pathology. They also believed that adult-directed sport was itself a panacea that would help lead young men away from gangs, pool rooms, saloons, and brothels toward new and more positive surroundings comprised of settlement houses, parks, and playgrounds where lads could be supervised in constructive team sports. Instead of becoming juvenile delinquents and hoodlums, boys would be trained through clean sports to become good citizens and dependable workers by improving their health, experiencing cooperation, and learning punctuality. [37]

Settlement houses promoted athletics from their earliest days. By the 1890s Hull House, located in the impoverished Near West Side of Chicago, had organized gymnastics and calisthenics classes to counter the deleterious influence of the crowded neighborhood. The gymnasiums attracted local youths, who wandered in and might stay long enough to be reached by boys' workers. Jane Addams, the director of Hull House, was well known for her support of athletics. Addams believed that open air sports "might both fill the mind with the imaginative material constantly supplied by the theater, and also afford the activity which the cramped muscles of the town dweller sorely needed." She believed that the teamwork learned from organized sports promoted a sense of community among boys from different backgrounds and taught lessons transferrable to the workplace. Team players were taught how to cooperate so they would not feel alienated when they got a highly specialized factory job, but rather gain a sense of accomplishment by recognizing how they were contributing to the success of the total project. [38]

Neighborhood youth mainly relied on the settlement houses for recreational purposes. Hull House, for example, sponsored boys' clubs for younger lads and bowling and billiard tournaments for older boys. Athletic exhibitions frequently preceded Saturday night dances. The gymnasium was one of its most popular facilities, and one observer claimed that Hull House was better known for its women's basketball clubs than anything else. Young men who wore Hull House's colors competed against various athletic organizations. The settlement was especially renowned for its Greek wrestlers, who won numerous local and national championships—so many medals and cups that Addams feared that "too much success may lead the winners into that professionalism which is so associated with betting and so close to pugilism." But she felt that the benefits outweighed the dangers: "Young people who work long hours at sedentary occupations, factories, and offices, need perhaps more than anything else the freedom and ease to be acquired from a symmetrical muscular development and are quick to respond to that fellowship which athletics apparently afford more easily than anything else." In spite of her pacifism Addams even allowed a paramilitary Greek society to organize and train at Hull House because "each lad believes that at any moment he may be called home to fight [Turkey] . . . . With such a genuine motive at hand, it seemed mere affectation to deny the use of our . . . gymnasium for organized drill." [39]

The popularity of competitive sports among settlement clientele was so great that leagues were formed that leagues were formed like the Inter-Settlement Athletic Association (ISAA) in New York (1903). The ISAA gained a lot of favorable publicity for the settlement house movement. Each member had on its staff a trained physical culture instructor who taught and supervised competitors. Among the most successful programs in the ISAA were the Henry Street and University settlements on the Lower East Side, where their Jewish members excelled at indoor sports like basketball, boxing, and wrestling. Most ISAA meets were held in the evenings to maximize the number of participants and spectators. The ISAA claimed, with considerable justification, that it reached more working youth than any other athletically oriented boy's program.[40]

Besides providing gymnasiums and organizing sports teams, settlement workers also ardently advocated improved public recreation. Jane Addams and other reformers fought for municipal programs to fill the glaring need for inner-city playgrounds, parks, and bathhouses and for hiring trained supervisors to organize and regulate public programs. Addams got involved in ward politics partly to defeat local alderman and committeeman Boss Johnny Powers, who was uninterested in securing more responsive aldermen. Inner-city politicians often felt threatened by recreational reformers and anyone else who gained influence over neighborhood youth, since they were the voters of the future. A Boston settlement house tried to alleviate this tension "by inviting the politicians to referee the games and to make speeches to the boys at our 'banquets,'" so politicos could appear as friends of local youngsters.[41]

In 1906 Jane Addams took her crusade to a national audience by helping to form the Playground Association of America, which sought to promote municipal playgrounds throughout the United States. The PAA was led by the ubiquitous Dr. Luther Gulick with Theodore Roosevelt as honorary president. Jane Addams was vice-president and the secretary was Dr. Henry Curtis, supervisor of playgrounds in the nation's capital. The PAA advocated the construction of small neighborhood parks where trained adults would supervise children's play. The organization's short-range goal was to tame the wild animals of the street and its long-term aim was "to shape a cohesive urban moral order" with the playground becoming a focal point of community pride and identification. The PAA justified its activities on the basis of the biological theory of play and a belief in the efficacy of environmentalism. Like settlement workers, the playground leaders believed they could reach inner-city youths, including street gang members, by giving them an opportunity to participate in competitive athletics and supervised play that appealed to their atavistic instincts. Adult-directed play would provide a safety valve for inner-city children, teaching them the principles of adjustment and cooperation essential for growing up and going to work.[42]

Before the turn of the century, fewer than ten cities had supervised recreation programs, but by the time the PAA was organized, projects were under way in forty-one cities. The PAA did an excellent job educating the public about the additional needs for municipal recreation facilities and contributed to the momentum for reform already established. By 1917, 504 cities had supervised recreation programs, mainly based on the Chicago model. Large cities established recreation commissions that investigated available public and private resources and needs and recommended new programs. One of the most successful endeavors by the New York commission in the 1910s was its procurement of additional recreation piers and their expanded use nearly year-round. Some were even equipped with swimming pools to give boys and young men an alternative to swimming in polluted rivers. Another improvement was the rapid expansion in the numbers of evening centers for working people from eight in 1900 to sixty-two in 1914. These facilities had become so popular that in 1914 there were 629 centers in 152 cities. [43]

Conclusion: The Limits of Adult-Directed Play

Professional educators and instructors at informal educational settings like playgrounds and settlement houses provided important services for urban youth at the turn of the century by administering and directing athletic programs, securing play space at public and semi-public facilities, and lobbying for their leisure interests. However, zealous boys' workers often exaggerated the possibilities for adult-directed recreation and underestimated the potential for self-directed growth among boys and teenagers who played out of the gaze of their elders. The emphasize on close supervision took some of the creativity out of play. Sports and games comprised an important component of the play activities that urban children enjoyed free of adult control. They spontaneously organized athletic contests and utilized whatever space was available, be it in a park, back yard, street, or alley. In deference to tradition and common consent, participants determined their own rules, allowing for exceptions whenever necessary to conform to the unique contours of a playing area, such as narrow streets or a short right field ("over the fence is out"), or flaws in the surface that caused a bad bounce ("hindoo"; "do-over"). Of course not all disputes were peacefully or amicably resolved. The resourcefulness and cooperation required by unstructured children's games have been recognized by sociologists and social psychologists as a means to provide participants with a valuable learning experience, superior to, and independent of, adult supervision. [44]

Recent studies of the YMCA, PSAL, and the playground movement have taken the reformers to task for failing to regulate the activities of the slum-dwelling ethnic youth who most needed their help. While playground leaders loved to quote statistics that apparently demonstrated that supervised recreation had a major impact against delinquency, the reality was that fewer than 10 percent of urban children even used the playgrounds, and they were mainly middle-class WASP children who lived near playgrounds and whose family values coincided with those taught by play leaders. Playgrounds in the inner city were seldom a quarter mile or less from children's homes, which was as far as they would walk to get to a play site. The middle-class appeal of the playground movement also extended to other organizations like the YMCA and the Boy Scouts. Slum children admired the ability to fight, spontaneity, and defiance of authority which conflicted with the values promoted by progressive reformers. Consequently, as Rader points out, play leaders had to compromise and become less overbearing if they wanted to attract these youngsters. The result was that sometimes the roughest boys and their gangs took over the playground space.[45] Youth workers hardly expected that the playground would become the scene of future gang conflicts as rival groups sought control over the neutral turf.

Rader astutely concluded that by 1920 the adult-managed sports movement was at a serious impasse. The YMCA, disillusioned with organized athletics, had already abandoned high-level sports; the PSAL had no impact on older ethnic adolescents out of school; and the PAA failed to regulate the leisure time of slum youth as it had promised to do. Evening recreation programs aimed at working young adults received only lukewarm municipal support, and settlement houses got the community to use their athletic facilities but usually on the clients' own terms. This was especially true at denominational houses frequented by Catholic and Jewish boys who would leave once any proselytizing began. Athletic leaders at the high school level dealt mainly with a homogeneous population of native white Americans who shared their values, and consequently sport was not needed to acculturate the student body.[46]

Professional educators after World War I became less certain of the character-building qualities of sport for children, although administrators, coaches and parents continued to assert sport's ameliorative functions for teenagers. Psychologists and physical educators no longer had confidence in instinct theory as an explanation of child behavior, and the latter began to wonder if the bad effects of boys' sport did not outweigh the benefits. By the 1930s they were opposing competitive sports for preadolescents. However, as Jack Berryman cogently notes, the rhetoric of sport had become so completely assimilated by the core society that parents and voluntary associations like the Little League and the Soap Box Derby were established to promote organized competition for children.[47]

"A New York Poolroom"—an illegal off-track betting parlor—drawn by W. A. Rogers. *Harper's Weekly* 36 (2 April 1892): 324.

American Derby Day at Washington Park, 1891. Photo by J. W. Taylor courtesy of the Chicago Historical Society (ICHi-13320).

"The Manhattan Athletic Club Headquarters—Drawn by Hobson Hawley." This well-equipped facility, located in New York City at 45th and Madison Avenue, opened in December 1890. *Harper's Weekly* 34 (3 November 1890): 864.

Chicago Turnverein class, c. 1885. Photo by Schollz, courtesy of the Chicago Historical Society (ICHi-14858).

Boys boxing in front of the gymnasium at the Chicago Hebrew Institute. Photo courtesy of the Chicago Historical Society (ICHi-17310).

"Across the Street from '4630 Gross.'" Children playing baseball at a neighborhood lot in Chicago. Photo courtesy of the Chicago Historical Society (ICHi-15015).

Jackson Park about 1900. The spectators at this ball game were extremely well dressed, which was common when people went out in public at the turn of the century. Photo courtesy of the Chicago Historical Society.

"One of the Tennis Courts." The City of New York, Department of Parks, *Annual Report, 1911* (New York: Martin B. Brown, 1912), 109.

"300 Tennis Courts in Prospect Park Appear to Be Appreciated." L. H. Weir, ed., *Parks: A Manual of Municipal and County Parks*, vol. 2 (New York: A. S. Barnes, 1928), frontispiece.

Vol. XXXV—No. 106.

THE NATIONAL
POLICE GAZETTE

THE OLDE. ILLUSTRATED

NEW YORK, SATURDAY, OCTOBER 4, 1879.

WEEKLY. ESTABLISHED 1846

THE GREAT WALKING MATCH

Price Ten Cents.

The start of the Astley Belt six-day, go-as-you-please pedestrian race at Madison Square Garden at 1 A.M. Monday morning, 22 September 1879. Courtesy of John Cumming.

"The New Madison Square Garden Building in Course of Construction," by Hawley and Snyder. *Harper's Weekly* 34 (12 April 1890): 281.

"A Chicago Pool-Room on Sunday," drawn by T. de Thulstrup. *Harper's Weekly* 36 (10 September 1892): 880.

Pool Hall interior, St. Louis, 1910. Photo by Lewis Hine courtesy of the International Museum of Photography at the George Eastman House, Rochester, N.Y.

Pinboys in subway alley, New York City, 1909. Photo by Lewis Hine courtesy of the International Museum of Photography at the George Eastman House, Rochester, N.Y.

Men bowling in downtown Chicago alley (possibly the Fischer Building) at the turn of the century. Photo by Dick Sale courtesy of the Chicago Historical Society.

Children playing ball in the street. Independent of adult intervention, they seem to be having a good time. Photo from the Chicago Commons Association, courtesy of the Chicago Historical Society (ICHi-18398).

Boys swimming in the East River, New York City. While these street urchins swam in the nude, often using the dog paddle to clear debris from their path, bathers at public beaches like Coney Island were more than amply clothed. Photo courtesy of the Bain Collection, Library of Congress.

Public baths, New York City, the East River, c. 1898. Public baths were a progessive reform to urban health problems and a safe and moral alternative to swimming in polluted rivers. Courtesy of the Musuem of the City of New York.

Roof playground, New York City, c. 1898. Since crowded Manhattan had few empty spaces in which to play, roof playgrounds were a valuable supplement. Courtesy of the Museum of the City of New York.

Children playing basketball at the Carnegie Playground on Fifth Avenue in New York City, August 1911. While apparently under adult supervision, they seem to be having a good time. Photo from the Bain Collection, courtesy of the Library of Congress.

The Power Brokers and the Business of Urban Sport

I can't see why Tammany shouldn't win. Tammany takes about everything into its reach as far as my observations go, and there doesn't seem to be any good reason why Tammany shouldn't take the richest plum of a racing meeting.

Mayor Hugh Grant of New York commenting on the victory of Tammany, a 40-to-1 shot in the lucrative Eclipse Stakes at Morris Park. *New York Times,* 7 June 1891.

MR. BONOMI. Do you recall that you fought Jesse Flores . . . on Sept. 23, 1948? . . . a world's light-weight bout, was it not?

MR. IKE WILLIAMS. Yes.

BONOMI. What was the amount of your purse?

WILLIAMS. $32,500.

BONOMI. And your manager . . . was . . . Frank "Blinky" Palermo, is that right?

WILLIAMS. That is right.

BONOMI. Did you see one red cent of that $32,500?

WILLIAMS. No . . .

BONOMI. The whole $32,500 disappeared?

WILLIAMS. The entire purse.

U.S. Cong., Senate, Judiciary Committe, *Professional Boxing: Hearings Before Subcommittee on Antitrust and Monopoly,* 86th Cong., 2d. sess., Pursuant to S. Res 238, Dec. 5–14, 1960 (Washington, 1961), 667.

CHAPTER 6

Urban Politics, Organized Crime, and the Commercialization of Professional Team Sport

The rise of commercialized professional spectator sport was the most significant development in post-bellum American athletics. In the antebellum era large crowds had occasionally gathered on the banks of lakes and rivers to watch rowing contests or traveled to distant racetracks to glimpse intersectional contests, but few entrepreneurs had tried then to capitalize on the spectatorial fascination with sports. However, once sport had become a popular urban leisure activity, sagacious businessmen recognized the possible profits to be made by promoting sporting events in urban areas which offered large potential audiences accustomed to paying for their entertainment. The modernization of sports and the development of highly specialized professional athletes whose excellence would attract crowds facilitated the process of commercialization. Entrepreneurs organized baseball leagues and racing circuits and constructed or rented baseball parks and enclosed tracks in which their promotions could be seen only by paying customers. Baseball, boxing, and horse racing, the three major professional sports, were dominated right from the start by professional politicians, generally political bosses, and close associates, either traction magnates or gamblers. This had important ramifications for urban political culture and was a central element in the nexus that evolved between urban machine politics and organized crime. This chapter will examine why politicians and underworld figures got involved in commercialized sport, how they utilized their power to secure control of professional sports, and what they did once in charge. We shall also analyze the process in which politicians eventually lost control of baseball to more respectable businessmen and were largely shunted aside in the formerly illegal turf and ring sports by vicious gamblers and bootleggers.

Boxing

The intimate connections between urban politicians and prize fighters that had emerged in the rough-and-tumble antebellum political campaigns, when boxers were used as intimidators, continued after the Civil War. Even though political machines were marshalling their supporters by more rational means, like patronage and the performance of services, they still occasionally relied upon shoulder hitters to convince citizens how to vote. Professional politicians and other members of the sporting fraternity continued to enjoy pugilism, but arranging matches was difficult since the sport was universally banned until the 1890s and thereafter was legalized in few locations, and usually just briefly, until the 1920s. During the period 1870–1920 machine politicians became a dominant force in the sport. They either owned major indoor arenas or protected their owners, had the clout to pull off fights of dubious legality, and used their influence to secure the legalization of prize fighting.

Boxing matches in the 1870s and 1880s usually either were impromptu barroom brawls or were organized on a personal basis by fighters or their managers in sporting taverns like Harry Hill's Lower East Side Dance Hall. Each combatant's backers would put up a stake, which would be held by the saloonkeeper or a local pol. Certain major bouts were arranged through the sporting press, especially Fox's *National Police Gazette*, which printed challenges by aspiring fighters. Fox himself arranged world championship bouts and contributed valuable belts for the winners.[1]

Promoters had to go to great lengths to stage their contests. The sites of major nineteenth-century fights were often not publicly reported for fear the authorities would break up the match. Fans learned by word of mouth where tickets were on sale (usually a sporting tavern) and then made their way to the secret location, either a back room of a saloon or such out-of-the-way sites as a barge, barn, or railroad siding. Fans attending a championship fight would head to the train station, where they bought tickets for the match and a train ride to an undisclosed destination, where the fight would be held. On 7 July 1889 the sporting fraternity gathered in New Orleans to attend the Sullivan-Kilrain title bout. Late that night the fans purchased tickets for ten and fifteen dollars and secretly rode off by train to the obscure town of Richburg, Mississippi, where a ring was laid out early the next morning. A future mayor of New Orleans refereed the match, proclaiming Sullivan the victor when Kilrain could not continue after the seventy-fifth round.[2]

The New York metropolitan area was the center of boxing in the early 1880s; Tammany influence and police payoffs enabled "exhibition" four-round bouts to occur. However, by 1885 reformers had succeeded in getting the police to repeatedly interfere in major fights, and local promoters gave up the business. The locus of the sport shifted to New Orleans, where promoters and politicians used a variety of means to circumvent the local proscriptive laws. The 1882 Louisiana laws against fighting only prohibited "personal combat with fists"; thus when gloved bouts were introduced a few years later, the courts upheld their legality. After a new law was passed forbidding gloved matches, Delta City mayors continued to grant permits for matches in return for a fifty-dollar "donation" to the city.[3]

Boxing soon became a popular elite participatory sport in New Orleans. Members of local athletic clubs relished the opportunity to attend professional fights so they could observe excellence in action in a setting free of the rowdyism and disorder that normally accompanied prize fights. Consequently, in 1889 the Young Men's Gymnastic Club and the Southern Athletic Club both arranged professional fights for the entertainment of their members. One year later the city council and the state legislature both passed laws permitting sparring exhibitions sponsored by chartered athletic clubs, implying a difference between such matches and the outlawed prize fight. These laws resulted in a crucial innovation in boxing promotion. Instead of the old system, in which matches were arranged by managers or middlemen like Fox, with purses coming from side bets, a new system developed, in which athletic clubs negotiated with managers, advertized bouts, secured sites, provided prize money, and met their expenses from gate receipts.[4]

The legalization of "glove contests" and the large purses offered top pugilists by New Orleans athletic clubs encouraged the promotion of major contests. For example, on 14 January 1891 nearly 5000 fans inside the arc-lit Olympic Club saw Bob Fitzsimmons take the world middleweight championship from Jack Dempsey and win a purse of $12,000. Twenty months later, the club organized one of the finest boxing shows in history, holding lightweight, featherweight, and heavyweight championship bouts on consecutive nights. The finale on 7 September 1892 pitted heavyweight champion John L. Sullivan against James J. Corbett in the first title match fought with gloves. The San Franciscan won a $25,000 purse, plus a $10,000 side bet in his shocking upset of the toughest man in the world. The three-day carnival was a huge success and netted the

Olympic Club over $50,000. Boxing remained a popular sport in New Orleans for two more years, until the death of a local hero on 14 December 1894. A few months later a suit filed by the state attorney general reached the Louisiana Supreme Court, which ruled that the boxing matches were patently prize fights and thus illegal. This marked the end of New Orleans as the national center of boxing.[5]

In the early 1890s prize fighting staged a revival in the New York metropolitan area. A number of politically influential entrepreneurs staged some boxing shows without fear of legal redress. The bouts were mainly held at Coney Island—a wide-open resort in the town of Gravesend, Kings County (popularly known as "Sodom-by-the-Sea"), that was fast becoming a major sporting center with racetracks and boxing arenas. The local political boss, John Y. McKane, a former Democratic president of the county, was concurrently president of the Gravesend town board, chief of police, and head of both the water and health boards. It was in his building that the Coney Island Athletic Club (CIAC), organized in May 1892 by various Kings County machine politicians, held its fights. They provided the necessary protection to enable the CIAC to become the leading boxing club in the United States and to prevent other clubs in the area from holding lucrative bouts unless they got a piece of the action. In its first fifteen months in operation, the CIAC promoted sixteen cards, which netted about $150,000. However, even the CIAC was not omnipotent; early in 1893 public pressure forced it to cancel a world championship heavyweight fight between Jim Corbett and Charley Mitchell.[6]

The New York-Brooklyn metropolitan area became the leading center of boxing in the mid-1890s, especially after the passage of the Horton Act in 1896 permitted sparring matches in buildings owned by athletic associations. The Horton Act had been shepherded through the state legislature by Senator Tim Sullivan, the boss of the Bowery and the number two man in Tammany Hall. Sullivan was enormously popular with his constituents for the services he provided, but allowed vice and organized crime to flourish in his district, where he was associated with such gangsters as Monk Eastman, Kid Twist, and Paul Kelly. Sullivan had been involved in boxing clubs prior to 1896 and subsequently monopolized prize fighting in Manhattan for the next few years. In Brooklyn, the New CIAC dominated the sport under the protection of Kings County Democratic boss Hugh McLaughlin. The Horton Act did not actually permit prize fighting per se, but the police rarely enforced the letter of the law because of the political influence of club owners, the cooperation of crooked Tammany police chief William Devery, and the judgment of police commissioner Theodore Roosevelt that the rough contest he attended at Sullivan's Broadway A.C. had complied with the law.[7]

Profits for promoters came mainly from box-office receipts. Bouts at athletic clubs cost a minimum of fifty cents, double the price of some of the cheap fights held in the rear of saloons. Tickets to top-flight matches normally ran from one to three dollars, but championship fights at the turn of the century could be scaled from five to twenty-five dollars. The single biggest gate in the Horton era was the Jeffries-Corbett fight at the New CIAC on 11 May 1900, which brought in $60,000. In addition to box-office receipts, another valuable source of profits was the sale of movie rights to championship fights.[8]

In 1900 the Horton Act was repealed by upstate Republican legislators opposed to the brutality of the sport, the gambling menace, the influence of Tammany in pugilism, and disorderly urban crowds. However, repeal did not mean the end of prize fighting: boxing survived secretly in saloon back rooms, barges, and club smokers, and through the guise of the "membership clubs," ostensibly private organizations which held three-round contests fought by club "members," to entertain their peers, who paid a one dollar "fee" to join the club. These clubs were controlled by a "boxing trust" that included leading Tammanyites like Tim Sullivan, whose National A.C. reputedly had 3,000 "members." By 1908 there were fifteen clubs holding weekly bouts, and as long as they did not blatantly advertise their bouts and attract too much public attention, the police would not interfere.[9]

Prize fighting elsewhere operated, if at all, under severe restrictions. By 1905 former boxing centers like Chicago had no boxing, and Philadelphia was limited to six-round matches. Some of the major bouts in the early 1900s were held in obscure, isolated mining towns like Goldfield, Nevada, where bored and lonely miners with a lot of ready cash flocked to Tex Rickard's first big promotion, which matched lightweight champion Joe Gans and Battling Nelson. The grueling bout was won by the champion on a foul in the forty-second round. San Francisco, the center of prize fighting in that decade, was the scene of more championship fights than any other city. State law permitted matches up to twenty rounds. Local promoters needed to go through Democratic boss Abe Ruef to get their licenses—at least until 1907, when he was sent to jail for corruption, which included taking bribes from boxing promoters. But there were limits to tolerance even in San Francisco, which lost the 1910 Jeffries-Johnson championship match because of adverse public reaction throughout the state. Rickard moved the bout to Reno, Nevada, where 20,000 spectators paid a record $200,000 in anticipation of seeing "The Great White Hope" regain the title for his race.[10]

In 1911, for the first time in years, New York's Democratic party controlled the governor's mansion and both houses of the legislature. This enabled Tammany politicians to pass the Frawley Act, which legalized ten-round no-decision boxing under the supervision of a state athletic commission. The unpaid but highly politicized commission was empowered to license principals, protect the safety of boxers, and secure adequate accommodations for spectators, but it failed to halt chicanery and gambling. Promoters, still either politicians or closely tied to politicians, continued to double as managers and seconds, which was a gross conflict of interest. They did not always pay off fighters and forced men seeking bouts at neighborhood clubs to sell tickets. Worst of all, fixed bouts continued to take place.[11]

By 1917 twenty-three states had legalized boxing; however, it was still severely restricted in the major metropolitan markets in which the sport received the bulk of its support. In San Francisco, formerly a major boxing center, a restrictive state law passed in 1914 permitted only four-round bouts, and in New York the sport was under strong attack by a coalition of urban reformers and upstate rural folk. In 1915 New York state politics had reverted to form, with the Republicans back in control of the governorship and the legislature. Governor Charles Whitman appointed a Republican-dominated athletic commission which was placed on salary, but that hardly improved the quality of their work. In 1917 the chairman was ousted for extorting money from promoters and managers, and the SAC's reputation was further soiled when a fighter died in a match attended by the other two commissioners. These events convinced Whitman to ban boxing, a politically astute move that symbolized to small-town anti-urban upstate voters that his party stood for tradition and high moral values, unlike the Democrats, who had long supported an immoral blood sport with dubious connections to political machines and the underworld. Whitman's proposal to halt boxing ran into trouble in the legislature, where there was a lot of support for the sport, particularly among the Democrats. At first defeated in his efforts at repeal, the governor secured his goal only after designating the bill a party measure. Repeal passed on strict party lines without a single Democratic vote in the Senate.[12]

Although some bouts were still held under the old membership dodge, the criminalization of boxing in New York was a severe blow to the sport. However, during World War I boxing was used to train soldiers for combat. Consequently, the sport's image improved; even the reform-minded *Times* became an advocate of pugilism. Republicans prevented the resumption of legalized boxing until 1920, when Senate minority leader James J. Walker, a loyal son of Tammany, successfully guided a bill through the legislature and got it signed by Democratic Governor Al Smith. The Walker Act allowed twelve-round matches, empowered judges to decide bouts that went the distance, and established an unpaid athletic commission to supervise the sport. The new law enabled New York City to regain its position as the national center of boxing, but in the ensuing years the mobsters, rather than the machine politicians, would dominate the game.[13]

Organized Crime and Professional Boxing

Boxing in the 1920s achieved its highest status following the passage of the Walker Act, the development of Madison Square Garden into the premier site for major contests, and the rise of popular boxing idols, particularly Jack Dempsey. Championship matches at the Garden and other major venues became social affairs that drew a glittering audience of male and female celebrities who would never before have been seen at a boxing show. Other state governments emulated New York's example, legalizing boxing in order to reap windfall revenues from admission taxes. In Illinois, for instance, where the sport had been banned since 1905, pugilism was legalized in the mid-1920s in anticipation of securing a lucrative world championship bout. In 1927 Chicago got just such a contest—the Dempsey-Tunney rematch at Soldier Field, which attracted the largest fight crowd in history.[14]

Ironically, just as boxing was becoming respectable, mobsters were replacing local politicians as managers and promoters. Gangsters had long been an integral part of the boxing subculture and the tough environment that had spawned the sport. They hung out at gymnasiums, bought ringside seats, and socialized with old friends active in the fight game. In the 1920s bootleggers like Waxey Gordon in New York often either became managers of up-and-coming fighters or operated covertly behind the scenes. Fighters sometimes welcomed such backers, who used their influence to help get good bouts; however, the gangsters occasionally threatened pugilists with violence. Hoodlums involved in boxing in the 1920s and 1930s included Dutch Schultz and Owney Madden in New York, Boo Hoo Hoff in Philadelphia, and Al Capone in Chicago. By the Depression the sport's connection with organized crime was an open secret. Mobsters like Madden, "Lucky" Luciano, Thomas Lucchese, and Phil Gagliano gave behind-the-scene backing to Italian heavyweight Primo Carnera, a huge man of limited boxing ability. They used their influence to build up Carnera's reputation over the bodies of carefully chosen patsies and paid-off opponents. Carnera managed to briefly become world champion (1933–34), enriching his backers but not himself. The bootleggers backed fighters because they enjoyed the celebrity status of associating with professional athletes, especially world champions, just as they liked to squire pretty young women to night clubs. Gangsters also made a lot of money from their share of the purses of contenders and champions and used their position to arrange betting coups by fixing fights.[15]

Between the mid-1930s and late 1950s the prime mover in professional boxing was Frankie Carbo, also known as the shadowy "Mr. Big." Carbo was a dangerous gangster whose arrest record included five murder indictments. In one case he was indicted, together with Bugsy Siegel and Lepke Buchalter, the head of Murder, Inc., for the gang land killing of Mo "Big Greenie" Schecter. They were eventually acquitted in 1942 after the state's key witness fell from a window to his death, despite twenty-four-hour police protection. Carbo started out in boxing in the 1930s, gained a virtual monopoly over the middleweight division, and then, over the next two decades, influenced all divisions. Because of his close ties to managers, matchmakers, and promoters, Carbo could arrange or prevent matches, and he used any means necessary to gain control of fighters, including having managers taken on car rides and giving them offers they could not refuse.[16]

Because Carbo was a convicted felon and therefore ineligible for a license, he could not personally manage a fighter. Instead he used front men, some of whom were Jewish businessmen, while others, such as Gabe Genovese (cousin of Vito Genovese, the head of organized crime in the 1950s) and Blinky Palermo, Philadelphia numbers king, had more questionable backgrounds. Palermo was best known as the manager of lightweight champion Ike Williams and of Sonny Liston before he became heavyweight champion. Williams had tried to manage himself in the mid-1940s but was blacklisted by the Boxing Managers' Guild and could not even get sparring partners, much less a fight. When Palermo became his manager, Williams immediately got good fights. Within a year he was champion. However, Williams's purses as champion (1947–50) always went directly to Palermo, and in at least three defenses, Williams received not one cent for his fights.[17]

Carbo controlled several of the leading matchmakers, such as Billy Brown at Madison Square Garden, because they got their jobs through him. Brown was constantly in touch with Carbo by phone, although he was discreet enough to use a public telephone instead of an office line. Brown, who could always be counted on to do his patron's bidding, at times arranged cards in which both main-event fighters were managed by Carbo's front men. Mr. Big's influence extended from the East to the West Coast, particularly to the Los Angeles Olympic Club, whose corrupt matchmakers and promoters often required managers of fighters who appeared at the LAOC to share their purses with them.[18]

One fighter badly stymied by this system was Jake LaMotta, the number one middleweight contender from 1943 to 1947. LaMotta had stubbornly tried to manage himself but lacked the necessary influence to get a title match and refused to allow Carbo to take him on. Finally, disgusted with his lack of progress, LaMotta accepted an offer from the Carbo camp to fix a fight against promising light-heavyweight Billy Fox, managed by Blinky Palermo. In return, LaMotta was guaranteed $100,000 and a title shot. The fight was a total sham: LaMotta refused to attack, going into an uncharacteristic shell, and Fox could not land any solid blows. The referee stopped the bout in the fourth round on a TKO, with most everyone in the audience sure that a fix was in. A subsequent investigation cleared La Motta, but the stink was so bad that he could not get his title fight until 1949. He then had to pay champion Marcel Cerdan $20,000 to get the match—$1,000 more than the challenger's share of the purse.[19]

Such chicanery flourished because prize fighting was virtually unregulated, especially outside of New York, which had the most responsible state athletic commission. Commissioners—usually political hacks—rarely enforced licensing rules, and their staffs lacked sufficient time or money to thoroughly investigate applicants for licenses. Since there was little interstate cooperation, men rejected for licenses in New York were often approved elsewhere. The absence of tight supervision made fixing a fight easy—either to facilitate a betting coup or to bolster the reputation of a young fighter. Clever trainers could overtrain a fighter so he would leave his fight in the gym, alter the pugilist's weight too rapidly and thereby weaken him, tape his hands too tightly so he would have difficulty maneuvering, or even dope his oranges. There were also less sophisticated and more direct methods—bribing fighters, managers, or referees (part-time employees who might not get rehired if uncooperative) and threatening the use of violence, which could never be taken as an idle warning.[20]

Besides his close ties to managers and matchmakers, Carbo also had important connections with the major promoters of the day, such as Sam Silverman in Boston, Benny Geigerman in New Orleans, Larry Atkins in Cleveland, and Mike Jacobs in New York (the leading boxing promoter in the country)—all upwardly mobile Jewish entrepreneurs. During his tenure at Madison Square Garden (1937–49) Jacobs staged 37.5 percent of all American championship fights. Carbo boasted in 1947 that he did everything for Jacobs except sign the contracts. In 1949 Jacobs retired due to ill health, and a new organization, the International Boxing Club (IBC), was created to promote major boxing matches. The principals were two extremely rich men—James Norris, president of Madison Square Garden, and Arthur Wirtz, a Chicago realtor and Norris's partner in the Detroit Olympia and the Chicago Stadium. Their junior partner was Joe Louis, who, in return for a share of the business, had retired as heavyweight champion and agreed to help stage a Tournament of Champions to select his successor. Between 1949 and 1953 the IBC staged 80 percent of all the championship fights held in the United States. In addition, it controlled many major arenas and dominated the lucrative television market. The networks broadcast fights on Wednesday, Friday, and Saturday. The principal sponsor was Gillette, which paid $100,000 for the privilege of hosting the Friday Night Fights. Since there were so many fights on television, the promoters needed a steady supply of quality fighters to fill the demand. Carbo was the man they counted on to supply the boxers through his various fronts. The IBC developed a cozy relationship with Carbo and even hired his wife as an $11,000-a-year consultant.[21]

In 1953 the Justice Department instituted antitrust proceedings against the IBC for monopolizing major boxing bouts. Two years later the courts ruled that the IBC had conspired to monopolize championship fights; it held exclusive contracts with virtually every contender, controlled key arenas and stadiums, and had negotiated preferential contracts with CBS. The case eventually went to the Supreme Court and resulted in the breakup of the IBC in 1959.[22]

The increased public attention given to boxing because of the IBC case and Senate investigations into organized crime failed to halt the use of strong-arm tactics by Carbo and other mobsters. Their targets included Nat Fleischer, publisher of Ring magazine. Once, when Fleischer failed to rank a particular Carbo fighter in the "top ten," he was warned that his magazine would be taken off the rack of every New York newsstand. Apparently this threat was never carried out, but warnings could not be disregarded. In 1952, when the great trainer Ray Arcel was promoting a number of televised boxing shows, he refused to do business with the corrupt International Boxing Managers Guild. As a result, he was severely beaten by a hoodlum wielding a lead pipe. In 1959 Carbo and his associates tried to muscle in on welterweight champion Don Jordan, and when Jordan's manager, Don Nesseth, refused to pay half of his manager's share to Blinky Palermo, Nesseth was told in no uncertain terms that a lot of people would be unhappy. His colleague Jackie Leonard, the promoter at Hollywood's Legion Stadium, soon received phone calls warning that he would be made an example unless Nesseth cooperated. Palermo, accompanied by some unsavory characters, visited Leonard a number of times, admonishing him once, "We'll get even," and later, "Your head's in a noose." When Leonard was subsequently beaten up by Palermo's goons, he went to the authorities. Carbo, Palermo, and their colleagues were arrested, indicted, found guilty of extortion, and given lengthy prison sentences.[23] Though the underworld continued to play a significant role in the sport, organized crime's control over boxing suffered a severe blow.

Thoroughbred Racing

Politics dominated not only the "sport of pugs," but also the "sport of kings." Despite the aristocratic image of the turf, church leaders and other moral reformers scrutinized racing severely because the sport was almost totally dependent upon betting for its appeal and survival. Moral objections, abuse of animals and the sport's close ties to machine politics and urban crime syndicates resulted in widespread banning of horse racing at the turn of the century, including for a period of time in Chicago, New Orleans, and New York. The survival of the sport depended heavily on the political influence of leading horsemen and professional gamblers. In those cities in which the turf was most successful, including Brooklyn, Chicago, New Orleans, New York, and St. Louis, it was dominated by politically active elites and machine politicians. New York's wealthy traction magnates like William C. Whitney, Thomas Fortune Ryan, and August Belmont II used their participation in racing to facilitate cross-class coalitions in the Democratic party that helped them protect their franchises. These rich sportsmen, along with machine politicians like Tammany boss Richard Croker and Tim Sullivan, owned and bred thoroughbreds, wagered heavily, and some even owned racetracks. Sullivan and other machine politicians were also prominent in the business of betting as organizers and protectors of bookmakers and off-track poolroom (betting parlor) syndicates. The elite and plebeian members of the sporting fraternity worked together on such issues of mutual concern as the legalization of on-track betting but could become bitter enemies when off-track betting cut into track attendance and harmed the prestige of the turf.[24]

In the 1870s all major American racetracks had important political connections to maintain legislative approval of gambling at the tracks. Members of the AJC in 1870 included not only club president August Belmont, chairman of the national Democratic party, but also Tammanyites Peter Sweeney and William Tweed. Tweed was also an investor in Monmouth Park Racetrack, established in 1870 by gambler Joseph Chamberlain, who was trying to make Long Branch, New Jersey, into a second Saratoga. Other interested parties included robber barons Jay Gould and Jim Fisk, Jr, who "practically owned the Legislature." In New Orleans, younger members of the Metarie JC who wanted to put the sport on a business-like basis formed a new organization, the Louisiana Jockey Club (LJC). The LJC raced at the old Union Course (later known as the Fair

Grounds) under the supervision of influential Republican politician Charles T. Howard, director of the infamous Louisiana State Lottery. The LJC tried to bolster attendance by introducing cheaper ticket prices and relying on the parimutuel system, first introduced in America at Jerome Park in 1871, which gave the track a direct and active role in gambling. Little is known about the profitability of the LJC, which made about $9,000 during the spring 1875 meet but was forced to close three years later because of the cost of purchasing and improving the Fair Grounds.[25]

Successful track operators needed to know not only how to balance their budgets, but also how to circumvent the various legal barriers to gambling, the backbone of the sport. In 1877, in response to the widespread wagering on the Tilden-Hayes election, the New York state legislature passed a law banning the old auction pool betting system. This was expected to hurt track attendance; however, the turf continued to flourish, largely because of the introduction of bookmaking. Unlike the auction system, in which large bettors could monopolize the wagering on favorites, the bookmaking system enabled a bettor to select any horse he wished at the odds publicly posted by bookmakers. The minimum bet was generally two dollars, less than the minimum five dollars under the parimutuel system, and helped democratize the sport.[26]

In the 1880s and 1890s political connections became even more prominent than ever before, especially among the various proprietary profit-oriented tracks that lacked the prestige and social cachet of the elite jockey clubs. These tracks ranged from modestly appointed facilities that put on a few stakes races to blatantly corrupt outlaw grounds that catered to low lifers. In the 1880s Coney Island became a major racing center for both elite and proprietary tracks in the New York metropolitan area. Local boss John Y. McKane was expected to protect the tracks from rigorous enforcement of the anti-gambling penal codes. His construction company received, hardly coincidentally, many lucrative projects at the new tracks. In June 1879 a politically well-connected hotel owner, William A. Engeman, established the proprietary Brighton Beach Racetrack, which by 1882 was netting $200,000 a year. It was followed a year later by the prestigious new Coney Island Jockey Club (CIJC), whose leaders—Leonard Jerome, August Belmont, William K. Vanderbilt, and Pierre Lorillard, Jr.—organized the important Sheepshead Bay Racetrack. Finally, in 1885 the proprietary Gravesend Track was constructed by the politically astute Dwyer brothers, noted plungers who had made a fortune as butchers. Under the protection of local Democratic politicians, pool selling flourished at these tracks. A Republican district attorney in Kings County originally tried to suppress racetrack gambling but failed to obtain a single conviction out of fifty-seven indictments. His Democratic successor never interfered during the racing season, conveniently waiting until the end of meets before making a show of compliance with the laws.[27]

In 1887 representatives of New York racing interests secured the passage of the Ives Anti-Poolroom Law, which forbade off-track betting but allowed wagering at the tracks. This caused a boom in racing and betting and led to the formation of the Metropolitan Turf Alliance (MTA) a year later. The MTA, an association of over sixty well-connected bookmakers, sought to monopolize the bookmaking privilege at New York tracks, which cost each of them as much as $100 a day. Its secretary was a young politician named Timothy D. Sullivan. In 1889 the racing boom also led John A. Morris to build palatial Morris Park Racetrack in Westchester, to replace Jerome Park, which the city had purchased for a reservoir. Morris, a politically well-connected member of an old New York family and father of a Tammany assemblyman, had made his fortune operating the Louisiana Lottery.[28]

The most infamous outlaw proprietary tracks were in New Jersey, in close proximity to New York and Philadelphia. In 1885 the Guttenberg Track opened in the town of Guttenberg, Hudson County, a short ferry ride from New York. Its principal owners were professional gamblers and machine politicians, including the Democratic county boss who used his clout to keep the track operating without interference even though gambling was illegal in the state. At the southern tip of New Jersey was the equally notorious Gloucester Racetrack, a ferry ride across the Delaware River from Philadelphia. Gloucester was opened in 1890 by the local Democratic boss, Assemblyman William A. Thompson, who was so powerful that in 1893 he got the starter at his racetrack elected speaker of the state assembly. These two outlaw tracks reputedly earned $2,500 a day. They were infamous for lacking any standards of integrity, permitting second-rate horses to run, allowing year-round racing, even during blinding snowstorms and dense fog, and having had a remarkably large number of dubious contests. In 1893 the Democratically controlled legislature legalized on-track betting; since the outlaw tracks were operating regardless of the law anyhow, this benefited mainly respectable Monmouth Park and the proprietary tracks near New York in Clifton and Elizabeth. The passage of the Parker Acts led to enormous public outrage against the turf which culminated in the surprising 1893 elections, in which the Democrats lost control of the legislature because of the gambling issue. In 1894 Republican foes of betting repealed the Parker Acts and effectively ended thoroughbred racing in New Jersey for nearly fifty years.[29]

Throughout the country it was difficult for proprietary tracks to operate without strong ties to local political bosses, but even those connections could not guarantee success. For example, in Chicago, the midwestern center of racing, the business-oriented tracks on the West Side were closely tied to prominent Chicago politicos. West Side Track was run in the 1880s by a syndicate of bookmakers who sold it in 1887 to Edward Corrigan, a prominent horseman who had considerable political influence in the city. Corrigan encountered a lot of opposition from politically well-connected bookmakers tied to Mike McDonald, a major power in Chicago's Democratic party and purportedly the head of organized crime in the city. In 1891 Corrigan left the city for a new site further west in Cicero, where he hoped to free himself from the entanglement of Chicago politics. His lease on West Side Track was assumed by a syndicate of Chicago's most influential gamblers, including Harry Varnell, John Condon, George Hankins, and Mike McDonald. Competition between the suburban Hawthorne Racetrack and the newly named Garfield Park was fierce. Both tracks occasionally let in spectators for free just to get bettors in. The bookmakers ran Garfield Park as an outlaw track and kept open until the onset of winter. They expected their political allies at City Hall, like aldermen John Coughlin and Johnny Powers, the "Prince of Boodlers," would protect them against reform opposition to their scandalous operations and community opposition to the prostitutes, pickpockets, and shoulder hitters who were attracted to the track and frightened respectable neighborhood residents. But the two inner-city ward bosses could not prevent crusading Republican Mayor Hempstead Washburne from closing the track in 1892. Two years later, the prestigious Washington Park course closed voluntarily in deference to public opinion, and in 1895 Hawthorne was closed through the efforts of the Civic Federation and other municipal reformers.[30]

Racing at this time was nearly banned in New York. A coalition of social reformers, clergymen, opponents of Tammany Hall, and racing fans alienated by greedy track operators and repeated rumors of fixes got the State Constitutional Convention meeting in September 1894 to adopt an article totally banning turf gambling, and when the draft was approved in a referendum, the end of racing appeared imminent. However, racing interests waged an all-out campaign to save the sport. Early in 1895 powerful friends in Albany passed legislation that created a state racing commission to supervise the sport in conjunction with the Jockey Club, a year-old elite organization that was single-handedly trying to save thoroughbred racing by establishing national standards of conduct and behavior and forcing horsemen to boycott tracks that did not meet its strict criterion. TJC president August Belmont II was appointed head of the new racing board.[31]

As important as political connections were in keeping racetracks open in the face of moral opposition to gambling, they were doubly important when it came to off-track betting. While betters who went out to the racetracks could at least be considered sportsmen interested in improving the breed, off-track gamblers were simply men out to make easy money. Betters who could not afford to visit the track or take time off from work took their business either to neighborhood bookmakers found at such male bastions as newsstands, barbershops, or saloons, or to off-track betting parlors. These poolrooms, distinct from billiard rooms, were located in vice districts like the Tenderloin in New York, certain inner-city residential neighborhoods, and even the CBD, and accepted bets as small as one dollar, which bookmakers at the tracks would not accept. The press and social reformers universally castigated poolrooms for ruining young clerks and artisans who wasted their hard-earned money gambling and were sometimes driven to embezzlement and other crimes to pay for their debts.[32]

Off-track betting occurred all over the country but was especially prominent in Chicago and New York, the nation's largest cities, which had great potential markets and powerful political machines to protect the professional gamblers. The poolrooms got their race results from Western Union, whose racing department made about $20,000 a week—the most profitable part of the company. In 1890 the telegraph company paid about $1,600 a day to each New York track for the exclusive privilege of transmitting race results, but when tracks realized they would be hurt in the long run by poolroom competition, the major New York racetracks decided to bar Western Union from their facilities. Wire service employees were forced to sneak into the tracks and use their ingenuity to report race results to confederates waiting outside.[33]

Despite the Ives Anti-Poolroom Law and the Saxton Act of 1893, which made the keeping of a poolroom a felony, New York's poolrooms operated with near impunity. Reformers like Anthony Comstock of the Society for the Suppression of Vice or the police instigated occasional raids, but the poolroom operators were well protected by Tammany mayors like Hugh Grant and Tammany-appointed judges and by payoffs to prominent politicians and policemen. Most raids served just for publicity or to close down rooms that were not paying off. Poolroom clerks, forewarned of an impending raid, would clear out before the authorities arrived. On the rare occasion when a poolroom operator or an employee was arrested, he was usually acquitted by a cooperative judge or given a token fine. By the mid-1890s the business was being masterminded by Tim Sullivan, who organized a poolroom trust that included such leading gamblers as "The Allen" and Frank Farrell, owner after the turn of the century of the city's most luxurious casino along with the New York Highlanders (Yankees). The syndicate controlled as many as 400 rooms, which paid from sixty to 300 dollars a week to stay in business. Although some poolrooms were hidden in the backs of saloons or cigar stores or under the guise of some other business like a bucket shop, most operated pretty openly. In 1902, when Sullivan went to Washington to serve in Congress, the syndicate's profits were estimated at $3.6 million. Three of his chief associates—Farrell, Peter DeLacey, and Jere Mahoney—each subsequently set up his own syndicate but kept closely tied to Sullivan, described by journalist Josiah Flynt as "the most scandalous individual in the pool-room Griff in the United States."[34]

Chicago did not have a city-wide gambling syndicate like New York's. In part this reflected the absence of a powerful city-wide political machine. Instead, at the turn of the century each of the city's three major geographical divisions, plus the Loop (CBD), had its own handbook chief, usually a neighborhood boss who dominated the poolroom business in conjunction with the local police captain. James O'Leary controlled the South Side, alderman Johnnie Rogers the West Side, Mont Tennes the North Side, and aldermen Hinky Dink Kenna and Bathhouse John Coughlin, plus others, the downtown area. They originally received race news from Western Union, but in 1904, Helen Gould, one of the company's leading stockholders, forced it out of the business on moral grounds. The successor was the Payne Telegraph Service, established by a former telegraph operator. In 1907 Tennes purchased the exclusive rights to the racing wire in Chicago for $300, and within two years had employed that monopoly to gain control of the city's handbook business. This was a remarkable accomplishment because Tennes was a political independent (though he did contribute huge amounts to mayoral campaigns) and also had to survive a vicious bombing war with his opponents. In the meantime, the Payne Company was struggling against gangsters who were trying to muscle in on its profitable business. Finally, in 1911, its chief rival, Tennes's General News Bureau, took over Payne. Tennes thus gained a near national monopoly over the racing wires and supplied race results all across the country. His most profitable outlets were in Chicago, where he serviced ninety outlets for $3,600 a week, and New York, where seventy poolrooms paid him a total of $4,000 a week. Chicago rooms that dared subscribe to a rival betting service were subjected to firebombings or were closed by the police on Tennes's behalf.[35]

Thoroughbred racing's greatest crisis came in the spring of 1908, when progressive Governor Charles Evans Hughes of New York mounted a full-scale campaign to eliminate on-track gambling, which he regarded as a moral outrage and a blatant violation of the state constitution, which had banned it in 1894. Thoroughbred racing was then enormously profitable, and the local tracks were coming off record grosses the previous season. The CJIC had taken in around one million dollars for a thirty day meet which yielded a profit of about $400,000, and the Brooklyn Jockey Club had done almost as well. The governor put his prestige on the line with his antigambling crusade, though at first few observers expected him to succeed because of the sport's popularity and its considerable political and economic clout, which included a $500,000 war chest for bribes and publicity. The Hughes-sponsored Agnew-Hart bill prohibiting track betting passed the Assembly but was defeated in the Senate by a tie vote based on party and urban-rural divisions. However, the governor persevered, and he gained the missing vote when a vacant senate seat from traditionally Republican western New York was filled in a special election by a candidate who shared his abhorrence of gambling. In June the governor convened a special session of the legislature, which passed the Agnew-Hart Act. This victory was described by a Hughes biographer as his "most dramatic venture in the area of moral reform."[36]

This important effort by urban progressives and conservative WASPs to exercise social control over city folk did not immediately succeed. The major metropolitan tracks stayed in business, though at great sacrifice (attendance dropped by two-thirds), by adopting the English system of oral betting. Since the bookies did not keep written records in this betting format, the police could not gather evidence that would stand up in court. In 1910 a new gambling law (the Agnew-Perkins Act) was passed with the intention of stopping oral betting by making track operators liable for any gambling violations at their tracks, even if they had no personal knowledge of the crime. This forced the local tracks to close, and there was no thoroughbred racing in New York until 1913, when the courts ruled that track managers were answerable only if they had wittingly permitted bookmakers to operate. The result was that Empire City (Yonkers) and the three Long Island tracks, including the prestigious Belmont Park (established in 1905), reopened, employing the oral betting system. However, the other facilities, including historic Sheepshead Bay, remained shut forever.[37]

Politics, Organized Crime, and the Revival of the Turf

Horse racing in America enjoyed a great revival after World War I. Between 1918 and 1920 purses more than doubled to $7.7 million and nearly doubled again by 1926, when they reached $13.9 million. In the 1920s the number of thoroughbreds doubled and the total number of races increased by 60 percent to 11,477. The rapid expansion of the turf owed a great deal to the growing political influence of new immigrants who worked together with the Irish to legalize racetrack gambling. These ethnic groups enjoyed gambling and opposed the efforts of rural WASPs to exercise social control over their behavior. State governments at this time were becoming receptive to the concept of legalized racing and on-track betting because of the clout of inner-city Democratic machines, the support of urban voters for gambling, growing pressure from racing interests, and the recognition that legalized betting could provide a valuable source of badly needed revenues. These factors all contributed to the complete resumption of racing in Chicago in the late 1920s. The former center of midwestern racing, Chicago's tracks had rarely operated after 1905 because of public fears of the gambling menace. In 1922 Hawthorne opened on the border of Stickney and Cicero, employing evasive oral betting schemes. Then in 1927 the state legislature legalized parimutuel betting, which led to the opening of the suburban Arlington Racetrack in 1927 and Sportsman's Park in Cicero in 1932. Both tracks initiated the parimutuel betting system, which by this time was regarded by bettors as the fairest and most honest, instead of bookmaking, which had damaged the turf's reputation by its ties to local political machines and organized crime. By the end of the 1920s, thirty-four tracks were in operation in the United States, of which 70 percent had opened since the war.[38]

The turf, like all other popular entertainments, was hurt by the coming of the Depression. Purses dropped, even for states races like the Preakness, by as much as 50 percent, and attendances also plummeted. Yet in the long run, the poor economy helped the sport because the urgent need of state governments for funds encouraged many legislators to vote to legalize racing. Underworld bribes also helped. The strongest support for racing still came from large cities in which two-thirds of the voters favored on-track gambling. In a 1933 California referendum which led to the resumption of racing there, 76.3 percent of San Franciscans supported legalization. Even in the more pietistic, WASPish city of Los Angeles, 60.1 percent voted for the referendum. In Illinois, Chicago machine Democrats and their underworld allies tried to go even further and legalize off-track bookmaking. In 1935 such a bill passed the legislature to raise money for teachers' salaries. Despite extraordinary political pressure from old family friends and political allies, Governor Henry Horner vetoed the measure. As punishment, the machine slated someone else as the party's candidate in 1936, but Horner, who had become a hero outside the city for his courageous stand, was renominated and reelected anyhow. By the end of the Depression thoroughbred racing was permitted in eighteen states, including such northern industrial states badly hit by the Depression as Michigan and Ohio as well as sunbelt states like California, Texas, and Florida, which hoped that legalized racing would promote tourism and thereby improve their economics.[39]

The politicization of the sport of kings did not end with the legalization of the turf. Jockey clubs and promoters who wanted to operate tracks needed political muscle to secure the necessary licenses and choice racing dates from their respective state racing commissions and thereafter needed to stay on good terms with the supervising body. Since strong political opposition could close tracks, they often sold stock to prominent public officials for a fraction of the market cost, provided jobs or contracts for patronage, gave politicos their insurance business, or simply bribed them in order to maintain their political leverage. For example, during the Depression Rockingham Park in Salem, New Hampshire, employed thirty-two state legislators, including the local political boss, the politico who had led the fight to legalize betting in the state, and the governor's brother. The justification was that all racetracks employed political workers and that the legislators had earned their small retainers. In nearby Rhode Island, publisher Walter E. O'Hara had a hard time keeping Narragansett Park in Providence open during the late 1930s because his political faction opposed Governor Robert E. Quinn and he used his money and the *News-Tribune* to bring down the governor. The state racing commission tried to take his license away but was blocked by the courts. Quinn followed up by declaring martial law at the track and temporarily closed Narragansett. Political connections were even more important in states where racing was illegal, like Missouri. Riverside Park, just outside Kansas City, was able to operate only because of connections to the Pendergast machine.[40]

In the 1930s and 1940s racetracks were usually operated as joint stock companies, though some were privately owned, and a few, like the New Orleans Fair Grounds, were run by not-for-profit organizations. The most prestigious tracks, such as Belmont Park, were controlled by elite jockey clubs dominated by scions of such old elite families as the Vanderbilts, Wideners, and Whitneys, who were more interested in improving the breed and less concerned about profits than entrepreneurial-minded owners. A love of sport and an eye on future profits undoubtedly influenced the Wideners and Whitneys to invest in Florida tracks like Gulfstream and Hialeah, which opened in the midst of the Depression. Several important tracks were also owned by men of new wealth, such as Benjamin Lindheimer, a politically connected realtor who operated Arlington Park from 1940 to 1960, in order to make money and enhance their social prestige. Lindheimer was an opportunist who had grown up with Governor Horner and served in his administration until he dumped him to support Chicago Mayor Edward Kelley's fight for legalized off-track gambling in return for the promise of a racetrack in the future. In Los Angeles the new tracks in the 1930s were owned by such Hollywood celebrities as Hal Roach, Bing Crosby, and Harry M. Warner.[41]

Racetracks were potentially very lucrative investments when located near large cities whose residents enjoyed gambling, where there was cheap mass transit, and when the management had the clout necessary to secure good racing dates. Even during the Depression a number of tracks turned profits—most notably Rockingham Park. Purchased for $100,000 in 1931, although it did not open until 1933, Rockingham earned $1.5 million over the next six years. The Salem track flourished because it was readily accessible to Boston, and Massachusetts proscribed horse race betting. Dividends were generally more modest elsewhere, although huge profits could be made by selling stock. Hollywood Park, established in 1938 by movie mogul Harry Warner, paid 20-percent dividends in its first two seasons, and 10 percent in the third. Nearby Santa Anita Racetrack, opened in 1934, earned back its capital investment in just one year. Stock-holders became accustomed to 25-to-30 percent annual dividends, and by 1947 the value of shares had escalated by 1300 percent. Racetracks even made money during the war, despite government-imposed restrictions such as on transportation. In 1944 New York's tracks, which in 1940 had finally been allowed to introduce parimutuels instead of bookmaking, made a 15 percent profit.[42]

After the Depression public interest in turf sports and gambling led to a revival of harness racing as an urban sport. For most of the century, with the exception of the Grand Circuit, the sport had been largely relegated to state fairs and rural tracks. The rebirth began in New York State in 1940 once parimutuel betting was approved and a harness racing commission was organized to issue licenses, set dates for meets, and otherwise su-pervise the sport. The most important site was Roosevelt Raceway, an abandoned half-mile automobile track at Westbury, Long Island, leased in 1940 by George Morton Levy, a politically prominent attorney. The track initiated dash races, instead of heat matches, to enhance betting oppor-tunities and night time racing to increase the chances for working-class fans to attend after work. Bettors reached Roosevelt by private automobile or public transportation. After the war its format became the model for other major facilities like Maywood Park (1946) just outside Chicago and Yonkers Raceway (1950).[43]

The new trotting associations and harness tracks were from the start closely associated with prominent political leaders and syndicate crime figures, who quickly made some extraordinary profits. The initial $25,000 investment by Levy and his partners in the Old Country Trotting Association was worth $14 million by 1954. Levy himself made $3 mil-lion in legal fees and stock appreciation. Levy and other racing moguls sold stock at bargain rates to legislators who helped pass the parimutuel laws and to other politicians in high places who could assist, or hinder, the track's operations. These secret transactions, often in the names of friends or relatives, were revealed in a 1954 Pulitzer-Prize-winning exposé by *Newsday*. In 1953, 35 percent of the stock in all the New York state harness tracks belonged to professional politicians, including all of the stock in the Buffalo Trotting Association, approximately 30 percent of the Nassau TA, and over 40 percent of the Yonkers TA. One who benefited most was J. Russel Sprague, the chief executive of Nassau County. In 1945 the Republican leader paid $2,000 for 40 percent of the Cedar Point Trotting Association, which got the seventh, and last, state license to conduct gambling harness meets. Ten months later Sprague sold his CPTA stock for $195,000. In 1947, after the CPTA went out of business, Sprague secured $1,000 worth of shares in its successor, the Nassau Trotting Association, which he sold in 1953 for $64,000. In 1950 he purchased $80,000 of stock in the new Yonkers TA, which paid him $88,000 in dividends over the next three years.[44]

The substantial profits, the excitement of the turf, and its historic connections with gambling attracted avid underworld interest. According to historian Humbert Nelli, a substantial number, if not the majority, of thoroughbred tracks in the 1930s "came under the influence or control of criminal syndicates," and the situation in harness racing was not very different. Hoodlums invested in the turf to gain prestige among their peers and greater acceptance in the broader society; to symbolize their financial success; to make legitimate profits from admissions, betting, parking, and concessions; to skim off money from a cash-rich business; to facilitate illegal gambling and fix races; to launder ill-gotten gains; and to secure jobs for members of their syndicates as subcontractors, ticket sellers, or labor racketeers. Labor racketeers extorted huge sums of money by shaking down high-paid track employees or by demanding payments from unions and management for "protection," or from track operators to prevent strikes and guarantee garbage collection. To keep the peace the tracks "hired certain corrupt union officials as labor consultants." Underworld threats could never be taken lightly; in 1953 a union leader at Yonkers was murdered in a struggle over spoils.[45]

Bootleggers, former bootleggers, and gamblers involved in the turf often got their first experience in the less glamourous sport of dog racing. The mechanical rabbit was invented in 1909 by Oliver P. Smith, who, in partnership with St. Louis politician Edward O'Hare, made the sport a success in the 1920s. O'Hare, who was convicted in 1923 for participation in a bootlegging operation, helped establish a track outside Kansas City in cooperation with local bootleggers and politicians and then moved on to Miami Beach to do the same with Phil Ball, owner of the St. Louis Browns. He was recruited in 1928 to operate the Hawthorne Kennel Club in Cicero for Al Capone, Frank Nitti, and other members of Capone's mob. Dog racing was illegal in Cicero, but with the backing of powerful gangsters and bribes in the proper pockets, the contests went on uninterrupted. The track's main problem was competition from the Fairview Track, owned by South Side mobster Bugs Moran, but that matter was largely alleviated after the St. Valentine's Day Massacre. Capone became a major figure in the sport and took charge of the International Greyhound Association, which in the mid-1930s controlled dog racing in Miami, Tampa, and Jacksonville, where it was not. In 1934 Eddie O'Hare orchestrated the legalization of dog racing in Massachusetts with the support of the governor, Boston Mayor James M. Curley, and legislative leaders who anticipated the creation of new jobs and badly needed revenue for local governments. Three dog tracks opened in the state in the 1930s, and in at least one the majority stockholders were former bootleggers.[46]

The influence of the mob was less pervasive in horse racing than with the greyhounds because the turf was older, better established, and more prestigious, but their presence was still very significant. In 1931, after racing was legalized in Florida, Canadian bootleggers financed the conversion of Tropical Park, located near Coral Gables, from a dog track to a horse racing track under the management of "Big Bill" Dwyer. Dwyer was a major bootlegger and partner of the notorious Frank Costello and owned the New York Americans hockey team and several nightclubs, including the Stork Club. Three years later the track was reputedly purchased by a syndicate that included Meyer Lansky, who was also involved in Gulfstream Park, bookmaker Frank Erickson, and several leading Chicago hoodlums. In the meanwhile, in 1932 in Chicago O'Hare expanded from dog tracks into a thoroughbred facility (Sportsman's Park) which he was operating at the time of his murder in 1939. After World War II the underworld got involved in harness racing and expanded their thoroughbred racing interests. Costello and Erickson's son and son-in-law owned stock in New York harness tracks. Detroit hoodlums Pete Licavoli and Joseph Zerilli ran Wheeling Downs in Wheeling, West Virginia, from 1946 until the mid-1950s, when they sold out to William Lias, a Prohibition era hoodlum, and Zerilli and his associates operated Hazel Park in Detroit in the 1950s and early 1960s. In Massachusetts, Raymond Patricia and Tony Lucchese controlled Berkshire Downs and Patricia also controlled Scarborough Downs. These gangsters were often closely allied to state politicians who had influence over the approval of license applications, the awarding of racing dates, and the operations of the state agency supervising the turf and to local politicos who controlled the various municipal services track operators might require. These connections were sustained by bribes, patronage opportunities, and the sale of stock at deflated prices.[47]

The racing boom led to a rapid growth in illegal off-track betting, especially during the Depression when "handbooks, horse-rooms, telephone offices, tipster bureaus and the racing wire-service began doing bigger business than ever before as millions dreamed of getting out of hock with the horses." The clientele was primarily working-class urbanites—typically Irish, Jewish, Italian, or black residents of the inner city—who bet one or two dollars a race. They regarded their gambling as highly rational behavior which provided them with an opportunity to utilize their "expertise" as rich people did in the stock market. These bettors preferred neighborhood bookies to the tracks; they could save time, travel expenses, and taxes by patronizing bookies, who also extended credit.[48]

Illegal off-track gambling was dominated by professional gamblers and ex-bootleggers. As Mark Haller has pointed out, "Bookmakers understood horse racing and the statistical skills necessary to balance the books. . . . Among bookmakers there were established relationships with race wires, with local tracks and with politicians." Gamblers not only had expertise in betting but also experience dealing with wagering clients. Bootleggers got involved in the business because they themselves were fans and betters who attended every big sporting event; many were former professional gamblers; and all recognized the huge profits available in a victimless crime that would not attract much public outrage. Haller points out that these gangsters came to gambling with the advantage of having working relations with the police and urban politicians, experience in the use of violence, and familiarity with organizational structures with regional and national connections.[49]

In the 1920s bookmaking underwent important changes. Instead of the old highly personal contact between bookie and client in the barbershop or saloon, there was widespread use of the telephone to transmit wagers. Furthermore, the old protected neighborhood bookmaking syndicates of the turn of the century had begun to die out and were replaced by the layoff system. Under this system bookmakers who had too much money bet on a particular horse would try to even off potential losses by betting on that horse with a bigger bookmaker. This system was reputedly pioneered by Arnold Rothstein and carried on after his murder in 1928 by Frank Erickson. Erickson's partner, ex-bootlegger Frank Costello, utilized his political protection to operate for over twenty years in Bergen County, New Jersey, without any interference. He himself owned a lot of stock in the Tropical Park Racetrack, where he would lay off a lot of his bets over the phone. After Prohibition, former bootleggers coordinated and sponsored bookmaking in metropolitan New York, Chicago, and Miami, usually in cooperation with old-time gamblers who they financed and provided with political protection. However, Haller has found little evidence that the old bootleggers extended their influence into the South or West during the 1930s and 1940s, although he argues they were crucial in maintaining regional gambling centers like Covington, Kentucky, and in creating new centers, especially Las Vegas after World War II.[50]

Until 1927 bookmakers still got their race results primarily from Mont Tennes, but that year he sold out to Moe Annenberg, who quickly developed a virtual monopoly over the wire services. Second-generation Jews whose family had migrated to Chicago from East Prussia in the 1870s, Annenberg and his brothers were circulation managers for the Hearst news chain at the turn of the century. That entailed recruiting young toughs who "persuaded" vendors to sell only Hearst papers and hide the rest. In the 1920s Annenberg established a communications empire by securing the two major racing papers, the *Daily Racing Form* and the *Morning Telegraph*, along with various tip and scratch sheets, and then added the racing wires. In 1940, when he was sent to jail for tax evasion, he gave up the racing wires. Two rival firms were organized to fill the vacuum—the Continental News Service by Annenberg's protégé, James Ragen, and Trans-America by Jake Guzik, one of Al Capone's chief lieutenants. The competition ended abruptly in 1946, when Ragen was assassinated and his company was taken over by Guzik's henchmen.[51]

Professional Baseball

Urban politicians played an influential role in professional baseball from its earliest days. However, unlike pugilism and the turf, which operated under severe legal constraints and social opprobrium, baseball did not need to circumvent antigambling laws or operate in violation of the penal codes. The national pastime, the preeminent commercialized spectator sport in the radial city, was regarded as a clean exciting game and the widely accepted baseball ideology depicted club owners as selfless, civic-minded businessmen who sponsored teams out of a concern for the public welfare. In reality owners were usually profit-oriented businessmen—typically professional politicians, friends or business allies of politicians, or traction magnates—just as involved in urban politics as other sports entrepreneurs. Although not all executives were members of urban political machines, in cities that had powerful bosses, teams were often affiliated with their organizations. Political connections helped club owners in a variety of ways, such as providing protection against interlopers, obtaining inside information, and securing preferential treatment from the municipality. These services greatly enhanced the security and profitability of an entrepreneur's investment in baseball.[52]

During the first three decades of professional baseball, when teams came and went with great regularity, nearly all major and minor league clubs had direct or indirect connections to urban politics. Ted Vincent examined the occupations of 1,263 officials and stockholders and found that nearly half were politicians, including 50 mayors, 102 state legislators, and countless judges, councilmen, and police commissioners—mainly professional politicians trying to profit from a new business venture in a field disdained by old money while picking up votes from fans who were grateful to them for sponsoring a popular entertainment. A number of politicians, especially those who founded new teams, were also civic boosters.[53] The first all-salaried team, the Cincinnati Red Stockings, was organized in 1869 by local boosters, under the leadership of businessman and politician Aaron Champion, whose goal was to use sports to publicize their hometown. The team was a great success on the field, going undefeated in 1869 (56–0–1) and winning its first twenty-five games a year later before suffering its first loss. The club did a great job advertising the Queen City but only broke even at the box office. Its example encouraged the formation of at least four other fully salaried teams in 1870, including the Chicago White Stockings, a club backed by leading business and political leaders who also wanted to use baseball to publicize the sophisticated and progressive character of their city.[54]

A year later the first professional league was organized, with franchises in ten cities which ranged in size from New York to Keokuk, Iowa. Financial support for the National Association of Professional Base Ball Players (NA) came mainly from politicians, businessmen, and other leading boosters. The owners in the player-oriented league were not looking for great profits (in 1875, when the Boston Red Stockings won the championship with a 71–8 record, it made $3,000 on a gross income of $37,000), but hoped to break even. However, most clubs in the shaky NA, which had twenty-eight teams in five years, lost money. It only cost ten dollars to join, some franchises were located in cities too small to support professional baseball, and teams in distress would just go out of business.[55]

In 1876 the NA was supplanted by the new National League (NL), whose eight owners were confident that, if properly managed, their sport could become a highly profitable urban entertainment. The NL planned to operate on sound business principles which included keeping out franchises with insufficient populations (75,000 residents was the minimum established) and charging high annual dues of $100. It also expected to avoid such other problems as gambling, fixes, and unequal competition caused by star players jumping to better-paying clubs. The NL's first years were very difficult; it encountered many of the same dilemmas as the NA, such as fixed games and uneven competition. In 1876 only the champion White Stockings made a profit and every team ended in the red a year later. The NL was plagued by unstable franchises as New York and Philadelphia dropped out in 1876, and St. Louis and Louisville a year later. In 1878 it had only six franchises including Troy, New York, whose population was well below the stipulated minimum. The NL resumed its eight-team structure in 1879 by adding Buffalo and Syracuse.[56]

Despite the struggling start of the National League, by 1882 professional baseball was popular enough to encourage the formation of a rival major league, the American Association (AA). Known as the "beer league" because franchise owners were either saloon keepers or beer or whiskey manufacturers, the AA started with just teams located in major markets whose total population exceeded the NL by 500,000. The association purposefully catered to the masses, and all but one of its teams outdrew the White Stockings, whose attendance was triple any of its sister NL clubs. In 1883 the AA added franchises in Columbus, Ohio, and New York City, while the NL, having learned its lessons the hard way, dropped Troy and Worcester in favor of New York and Philadelphia.[57]

The 1880s were prosperous years for professional baseball. NL attendance and profits increased annually from 1882 to 1889. Between 1885 and 1889 alone, the league's teams earned about $750,000 led by Chicago, whose profits averaged about 20 percent of its gross in those five years. By 1887 the club already had $100,000 in the bank. Attendance in the 1880s was correlated to the quality of team, size of the city, and the cost of tickets. The highest single year attendance was 353,000 by Brooklyn (AA) in 1889 during a heated pennant race, which it won, and despite a fire that destroyed its field early in the season. Owners also profited from the sale of players, concession privileges, and rental fees when they leased their grounds for other popular entertainments. Their main expense (59 percent) was player salaries, and owners used various means to keep down wages, particularly the reserve clause and gentlemen's agreements with fellow owners to keep wages to a maximum of $2,000. However these understandings were often broached, and stars received up to $6,000. The average veteran's wage in the decade increased from about $1,500 to $2,500 and was further accelerated by the competition of the Players' League in 1890. But the Players' League only lasted one season, and after the remaining leagues merged in 1892 to form a twelve-team NL, ballplayers were placed in a vulnerable position. Wages dropped drastically and a new $2,400 maximum was strictly enforced. By 1893 the NL was again profitable, though four weak franchises had to be dropped in 1899.[58]

After the turn of the century baseball's profitability greatly increased as the sport grew quickly in popularity. The number of professional leagues rose from thirteen in 1899 to forty-four by 1912, with teams located all over the country in cities of all sizes. A new major league (the American League) formed in 1901, and attendance in the big leagues doubled between 1901 and 1908. Major league owners made very substantial profits. Between 1901 and 1911 the Chicago White Sox, owned by former player and manager Charles Comiskey, a son of a former Chicago city council president, earned over $700,000. Across town, the Cubs were also making enormous profits. At the end of 1905 sporting goods tycoon and ex-player Albert G. Spalding sold the team to Charles W. Murphy for $105,000. The purchase was financed by Charles P. Taft, whose brother was secretary of war. In the following season the new owners made $165,000! Between 1907 and 1913 their earnings reached $810,000—about an 800 percent return on their original investment. The most valuable franchise in the sport, the New York Giants, made about $100,000 a year from 1906 to 1910 and over $150,000 in 1913. In 1919 the team sold for $1 million, which turned out to be a very good buy; in 1920, one year after Sunday baseball was legalized in New York, the club made $296,803, a new league record. However, the Giants' owner was jealous because his tenants, the Yankees, earned $373,862, which set a new major league record. Their main attraction was Babe Ruth, just acquired from the Red Sox, who hit fifty-four home runs, nearly double his year-old mark.[59]

The profitability of baseball teams, the opportunities for honest graft and patronage for supporters (ranging from a job as ticket seller to lucrative excavation and construction contracts), and favorable publicity, not to mention their own interest as baseball fans, encouraged machine politicians to play a prominent role in the national pastime. In Philadelphia, for instance, members of the city's Republican machine operated the Athletics from the 1860s until the club's demise in 1892. In New York Tammany had a very strong influence that began in the 1850s, when it sponsored amateur nines—most notably the Mutuals—and continued after baseball became professionalized. The Mutuals, one of the leading amateur teams in the 1860s, were supported by Boss William M. Tweed, who got municipal appropriations for the team and city jobs for the players. The team was one of only three that played all five years of the NA's existence. The board of directors then included the county sheriff, two judges, a number of aldermen, and six state legislators. The Mutuals were charter members of the NL, operating as a player-controlled cooperative, but were kicked out of the league for failing to make a costly western road trip late in the season. New York went without major league baseball until 1883 when

Tammanyites John B. Day and Joseph Gordon were awarded franchises in both the National League and the American Association. They devoted most of their attention to the Giants (NL) since they could charge twice as much for tickets. In 1885 they sold the Mets (AA) to a Staten Island traction magnate who hoped to use the team to increase traffic on his ferry line. But the scheme failed and the team disbanded two years later. Day and his partners, badly drained by the Players' League war, sold the Giants in 1891 to a syndicate of Republican politicians who had financed the city's PL team. Tammany regained control of the Giants four years later, when Andrew Freedman, an intimate friend and business partner of Boss Richard Croker, who was a member of Tammany's powerful Finance Committee and a future treasurer of the national Democratic party, purchased a majority share in the team for $48,000.[60]

Freedman ran the Giants as if they were an adjunct of the machine, bullying fellow owners into accepting various demands for special treatment and getting into fights with players, umpires, and journalists. Disappointed with his profits and the team's mediocre play, and subjected to considerable abuse from fans, the press, and fellow owners for mismanaging and encouraging rowdy baseball, Freedman decided to sell out and devote himself to the financing and building of the New York subway system. In 1902 he sold most of his stock for $125,000 to John T. Brush, the former owner of the Cincinnati Reds. Brush had sold the Reds to a local syndicate comprised of Republican boss George B. Cox, water works commissioner August Herrmann, and mayor Julius Fleischmann, who had ostensibly threatened to cut a street through his ballpark. However, the Giants continued to be regarded as the "Tammany" team, and in 1919 Brush's heirs sold the club to Tammanyite Charles Stoneham, a crooked bucket-shop operator politically protected by Governor Al Smith and former county sheriff Tom Foley, a prominent Manhattan political boss. The go-between in the sale was said to have been the notorious gambler Arnold Rothstein, who was Stoneham's partner in a rum-running deal and an Havana racetrack and supposedly the fixer of the 1919 World Series.[61]

When the American League tried to move into the potentially lucrative New York market, they were blocked at first by Freedman, who did not want the competition and used his political clout and influence in the real estate business to keep out any interlopers. Freedman held leases on all possible park sites and had the power to have streets cut through sites he did not control. In December 1902, when the junior circuit apparently was going to get help from the company constructing the subway in finding a place to play, Freedman used his position on the board of directors to veto the scheme. As a result the AL could not break into New York until it granted a franchise to a Tammany syndicate that could counter Freedman's power. The franchise, headed by poolroom king Frank Farrell and former police chief William Devery, a corrupt protegé of Tim Sullivan and Boss Croker, cost $18,000. In 1915 they sold the club for $460,000 to brewer Jacob Ruppert, Jr., and his partner, construction engineer C. Tillinghast Huston. Ruppert, a renowned horseman and member of the social elite, was also a long-time Tammanyite, had worked on its powerful finance committee, and served four terms in the Congress. [62]

It was not happenstance that every American and National League team between 1900 and 1920 had owners with important political connections, a condition undoubtedly replicated in most minor leagues as well. A cordial working relationship between team owners and local politicians was invaluable to a club's financial success. Clout deterred interlopers and gained access to the best possible data on property values, land uses, and mass transit—essential when teams were selecting new grounds. Clout helped teams stay open on Sundays or get new laws passed to legalize Sunday ball. Political influence secured preferential treatment in municipal services, fees, and assessments. In Cincinnati, for instance, the Reds paid just $100 for its license until 1912, when the machine was overthrown and the new reform mayor raised the levy to $750. An owner without protection was vulnerable to political pressures and harassment: his park could be subjected to an unusual number of careful inspections by the fire marshals or unfairly charged high fees, which would encourage the owner to sell out to men with political protection. [63]

Among the more mundane, yet essential, services municipalities provided was police protection. Police assigned outside the ballparks kept traffic flowing, maintained order among fans waiting on line for tickets, and prevented ticket scalping. Even though private property was outside police jurisdiction, teams with a lot of clout could also get officers assigned inside the field to prevent gambling and keep order. At the turn of the century Chicago and New York teams saved a lot of money because city police were deployed inside the local ballparks at no cost to the management. A New York reform police commissioner halted the practice in 1907, but it continued in Chicago for decades. [64]

After the 1920s the political connections of baseball magnates declined as older owners retired and sold out to a new cohort of independently wealthy men for whom baseball was more a diversion than a business. By then franchises seldom needed special political clout (though like all other urban businesses, they still welcomed preferential municipal treatment), since the sport was firmly established. The major cities all had expensive modern ballparks in place and, once Sunday baseball had been achieved, few pressing political problems. The national pastime was too popular and well esconced for urban politicians to dare threaten the security of their home team. And whatever fears owners had of possible governmental interference on the national level were alleviated in 1922, when Supreme Court Justice Oliver Wendell Holmes, Jr., ruled that organized baseball was exempt from antitrust legislation.

Conclusion: Sport, Crime, and Urban Politics

Commercialized professional spectator sports in the industrialized radial city were controlled mainly by urban politicians and various close associates who had the power and influence needed to facilitate the operation of their sports businesses. A business dominated by Irish-Americans and enterprising members of other white ethnic groups, it was in many ways like the movie industry, which was also largely shunned by old wealth but open to men of ability regardless of social background. Until the 1920s baseball franchises were operated by professional politicians and traction magnates who were often political powers in their own right. The turf and prize fighting, which were often illegal or permitted to operate only at the pleasure of local authorities, were also influenced by machine politicians, typically in collusion with bookmakers and other organized crime figures. Yet at the same time social elites, often transit executives, were also prominent in the turf.

The politicians involved in professional sport were predominantly ethnic machine politicians who were leading figures in the bachelor subculture and as youths had been active participants and fans. They got involved in the business side of sports because of the opportunities to make money, obtain patronage, enhance prestige among peers in the sporting fraternity, and provide a valuable service to constituents who enjoyed commercialized entertainment or hoped to secure fame and fortune through sports. By owning baseball franchises, boxing clubs, racetracks, and poolrooms and by racing horses, managing fighters, and backing bookmakers, machine politicians had many opportunities to utilize their clout to protect their investment and hurt their competition. Political bosses, who had a reputation for being able to get things done, successfully galvanized the various and changing social forces in the late nineteenth and early twentieth centuries to enhance the success of their sports enterprises. They took advantage of inside information to build ballparks and tracks at accessible sites serviced by the new electric trolleys and subways, used political clout to protect their outdoor edifice or boxing club from competition, and operated protected poolrooms without fear of police interference. Local magistrates affiliated with the machine supported the sporting life when issues of personal freedom were brought before them, and allies in the state capital protected urban sporting interests against legal restrictions and worked to secure the legitimization of currently proscribed activities. As a result, politician-sportsmen provided exciting entertainment to urbanites who paid for their vicarious recreation either by purchasing tickets to watch professionals box or play baseball or by betting on sporting contests.

Sportsmen like Tim Sullivan made money from sports, gained jobs and contracts for the machine, and became celebrities, but not necessarily respectable, even though they mixed with members of the slumming elite who needed political aid to facilitate some of their favorite pastimes. Professional politicians like John Morrissey and Richard Croker craved acceptance and recognition by the social elite and tried to emulate their behavior. But while the Belmonts, Lorillards, and Jeromes might race with the Crokers and gamble with the Morrisseys, they would never invite them home for dinner with the family. Ownership of a baseball team could provide public recognition of a magnate's public spiritedness, as it did for Frank Farrell, but that alone would not assure acceptance by the elite. Before the 1920s club owners were seldom members of the social set but rather men of more modest means and standing, seeking financial profits and social acceptance in a business shunned by old money, but thereafter respectable money found its way into baseball.

The nexus between organized crime and machine politics was much stronger in horse racing and boxing, sports that were illegal for long periods of time, primarily because of the gambling and brutality of the contests. The politicians were the senior partners in this symbiotic relationship until the 1920s, when organized crime leaders took over the dominant role. Inner-city politicians came from the same social background and neighborhoods as syndicate crime figures, who might have been their boyhood friends. As they grew up they still socialized together and depended upon each other for favors and services. Politicians needed the criminals' money, power, and access to election workers, and in return the hoodlums needed protection for their betting operations and other illicit activities. These connections were so close that in many circumstances it was difficult to tell the gambling kingpins from the politicians without a scorecard.

There were important differences in the underworld's relationship to the turf and prize fighting. While boxing was always a lowlife sport, the turf was originally dominated by the social and economic elites who were actively involved in politics. The elites controlled great prestigious tracks, but in the late nineteenth century bookmakers established more plebeian proprietary tracks. Legal bookmakers were essential to the late-nineteenth-century racing scene: without betting horse racing would die.

Organized crime was mainly interested in off-track betting, which was illegal and enormously profitable. It provided a major source of underworld revenue and operated with little interference from the authorities because of political protection and few complaints from a satisfied clientele. Once racing was widely legitimized in the 1920s and 1930s and tracks eliminated the need for bookmakers by adopting the parimutuel system, political connections were still essential to secure good racing dates and maintain good relations with state racing commissions. These commissions failed to exercise sufficient control over thoroughbred and harness racing to keep underworld elements (primarily old gamblers and bootleggers) from gaining control of certain racetracks, which they proceeded to manipulate for their own corrupt interests.

The underworld influence in boxing was more pervasive and less ambivalent. Prize fighting was always wide open for criminal exploitation; even after it was legalized, hoodlums had no problem in circumventing the weak governmental agencies. Since pugilism had always recruited its principals from the same social groups and geographic localities that bred mobsters, rich and powerful figures from the neighborhood (gangsters) naturally gained influence over local young men trying to work their way up with their fists. Leaders in syndicate crime possessed not only the wealth and symbols of achievement that inner-city boys sought but also the power and influence (in cooperation with machine politicians before the 1920s, independently thereafter) to shape a boxer's career. In the 1920s, as boxing became legalized and political machines weakened, gamblers and bootleggers took over total control of the sport. Men in the boxing subculture knew that powerful gangsters could make or break their careers and, if they did not cooperate, could break their bodies. Hoodlums employed the same techniques to gain control of the sport as in their other endeavors like loan sharking and labor racketeering, with similar results. Their success meant entertainment, money, and an enhanced status with their peers. Underworld control was both overt and covert and was for years largely corrupt and totally dominating at the highest levels of the sport.

CHAPTER 7

Spectator Sport and Semipublic Space

Profit-oriented spectator sporting events were almost always staged at semipublic buildings owned or leased by contest promoters. Before the Civil War there had not been much call for such structures, outside of taverns and a few race courses, but the great boom in spectator sports in the late nineteenth century created a demand that entrepreneurs sought to satisfy by utilizing and adapting standing edifices and constructing specialized new ones. Promoters utilized indoor facilities and covered arenas for such sports as boxing, cycling, and marathon running and outdoor enclosures for contests that needed a lot of space, such as baseball and horse racing. The new structures were at first often cheaply built, dangerous firetraps, but because of fire codes, competition from other amusements, and increased success (which resulted in larger seating capacities for stabilized enterprises), sports facilities around the turn of the century would be sophisticated and expensive edifices costing hundreds of thousands, and eventually millions, of dollars. This chapter will examine the development of the semipublic sports facility, primarily in metropolitan New York and Chicago. We will focus on the changing physical character of semipublic sports buildings, the variables that determined their location, the impact of semipublic facilities on surrounding land uses and property values, and the composition and behavior of crowds that attended sporting events.

The Indoor Sports Arena

A wide variety of semipublic facilities were utilized for indoor spectator sports, especially for sports like boxing or basketball, which did not require much space. Illegal boxing matches staged in cities or nearby suburbs might take place in barns, on river barges, or in back rooms of sporting saloons located in the roughest part of town. For example, in the 1870s and 1880s, when boxing was forbidden in New York, one of the most prominent sites of matches was Henry Hill's Dance Hall, a Lower East Side sporting saloon popular among the sporting fraternity. Fight fans paid from twenty-five to fifty cents to see bouts, which included John L. Sullivan's first New York fights. In order to deter police interference, contemporary matches between well-known fighters would be promoted as "exhibitions" instead of as prize fights, which were illegal. Those contests drew such large crowds that they were held in opera houses, mechanic institutes, theaters, or public armories, usually in or near the heart of the city's entertainment district. In the 1880s and 1890s only a few large cities, such as Boston, Brooklyn, Chicago, New Orleans, New York, Philadelphia, St. Louis, and San Francisco, had sufficient numbers of sports fans and large enough facilities to stage sports that required a lot of space, such as major cycling races or six-day go-as-you-please pedestrian contests. And even fewer outside metropolitan New York, Chicago, New Orleans, and San Francisco could afford specialized indoor sports facilities whose main business was spectator sports.[1]

The preeminent locus of indoor sport was New York's Madison Square Garden, which surpassed all other arenas in its ambiance, the quality of competitors, the amount of purses, and the size of crowds. The Garden was located at 27th and Madison, adjacent to Madison Park in the heart of an attractive, well-to-do neighborhood, surrounded by luxury hotels and expensive town houses owned by Leonard Jerome and his ilk. In 1871 the lots housed a railroad shed and stable belonging to the New York & Harlem Railroad, owned by Cornelius Vanderbilt, who had just moved his operations to Grand Central Station. Two years later P. T. Barnum leased the property for his Great Roman Hippodrome. Then bandmaster Patrick S. Gilmore rented the Garden for boxing matches, marathon running races, the first Westminster Kennel Show (1877), political conventions, and the circus. In 1879 William K. Vanderbilt took over the family's site with the intention of emphasizing athletic promotions.[2]

Vanderbilt renamed the building Madison Square Garden (MSG) and made it into one of the foremost sports centers in America. The first major events were long-distance races like the Astley Belt Series in July 1879. The promoters were charged $10,000 to rent MSG for the six-day spectacle, and they in turn charged fifty cents for admission. As in all other arenas, the air inside was full of smoke, and on behalf of the long-distance runners, smoking was forbidden on the ground floor. Up to this time indoor semipublic facilities were poorly illuminated by gas or kerosene lamps, which provided a flickering light. Thomas A. Edison described the gas lighting at Gilmore's Gardens as "so unpleasant . . . that . . . every gas jet is ventilated by small tubes to carry away the products of combustion." Edison was hardly an unbiased observer, since he had recently invented the incandescent light bulb along with a system of parallel circuitry so that outlets could be independently operated, but he was correct. Perhaps not coincidentally, since Vanderbilt's father was a major financier of the Edison Electric Light Company, the landlord decided to install electric lights, both to improve the ambiance of the Garden and to promote the new technology. However, the pedestrians rebelled against electric lighting, which they felt was *too* bright, and gas lighting was temporarily restored. Nonetheless, arenas across the country soon switched to electric lighting because it was safer and provided better illumination. They mainly used arc lighting, which had become widely feasible after the invention of the dynamo. By 1890 the use of electricity had become commonplace at major indoor sports facilities, and it helped attract spectators and participants to athletic clubs, armories, gymnasiums, and YMCAs.[3]

In addition to pedestrianism popular sporting affairs at MSG included boxing, amateur track and field, and the prestigious Horse Show, which began in 1885. In the early 1880s, Vanderbilt relied a lot on boxing matches to fill the arena. The main attraction was John L. Sullivan, once he became champion. His first exhibition there, on 17 July 1882, was a sellout, and his fight on 14 May 1883 against Charlie Wilson attracted a large crowd, including many well-to-do patrons. But on 17 November 1884 Sullivan's match with Alf Greenfield was broken up by the police, as was a rematch with former champion Paddy Ryan on 19 January 1885 before 10,000 spectators. The result was the end of boxing in New York City for a decade.[4]

Madison Square Garden was a big money loser for Vanderbilt, and in 1887 he decided to raze his "patched-up, grimy, drafty, combustible old shell." Members of the Horse Show Association, including Frank Sturgis, William F. Wharton, and J. P. Morgan, built a new Garden on the old site at a cost of $3 million. The new edifice was designed in a moorish style by the renowned architect Stanford White. Its auditorium was eighty feet high with seats for 8,000 (and space for more on the floor)—at the time the largest in the United States. The new building also had a 1,200-seat theater, a 1,500-seat concert hall, the largest restaurant in New York, a roof garden cabaret, and apartments in its 320-foot tower, which made it the second tallest edifice in New York. Placed atop the tower was Saint-Gaudens's thirteen-foot-tall sculpture, *Diana*. The Garden was immediately regarded as one of the great institutions of New York, along with Central Park and the Brooklyn Bridge.[5]

The new MSG cost $240,000 a year to maintain and at a daily rental of $1,500 had a difficult time attracting sufficient numbers of events. The main events were long-distance cycling races, the National Horse Show, boxing, wrestling (after 1900), and physical culture exhibitions. By the turn of the century the owners wanted to sell out because they were losing too much money. The local press demurred, pointing out that as a convention center MSG had many important civic and municipal functions and that many of its promotions could not be duplicated elsewhere. "It is safe to say," editorialized the *Times*, "that it is the municipal possession which is most envied . . . by citizens of the other great cities." The *Times*, recognizing that there was not enough public demand for MSG "to sustain it as a moneymaking enterprise," urged that it be saved by benefactors like those who supported the city's zoo, botanical gardens, and the Public Library. [6]

Although the Garden monopolized major indoor sporting events that required a lot of space, it had a lot of competition from gymnasiums and smaller arenas for the boxing trade. In the early 1890s, before boxing was legalized in the state, there were about a dozen fight clubs in Brooklyn and some others located throughout the metropolitan area. After the Horton Act, most big matches were still fought at Coney Island sites, at the Garden, and at two Manhattan clubs controlled by Tim Sullivan. There were also many small neighborhood gyms distributed throughout the city, mainly in midtown Manhattan, which was the center of the entertainment district, and in such lower-class communities as the Lower East Side, Harlem, and the South Bronx. The quality of these neighborhood clubs ranged from small-time operations like the Sharkey AC, which featured club fighters and sat a few hundred, to major arenas like Billy Gibson's Fairmont in the Bronx, which seated over 3,000. When the Frawley Act was passed in 1911, about thirty boxing clubs were in operation. Over the next few years as many as forty-nine professional gymnasiums or arenas were in operation at any time. [7]

In the early 1900s, because of competition from other boxing facilities and its limited number of alternate attractions, MSG struggled to survive. In 1911 the Garden was sold for over two million dollars to businessmen who expected that the legalization of boxing would turn things around. But it did not, and in 1916 they went bankrupt. After the passage of the Walker Act in 1920 interest in the Garden revived, and several politically well-connected syndicates organized to gain control. A ten-year lease for $200,000 a year was awarded to sports promoter Tex Rickard, who was financed by circus magnate John R. Ringling and politically backed by Governor Al Smith. In 1916 Rickard had promoted the Willard-Moran heavyweight championship fight at MSG; it drew a Garden record $152,000. He recognized the arena's potential and through his imaginative leadership helped make MSG the mecca of prize fighting, a center for political conventions, and a site of varied popular entertainments for New Yorkers with discretionary income. Rickard was enormously successful. Between 1920 and 1925 boxing alone brought in $5 million. Rickard employed the talents of charismatic pugilists like Benny Leonard and Jack Dempsey to expand his audience beyond the boisterous blue-collar fans in the galleries and the blue bloods, politicians, and gangsters at ringside to include millionaires, glamorous personalities, and respectable middle-class men. At the end of 1925 he moved his operations uptown to a new six-million-dollar Garden located at Fiftieth and Eighth Avenue in the theater district. It had a seating capacity of 18,500 for boxing and 17,442 for ice hockey.[8]

Public behavior at indoor sporting events often reflected the quality of the auditorium and the character of the sport. All things being equal, more decorum could be expected in roomy, well-appointed facilities like Madison Square Garden than in crowded taverns or gymnasiums. Order certainly reigned when elegant, well-mannered audiences attended prestigious events like the horse show at the Garden, but rowdy behavior was common even at the Garden for prize fights and pedestrianism, which until the 1920s attracted motley male-only crowds. In smaller gymnasiums the violent and emotional nature of boxing infected spectators seated close to the action, especially if they were betting on the outcome or rooting for a hero with whom they and the rest of the crowd had a strong collective identity. Riots often erupted when overly ardent, disruptive fans brought into the arena their ethnic animosities, which simply heated up when interethnic matches embodied rivalries that existed in their neighborhoods. In New York City in the decade before World War I club fights between Irish and Jewish pugilists occasionally resulted in wild disorder among the spectators—people threw chairs into the ring, seconds jumped into the ring, fist fights broke out among onlookers—that required police reinforcements to put down. Riots often occurred when police broke up a bout or especially when a referee made a decision that adversely affected bettors or a fighter popular with the audience. Fans who attended obviously fixed fights felt cheated and could become violent. In 1904, for example, spectators rioted in a Philadelphia arena after light-heavyweight champion Jack Root floored Tommy Ryan by a slap to the face. Police had to escort the principals through an angry mob to their dressing rooms.[9]

Mismanagement also caused disturbances at boxing matches. Promoters sold as many tickets as possible for popular matches and did not worry about overcrowding or inadequate security. They also engendered hostility by raising prices at the last minute. All of these problems occurred on 30 August 1911, when MSG resumed boxing after the passage of the Frawley Act. The Matt Wells—K. O. Brown lightweight fight drew an overflow crowd that the management was unprepared to handle. The crowd was so thick that ticketed fans had a hard time getting into the Garden, and once inside, getting to their reserved seats. Fans who had bought gallery tickets for $1 discovered a $2 surcharge before they could get in. Their displeasure was surpassed by that of the thousands of people who could not get tickets. Only thirty policemen had been assigned to the Garden for crowd control; over 200 more had to be brought in to calm the crowds outside and stop the fighting inside among ticket holders scrambling for seats.[10]

The Outdoor Sports Park

Outdoor sports structures were needed primarily for athletic contests that required a lot of open space or attracted huge crowds. A few were temporary structures, like the 91,000-seat grandstand put up for the Dempsey-Carpentier heavyweight championship fight of 2 July 1921 in Jersey City. Tickets were scaled from $50 down to $5.50 and brought in a then-record $1.8 million. Certain permanent structures like the Indianapolis Speedway, which drew a crowd of 80,000 as early as 1911, or college football fields were used just a few days a year. The first modern college facility was Harvard Field, a 38,000-seat concrete-and-steel structure built in 1903 in Cambridge for $250,000. Its success depended not only on student and alumni support but also on the vicarious identification of middle-class Bostonians with the Crimson. A decade later the 67,000-seat Yale Bowl was built for $400,000. Similar projects soon followed at Syracuse, Princeton, and Chicago—football powers located in metropolitan areas or college towns where they tried to make the sport a money-making proposition while bolstering their own reputation and that of their city. The construction fever spread in the late 1910s to public institutions like the University of Michigan, which fabricated a 46,000-seat wooden facility, enlarged a decade later to 87,000.[11] Finally, there were the semi-public structures used on a more regular basis, namely racetracks and baseball parks.

The outdoor semipublic sports facilities were nearly always located far from the urban core, usually on the suburban fringe or, in the case of the turf, often outside the city limits. By contrast major indoor semipublic sports buildings were generally very accessible, even to a walking public, because they were usually in or near the CBD, and smaller clubs were located near the homes of their clientele. Baseball and racing fans needed good public transportation to get to the distant sites. They took advantage of the mass transit systems developing in urban areas all over the country in the late nineteenth century. By 1890 electrified streetcars traveling twelve miles per hour were supplanting horsecars. Trolley car mileage in

America increased from 1,260 miles in 1890 to 22,000 twelve years later. An even more advanced vehicle was the subway, introduced in Boston in 1897 and New York in 1904. In the nineteenth century the high cost of transportation limited public transit to the middle classes, who could afford the carfare to commute to work or ride to their favorite amusements. But by the early 1900s everyone but the very poorest slum dwellers could afford streetcars at five cents a trip, including a free transfer.[12]

The location of commercialized semipublic outdoor sports facilities was directly tied to the routes of streetcar lines. Routes radiated outward from the CBD toward new residential neighborhoods and popular destinations like municipal parks or privately owned recreational facilities, often operated by the traction companies. Over fifty transit firms in the late nineteenth century sponsored amusement parks at the end of their routes to encourage ridership. Urban amusement parks had thrilling rides, amusing sideshows, and a variety of sports facilities ranging from roller-skating rinks and shooting galleries to velodromes for cycling and tracks for professional sprint racing. In the 1870s and 1880s eastern cities like Boston, Brooklyn, Hartford, Hoboken, Paterson, Philadelphia, and Providence had enclosed running tracks at their amusement parks. The best known was D. E. Rose's Roman Amphitheater at Coney Island, an expensive forty-cent ride from New York. On weekends working-class athletes competed all afternoon in elimination sprint races for purses up to $100. The contests drew as many as 2,000 spectators, many of them friends of competitors who paid twenty-five cents to cheer on their chums. These spectators were probably single young men with no responsibilities, since the cost of the outing was nearly equal to a full day's wages for an unskilled worker.[13]

Racetracks were also located at a substantial distance from the CBD. Since the circumference of the running surface ranged from half a mile to a mile and a half, they required enormous space. Yet most were used only for several weeks or a few months at most because racing seasons were short, although there were exceptions like the mercenary Guttenberg and Gloucester tracks, which stayed open all year. In 1870 none of the prestigious New York tracks were even located in the city. Saratoga and Monmouth were in distant resort towns while the only major thoroughbred track in the metropolitan area was Jerome Park in the Fordham section of Westchester. The main means of reaching Jerome Park in the 1870s was by either costly carriage or an expensive train ride from Grand Central Depot. When the Coney Island tracks were getting going in the early 1880s, racing fans had to endure a forty-cent hour-long train ride to that resort area. Traveling time from mid-town Manhattan was cut in half for sportsmen when Morris Park was opened in 1889. It was located in

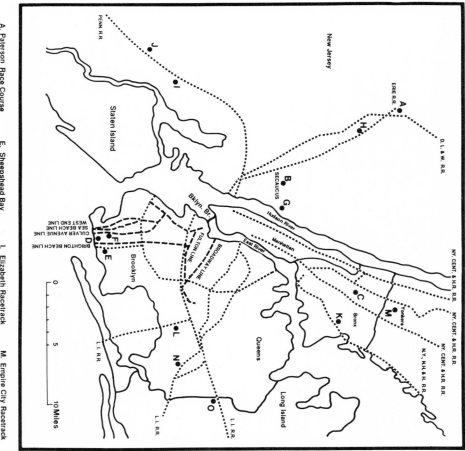

5. The Thoroughbred Racetracks of Metropolitan New York, 1863–1910.

A. Paterson Race Course (1863 - 1869)

B. Hoboken Race Course (1864 - 1868)

C. Jerome Park Race Course (1866 - 1891)

D. Brighton Beach Racetrack (1879 - 1910)

E. Sheepshead Bay Racetrack (1880 - 1910)

F. Gravesend Racetrack (1885 - 1910)

G. Guttenberg Racetrack (1885 - 1893)

H. Clifton Racetrack (1887 - 1893)

I. Elizabeth Racetrack (1889 - 1893)

J. Linden Racetrack (1889 - 1893)

K. Morris Park Racetrack (1889 - 1904)

L. Aqueduct Racetrack (1894 -)

M. Empire City Racetrack (1900 - 1942)

N. Jamaica Racetrack (1903 - 1959)

O. Belmont Park Racetrack (1905 -)

R.R. ·············

BRT ------------

Westchester, east of the Bronx River near the New Haven Railroad, in a section that was annexed by New York six years later. Many New Yorkers, particularly the lower-class bettors, preferred the nearby New Jersey proprietary tracks, which were more accessible than the Coney Island tracks. Guttenberg was a short ferry ride from Manhattan, and not too much further away were the proprietary tracks in Clifton and Elizabeth, owned by the same families who controlled the profit-oriented Coney Island courses. Their owners knew how important accessibility was to their clients. When the Jersey tracks were closed in 1894, after the legislature banned horse-race gambling, the next four tracks built in the metropolitan area were either in or adjacent to Queens, which became a borough of New York in 1898, or in the city of Yonkers, just north of New York. The most important of these sites was Belmont Park, built in 1905 at the border of Queens and Nassau counties—about twenty miles from Times Square, an hour by train. These distant locations were selected for the cheap real estate and improved transportation.[14]

Tracks in other metropolitan areas were also located far from the CBD, although not as far as in New York. In Chicago, for instance, the prestigious Washington Park was originally located outside the city until 1889, when Chicago annexed the Town of Lake. The track was on the border of the southern end of the suburban park system, about six miles from the Loop. Washington Park was reached by cable cars, an elevated railroad, and by carriages that rode through some of Chicago's most fashionable neighborhoods. The city's two proprietary tracks were then located west of the CBD. Garfield Park was situated at the city limits adjacent to the park from which it took its name, a thirty-minute streetcar ride from the Loop. Hawthorne, its rival for the mass audience, was just outside of Chicago in the town of Cicero, yet the train ride there cost five times as much as the trip to Garfield Park.[15]

The facilities at race tracks varied from the spartan accommodations at cheaply constructed plebeian tracks with small grandstands seating 2,000 to expensively appointed resorts with lavish clubhouses and 10,000-seat grandstands. In 1866 Jerome Park led the way, with its extravagant ballroom and dining room, a clubhouse open year round, and overnight accommodations which made it virtually a luxury hotel and club for wealthy New Yorkers and their wives and daughters. Jerome Park provided a model for other prestigious tracks around the country, like the Fairgrounds (New Orleans), Sheepshead Bay (Brooklyn), and Washington Park (Chicago), which all had large grandstands with separate sections for jockey club members, ladies, and the masses, along with cheaper standing room in the infield, to prevent the mixing of classes and pollution from the riff raff. In 1884 the Washington Park track cost $150,000, which included

$40,000 for the grandstand and $50,000 for the clubhouse. Even grander was Morris Park; its 1.375-mile track was the longest in the country, and its 15,000-seat grandstand, the largest. A palatial structure, it quickly became an important resort for the social set. Beginning in 1895 the track was operated by the elite Westchester JC led by August Belmont II and James Keene, but various problems, including an insecure lease, encouraged them to move to Long Island, where they built the even more opulent Belmont Park at a cost of $2.4 million. The track was 1.5 miles in length and the 650-foot grandstand was the finest in America. Belmont had a lavish clubhouse with dining rooms, bedrooms, and balconies from which club members could view the races. [16]

Even disregarding betting losses, attending the track generally cost more than any other sport before the 1920s, with the exception of boxing championships. Transportation was expensive and ticket prices were high. The cheapest plebeian track usually charged fifty cents for admission and another fifty cents for a grandstand seat. In the late nineteenth century the higher quality proprietary tracks and the elite tracks generally charged seventy-five cents for admission plus another $1.25 for a seat. In the early 1900s prices were as high as three dollars, which became the standard rate at Belmont Park. Women were usually admitted at a reduced rate, and on occasion, when business was bad, outlaw tracks and even respectable facilities might admit fans to the infield for free. Thereafter ticket prices did not go up very much. In the 1940s, for instance, major tracks only charged $1.50 for admission, although a seat in the clubhouse was $4. [17]

In the late nineteenth century weekday crowds usually averaged just a few thousand spectators, but on opening days, holidays, and Saturdays, when valuable stakes races were accompanied by considerable pageantry, crowds at prestigious tracks might range from 10,000 to 20,000. After the turn of the century, crowds got even larger, such as the 35,000 in attendance in 1913 when Belmont Park reopened. By the 1930s major stakes races drew crowds in excess of 50,000, and New York tracks had weekday crowds that surpassed 15,000, carried to distant tracks on Race Track Specials. Races usually started around 2 or 2:30 P.M., although as early as the 1880s a number of proprietary tracks had installed lights to increase their potential working-class audiences. [18]

The conduct of crowds at the races was generally very good except for the plebeian outlaw tracks like Guttenberg and Garfield Park that thrived mainly in the 1880s and early 1890s. Their audiences, drawn almost totally from the lower classes, included criminals, ladies of ill repute, and various rowdy elements. Racing fans coming and going from these tracks were known to terrorize nearby residents and streetcar riders. Riotous behavior occasionally occurred inside the outlaw enclosures in response to races thought to have been fixed or dishonest work by the bookmakers. Crowd control was seldom a problem at the respectable tracks, which drew their spectators from a higher cross-section of the community. Pinkerton guards were employed to look out after pickpockets and other lowlifers, and ticket pricing policies prevented social inferiors from rubbing shoulders with fashionable young women. The crowds for important races at the turn of the century not only included celebrities like machine politicians, entertainers, and the social elite, but were

mainly composed of people in comfortable financial circumstances: lawyers, brokers, the element that speculates in Wall Street, merchants, salesmen, "sport" young clerks with their week's salaries in their pockets, members of the leisure class with time to kill, and men who own or control small shops, such as grocers, butchers, restaurateurs, saloonkeepers. Comparatively few men in positions of financial trust, such as bank employees, are in the crowd. These men realize that if they were seen frequently at the races, they would fall under suspicion and their discharge might quickly follow. And there are practically no laborers—the racing game demands people with money—and very few of the well paid skilled workmen, who are much less prodigal in their spending than salesmen or young professional men of the same earnings.[19]

By the early 1950s the turf was the most popular spectator sport in America by number of admissions. In the 1970s track goers at the thoroughbred races were mainly middle-income Catholics and Jews who lived in suburbia near the tracks and did not regard gambling as sinful. The turf also attracted a large working-class urban ethnic audience, who were particularly drawn to night-time harness racing after World War II. They had greater access to racing than ever before because of cheap tickets and improved public (trains, express subways, and buses) and private (chartered buses) transportation.[20]

The Baseball Parks

The most important semipublic sports edifices were professional baseball parks, which by the early 1900s were located all over the country and attracted the greatest number of spectators. They were also used for various other sports and pleasures, ranging from college football and wild west shows in the 1880s and 1890s to prize fights by the 1910s. Nineteenth-century enclosures were almost exclusively wooden because of the cheap cost and because teams frequently moved from site to site, usually outward towards cheaper peripheral locations, and thus it did not pay to build expensive semipermanent ball parks. Further, franchises, especially in the minor leagues, did not always last very long. However, in the first decade of the twentieth century, as the sport became increasingly popular and stable and a good investment, owners in large cities began building expensive and permanent fire-resistant ball fields on the urban periphery. These new structures were safer, more comfortable, and much larger. The increased seating capacity promised even better profits in the future.[21]

The location of the wooden ballparks was determined by the cost of buying or renting the site and by its accessibility to mass transit. Virtually no professional ballpark was located within walking distance of the CBD because such property was too valuable and expensive to sit unused for 80 percent of the year. Local traction interests were closely tied to ball clubs in a mutually beneficial relationship. One historian has estimated that, before 1900, 15 percent of the businessmen involved in baseball were traction executives. Transit companies in seventy-eight cities, mainly in the minor leagues, were financially involved in the national pastime. There was even an association in 1899 known as the New England Trolley League. In many smaller cities the traction people were about the only ones with sufficient capital to sponsor professional baseball. Streetcar firms also tried to help out local franchises with subsidies and favors, like grading the field or even building the team a ballpark. Baseball fields were commonly located at the terminus of streetcar lines and owned by local transit lines that anticipated an increase in ridership. Their streetcars heading in the direction of the ballpark would have signs on the front cars announcing scheduled games. In Atlanta the city's leading streetcar company purchased the Crackers in 1906 and almost immediately moved the team from the 2,000-seat city-owned field to a new 6,800-seat ballpark located at the end of one of its routes, directly across the street from its amusement park.[22]

Close connections also existed between major league teams and local traction interests. In the late 1890s the Cleveland Spiders were owned by traction magnate Stanley Robison, who arranged for fans traveling to the game by trolley to purchase a round-trip ticket and admission to the game right on board. The Brooklyn NL Club was owned from 1891 to 1898 by traction magnates who moved the club from South Brooklyn to Brownsville, which was serviced by their trolley line. The team was soon nicknamed the "Trolley Dodgers" because fans had to walk carefully to avoid the traffic. In 1898, when the new president and principal owner Charles Ebbets moved the club back to its old neighborhood, across the street from

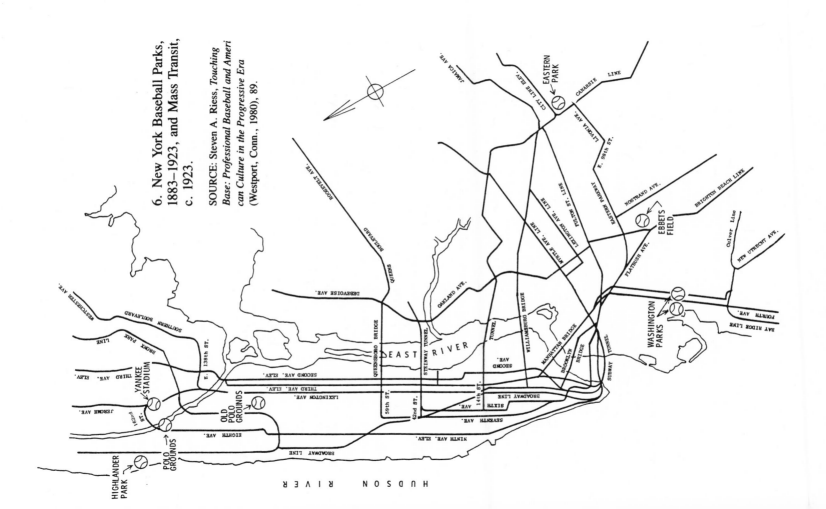

6. New York Baseball Parks, 1883–1923, and Mass Transit, c. 1923.

SOURCE: Steven A. Riess, *Touching Base: Professional Baseball and American Culture in the Progressive Era* (Westport, Conn., 1980), 89.

an earlier site, the switch was financed by local transit firms eager to recoup lost business.[23]

One of the most important decisions team owners ever made was what was the ideal site for their ballpark, and they used their close ties to local political and traction leaders to secure the best possible information about property values, transportation routes, and future developments. Teams in the nineteenth century moved often because they wanted cheaper and more accessible sites, hoped to avoid neighborhood hostility, or were being pushed out by politicians who threatened to cut streets through the field because they were not getting enough passes or other favors. The New York Giants, for example, played at four different fields between 1883 and 1891. Even though the team was politically well connected, it was forced out of the old Polo Grounds near Central Park after disgruntled aldermen had a street opened through the site.[24]

The trials and tribulations of securing a good ballpark site was exemplified by the geographic mobility of the Chicago White Stockings, who played in six different sites between 1870 and 1894. The major reason for its switches were improvements in mass transit which enabled the owners to move in the direction of the city's periphery without raising traveling times. In 1870 Chicago's first professional team played inside the Dexter Park Racetrack, more than six miles southeast of the CBD, an hour-long ride by horsecar. A year later the club joined the NA and played at Lake Front Park, a small site in a public park close to the CBD. During the Great Chicago Fire the field burned down, and the city went without an NA franchise for two years. In 1874 a new team was established and played at the Twenty-third Street Grounds, three miles south of the new CBD. It was reached by horsecar until 1877, when a new steam-powered train cut traveling time in half. One year later political friends of owner William S. Hurlbut arranged for the club to return to the old convenient lake-front location, where a second Lake Front Park was built. In 1883 a model ballpark was constructed there by Hurlbut's successor, former star pitcher Albert G. Spalding. The handsomely built $10,000 field seated 10,000 fans and had a band pagoda built near the main entrance. The size and shape of the parcel severely restricted the playing dimensions: left field was 180 feet from home plate; right field, 196; and center field, 300, making for the smallest playing surface in major league history. One result was that in 1884 Ed Williamson hit twenty-seven home runs, a record that lasted until 1919. In 1885 legal problems that stemmed from the private use of what was originally federally donated land forced Spalding to relocate. The team moved to the West Side, then the most heavily populated section of town, where Spalding built the $30,000 Congress Street Grounds. The brick-fenced wooden structure was constructed on an expensive lot that rented for $7,500 a year in an attractive middle-class neighborhood. Local residents opposed the park as a threat to their safety and tranquility but could not halt the project. The grounds were reached from the CBD by a slow 4-mph horsecar and a faster, more expensive steam-powered commuter rail line that made the trip from downtown in fifteen minutes.[25]

In 1891 Spalding decided to split his season between the West Side and the South Side, which was undergoing a boom in anticipation of the coming Columbian Exposition. Spalding leased the Thirty-fifth Street Grounds, used the year before by the defunct Brotherhood League. The field had excellent transportation to the Loop via a 15-mph elevated steam railroad. But Spalding was soon dissatisfied with this arrangement because he was carrying a high rent at the Congress Street site and because his lease proscribed Sunday ball at the South Side field. Spalding decided to build a field at a site he owned west of the Congress Street park. The new $30,000 West Side Park was located in a native-born middle-class residential section, a mere seven minutes from the Loop via a new steam-powered elevated line. In 1893 it was used just on Sundays but became the White Stockings' sole home a year later.[26]

The wooden baseball parks were extremely dangerous structures, often poorly constructed of flimsy materials by contractors cutting costs and depending on payoffs or clout to prevent careful inspections. In 1894 there were at least five fires in major league parks. St. Louis alone had six fires in a decade. Between 1900 and 1911 there were again at least five fires in major league parks. Fortunately, there were few serious injuries. However, there were episodes when strong winds knocked down walls or stands collapsed due to overcrowding with tragic results. The worst disaster occurred in 1903 at Philadelphia's Baker Bowl, when a wooden railing gave way, causing twelve deaths and hundreds of injuries.[27]

Because of such tragedies as the collapse of a section of Baker Bowl and the Iroquois Theater fire in Chicago, also in 1903, in which 602 people died, urbanites in the Progressive era were very conscious of the need for safety in semipublic buildings. Municipalities throughout the country rewrote building codes to tighten up regulations regarding construction materials and safety standards in semipublic buildings. Chicago's revised building code of 1911 actually had specific sections for baseball fields that required the use of fire-resistant materials, annual inspections, and easy egress through open aisles and limited the number of tickets sold to their seating capacity.[28]

The technological know-how needed to construct fire-resistant parks was available by the 1880s, and in 1887 the Philadelphia Phillies utilized fireproof materials in sections of their new 18,000-seat field. A number of

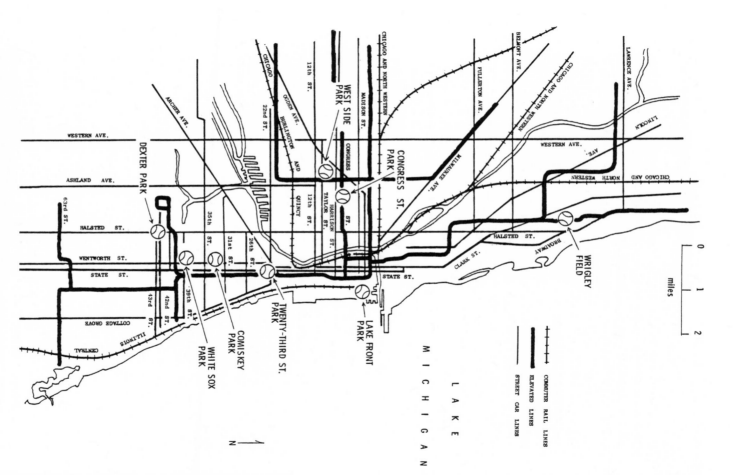

7. Chicago Baseball Parks, 1870–1916, and Mass Transit, c. 1915.

SOURCE: Steven A. Riess, *Touching Base: Professional Baseball and American Culture in the Progressive Era* (Westport, Conn., 1980), 87.

parks were subsequently built with steel and concrete, but the cost was too high and the profit potential too low to build fully fire-resistant parks. By 1908 circumstances changed as the growing popularity of the national pastime and a decline in construction expenses encouraged magnates to adopt a new policy. The decision to build modern fire-resistant parks symbolized a recognition of the maturity and stability of the baseball business. Construction of the new buildings was an expensive proposition that would cost several times the $75,000 that Hilltop Park, 16,000-seat home of the Highlanders (Yankees) and the last wooden major league edifice, had cost. Furthermore, the modern parks could not be readily dismantled and rebuilt elsewhere if the site did not work out. Consequently, it was crucial that a team use its clout to secure the best possible information about potential fields, including data on property values, anticipated future land uses, current and planned mass transit facilities, and the social character of the neighborhood, so the owners could make an intelligent choice. Once the location was selected, most teams secured long-term leases, which were necessary to guarantee a large investment against capricious landlords who might otherwise subdivide for apartments or squeeze the team when the lease was up.[29]

Shibe Park, built in Philadelphia in 1909, was the first fully modernized baseball field. Constructed totally of concrete and steel, except for its brick wall, it had 20,000 seats in a double-decked grandstand that cost about $500,000. A second "palace of the fans" to open that year was Pittsburgh's Forbes Field, located in the city's leading residential section. It had three decks and such modern facilities as elevators, telephones, and electric lights. An important safety feature was the use of inclined ramps instead of stairs to facilitate crowd movement. In all, ten new major league parks were built between 1909 and 1916, and improvements were made in the others, except for Baker Bowl, using inflammable materials. The oldest still in use are Tiger Stadium and Fenway Park (both 1912) and Wrigley Field (1914). Teams in large minor league cities like Newark, San Francisco, and Toledo, which had sufficient populations to merit a big investment in their team's future, also constructed concrete and steel structures in the 1910s.[30]

The imposing new structures were designed by professional architects in the imperial style of the old Roman stadia. They were intended to be functional rather than artistic, but some consideration was given to their appearance. The new Polo Grounds (1911) had facades on two of its decks with friezes depicting a martial display of shields and garlands, while Comiskey Park (1910) had fountains, and Shibe had Roman columns. The dimensions of the interiors were all highly unique, a function of the spatial configuration of the lots. The Polo Grounds probably had the oddest shape, with left field 279 feet from home plate; center field, 480; and right field, a mere 256 feet. These dimensions strongly influenced strategy and play. The ballparks were still green oases in the concrete cities and contributed in a small way to the City Beautiful movement, although billboard advertisements did detract from the rustic image. The owners anticipated the new structures would help them compete with other urban entertainments like lavishly decorated and comfortable vaudeville theaters, new movie palaces, and magnificent amusement parks. They also gave them an excuse to drop most cheap sections, if not to raise ticket prices.[31]

Nearly all of the new ballparks were located on the urban periphery, where land was relatively inexpensive and where the neighborhood was either underdeveloped or middle class. The ballparks were located on the urban periphery, built in the CBD was Navin Field in Detroit (located on the site of the old Bennett Park), and the only grounds located in working-class areas were Comiskey Park and League Park in Washington, which was in a black area. Both were in areas historically connected with baseball, the former just four blocks from its previous home. More representative were the locations of the Cubs and the New York teams. Through 1915 the Cubs played at West Side Park, which was by then in a deteriorating neighborhood populated by first-and second-generation new immigrants. After the demise of the Federal League that year, the owners of the ChiFeds were allowed to buy the Cubs from Charles P. Taft. They moved the franchise to the new Federal League park (Wrigley Field), built in 1914 in the middle-class Lakeview community on the North Side of the city, six miles from the Loop. The North Side was just beginning to get good mass transit, and a new el station was located across the street from the field.[32]

The 32,000-seat Polo Grounds (eventually expanded to 54,000), built in 1911, was the first modern ballpark in New York. It was located at 155th Street in Washington Heights, on the site of an earlier Polo Grounds constructed in 1890 but destroyed by fire twenty-one years later. In the 1890s the Heights was a forty-five-minute trip from Wall Street and was just becoming a popular middle-class residential area. In 1913 Ebbets Field was completed in an undeveloped cheap section of Flatbush that Charles Ebbets had secretly purchased in small parcels for $100,000. The total cost of the new park came to $750,000, which almost bankrupted the Dodgers' owner. His choice for a playing field was derided by experts, but the former Brooklyn councilman astutely recognized the future potential of Flatbush, which soon became a popular residential area. The field was four miles from the Brooklyn Bridge and blessed with excellent transit service, making it accessible to most of the borough. In 1913 the city's third just twenty minutes by subway from Wall Street.

team, the Yankees, lost their lease to Hilltop Park, which was torn down for apartment buildings, and became renters at the Polo Grounds. The high rent, which eventually reached $100,000 a year, the jealousy of Stoneham once the Yankees became successful, a desire for their own identity, and declining construction costs in the early 1920s encouraged the American Leaguers to build their own park. The $2.5 million Yankee Stadium was built in the Bronx in 1923, and it marked the end of the era of the new modern ballparks. The owners had wanted a site in Manhattan, but that was not feasible because of high real estate prices and the huge costs of excavating the granite bed that covered the borough. Back in 1903 it had cost $200,000 just to dig out the site for Hilltop Park. The West Bronx was a feasible site for a ballpark because in 1917 the East Side subway had been extended into the borough along Jerome Avenue, making the field just sixteen minutes from midtown Manhattan. The Stadium was the first triple-decked field and the largest baseball park, with a seating capacity of 63,000—well above the major league average of 25,000.[33]

The "House that Ruth Built" was the first park referred to as a "stadium," although some football fields were already using that terminology. The new nomenclature symbolized a subtle and significant shift in the relationship between the national pastime and urban society. Instead of titling the site a "park," "field," or "grounds," rural metaphors reinforcing the arcadian ideology of baseball, the new terminology indicated an identification with the urban milieu. This was apropos, since the 1920 census had reported that most Americans were urban residents. The term "stadium" indicated an emphasis on the massive quality of the structure and the advanced technology used to construct it—themes more appropriate to complex urban societies than to simple agrarian communities. Professional baseball had become a part of the modern industrialized city. Nevertheless, it was still perceived as the embodiment of traditional rural symbols, beliefs, and values relevant to the needs of urban Americans.[34]

Residents of established communities generally opposed the introduction of baseball teams into their neighborhoods for fear they would bring in noisy and disorderly crowds, lower property values, and attract deleterious land uses. In some cases, as on the North Side of Chicago, community groups fought the presence of a baseball park but were unable to block construction. On the other hand, businessmen and property owners of undeveloped sites selected for ballparks were usually ecstatic because of the anticipated rise in property values and the opportunities for entrepreneurs to cater to the baseball crowds.[35]

The impact on the communities turned out to be neither as bad as residents feared nor as profitable as speculators anticipated. The presence of a ballpark like Wrigley Field did not drastically alter its surrounding neighborhood, which to this day has maintained its residential character. The most visible impact on land uses occurred within a block or two of the entrance, where parking lots and businesses like restaurants, souvenir shops, and taverns were opened. Beyond there, the field had little economic impact. A similar situation existed on the South Side near Comiskey Park. In New York the Polo Grounds had hardly any impact on Washington Heights, which remained an attractive residential community for decades, perhaps because it was so cut off from its neighbors by natural boundaries like Coogan's Bluff and artificial barriers like the Speedway. Along with the impact on land uses, there was also not much of an impact on property values. The only exception was a corner east of the main entrance of Comiskey Park, which nearly tripled in value in five years in anticipation of stores moving in to cater to the baseball trade.[36]

The influence of Ebbets Field and Yankee Stadium on their neighborhoods appears at first glance to have been far more economically important, but that was not the case. Soon after the Dodgers moved to Flatbush, it became a popular residential area and homes were built within walking distance of Ebbets Field. Property values in the vicinity of the park rose dramatically in the 1910s and 1920s, but at the same pace as the rest of Flatbush, which tripled in each decade. The area's rapid expansion as a bedroom community, not Ebbets Field, was the basic cause of the rising neighborhood property values.[37]

Yankee Stadium was built at the same time that an enormous building boom was underway in a section of the West Bronx that had previously been largely vacant. While some sportswriters attributed this to the coming of the ballpark, the real reason was the huge demand that existed then for good cheap housing in neighborhoods accessible to jobs in Manhattan. Upwardly mobile families were attracted to the broad tree-lined Grand Concourse with its well-built new six-story apartments and ready access to downtown on the Jerome Avenue line. Yankee Stadium did not create the construction boom, but its presence did provide a positive psychological support for real estate investors and advertisement for the neighborhood. Small businessmen gained confidence in the area and fans provided trade for the restaurants, bars, and garages that opened across the street from the ballpark. Property values on the major commercial streets in the vicinity increased four-fold and more between 1920 and 1930 mainly because of the new elevated station at 161st and Jerome Avenue and other new local institutions like the county government offices.[38]

Baseball Crowds and Their Behavior

While contemporaries exaggerated the extent to which bootblacks rubbed shoulders with judges and bakers with merchants, the national pastime did attract the broadest audience of any major spectator sport. There was not much intermingling in the stands, but crowds included people from all ages, ethnicities, genders, and socioeconomic levels. As one journalist claimed in 1883:

A glance at the audience on any fine day at the ball park will reveal the presence of representatives of all respectable classes. Telegraph operators, printers who work at night, traveling men who go out on the road at nightfall, men of leisure . . . , men of capital, bank clerks who get away at 3 P.M., real estate men who can steal the declining hours of the afternoon, barkeepers with night watches before them, hotel clerks, actors and employees of the theaters, policemen and firemen on their day off, strangers in the city killing time, clerks and salesmen temporarily out of work, steamboat captains, clerks and mates, merchants in a position to leave their stores with a notice to the bookkeeper that they will not be back today, call board operators who need recreation after the experience of the noon hour . . . , workingmen with the lame hand, butchers, bakers, candlestick makers, mechanics out on strike, lawyers in droves, an occasional judge, city officials . . . and . . . doctors . . . [39]

Nonetheless, until 1920 professional baseball was mainly a middle-class spectator sport which was reflected in its popularity with women, who in the late 1910s comprised over 10 percent of audiences. The precise social composition of crowds varied from city to city depending on cost, availability of Sunday games, and competition from other pastimes as well as on each town's social structure. In Cleveland, for example, a city with a large industrial work force, working-class attendance was lower than might be expected on Saturdays because of local interest in amateur baseball, which was cheaper and often more accessible than the Indians' Lake Park. Thus on 19 September 1914, a crowd estimated at 83,000 turned out for the amateur city championship between Telling's Strollers and Gus Hanna's Street Cleaners. Cleveland had Sunday ball beginning in 1911, but the working class was very selective in their attendance and showed up in large numbers only if the Indians had done well that week. But during the 1920s rising standards of living, the cheap cost of tickets, Sunday ball, and the introduction of night baseball during the Depression made it increasingly a lower-class sport. [40]

The size of crowds in the nineteenth century, for which we do not have reliable records, was generally quite modest. In 1883, for example, Philadelphia averaged under 1,000 spectators a game, and one year later the championship Providence nine, led by fabled "Hoss" Radbourne, drew under 1,000 fans for some home dates. Attendance was price-elastic: the Phillies started out in 1883 charging fifty cents for tickets and increased attendance four-fold by cutting prices in half. In 1890, when there were three competing major leagues, the Players' League averaged 1,844 per game and the NL about 1,500. After the AA merged into the NL in 1892, the average surpassed 2,000. Contending teams in large cities usually drew best. In 1889, when the Brooklyn franchise won the AA pennant, it averaged over 5,000 a game, reputedly a nineteenth-century record. In 1894 the second place Giants, winners of the postseason Temple Series, led with 2,500—about six times as many as the hapless Cleveland Spiders. In 1899 the Spiders actually averaged less than 200 a game while compiling a record of 20–134 after their owner shipped off his best players to bolster his brother's team in St. Louis. The games on weekends and holidays drew the largest crowds; by the mid-1880s, holiday and Sunday games attracted 5,000 to 10,000 spectators in the bigger cities. Memorial Day was usually the single most popular date for baseball: in 1887, 30,000 New Yorkers attended the morning or afternoon games at the Polo Grounds. The single largest crowd was the 27,489 Chicagoans who jammed West Side Park in 1899 for a Sunday game. Nonetheless, the seating capacities of major league parks were seldom taxed in the 1890s, and the rare sell-out crowds were accommodated with space on the huge playing fields. [41]

After the turn of the century booming attendances reflected growing popular interest in baseball. By 1901 the average NL team drew about 3,400—more than a 50-percent increase compared to 1892. But the attendance was unevenly distributed. Between 1901 and 1910 the Giants drew 20 percent of total admissions compared to just 6.2 percent for Boston. In 1908, for instance, the Giants averaged 13,000 at home while coming in second (it was the year of the Merkle "boner"). In general, teams with the best records did best at the box office. Consequently, the Yankees did poorly at the gate despite their favorable location. On the other hand, once they got Babe Ruth and could play on Sundays, the team became an instant hit. In 1920 the club established a major league record with 1,289,422—double their attendance the year before. Building large new parks did not guarantee big crowds once the novelty wore off. The 40,000-seat capacity of Braves Field, completed in 1915, was seldom taxed because of the mediocrity of the team. But teams like the Yankees, Giants, and Cubs did utilize their capacities. In 1923, when Yankee Stadium opened, 63,000 filled the park on Opening Day and the three World Series games there that year drew between 55,000 and 62,817 spectators. The Cubs had one of the smallest parks in the majors yet their pennant-winning club in 1929 established attendance records in 1929 and 1930 that lasted until 1946. Over all, a team that won two-thirds of its games between 1920 and 1950 would attract nearly 18 percent of its league's attendance, while a team which won two-fifths of its contests got only about 9 percent (12.5 percent being average).[42]

In the early days of professional baseball the behavior of crowds caused enough problems that the NL always required host teams to secure police protection to prevent antisocial behavior in the stands. Baseball had a reputation for honesty and did not attract the same kind of rowdy spectators who attended boxing matches or the gambling crowd that frequented the track; nonetheless, problems did exist, as at any other setting in which large crowds gathered in a congested area. Fans waiting outside to purchase tickets were known to get unruly and once inside the enclosure might become nuisances or even get into fights with other spectators. In small wooden parks security problems were exacerbated by the proximity of the seating area to the players and umpires, who could hear many of the epithets issued at them by boisterous fans. Few of these problems were ever fully eliminated, but baseball has generally been free of disorderly crowd behavior since the early 1900s.[43]

The major causes of rioting inside ballparks were unpopular decisions by an umpire who "robbed" the home team of an apparent victory. There were several episodes of violence against umpires, especially in the 1880s, when umpires had not yet earned public respect. In 1884, for example, a crowd in Philadelphia mobbed an umpire after he could no longer take the fans' abuse and threw a bat at some spectators. In New York on 8 August, in a rescheduled game between the local nine and Boston played without league umpires, a Boston player substituting as umpire blatantly cheated on behalf of his teammates, enabling them to make up a four-run deficit in the eighth inning. After all the New Yorkers were retired on strikes in the bottom of the inning, he called the game off at the behest of his team captain. Several spectators then rushed onto the field and attacked the umpire until the police escorted him to safety. Such disorderly behavior led the Baltimore owners to install barbed wire around the field to keep spectators off. Attacks on umpires did not cease until about 1907, when one umpire was almost killed by a soda bottle tossed from the stands. Around that time the leagues began strongly backing the umpires, fining abusive players and ejecting obnoxious fans. Once players and fans were socialized to respect the authority and integrity of umpires, crowd behavior modulated. Spectators could still see umpires as villains and berate their close calls, but when they screamed "Kill the Umpire," they no longer meant it literally.[44]

American baseball fans learned to accept unfavorable decisions and live with defeats because they did not have their entire world view wrapped up in their hometown teams. Supporters of rival clubs usually lived in different cities and were spared face-to-face confrontations. Furthermore, fans of different teams shared the same basic social values and beliefs, and thus sports contests did not symbolize any deep-seated antagonisms. Supporters could sit in the stands together, argue about their heroes, chastise the umpires, and shake hands once the contest was over. By contrast, soccer crowds in Europe and Latin America have always been far more violent in their behavior. Soccer contests abroad symbolize international, class, religious and ethnic rivalries between fans who do not share the same core beliefs. Thus adverse decisions by referees may mean the loss of national honor or community pride to unforgiving spectators, and it is necessary to protect referees by the use of barbed wire, moats, armed security and steel doors to their locker rooms. There has also been a lot of disorder outside soccer stadiums and inside the stands among fans whose teams come from the same or nearby communities, especially when they represent different ethnic and religious groups who have little in common. Soccer matches in Glascow between Rangers (Protestant) and Celtic (Roman Catholic) have become notorious as the scene for the acting out of mutual distrust and hatred. Nothing approaching this ever occurred in baseball despite rabid intra-urban rivalries like the Dodgers and the Giants.[45]

The other major cause of collective disorder was overcrowding. In the wooden-park era, in the days before strict fire codes were implemented, teams never had any qualms about selling as many tickets as possible. Sellouts were not common, but on those days patrons might end up standing in the aisles, obstructing the view of other fans and creating a dangerous hazard if a fire broke out. At times certain sections of the stands were overloaded and collapsed. More people would be hurt in the rush for safety than from fire or falling debris. The usual response to overflow crowds was to let many spectators on to the playing field. Although they were separated from the play by a rope hung around the field, the standees obstructed the view of seated patrons and commonly got in the way of ballplayers and interfered with the game. On such occasions security guards were usually too few and too frightened to take charge when a crisis occurred. On Opening Day, 12 April 1912 at Brooklyn's Washington Park, part of an overflow crowd encroached on the field of play and disrupted the game. When private security guards could not keep order, Mayor William Gaynor ordered city police into the ballpark. Chaos resulted, halting the game after the sixth inning. Construction of large new modern ballparks, which had sufficient seating capacities to satisfy demands for tickets, and enforcement of strict new fire codes against overcrowding and standing in the aisles solved these problems.[46]

Conclusion: Sport and Semipublic Space

Semipublic sports facilities were essential in the development of commercialized spectator sports; they restricted spectatorship to paying customers and thereby encouraged the promotion of professional sports. Before the Civil War there were few such places outside of the back rooms of taverns and racetracks, the only prominent enclosures devoted exclusively, or almost exclusively, to sports. In the 1870s a remarkable expansion in the number and variety of semipublic sports structures reflected the concurrent sporting boom. The main constructions were outdoor edifices for baseball—normally rudimentary structures—and fashionable accommodations for prestigious race courses. Entrepreneurs began to build indoor sports facilities, usually in the urban core—depending on their clientele, in either the slums or the theater district. Because of the high overhead, expensive facilities frequently showcased a variety of popular entertainments.

The owners or lessees of these semipublic buildings were usually very rich men with political influence or professional politicians with clout. Political connections provided the operators the best possible information about transportation developments, real estate costs, and land uses—essential to make the most astute choice of a site for commercialized sport. Political influence also protected the investment against potential competitors, troublesome inspections, police interference, and such unforeseen problems as the opening of a street through the lot. Clout and inside information were especially important for baseball club owners in the early 1900s, when the sport enjoyed a great boom which encouraged magnates to build expensive, fire-resistant stands to provide greatly increased seating capacities in safe, comfortable surroundings. The teams had to build the new grounds on economical sites, either rented or purchased, in stable neighborhoods that had a promising future and were well serviced by cheap public transportation.

The modern baseball parks, the prestigious and elegant racetracks, and the large sports arenas constructed in major cities in the 1920s and 1930s became civic monuments and symbols of their city's cosmopolitan character. Although these facilities were nearly all privately constructed and operated, local communities identified with these structures as if they were public trusts operated by management on behalf of the city (though no one wanted a sports facility built in *their* residential neighborhood).

In an urban area aspiring to first-class status, a major league team playing in a large modern stadium was as vital as a symphony or an art museum. Five cities had the prestige of supporting multiple major league franchises, and most of the teams had their own ballparks. New York, befitting the nation's leading city, had three teams and by 1923 three ballparks.

The semipublic sports building not only provided a site for commercialized spectator sport and bolstered local boosterism but also tested the American myth of social democracy. Because of improved standards of living, the decline of Sunday blue laws, cheap ticket prices, and enhanced mass transit, people from all social classes were increasingly able to attend sporting contests. Of course, social classes did not rub shoulders in the stands; they normally sat in separate sections depending on the price of tickets. By the 1920s all but the most expensive sporting contests were accessible to most urbanites, if only on an occasional basis. In the popular mind the semipublic buildings belonged to everybody. Just as the Brooklyn cab driver could enjoy the rituals of sport at Ebbets Field, the Detroit assembly-line workers at Ford could partake of the ambiance at the Olympia or Tiger Stadium, and the Chicago cop could relax with his friends and family at "Beautiful Wrigley Field."

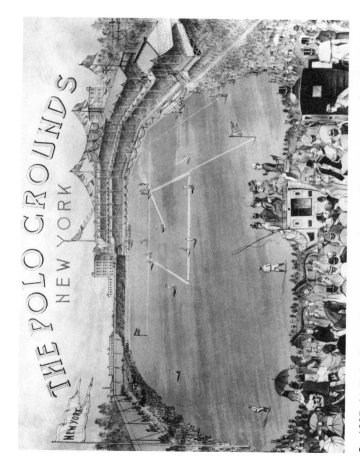

In 1887 the Polo Grounds—the original home of the New York Giants Baseball Club—extended from Fifth Avenue to Lenox Avenue between 110th and 112th streets. Lithograph courtesy of the New-York Historical Society, New York City.

The Polo Grounds, New York, c. 1900, the view from the 8th Avenue side across the baseball field to the grandstand. This field, built in 1890 and destroyed by fire in 1911, was located west of 8th Avenue between 157th and 159th streets, below Coogan's Bluff, from which fans could watch for free. Note the carriages parked in the outfield. Photo courtesy of the New-York Historical Society, New York City.

West Side Park, Chicago, 23 July 1904. Located at Polk Street and Wood Avenue, this field was the home of the Chicago National League club from 1893 through 1915. Note the advertisements on the right-field wall. Beyond the grounds the neighborhood was becoming quite congested. When large crowds attended games at the small old wooden ballparks, fans were often admitted onto the playing field, confined to areas roped off in the outfield and along the foul lines. Both photos courtesy of the Chicago Historical Society (ICHi-03976).

Shibe Park in Philadelphia. The first concrete and steel major league park, it was the home of the Philadelphia Athletics from 1909 to 1954 and the Phillies from 1938 to 1970. Note the use of pillars in this classically inspired structure. Courtesy of the National Baseball Library, Cooperstown, N.Y.

Comisky Park, Chicago. The White Sox field at 34th and Shields Avenue was built in 1910 and is scheduled to be replaced in 1991 by a new field located in the present parking lot. The Sox are identified as a South Side institution, but the grounds are readily accessible to Chicagoans and suburbanites via the el and the interstate expressway system, and the site provides plentiful parking. Courtesy of the Chicago White Sox.

Wrigley Field, Chicago. The Cubs' home at Clark and Addison was built in 1914 for the Chicago Whales of the Federal League, and the Cubs moved in two years later. Regarded as the most intimate major league ballpark, with a seating capacity of merely 35,000, it is located in a densely populated residential neighborhood where there is virtually no parking. Fans relied mainly on the nearby el for access. The introduction of night baseball on 8 August 1988 was strongly fought by the local community, which was worried about rowdyism and competition for scarce parking spaces. Courtesy of the Chicago Cubs.

SPORT IN THE SUBURBAN ERA, 1945–80

. . . I never talked with anybody . . . about the Dodgers ever leaving Brooklyn until I was given very excellent reason to believe the thing was not going to be processed in Brooklyn, and euchred myself . . . in a position where I had sold my ball park and I had to have a place in which to play ball . . . .

. . . .

I have never asked the city of New York to build me a ball park, to give me land, to give me a subsistence or a subsidy, nor have I asked Los Angeles or anyplace to do it.

> Walter O'Malley testimony, U.S., Cong., Senate, Judiciary Committee, *Organized Professional Team Sports, Hearings before the Subcommittee on Anti-trust and Monopoly*, 85th Cong., 2nd sess. (Washington, D.C., 1958), 860.

[T]he strongest argument to me for bringing big league baseball to Los Angeles was the intangible benefits. . . .

Psychologically, it was a great boost for Los Angeles and the West. . . . We just were not big-leaguers in any way. . . . To cap it all, that we had taken this team right out of New York under their own noses, added more vinegar.

. . . .

In late May [1957] I went to Brooklyn to see O'Malley. I explained that we couldn't raise the money to build a ball park, but suggested that we would try to get him the land at Chavez Ravine for a nominal cost, and he could build his own stadium. He hit the ceiling. "I already have one ball park there!" he exclaimed. "What am I going to do with two?"

> Norris Poulson Memoirs, Oral History Collection, UCLA, Los Angeles, Calif., pp. 333–34, 341.

CHAPTER 8

Urbanization, Suburbanization, and the Business of Professional Team Sports

The changing geographical dimensions of American cities since World War II have had an enormous impact on the recent history of professional team sports. Until the 1950s top-level professional sports franchises were almost exclusively located in the urban Northeast and Midwest, where they were connected to each other by rail lines. But the rise of large metropolitan centers in other regions, quickly reached by airplanes, encouraged established teams to relocate, prosperous leagues to expand, and new associations to organize. This was a radical change for baseball and hockey, whose franchises had been extremely stable for decades, but not for professional football and basketball, whose teams had been historically less stable. A second major spatial shift for professional sports clubs was the relocation of their playing areas within their home cities. By the late 1950s, when many of the aging ballparks and arenas needed expensive refurbishment or complete replacement, owners turned to local governments for new facilities. These new public grounds and arenas were major municipal expenditures, rationalized as a means to enhance the city's image, promote commerce, and encourage local development. The geographic mobility of franchises proved to have important ramifications, not only on profitability but also on land use patterns, community psychology, and local politics.

The Location of Professional Sports Franchises

The NBA, the NFL, and the Search for Stability

By the end of World War II professional basketball had existed for nearly fifty years, but on a highly regional and modest level. It dated back to the National Basketball League (1898), whose clubs were all located in the Philadelphia metropolitan area. The first significant organization was the American Basketball League (ABL), founded in 1926 with franchises in eastern and midwestern cities that ranged from New York to smaller cities like Rochester and Fort Wayne, a pattern that continued into the first decade of the NBA. The ABL survived until 1931, suffering from limited press coverage, unbalanced competition, the absence of such top pro teams as the black Harlem Rens, and, finally, the Depression. Touring clubs like the Rens and the Harlem Globetrotters kept professional basketball alive and weekend leagues were subsequently organized; a new ABL in the East (1934) and the National Basketball League (NBL) in the Midwest (1937). The latter, predominantly an industrial league, was organized by Akron's Goodyear and Firestone recreation directors. NBL teams played in cities ranging in size from Chicago to Sheboygan. During the Depression pro basketball was a distinctly minor sport, overshadowed in big cities by intersectional college doubleheaders staged at Madison Square Garden, the Chicago Stadium, and other major indoor arenas.[1]

A major step in making basketball a big-time professional sport came in 1946, when businessmen who controlled the eleven best eastern and midwestern arenas organized the Basketball Association of America (BAA). They hoped to develop a new attraction to complement the other sports contests and shows staged in their facilities, which averaged 12,000 seats. Although few of them were experienced basketball men, all were veteran promoters who had excellent press connections and who were accustomed to putting on big shows. The BAA, which had on paper many advantages over the two regional leagues, virtually destroyed the ABL; however, the NBL proved more competitive than anticipated. Even though its arenas held only about half as many seats, with as few as 2,500 for Oshkosh, it had some excellent players like George Mikan, and its owners were civic minded and less profit oriented. Loyal fans appreciated management's efforts to provide high-quality sport with small-town informality that encouraged community pride.[2]

Professional basketball struggled in the late 1940s; few teams made money. Consequently, in 1949 the two leagues merged, forming a seventeen-team National Basketball Association (NBA) with clubs in such major markets as New York, Chicago, and Philadelphia but also in Anderson, Indiana, Waterloo, Iowa, and Sheboygan. Several of the franchises, particularly those in small towns, were weak from the start; six teams dropped out the first year—not only those from small towns but also Chicago's. By 1954 the NBA was down to eight clubs, but the shaking-out process was not yet over. The smaller cities were barely surviving because of their relatively limited potential audience and league policy that all gate receipts went to home teams. That was very good for the New York Knickerbockers, but not so good for the Fort Wayne Pistons. Consequently in 1957 the Pistons moved to Detroit, and Rochester to Cincinnati. Syracuse was then the only small city in the NBA, and in 1963 the Nationals moved to Philadelphia to fill the void created a year before when the Warriors had moved to San Francisco.[3]

Professional football also started out as a regional sport. When the American Professional Football Association was formed in 1920 (renamed the NFL two years later), only the Rochester and Buffalo teams were located outside the Midwest. The NFL expanded slowly into the East: though there were already teams in towns like Rock Island and Kenosha, there was no franchise in New York until 1925. The early NFL was very unstable; there were thirty-six different franchises between 1921 and 1932, with as many as twenty-two in 1926. Franchises were cheap (ostensibly $100 when the league was founded, though no one paid the fee) but were not profitable because the professional game was not very popular or much respected. The typical home attendance for the Chicago Bears, one of the best teams in the early 1920s, was only about 5,000, even though general admission cost just fifty cents. All teams had a hard time surviving (in 1928 the New York Giants reputedly lost $54,000), especially clubs in minor towns that had smaller potential audiences. The smallest city in the league in 1925 was Pottsville, with 22,000 residents located in the hard-coal region northwest of Philadelphia. The Maroons provided a sense of community identification for its working-class residents, who were badly divided by ethnicity and religion, but the population base was too small and the club folded in 1929. By 1934 Green Bay was the only small city left in the NFL.[4]

At least until the late 1930s, professional football was still very much a minor sport whose owners, like George Halas, had to survive by their wits or perhaps their political or other connections. Two owners heavily involved in local politics were bookmaker Tim Mara, a Tammanyite who founded the Giants in 1925, and gambler Arthur Rooney, a Pittsburgh pol who established the Steelers in 1933 in anticipation of the passage of laws permitting Sunday sports. A third NFL patriarch with questionable associations was Charles Bidwell of the Chicago Cardinals, owner of Sportsman's Park. Bidwell's partner in the track was his attorney, Eddie O'Hare, a director of the Cardinals who had fronted for Al Capone at the Hawthorne Dog Track.[5]

Once World War II ended, the NFL appeared on the brink of stability and big profits. This encouraged the formation of a rival, the All-American Football Conference (AAFC), whose owners, many of whom had previously failed to get NFL franchises, hoped to share in football's future. They established teams in three NFL cities and in such previously unexploited big cities as Miami, Los Angeles, and San Francisco—now viable sites for clubs because of transcontinental air service and the need to make just one round trip a week. As a result the NFL's Cleveland Rams moved to Los Angeles, even though it was over 2,000 miles from the next closest league city. The Rams played in the huge Coliseum and were an instant success, averaging crowds of 38,700 to lead the NFL. However, the AAFC's Browns, who had moved into the vacated Cleveland market, did even better, averaging 57,000.[6]

The AAFC lasted four seasons. After the 1949 campaign its three most successful teams (Baltimore, Cleveland, and San Francisco) were absorbed into the NFL, which took a few years more to stabilize. Baltimore dropped out in 1951, and a year later the New York Yanks moved to Dallas, an untapped market where football was the rage. However, the professionals were a big flop; after four games the team left town to finish the season on the road. The franchise ended up in Baltimore a year later, after local boosters miffed at the loss of their club in 1951 mounted a public relations campaign to prove their city was ready for the NFL. By then the league had become quite stable: total attendance reached two million in 1952 and doubled a decade later, with additional revenues coming in from increasingly lucrative television contracts. The result was just one franchise shift over the next twenty-five years, when the Cardinals, who were the "second" team in Chicago, moved to St. Louis in 1960.[7]

Baseball and the Quest for Greener Pastures

The long-term instability of NBA and NFL franchises was a far cry from the pattern exhibited by major league baseball and the National Hockey League. From 1922, when the NHL was founded, until 1966, when expansion occurred, there were only twelve franchises (seven American), and all that were in business in 1966 had been in the same city for at least forty-one years. Of course, hockey was a relatively minor American sport with surviving NHL franchises in just Boston, Chicago, Detroit, and New York, where they were owned by businessmen who controlled local sports arenas and wanted hockey to fill up open dates. By comparison, twenty-five NBA and BAA franchises were lost or abandoned between 1947 and 1972. The NHL's stability reflected the limited regional appeal of the sport in the United States, the expenses entailed in building and maintaining arenas with the capacity for ice hockey rinks, and the high rate of profitability for established teams, which discouraged thoughts of change. The stability of the national pastime was even more impressive and far more significant. While many clubs had come and gone in the sport's early days, between 1903, when the Yankees joined the AL, and 1952 not a single team dropped out or moved to a new city. However, in the minor leagues teams and leagues came and went with great regularity because of internal factors like team quality and spectator interest and external variables like economic fluctuations and, after World War II, the televising of major league baseball. The stability of the big league teams reflected the sport's advanced level of modernization, strong traditions of hometown loyalty, extensive investment in ballparks, and the rules of organized baseball that originally required unanimous consent before franchise shifts could be approved.[8]

Bill Veeck was the first major league owner to seriously consider a franchise shift. His St. Louis Browns, always one of the worst and least profitable teams, were the "second" team in their city after the popular Cardinals. They drew only about 250,000 fans a year, which was exceeded by several minor league teams. Additionally, the Browns' broadcast revenues were a meager $9,000 compared to the Brooklyn Dodgers, who earned $580,000 for media rights in 1951. In 1952 Veeck tried to move the club to Milwaukee, where he had once owned a ball club, or to Los Angeles, which was boosting itself as a potential major league site. However, the maverick owner was voted down by the other magnates.[9]

One year later the league approved a transfer for the Boston Braves to Milwaukee. The lowly Braves, the weakest franchise in the NL, was the only big league club to have lost a significant amount of money between 1920 and 1950. Unable to compete with the Red Sox, owner Lou Perini relished the move to a city which put at his disposal a new $6.6 million stadium, which was sure to bring in more fans and lucrative media contracts. The Braves were an immediate success, drawing a record 1.8 million spectators in their first season. Such results convinced the AL in 1954 to approve the shift of the Browns (recently sold by Veeck) to Baltimore, a city with a great minor league tradition and a publicly financed stadium. A year later the dismal Philadelphia Athletics moved to Kansas City, where the municipality spent $3 million to upgrade the local minor league park. The migration of the Braves, Browns, and A's left just New York and Chicago with multiple franchises.[10]

The shifted teams all did well the first year in their new homes as fans came out to enjoy the novelty of major league baseball. Because the Washington club was located close by, the Orioles had a small region to draw upon, but the Braves and A's were able to draw from wide geographic areas and enjoyed large nodal zones for broadcasting. However, only the Braves were able to sustain their success and continue to set attendance records because they had excellent teams which had won consecutive pennants in 1957 and 1958 and the World Series in 1957. Neither the Orioles nor the Athletics were pennant contenders and quickly suffered more than a 20-percent drop in attendance.[11]

The single most important franchise shift in the 1950s, and surely the most shocking, was that of the Dodgers in 1958 from Brooklyn to Los Angeles. No professional sports franchise had been as closely identified with its host city as the Dodgers were with Brooklyn. The club was by a wide margin the most important institution in the borough and for all Americans it symbolized the character, culture, and ethnic diversity of Brooklyn, whose population was outnumbered by only four other cities.

In the early 1950s the Dodgers were the most profitable franchise in baseball, drawing huge crowds and enjoying the most lucrative media contracts in the sport. However, owner Walter O'Malley was a greedy, unsentimental businessman, concerned about the future economic viability of the franchise. He wanted the city to help him replace the deteriorating 35,000-seat Ebbets Field, one of the smallest in the league, at a new site in a better neighborhood more accessible to subway lines and with better parking facilities. As more middle-class fans moved to the suburbs, the automobile was becoming the prime mode of transportation to ball games.[12]

Negotiations with park commissioner Robert Moses for a new and more accessible ballpark got nowhere, so O'Malley turned his attention to Los Angeles. By the fall of 1956 Mayor Norris Poulson was urging him to move to the coast and recommending Chavez Ravine, a large, nearly vacant area adjacent to the downtown and near three freeways, as a possible location. O'Malley saw Los Angeles as a huge unexploited territory ripe for developing, with millions of potential fans living within driving distance and even more possible customers for pay-television broadcasts.[13]

The Dodgers' move west was facilitated by the decision of the New York Giants to join them on the West Coast in San Francisco, which meant that the expense of transcontinental travel for NL teams would be alleviated. The Giants had always been extremely successful both on and off the field, but after their 1954 world championship, attendance had sharply slumped. Owner Horace Stoneham felt that a lot of the problem was the declining neighborhood around the Polo Grounds and the lack of adequate parking and was also worried that the Los Angeles Dodgers would not be the kind of draw the Brooklyn Dodgers had been. Once the Dodgers had committed themselves to Los Angeles, San Francisco seemed a logical location for the Giants. It was the site of an old Giants farm team, and boosters led by the mayor wooed the club with the promise of a new municipal stadium.[14]

In November 1957 O'Malley agreed to trade Wrigley Field, the playing field of the minor league L.A. Angels, to the city in return for a 300-acre site in Chavez Ravine and pledges by the city and county to spend up to $5 million for public improvements, including access roads to the freeways. There was a lot of public opposition to this sweetheart deal because the city land had an estimated commercial value of $18 million, was the only decent-sized vacant public lot near downtown, and was required by law to be used for a "public purpose," which in many people's minds was public housing. A referendum held to approve the contract got a lot of support from local boosters and the print media, but television spokesmen were more skeptical because of their fears of pay-TV. A last-minute telethon arranged by local celebrities helped secure passage by just 24,000 votes out of a record 667,000 ballots.[15]

O'Malley had hoped that the city would further assist him by building a new ballpark, but it refused to, based on the community's traditional hostility to bond issues and the sharp divisions created by the trade of Chavez Ravine. So O'Malley built the $15.5 million Dodger Stadium on his own. The 56,000-seat structure was completed in 1962 (the Dodgers playing in the meanwhile in the Coliseum) and is the only privately financed big league park built since 1923. O'Malley's move west turned out to be enormously profitable: attendance in the 1980s annually exceeded three million. The city also benefited with an important new source of entertainment, certification of its status as a first-class city, and the realization of taxes on Chavez Ravine. The only losers were the poor citizens who did not get public housing and the two million residents of Brooklyn.[16]

The Era of Expansion 1960–76

Before 1960 virtually the only time new cities got major sports franchises was when established clubs moved to new locations. However, in the 1960s and 1970s the number of cities with big league franchises increased substantially as the leagues expanded. The number of major league baseball teams increased from 16 to 26; the NFL from 13 to 28, the NHL from 13 to 21, and the NBA from 8 to 23. Expansion was the product of political pressures, competition from rival leagues, and anticipated profits from franchise fees and higher media rates for owners of established teams. Sports entrepreneurs, well aware that by 1970 nine of the twenty largest cities were located in the sunbelt, established their new franchises in untapped, rapidly growing cities like Dallas, Houston, Los Angeles, and Phoenix.

The main political pressure in favor of expansion came from Washington; entrepreneurs feared that Congress might enact antimonopoly laws against the major sports leagues for limiting the number of franchises and thereby keeping big-time sports out of many cities. This concern came to the fore in 1961 when the Washington Senators moved to a suburb of Minneapolis in quest of greater profits. Leaders of organized baseball feared that the loss of the local club might encourage Congress to eliminate the sport's special exemption from antitrust legislation. Consequently, the AL quickly added two new franchises—one in Los Angeles and the other in the nation's capital—to mollify the Congress.

Far more important in promoting expansion was the rise of new sports leagues. The most important new league was the American Football League (AFL), organized in 1960 by businessmen previously rebuffed in efforts to secure NFL franchises because NFL owners feared spreading their sport too thinly. Six of the eight AFL teams were located in metropolitan areas that had had no football teams and just two in cities that had NFL franchises. The strategy was to survive long enough to force a merger—a formula that subsequent interloping leagues would adopt. The NFL responded by expanding into Minneapolis—St. Paul to preempt that important market and into Dallas to compete with the local AFL club for that potentially lucrative location. In its early years the AFL struggled badly, but survived on a national television contract with ABC. Then in 1964 the league signed a lucrative five-year, $42-million contract with NBC which financed a full-scale salary war that directly led to a merger with the NFL in 1966.

A lot of the reticence against expansion was fear of changing a profitable status quo by presenting the public with a weaker product and diluted rivalries. This was especially true of the NHL, a cartel that filled 94.5 percent of its seats in the early 1960s. However, league executives and team owners soon learned they could make a lot of money adding new teams by charging exorbitant entrance fees and indemnities and broadening the TV audiences for their sport. For example, when the AFL merged with the NFL, it was assessed $18 million for permitting the Raiders and the Jets to play within the territorial limits of the 49ers and Giants. In addition, entrance fees for new teams rose from $2 million in 1960 to $18 million in 1976. The first major league expansions clubs were charged $1.8 million in 1961 plus $75,000 per player drafted to stock their rosters. By the end of the decade the cost had gone up to $5.25 million in the AL and $10 million in the NL plus $7 million for the forty players drafted by them from the established teams.[17]

The expansion of hockey, and to a lesser degree basketball, was tied to the hopes of securing a network television contract. In 1966 the NHL decided to emulate the other major sports by increasing the number of teams. The main purpose of doubling the number of clubs and locating them in such cities as Atlanta, Los Angeles, and San Francisco—none of which had any tradition of winter sports—was to take advantage of their valuable television markets. League owners believed that an NHL with major cities situated across the country would be a far more attractive package for television than the old league with just Boston, Detroit, Chicago, and New York.[18]

Making Semipublic Space Public: Governmental Subsidization of Stadiums and Arenas

Beginning slowly in the 1950s, mayors and other community leaders vigorously sought to maintain or attract professional teams by building expensive municipal stadiums or arenas and promising advantageous leases and other financial inducements. They hoped to certify their city's metropolitan status, create a positive attitude for tourism and commerce, and enhance their own civic image. Before this time very few major sports franchises played in edifices that were not privately operated. In baseball, for example, the only exception were the Cleveland Indians, who first played in the 80,000-seat Municipal Stadium in 1932. But by the early 1960s sports businesses were rapidly moving their operations into publicly paid-for stadiums as a matter of course. By 1970–71, 69.7 percent of all facilities used by major league sports teams were publicly owned; 23.7 percent were privately owned; and the rest (6.6 percent) were university affiliated. The only major sport that mainly used private facilities was hockey (66.7 percent), which historically had been played in large multipurpose buildings like Madison Square Garden. Back in the 1920s promoters who controlled those arenas had introduced hockey to fill up open dates. However, a minority of baseball stadiums (30.4 percent), football fields (22.6 percent), and basketball courts (16.3 percent) were privately owned. By 1988 the proportion of privately controlled baseball parks had declined to just five out of twenty-four (20.8 percent) and the football fields to two out of twenty-eight (7.1 percent).[19]

In the 1950s the old ballparks built between 1909 and 1916 were dilapidated and in need of expensive repairs. Furthermore, the surrounding neighborhoods were deteriorating and increasingly inhabited by new poor ethnic groups whose presence was unsettling to many middle-class sports fans. The widespread demand among growing young cities for sports franchises created an enviable situation for baseball teams seeking greener pastures; communities bid against each other to secure a ball club. The main selling point were provisions for a new or refurbished publicly owned ballpark, where the rent was cheap, the site was accessible to car drivers, and the surrounding neighborhood was safe and attractive.

Until recently, the debate over the building of public sports palaces was usually one-sided. While some critics argued that sports teams were businesses and should pay for their own facilities, city fathers, local boosters, and sportswriters generally favored opening up the public purse for a worthy project like a new ballpark or civic arena. The money spent would be a sound investment in their city's future, providing a great psychological boost, promoting confidence and hometown pride, and encouraging economic development. For example, when New Yorkers debated whether or not to rebuild Yankee Stadium in the early 1970s, politicians argued that it would help attract tourists, fill up hotels and restaurants, and revitalize its neighborhood and the rest of the borough. As Bronx borough president Robert Abrams asserted, a new stadium would generate the kind of electricity the city needed, "not only in real dollars, but in spirit. We're in a psychological crisis. Decisions are being made every day to come to New York, to leave New York, to invest in New York." Abrams argued that fixing up the ballpark would be interpreted as a message to local businessmen that the city was on the way back from its fiscal crisis.[20] In less established cities, investing in local sports arenas was a means of gaining widespread positive publicity. In 1977 San Antonio's mayor justified a $3.7-million improvement of the Convention Center, the home of the Spurs basketball team. "We have a great opportunity through the gaining of national stature on the sports scene. This will help attract industry and assist our economy." Rare was the urban politician who opposed expensive sports construction projects and ran the risk of being identified as an unprogressive killjoy who let a beloved team leave town or failed to bring in a much desired sports franchise.[21]

Once a community decided to build a new playing facility and the local movers and shakers had lined up behind the project, the next problem was to find a suitable location. In the past ballparks were built on the suburban fringes in middle-class residential areas; arenas, in entertainment zones in or near the CBD where there was a lot of nightlife. In both cases the buildings were at places with excellent mass transit. In the last two decades many of the new sports palaces and stadiums have been constructed both in the CBD, like the Omni in Atlanta and Joe Louis Arena in Detroit, and, increasingly, in suburbs—a major innovation. The Forum (Inglewood, California), the Brendan Byrne Arena (the Meadowlands in New

Jersey), and the Nassau County Coliseum (Uniondale, New York) are three of the most important suburban arenas, all situated where they would be accessible to the well-off suburbanites who comprise a major portion of indoor sports audiences. By 1970 one-fifth of the new baseball and football stadiums were also being built in suburbs like Bloomington, Minnesota, and Arlington, Texas, and the trend has continued to grow in that direction with facilities for football like Giants Stadium in the Meadowlands. Those ballparks built within the city limits are usually in or near the CBD—as in Atlanta, Cincinnati, Philadelphia, Pittsburgh, St. Louis, and Seattle—which had almost never been the case before, at least not in this century. Urban planners advocated downtown sites to promote civic development, save the CBD, and build confidence in the city's future. They are located near major downtown hotels to promote tourism; some also serve as convention centers. While centrally located, the new urban parks are not necessarily well serviced by mass transit but are always situated along major highway interchanges, to facilitate suburban attendance, and have excellent parking facilities. Parking is normally a scarce commodity in the CBD, so this goal is hard to achieve. Pittsburgh, for instance, originally had just 4,000 parking spaces at Three Rivers Stadium; Seattle's Kingdome, built in 1975, just 2,500. In Cincinnati the architects dealt with this problem by providing parking space underneath Riverfront Stadium.[22]

Once a site was chosen, the final, and greatest, problem was raising the money for construction, which has reached staggering levels. A number of private indoor arenas were built in the 1960s, like the $16-million Forum and the $43-million, thirteen-story Madison Square Garden on the former site of Penn Station in midtown Manhattan (later nearly torn down because the land is too valuable). These structures are used year-round and generate most of their revenue from nonsporting events. The skyrocketing cost of such structures can be afforded only by international conglomerants like Gulf & Western, which had planned to build a new Madison Square Garden next to the Javits Convention Center in Manhattan, or by governmental agencies like the New Jersey Sports and Exposition Authority, which paid $76 million for the 20,000-seat Brendan Byrne Arena. The expense of outdoor grounds is usually far greater; consequently, no privately owned major league baseball park has been built since 1962.[23]

Most stadiums built in the late 1960s and early 1970s cost from $40 million for simple single-purpose open structures to $60 million for complex multipurpose domed facilities. The cheapest publicly financed outdoor facility was the 70,000 Rich Stadium in Buffalo, built exclusively for football for $23.5 million after the Bills had threatened to leave town. More representative were multipurpose open-air stadiums like Three

Rivers in Pittsburgh, which cost $35 million, and Riverfront in Cincinnati, which cost $41 million. While construction costs varied from region to region, they escalated rapidly everywhere. In 1970 Three Rivers cost $700 per seat to build, while just five years before Atlanta's Fulton County Stadium had only cost $314 per seat. Projects planned at relatively reasonable rates (which had helped convince the public to support them), like the renovation of Yankee Stadium, often ended up with huge overruns. In 1971, when the city took over the stadium, it announced that refurbishment would take a year and cost $24 million. By the time the final bills were in, the renovations, along with a new multilevel garage and a new highway access ramp for car-driving (i.e., suburban) fans cost over $100 million. And the football Giants had vacated the Bronx, moving across the river into New Jersey.[24]

The Houston Astrodome, constructed for $45 million in 1965, was a model for subsequent domed stadiums. The Astrodome was built as a civic monument that was anticipated to become a center for public entertainment and an attraction for conventions and other businesses—expectations that were overly optimistic. The price of domed stadiums went up even faster than that of open-air structures, with the exception of the Pontiac Silverdome, located twenty-five miles north of Detroit. It cost $690 a seat—actually well below the average of $802 for the previously built open-air stadiums. This was the result of careful control and monitoring of expenses and the utilization of the newest and most innovative construction methods. Instead of a rigid roof, the structure was covered by fabric supported by hot air. The Silverdome might have proved the wave of the future, but in the winter of 1985 the roof collapsed from the weight of snow, which shook public confidence in its safety.[25]

The fiscal responsibility exercised by the Pontiac project was certainly not duplicated in the construction of the New Orleans Superdome. The Superdome was originally planned to be a 55,000-seat edifice which would cost $35 million and be self-supporting, but foolish booster pride caused a change in plans. The agency building the structure, the Louisiana Stadium and Exposition District (LSED), was given a virtual blank check by the legislature and constructed a 97,000-seat enclosed field which cost $163 million. The revised plans were justified by the unrealized expectation of a major league baseball tenant and the overly optimistic consultant reports on anticipated use of the Superdome.[26]

Public support of private franchises extended beyond the construction of ballparks and arenas to include the underpricing of rents and various fees, direct subsidies such as purchasing broadcast rights, and indirect subsidies such as undertaking the cost of constructing highways and exit ramps and giving up revenue because the stadiums were tax exempt. Economist Benjamin Okner estimated that in 1970–71 sports teams received indirect subsidies worth $8.8 million from municipal governments. He found that direct subsidies to indoor arenas were relatively small, but the typical outdoor stadium received an annual subsidy of about $400,000.[27]

Recent studies have pointed to the escalation of subsidies granted to sports franchises. A 1978 *Sports Illustrated* study on the economics of sport estimated that local governments were underwriting team sports by $25 million a year. During the 1970s teams normally paid less than 10 percent of their gate receipts to their landlords. The best deal of all belonged to the Milwaukee Brewers. In 1970 they were brought in from Seattle, where the Pilots had floundered as an expansion team. In the community's haste to get a big league franchise, the county agreed to charge $1 for the first one million admissions, and then just 5 percent for the next half million. Thus, in 1977, when the Brewers drew 1.1 million fans who paid an average admission of $3.68, the county received just $21,149. A much more equitable arrangement existed in Philadelphia, where the Phillies paid over $1 million to rent their municipal park. In New York the Yankees had an exceptionally favorable contract with their lessors. When George Steinbrenner purchased the Bronx Bombers from CBS in 1973, he had the city rewrite his lease to include a clause that permitted the Yankees to deduct maintenance costs from their rent. In 1976, when the Yankees grossed $11.9 million, they would have paid the city $854,504 if the original terms were in effect. But after the calculations were made according to the new lease, the city ended up *owing* the Yankees $10,000. One year later, when the team grossed $13.4 million, the city's return was just $170,681, or less than 1.5 percent of the gross.[28]

The economic impact of the heavy subsidization of professional team sports by local governments has fallen well short of exaggerated booster expectations. The highly positive predictions of private consultants (those who made negative reports were usually fired) have been far out of line with actual results, often because they overestimated the numbers of out-of-town fans and underestimated the alternative entertainments available to urban residents. Advocates of municipal stadiums also relied too heavily on the dramatic economic consequences of spectacles like the World Series and the Superbowl. The later worth purportedly $80 million to San Francisco in 1985. Even if the estimated yield is correct, such occasions are rare events which might occur in a city once or twice in a decade, if ever. Superbowls are not held in the home park of competitors, but in either resort cities or towns with domed stadiums. Cities like

Miami, New Orleans, and San Francisco are going to have high rates of hotel occupancy in mid-January regardless of the location of the Superbowl.[29]

Since open-air stadiums are vacant most of the year, it is nearly impossible for municipal governments to make up their subsidy and doubtful that any of them make a profit. Even an indoor structure like the Astrodome has been under-utilized and did not pay for its own cost. The high fiscal cost to a city of subsidizing professional team sport has been well documented by economists Mark S. Rosentraub and Samuel R. Nunn in their study of the Dallas suburbs of Arlington and Irving. In 1972 Arlington convinced the Washington Senators to move there by building them a $20-million stadium and establishing a corporation to buy media rights to the ball games for $7.5 million. Irving wooed the Cowboys from Dallas by raising a bond issue to pay for a new $25-million stadium after the club had failed to convince the Dallas municipal government to build them a football field. The suburban leaders recruited the franchises in hopes of gaining prestige, revenue, and entertainment for local residents, much the same way they sought to attract industry and businesses to improve their community's tax base and quality of life. All the profits acrued from Texas Stadium between 1972 and 1975 were completely eaten up by operating expenses. Enough profits were made a year later to retire stadium bonds for the first time, but there was still no marginal revenue left over for the city. Despite all the traffic passing through, neither city was able to make much money from sales taxes, and in fact whatever financial benefits resulted spilled over into adjacent cities. Paying for the baseball field left Arlington with the lowest bond rating of any Texas city in its class.[30]

If cities did not benefit financially from subsidizing professional sports, were the neighborhoods surrounding ballparks improved by their presence? Despite the promises made by urban politicians and civic boosters when they first drew up their long-range plans, the new sports palaces have had little impact on their surrounding area. In Pittsburgh, for example, the city assured the public that along with the completion of Three Rivers Stadium there would be road improvements as well as a new park, a marina, a hotel, and restaurants in the neighborhood, but none of those plans came to fruition. In the Bronx, where community improvement was the primary justification for refurbishing Yankee Stadium, there have been no apparent benefits to local residents and merchants. "That's an isolated place over there," pointed out a storekeeper to journalist Robert Lipsyte; "people just drive in and out." While there was money for new access ramps to the highway, no funds were appropriated to fix up the public park located behind the stadium, which would have improved security for residents and bolstered their spirit. Few observers would disagree with Lipsyte's judgment that the $100 million project failed to anchor the borough's rehabilitation and failed in its symbolic goals of restoring public confidence in the city and halting white flight to suburbia.[31]

Two sports facilities that did have an apparent ameliorative impact on their neighborhoods were Busch Stadium in St. Louis and the Meadowlands Complex in East Rutherford, New Jersey. Built by a subsidiary of the brewery that owns the Cardinals, Busch Stadium was located in the old Skid Row section, in conjunction with parking areas and a huge hotel. A second major hotel and office buildings soon followed in its wake. However, this was just one part of the city's major effort at rejuvenating the downtown, best symbolized by the Gateway Arch, built in 1965 before the stadium was completed. The Meadowlands Complex, just five miles from New York City, includes the 76,500-seat Giants Stadium and the 35,000 seat Meadowlands Racetrack, built in 1976 at a cost of $302 million, along with the Brendan Byrne Arena. Previously a vacant dumping and trucking area, the site had enormous potential because it was an hour's drive from twenty million people. The master plan, originally drawn up by the Hackensack Meadowlands Development Commission in 1971, foresaw the construction of office buildings, factories, hotels, and housing in addition to the sports complex. A lot of these projects have been completed or are on schedule for completion. While the commission does not claim that development could not have occurred without the presence of the sports complex, it does believe that its presence and the publicity directed towards the area helped accelerate the rate of capital investment.[32]

Urbanization and the Dimensions of Profitability

Many factors go into determining the profitability of a particular sports team. These include the popularity of the sport (especially crucial for national television contracts), public subsidies, the character and business orientation of the ownership, gate receipts, and hometown variables. In general, baseball was the most profitable team sport until the late 1960s, when it was supplanted by professional football, largely because of its lucrative television contracts which reached $50 million in 1970 and $164 million in 1977.[33]

The degree to which hometown variables influence attendance is not the same in all sports. The size of the home city was not a crucial variable in the old NHL before expansion or the new NFL after expansion because the demand for seats exceeded or nearly exceeded availability. Before 1966 the NHL clubs sold out nearly 95 percent of their seats, while by

1970 two-thirds of the NFL teams nearly always sold out. Green Bay's small population had no negative impact on ticket sales since it generally sold out its 50,000 seat stadium. The primary factor in attendance differentials among NFL teams has become the home field seating capacity. This has encouraged some relocation of teams to stadiums that hold more seats and generate greater profits.[34] In 1983 the Raiders moved from Oakland to the Los Angeles Coliseum, which had 40,000 more seats than their old field. A year later the Colts moved to Indianapolis, attracted by various concessions from the local government, which had built a new park with a seating capacity that surpassed the old Baltimore field. Finally, in 1984 the Jets moved from Shea Stadium to Giants Stadium, mainly because there were 20,000 more seats at the Meadowlands park.

While the size of the home city was not important in football or hockey, it has been crucial in baseball and basketball, where ticket demand is highly elastic. Teams in large metropolitan areas were far more likely to make money than those in smaller cities because of the greater potential ticket-buying audiences. The best drawing baseball teams were usually in New York, Chicago, or Los Angeles, which each had two teams. Economist Roger Noll estimated that in order for an average team in the early 1970s to draw one million fans, which was regarded as the break-even point, it had to be located in a Standard Metropolitan Statistical Area (SMSA) of 1.9 million residents. As the SMSA's population increased by one million, its team could expect to draw about 237,000 more customers. The relationship of urban size to attendance was quite similar in basketball. In the early 1950s, when the NBA included such mid-sized cities as Fort Wayne, Rochester, and Syracuse, there was a high correlation between city size and profitability.[35]

The ability of baseball and basketball teams to take advantage of their potential audiences was closely tied to quality of play—a situation that was not paralleled in football, in which mediocre teams in the 1970s like the Chicago Bears sold out despite their poor showing on the field. Whereas an average-quality major league team needed to be located in an SMSA of 1.9 million to draw one million fans, low-quality teams needed a population base of 2.9 million to reach the same attendance level. Only New York, Chicago, Los Angeles, Detroit, Philadelphia, and Boston were large enough to draw well with consistently losing teams. On the other hand, winning bolstered attendance substantially, especially in the year after a pennant victory, because season tickets and early spring crowds would increase substantially in anticipation of the forthcoming campaign. The degree of appreciation varied according to the size of the SMSA; a pennant in New York was worth as much as seven times in ticket sales what it was worth in a smaller town. In the case of basketball, Noll argued that winning was twice as important as in baseball, even though NBA races are seldom close and relatively meaningless since most teams make the playoffs. Thus in the early 1970s, when the New York Knickerbockers had one of the finest teams in the NBA, the high quality of play combined with expensive ticket prices in the nation's largest city to make the club the most profitable of all sports franchises. But on the other hand, when the Knicks had inferior teams on the court, fans did not come out to see them play.[36]

The quality of a team was improved when it added a star player; attendance would go up as more fans came to the park because of his charismatic and excellent play and because the club's record got better. The increased gate varied substantially from city to city. Noll estimated that adding a top baseball player to a team in a small city increased attendance by about 6 percent, while adding a star like Reggie Jackson to a New York team could improve the box office by about 500,000 admissions—a remarkable increase at a time when 2 million was close to the league record. Thus it made a lot of sense for teams in major markets—like the Yankees, Phillies, and Angels—to get heavily involved in bidding for free agents in the 1970s because the addition of a star player, even at a high salary, was a good investment. It was probably not for the Seattle Mariners or the Kansas City Royals.[37]

The addition of a star player was even more valuable in basketball, a sport in which star players have the greatest direct impact on their team's winning record. In 1970 adding a new star to a professional basketball team located in the average-sized city was worth over 1,650 extra admissions per game, plus almost 700 more if he helped improve the club's record by ten games. For example, the addition of Artis Gilmore to the Kentucky Colonels of the American Basketball Association in 1971 was worth about 3,000 tickets per game, or $250,000 a year. The value was even greater in New York, where the addition of a star was estimated by Noll to be worth 320,000 tickets over the course of a season. However, in the early 1980s, when the average player earned $185,000 and stars got over $1 million, management was less likely to recoup such expenses through increased revenues, but still felt compelled to pay huge salaries to maintain their audience. There is probably more pressure in basketball to please the home town fans than in baseball or football, since the host club keeps all the gate and shares nothing with the visiting team.[38]

Attendance at baseball and basketball games was also affected by variables reflecting the quality of urban life—income, race, the age of a sports structure, and the character of its neighborhood. Noll found an inverse correlation between baseball attendance and income but a positive correlation for basketball. In the early 1980s baseball tickets averaged about $3.50, which was well below tickets for other sports; football, for instance, cost about four times as much. On top of this, fans had to add the cost of food and parking, the latter alone costing upwards of five dollars or more.[39] Such costs helped make baseball far more a working-class spectator sport than football, basketball, or hockey.

The construction of new stadiums had a very positive impact on attendance. For example, when the Phillies moved into their new park in 1971, attendance immediately doubled. Noll estimated that an average-quality team in a typical major league city stood to gain 378,000 extra admissions by moving into a new facility. The novelty of the new ballpark was a big attraction: perhaps fans felt they were getting more for their entertainment dollar in a safer, cleaner, and more comfortable sports palace. However, the novelty wore off in due course.[40]

Noll found a negative correlation between attendance at baseball and basketball games and the presence of a large black population. Impressionistic evidence suggests that blacks are underrepresented at professional spectator sports, presumably because of the expense. The limited black attendance has been a crucial concern for NBA executives, whose sport is so dominated by black athletes, and competent white players are in great demand as gate attractions.[41]

Noll did not identify a direct linkage between urban decay and racial composition but pointed out that cities which have old downtown arenas situated in unsafe neighborhoods and old baseball parks in undesirable neighborhoods were mainly large northern and midwestern cities with relatively large black populations. Certainly, stadiums and arenas located in safe locations will normally draw better than those in dangerous sites. In the mid-1960s the Chicago White Sox almost left town because so many fans were afraid to travel to Comiskey Park, which is across the street from the city's Black Belt. One of the major reasons that owners demanded new ballparks from local governments was to escape their declining surroundings, a fall caused not by the aging of inner-city communities.[42]

The size of big league cities affected not only attendance but also local broadcasting revenues, an essential component of profitability in baseball. Major league clubs first began selling the rights for radio transmission of games in 1933, with some reticence, afraid that free radio would cut into live attendance. By 1939 all teams had radio contracts; the most lucrative was held by the New York Giants, who sold their rights for $110,000 a year. When television was introduced to a mass audience after the war, sports coverage became an early staple. Sixteen percent of air time in 1949 was devoted to sports. Football first went on television in Los Angeles in 1950, after the sponsor guaranteed to make up any lost box-office revenues. Attendance dropped by half, to 158,000. Consequently, home games were blacked out in 1951, and attendance at the Coliseum soon returned to the pre-TV level. In the 1950s NFL teams made their own local arrangements, which varied widely from the $158,000 for the football Giants to a mere $15,000 for the Chicago Cardinals, who lagged far behind the Bears in the hearts of Windy City fans. In the 1960s the NFL moved to network packaging. [43]

The televising of major league baseball games in the late 1940s developed new fans and bolstered attendance at big league games but virtually destroyed the minor leagues, whose attendance dropped from 42 million in 1949 to 15.5 million eight years later. Local broadcasting revenues in 1950 were a modest $3.4 million but more than doubled a decade later to $9.4 million. By 1970, when the number of teams had increased from 16 to 24, total revenues went up to $21.85 million. During that ten-year span the average revenue per team increased from $585,000 to $910,000. But these yields were unevenly divided, with the biggest metropolitan areas having the largest nodal zones usually getting the lion's share. However, there were important exceptions—namely, the Cubs and Red Sox, who played in big metropolitan areas with major media markets but lacked aggressive, profit-oriented owners to effectively bargain with the media. A leading expert on sports broadcasting estimated that in the 1960s these two clubs earned from $156,000 to $337,000 a year less than they should have considering their large viewing audiences. Local revenues were also a function of ratings, which were closely tied to team performance. After the Yankees finished last in 1966, the new TV contract was worth $250,000 less than the prior one. On the other hand, after the Reds won a pennant in 1970, their fee rose by $400,000. [44]

Broadcasting opportunities have had a major impact on franchise shifts in the major leagues. In 1961, when the Senators deserted Washington, D.C., for Bloomington, Minnesota, the main reason was that their new media contract was worth triple the old one, signed when they were in competition with the Baltimore Orioles for media coverage. Five years later the Milwaukee Braves moved to Atlanta primarily to take advantage of the huge Atlanta television market that blanketed the Southeast. The most the Braves had ever made from television in Milwaukee was $500,000, but they were guaranteed $1.2 million in the Gate City. In 1967, when the Athletics left Kansas City for Oakland, an important inducement was the offer of a combined radio-television package worth $705,000, compared to the paltry $98,000 back in Kansas City. [45]

By the end of the 1970s there was still a sharp imbalance in local media revenues, though it was somewhat offset by baseball's network television contracts, worth $970,000 to each club in 1978. The top-grossing club that year was the Red Sox, no longer under "benevolent" ownership, which grossed $2.5 million through its monopoly of the valuable New England market. On the other hand, Kansas City was still on the bottom, earning just $350,000 because, as their general manager noted, "our market is the smallest and most diffuse in the nation." The six top-grossing clubs averaged $1.8 million and were all located in major markets. The bottom six, which included such excellent teams as the Orioles, Brewers, and Royals, were all in minor markets and averaged slightly more than $600,000. The size of the market, not the quality of the product, determined a team's broadcasting revenues. [46]

Conclusion: Urbanization and Professional Team Sports

The spatial dimensions of professional sports franchises and their playing areas have undergone important changes since World War II. Virtually all clubs are located in major metropolitan areas, accessible to large numbers of possible "live" spectators or television viewers. Unstable leagues became more solid as they weeded out franchises in smaller cities and, along with the formerly stable associations, expanded into new markets in the West and the sunbelt to take advantage of population growth there. A number of franchises migrated west from older declining eastern cities, which had either small populations or more than one team in the same sport. They were mainly pulled by the new towns, which offered fans hungry for live entertainment, lucrative media contracts, and local governments willing to provide financial subsidies including new stadiums, rather than pushed from their old towns, which were nearly always anxious to keep them.

The location of spectatorial sporting sites, their physical character, and their ownership underwent important changes, especially in the 1960s and 1970s. Ballparks and arenas had to be constructed in cities that secured major league franchises and older edifices that housed the established teams needed to be replaced. In the past, such buildings had been privately built and operated, but in this era the costs were often too great for team owners; hence the great preponderance of new sports facilities were built by local governments. Public leaders believed such expensive projects enhanced their community's economic well-being, bolstered local pride, and boosted the city's reputation. Sports executives learned to manipulate public fears of losing a franchise or hopes of gaining one to secure the use of modern new parks (many of which looked the same) with all the latest features for minimal rent. Teams in the rustbelt moved from declining neighborhoods into the CBD or the suburbs; the local citizens paid the cost to keep the teams in town. The new sites were chosen because of accessibility by highway to suburban fans and because the ballparks or arenas were expected to become focal points for downtown redevelopment or suburban development. Such rippling benefits seldom occurred, yet urban planners, civic boosters, and sports fans have been very slow to recognize and criticize the high price paid to subsidize sports teams, which are private businesses, to provide entertainment and psychic rewards to their community.

Conclusion: Urbanization and the Rise of American Sport

The process of urbanization was both the crucial factor in shaping the rise of organized sport and a major influence in shaping the growth of recreational sports. The salient characteristics of modern sport first emerged in cities, where sporting structures and facilities were established, sport became institutionalized, and athletes competed in organized and unorganized games. Yet the city was more than simply a backdrop or site for the flowering and maturation of sport or a catalyst for those changes. The principal social and cultural elements of urbanization (its physical structure, social organizations, and belief and behavior systems) that combined to produce organic urban communities also strongly influenced the direction of American sport history. At the same time the development of American sport influenced the process of city building and helped shape the path of urban development.

The impact of urbanization on sport can be traced as far back as the Colonial and early Republic eras, when only 5 percent of the American population lived in cities. While early American sport was affected mainly by frontier conditions, old-world traditions, and various prevailing ideologies, the importance of urban communities to sport far transcended sheer numbers. The first cities were small centers of concentrated populations, which provided potential players and spectators and sporting sites close by, and in which a secular cosmopolitan culture developed that regarded sport in a positive light. Voluntary sports organizations were established to encourage sociability and social segregation. Publicans became the first sports entrepreneurs; they promoted sporting contests to attract men to their taverns, where they could sell them liquor. Sporting pastimes were subject to municipal approval, and local governments proscribed contests that endangered life and limb, crowded thoroughfares and hindered commerce, and undermined prevailing standards of morality.

In the period from 1820 to 1870, as the pace of urbanization accelerated, the process of city building had a far more significant influence on sport. Although most walking cities still had a lot of accessible open space, urbanization resulted in increased anomie and anonymity in larger, wealthier, and more densely populated cities. A large pool of potential athletes and spectators from different social backgrounds encouraged the formation of discrete sporting subcultures and the establishment of enclosed semipublic sports facilities to satisfy the demand of sports fans with discretionary income to view excellent sporting competition.

The dominant sporting culture at the start of this era was the sporting fraternity, who enjoyed blood and gambling sports that developed and displayed their masculinity and athletic prowess. Living in the large, anonymous cities freed single men from conventional morality and encouraged them to participate in a flourishing male bachelor subculture that emphasized a premodern life-style free of time-work discipline. By mid-century an important nexus was established between the sporting fraternity and machine politicians, who provided protection for sportsmen involved in illegal sports and in return received financial contributions, campaign workers, and votes.

One important response to the rapid pace of urbanization and the hegemony of the sporting fraternity was the development of a positive sports creed that addressed many of the problems generated by the process of city building. Social critics decried the quality of life and the social values in overcrowded, immigrant-infested, pathological cities. They belittled the materialism, artificiality, and immorality of urban life, which they contrasted to the morally and physically superior life of hardworking rugged yeomen farmers whose pastoral values had made America great. Social reformers advocated moral sports and other wholesome recreations as a solution to urban pathology. In the face of the apparent breakdown of morality due to the loss of the close-knit small town and intimate family life, ready access to vile amusements in anomic neighborhoods, and growing public health problems, the new sports ideology provided an alternative, a substitute for the lost frontier and small-town life, which would raise morality, build character, and improve health. The ideology encouraged the growth of elite and middle-class voluntary sports associations and of ethnic athletic clubs by rationalizing the social value of physical culture. These organizations arranged contests, established rules, and secured playing fields and other facilities. They also provided a community for people with similar social backgrounds which helped them maintain social distance from nonmembers and sustain their particularistic culture. The sports creed also encouraged the rise of the municipal park movement. Few public parks were developed in the antebellum era, when city governments were weak and just beginning to get the authority to provide for essential municipal services, but the movement eventually had a significant impact on urban planning, property values, and public transit routes.

The impact of urbanization upon sport was greatest and most dramatic in the era of the industrialized radial city. The large centralized populations of major cities provided the necessary audiences for a boom in commercialized spectator sports, and even small and mid-sized cities supported minor league baseball. But population growth was just one variable. The process of city building influenced sporting developments in nearly every conceivable way—most notably, changing spatial patterns, expanding municipal operations, the formation of class and ethnically defined neighborhoods, innovations in public transportation, the rise of political machines, the development of voluntary status-oriented sports associations, changing value and belief systems in a nation torn between an agrarian past and an urban present, and evolving forms of individual and group behavior on playing fields and in the grandstands.

The importance of athletics to city folk was stressed by the widely accepted positive sporting creed which by the turn of the century had become the conventional wisdom. Athletics and, in particular, team sports were regarded as symbols of democracy and as integrative mechanisms which taught traditional small-town values to urban youth. Many agencies tried to implement the ideology to Americanize and assimilate urban boys, especially impoverished second-generation inner-city lads. Although the reality of sport was far different from its public mythology, the creed operated as a cultural fiction as Americans tried to employ sports to alleviate various social problems. Industrialists used sport as part of their welfare capitalism program to fight unions and exercise social control over employees, and youth workers relied heavily on sport as a means of indoctrinating slum lads with traditional values and behavior. Reformers saw sports as a moral alternative to the vile amusements of the streets and believed they could blunt the negative influence of the streets by getting poor youth to watch or play clean sports under adult supervision. The result should be the transformation of wild delinquents into conforming, hard-working, moral, and patriotic adults.

Urbanization's impact upon sport in the radial city was particularly crucial because of changing spatial relations. Accessibility to outdoor recreational areas had begun to be a problem in the antebellum period but was a crucial factor in the large industrial cities. Many old playing sites were lost forever to alternate land uses as the inner city became increasingly crowded, central business districts were developed, and cities grew centrifugally to encompass outlying territory beyond their former borders. Old ball fields were developed for residential or commercial purposes; docks became too dangerous for swimming; and downtown streets, too busy for informal street games. Even on the urban periphery, empty lots were cut up for exploitation and old fishing streams were polluted by industrial waste. The securing and preservation of public space for municipal parks became important social and political issues in cities across the country, especially in older eastern and midwestern towns. Following New York's example, cities began taking an active role in the recreation of their residents by establishing municipal parks. The first were suburban parks in outlying sections of town, where they improved property values and provided beautiful vistas for middle-class neighbors but were inaccessible to inner-city residents, who needed such facilities the most. Consequently, in the late nineteenth century social reformers, inner-city residents, and their political representatives formed a small parks and playground movement that resulted in the construction of small, expensive inner-city parks where the space was used according to community needs. But the supply of public facilities did not keep up with local demands. City governments spent a lot of money building or improving public recreational space, especially during the Depression through programs like the WPA, yet could not satisfy the enormous needs in the inner city for safe public play space. The park movement failed to break down class, ethnic, or racial insularity or promote social integration, and some parks actually became battlegrounds between hostile neighbors.

The lack of space for play and sport in the urban core limited the sporting options of local residents, who relied mainly on their own localities as the locus for sport. They preferred contests that fit in best with their lack of space, privacy, and funds. Boys living in slums had to play outdoors in crowded streets or alleys and indoors in public schools, quasi-public settlement houses, and semipublic billiard halls and bowling alleys. Their favorite sports reflected their environment; they were cheap and required little space. By the 1910s and 1920s billiards and bowling were widely enjoyed at pool halls and bowling alleys located in working-class neighborhoods, where they were popular hangouts for street-corner youth. Young men frequented these semipublic sites to demonstrate their prowess in a setting that provided sociability and the privacy they were denied at home. They played basketball at neighborhood settlements and learned boxing at the settlements or local gyms. Boxing was especially appropriate—a functional skill for youth living in tough neighborhoods: it taught them to protect themselves against young men from rival ethnic groups, and it might provide an alternate avenue of social mobility.

Changing spatial relationships had little impact on the sporting pleasures of the elite and actually enhanced the recreational opportunities of the middle class. The rich readily escaped urban blight by hiding from it at their prestigious downtown or midtown athletic clubs or by traveling via expensive carriages, private automobiles, or trains to their private country clubs or elegant racetrack clubhouses. In the 1890s middle-income residents of the urban periphery and lower-middle-class residents of the zone of emergence escaped the cities on bicycles and, subsequently, in automobiles. Furthermore, they lived in the vicinity of the large suburban parks or at least near mass transit lines that went out to the parks where they enjoyed baseball, tennis, and other outdoor sports.

Urbanization continued to encourage the development of voluntary sports associations. As in the past the elite could certify their status by associating with others of similar stature in highly selective men's sports clubs, but unlike the past cities had become too large to allow residents to know everyone worth knowing on a first-name basis. Country clubs and athletic clubs provided a venue to make those connections while simultaneously escaping the parvenues. The middle class was also very actively involved in voluntary sports clubs by the 1890s, although the heyday of middle-class clubs did not come until the 1920s, when upwardly mobile businessmen organized their own restricted country clubs. These clubs not only sponsored expensive sports like golf but provided places to make valuable social and business contacts, assure members' social prestige, and create a sense of community—a rare commodity in new and growing American cities. Ethnic sports organizations also sought to promote a community, but one that sought to maintain their European heritage, facilitate adjustment to life in America, and pass on their culture to the next generation. These ethnic organizations sought to limit or at least supervise structural assimilation, which was precisely the opposite goal of reformers who wanted to use athletics to facilitate acculturation and structural assimilation. Ethnic clubs were located where their members lived, either in the slums or zones of emergence, where they provided private space for their members and, in certain cases like the turnhalles, for the entire community.

Finally, urbanization was crucial in the rise of commercialized spectator sport. After the Civil War sport's increasing popularity as urban entertainment plus a population boom encouraged entrepreneurs to build or rent indoor athletic facilities or enclose outdoor fields to which they charged admission fees. Intercity sports leagues were established, made feasible by interurban railroad transportation. Sports that did not require much space, like boxing, pedestrianism, and basketball, were staged in arenas, auditoriums, and gymnasiums which ranged in quality from dimly lit firetraps located in urban slums to brilliantly lit architectural landmarks like Madison Square Garden, located in the CBD or other very accessible sites. Because of the need for huge tracts of inexpensive land, the outdoor ballparks and racetracks were located on the urban periphery or in the suburbs. Since they were beyond walking distance from the CBD, it was essential to situate them near public transportation. The accommodations at racetracks ranged from the elegance of prestigious courses to the more spartan ambiance at bookmaker-run proprietary courses. The early baseball parks were dangerously constructed wooden structures with small seating capacities, but beginning in 1909, as major league baseball became very profitable, expensive modern fireproof grandstands were built. These edifices were semipublic monuments that testified to the forward-looking character of their cities.

Baseball, boxing, and the turf were all closely tied to urban politics. Professional baseball teams throughout the country were owned by local politicians (often machine politicians, if there was a machine in town) or their close associates like traction magnates, at least until the 1920s and often longer. These teams provided the hometown with a prized source of civic pride and an agency for promoting a sense of community. The turf was even more connected to politics because of its uncertain legal status due to its connections with gambling. The leading members of the prestigious jockey clubs were often heavily involved in politics and had powerful political allies, including machine bosses, while the owners of the outlaw proprietary tracks were often machine bosses or their closest cronies. Boxing was totally controlled by big city bosses, who arranged the fights, managed the pugilists, and controlled the arenas. These commercialized sports needed political influence for several reasons. Clout helped promoters secure the best possible sites for their semipublic structures, provided protection against competition, and secured special treatment from local governments. This was especially crucial for illegal sports whose appeal depended heavily on gambling. Illegal off-track betting was controlled by politically connected gambling syndicates that were protected against the criminal justice system by their associates in the machine. After the 1920s the influence of politicians declined in commercialized sport. The principal political problems of baseball had been resolved, and the sport was well respected and solidly entrenched. In racing and boxing, which were both widely legalized in the 1920s and 1930s, politicians were supplanted by gangsters, who ruthlessly moved into central positions in these sports to advance their illegal gambling interests and otherwise exploit the business opportunities of these pastimes.

The major changes wrought by urbanization since World War II include the complete ghettoization of the inner city, the decline of the old industrial eastern and midwestern cities, the rise of the sunbelt, and suburbanization. These developments have had a big impact on athletic participation and a huge influence on professional team sports. The historic inner-city sports are now totally dominated by blacks, who see athletics as one of the few escape routes from the ghetto and whose sporting options are still curtailed by inadequate outdoor space and underfunded interscholastic athletic programs. Instead of the Jewish, Irish, and Italian fighters of the past, prize fighters are now mainly black and Hispanic. Ironically, as the white ethnics and other urbanites moved to suburbia, their children could enjoy many more sporting choices because of the availability of space, afterschool programs, and well-financed high school athletic programs. But their sons, who now have many potential routes to success, do not have the same motivation to succeed in sports as their fathers.

The most visible impact of recent urbanization on sport has been the creation of new professional teams and leagues to exploit previously virgin territory and the geographic mobility of established franchises, either within their own metropolitan areas, or to totally new locations. The growth of new metropolises, air travel, and the construction of all-weather enclosed stadiums has greatly broadened the pool of potential new professional sports franchises.

When professional sports leagues were first founded, there was generally a lot of flux as weak teams came and went and other teams chose to leave unprofitable towns for more rewarding cities. Prior to the 1950s a sports franchise usually moved from a smaller city to a larger one simply because the new site had more potential fans. However, since the 1950s, established teams have relocated in wealthier cities with large media nodal zones promising fat radio and television contracts and local governments and community boosters guaranteeing big subsidies. Older declining cities tried to keep their teams from leaving; such a loss reflected poorly on their progressive character, hurt their economies, and destroyed public confidence. On the other hand, the new booming metropolitan areas actively courted professional franchises to promote local commerce and to certify their new cosmopolitan status. The process of saving or attracting sports franchises became an important task for urban politicians and other civic leaders concerned with boosting home town pride, business, and reputation. While urban politicians were no longer sports entrepreneurs, they did get local governments to subsidize the city's old franchises or else they pulled strings to facilitate construction projects to attract new clubs. Wily politicos got city or county governments to build multi-million-dollar public sports arenas and stadiums, which were leased for rents well below fair market value, and to provide other assistance such as tax relief or improved highways and exit ramps.

Urbanization not only influenced which cities maintained, lost, or acquired sports franchises but also played a crucial role in the location of sports facilities in each particular city. The changing spatial parameters of the modern city have led owners and urban planners to select sites different from those formerly utilized for arenas and stadiums. They have followed the middle-class white population to the suburbs and constructed a notable proportion of new facilities near suburban traffic interchanges instead of on the urban fringe close to mass transit routes. Municipal planners have also chosen sites in the heart of cities, which was not previously done because of high real estate costs. Local governmental leaders have built stadiums in the downtown area (near major traffic interchanges) in the hopes they would restore confidence in the CBD, encourage the growth of commerce and tourism, and symbolize a renaissance for their declining cities. Municipal and business leaders have sought to utilize popular interest in sport to guide urbanization toward a more favorable direction than their declining towns had recently enjoyed.

Sport, then, is not merely a recreational activity that happened to take place in cities, but is an institution that has been shaped, reshaped, and further molded by the interplay of the elements comprising the process of urbanization. While cities across the country differ in population, physical size, regional location, climate, wealth, and ethnic demographics, the development and influence of sport and sporting institutions in major metropolitan areas has been pretty much the same. In addition, America's sports institutions have been not simply a product of urbanization but have themselves deeply influenced urban change, usually for the better, in distinctive and visible ways.

Notes

Introduction

1. The first historians to consider the relationship between city and sport saw athletics as a safety valve that provided an escape from oppressive industrialized urban life. See, e.g., Frederick L. Paxson, "The Rise of Sport," *MVHR* 4 (Sept. 1917): 143–68; Arthur M. Schlesinger, *The Rise of the City, 1878–1898* (New York, 1938), 79; Foster Rhea Dulles, *A History of Recreation: America Learns to Play* (Englewood Cliffs, N.J., 1965), 136; John Higham, "The Reorientation of American Culture in the 1890s," in *The Origins of Modern Consciousness,* ed. John Weiss (Detroit, 1965), 27; Fritz Redlich, "Leisure-Time Activities:

A Historical, Sociological, and Economic Analysis,'' *Explorations in Entrepreneurial History,* 2nd series, 3 (1965): 3–23; Dale A. Somers, ''The Leisure Revolution: Recreation in the American City, 1820–1920,'' *Journal of Popular Culture* 5 (Summer 1971): 125–47, and idem, *The Rise of Sports in New Orleans, 1850–1900* (Baton Rouge, 1972), 275. Recent synthetic overviews of American sport history have argued that the rise of organized sport was the joint product of industrialization and urbanization. These scholars were mainly interested in the development of sporting institutions and were concerned with the city mainly as a catalyst or as the site where these institutional changes occur. See, e.g., John R. Betts, *America's Sporting Heritage, 1850–1950* (Reading, Mass., 1974); John A. Lucas and Ronald A. Smith, *Saga of American Sport* (Philadelphia, 1978), and Benjamin G. Rader, *American Sports: From the Age of Folk Games to the Age of Spectators* (Englewood Cliffs, N.J., 1983). For an excellent critique of the literature on sport and the city, see Stephen Hardy, ''The City and the Rise of American Sport: 1820–1920,'' *Exercise and Sports Sciences Review* 9 (1981): 183–219.

2. Louis Wirth, ''Urbanism as a Way of Life,'' *American Journal of Sociology* 44 (July 1938): 3–24; Roy Lubove, ''The Urbanization Process: An Approach to Historical Research,'' *Journal of the American Institute of Planners* 33 (Jan. 1967): 33; Eric E. Lampard, ''American Historians and the Study of Urbanization,'' *AHR* 67 (Oct. 1961): 60–61; idem, ''The Dimensions of Urban History: A Footnote to the 'Urban Crisis,' '' *Pacific Historical Review* 39 (Aug. 1970): 268 n.13; Theodore Hershberg, ''The New Urban History: Towards an Interdisciplinary History of the City,'' in *Philadelphia: Work, Space, Family, and Group Experience in the 19th Century* (New York, 1981), 7; Michael Ebner, ''Urban History: Retrospect and Prospect,'' *JAH* 68 (June 1981): 71–79.

3. Sport history monographs that emphasize the dynamic interplay between urbanization and sport include Steven A. Riess, *Touching Base: Professional Baseball and American Culture in the Progressive Era* (Westport, Conn., 1980); Stephen Hardy, *How Boston Played: Sport, Recreation, and Community, 1865–1915* (Boston, 1982); and Melvin L. Adelman, *A Sporting Time: New York City and the Rise of Modern Athletics, 1820–1870* (Urbana, Ill., 1986).

4. On urban colonial sport, see Nancy L. Struna, ''Puritans and Sports: The Irretrievable Tide of Change,'' *JSpH* 4 (Spring 1977): 1–21; idem, ''The Cultural Significance of Sport in the Colonial Chesapeake and Massachusetts'' (Ph.D. diss., University of Maryland, 1979), chaps. 1, 4; Hans-Peter Wagner, *Puritan Attitudes towards Recreation in Early Seventeenth Century New England, with Particular Consideration of Physical Recreation,* Mainzer Studies zur Amerikanistik, Ban 17 (Frankfort am Main, 1982), which is largely summarized in Peter Wagner, ''Puritan Attitudes Towards Physical Recreation in 17th Century New England,'' *JSpH* 3 (Summer 1976): 139–51; Winton U. Solberg, *Redeem the Time: The Puritan Sabbath in Early America* (Cambridge, 1977), 86–87, 107–10, 170, 207, 214, 219; Carl Bridenbaugh, *Cities in the Wilderness: Urban Life in America, 1625–1742* (1938; rep. New York, 1955), 119–20, 274–76, 278, 426–28, 435, 438, 441; idem, *Cities in Revolt: Urban Life in America, 1743–1776* (1955; rep., New York, 1964), 153, 167, 170, 363–66; Ruth E. Painter, ''Tavern

Amusements in Eighteenth Century America," *Americana* 2 (1916): 92–115; J. William Frost, *The Quaker Family in Colonial America* (New York, 1973), 207–10; J. Thomas Jable, "Pennsylvania's Early Blue Laws: A Quaker Experiment in the Suppression of Sport and Amusements, 1682–1740," *JSpH* 1 (Fall 1974): 107–21; Rhys Isaac, *The Transformation of Virginia, 1740–1790* (Chapel Hill, N.C., 1982), 94–104, 118–19, 132, 247; Jane Carson, *Colonial Virginians at Play* (Charlottesville, Va., 1965), 14–47. On the early Republic, see J. Thomas Jable, "The Pennsylvania Sunday Blue Laws of 1779: A View of Pennsylvania Society and Politics during the American Revolution," *Pennsylvania History* 38 (1976): 413–26; Jennie Holliman, *American Sport, 1785–1835* (Durham, N.C., 1938), 108–17; Soren Steward Brynn, "Some Sports in Pittsburgh during the National Period, 1775–1860," *Western Pennsylvania Historical Magazine*, pt. 1, 51 (1968): 345–68, pt. 2, 52 (1969): 57–69.

Chapter One

1. Howard P. Chudacoff, *The Evolution of American Urban Society*, 2nd ed. (Englewood Cliffs, N.J., 1981), 32, 62–63; David R. Goldfield and Blaine A. Brownell, *Urban America: From Downtown to No Town* (Boston, 1979), 14.

2. Benjamin G. Rader, *American Sports: From the Age of Folk Games to the Age of Spectators* (Englewood Cliffs, N.J., 1983), 31.

3. Melvin L. Adelman, "The Development of Modern Athletics: Sport in New York City, 1820–1870" (Ph.D. diss., University of Illinois, 1980), 70, 572, 684; Rader, *American Sports*, 33–34, 53; Dale A. Somers, *The Rise of Sports in New Orleans, 1850–1900* (Baton Rouge, 1972), 52–53; Patricia C. Click, "Leisure in the Upper South in the Nineteenth Century: A Study of Trends in Baltimore, Norfolk, and Richmond" (Ph.D. diss., University of Virginia, 1980), 93, 102, 112.

4. Melvin L. Adelman, *A Sporting Time: New York City and the Rise of Modern Athletics, 1820–1870* (Urbana, Ill., 1986), 59, 141–42, 237, 252–53; Click, "Leisure in the Upper South," 101; Elliott J. Gorn, "'Good-Bye Boys, I Die a True American': Homicide, Nativism, and Working-Class Culture in Antebellum New York City," *JAH* 74 (Sept. 1987): 388–410; Herbert Gutman, "Work, Culture and Society in Industrializing America, 1815–1919," *AHR* 78 (June 1973): 531–88.

5. Bruce Laurie, *Working People of Philadelphia, 1800–1850* (Philadelphia, 1980), 54–60; Paul Faler, "Cultural Aspects of the Industrial Revolution: Lynn, Massachusetts, Shoemakers and Industrial Morality, 1826–1860," *Labor History* 15 (Summer 1974): 381, 383, 393–94; Alvin F. Harlow, *Old Bowery Days: The Chronicle of a Famous Street* (New York, 1931), 193, 202–3; Richard B. Calhoun, "From Community to Metropolis: Fire Protection in New York City, 1790–1875" (Ph.D. diss., Columbia University, 1973), 133.

6. Rader, *American Sports*, 97–98. On Irish-American sport, see Carl Wittke, *The Irish in America* (Baton Rouge, 1956), ch. 24; William V. Shannon, *The American Irish* (New York, 1963), 95–102.

7. Adelman, *Sporting Time*, 220–21, 225–26. On the sporting functions of

the mid-nineteenth century tavern, see Herbert Asbury, *Sucker's Progress: An Informal History of Gambling in America from the Colonies to Canfield* (New York, 1938), 178–81; Harlow, *Old Bowery Days*, 296–301; H. A. Christie, "The Functions of the Tavern in Toronto, 1834–1875, with Special Reference to Sport" (MPE thesis, University of Windsor, 1973).

8. Adelman, *Sporting Time*, 222, 228; John C. Schneider, *Detroit and the Problems of Order, 1830–1880: A Geography of Crime, Riot and Policing* (Lincoln, 1980), 42–43, 94.

9. A plank was three feet wide and fifteen to sixty feet long. Men or women would walk the plank for a period of time, such as 100 hours, to win a bet. On plank walking, see John Cumming, *Runners & Walkers: A Nineteenth-Century Sports Chronicle* (Chicago, 1981), 48–49.

10. Adelman, *Sporting Time*, 241–42; Herbert Asbury, *The Gangs of New York: An Informal History of the Underworld* (New York, 1970), 49–51; Martin and Herbert J. Kaufman, "Henry Bergh, Kit Burns, and the Sportsmen of New York," *New York Folklore Quarterly* 28 (1972): 15–20.

11. For a perceptive analysis of gouging and honor on the frontier, see Elliott J. Gorn, " 'Gouge and Bite, Pull Hair and Scratch': The Social Significance of Fighting in the Southern Backcountry," *AHR* 90 (February 1985): 18–43. For an excellent survey of antebellum fighting, see Elliott J. Gorn, *The Manly Art: Bare-Knuckle Prize Fighting in America* (Ithaca, 1986), chaps. 1–4. See also Adelman, *Sporting Time*, 229–35.

12. Adelman, *Sporting Time*, 235–37; Edward K. Spann, *The New Metropolis: New York City, 1840–1857* (New York, 1981), 346.

13. Adelman, *Sporting Time*, 235–37; Gorn, *Manly Art*, chap. 4; Spann, *New Metropolis*, 346.

14. Gorn, *Manly Art*, 108–27; Adelman, *Sporting Time*, 80, 223, 237; Nat Fleischer, *The Heavyweight Champion: An Informal History of Heavyweight Boxing from 1719 to the Present Day* (New York, 1961), 55–62; *NYT*, 2 May 1878; Adelman, "Modern Athletics," 572–75.

15. Roland T. Berthoff, *British Immigrants in Industrial America, 1793–1850* (New York, 1958), 149; Daniel J. Walkowitz, *Worker City, Company Town: Iron and Cotton Worker Protest in Troy and Cohoes, New York, 1855–1884* (Urbana, Ill., 1978), 178n35; Adelman, "Modern Athletics," 263–64; Rader, *American Sports*, 90–91. On the Anglo-American trans-Atlantic sporting fraternity, see Rader, *American Sports*, 35, 52, 149–50; John R. Betts, *America's Sporting Heritage, 1850–1950* (Reading, Mass., 1974), 19–20, 47, 195; John A. Lucas and Ronald A. Smith, *Saga of American Sports* (Philadelphia, 1978), 96, 109, 111, 137–39.

16. Adelman, "Modern Athletics," 265–70, 286, 300–301.

17. George B. Kirsch, "American Cricket: Players and Clubs before the Civil War," *JSpH* 11 (Spring 1984): 28–29, 32–34, 41; idem, "The Rise of Modern Sports: New Jersey Cricketeers, Baseball Players, and Clubs, 1845–60," *New Jersey History* 101 (Spring-Summer 1983): 57, 60–62.

18. Berthoff, *British Immigrants*, 151 (quote); Gerald Redmond, *The Caledonian Games in Nineteenth-Century America* (Rutherford, N.J., 1971), 36–41,

49–56, 112–15; Rader, *American Sports,* 90; Adelman, "Modern Athletics," 538–40; *Boston Daily Globe,* 29 Aug. 1879 (quote), in Redmond, *Caledonian Games,* 39.

19. Goldfield and Brownell, *Urban America,* 153–55; Chudacoff, *Urban Society,* 52, 54, 104, 105; Kathleen Neils Conzen, *Immigrant Milwaukee, 1836–1860* (Cambridge, 1976).

20. Henry Metzner, *A Brief History of the American Turnerbund* (Pittsburgh, 1924), 8–9; Horst Ueberhorst, *Turner Unterm Sternenbanner: Der Kampf der Deutsch-Amerikanischen für Einheit, Freiheit, und Sociale Gerechtigkeit, 1848 bis 1918* (Munich, 1978); Susan Hirsch, *Roots of the American Working Class: The Industrialization of Crafts in Newark, 1800–1860* (Philadelphia, 1978), 100; Carl Wittke, *Refugees of Revolution: The German 48ers in America* (Philadelphia, 1952), 147–48; R. Von Raumer, "Physical Education," *American Journal of Education* 8 (1860): 203.

21. Conzen, *Immigrant City,* 79–80; Hirsch, *American Working Class,* 99. Data on national turner memberships was computed from Hugo Gollmer, *Namensliste der Pioniere des Nord-Amerik Turnerbundes der Jahre 1848–62* (St. Louis, 1885), and on Chicago turners from Theodor Jannsen, *Geschichte der Chicago Turn-Gemeinde* (Chicago, 1894), 9–13, used in conjunction with the *Chicago City Directory, 1854–1860* (Chicago, 1854–60).

22. Allan Stanley Horlick, *Country Boys and Merchant Princes: The Social Control of Young Men in New York* (Lewisburg, Penn., 1975), 122, 125–26, 131, 136–37. For discussions of American elites, see E. Digby Baltzell, *Philadelphia Gentlemen: The Making of a National Upper Class* (New York, 1958); and Frederick C. Jaher, *The Urban Establishment: Upper Strata in Boston, New York, Charleston, Chicago, and Los Angeles* (Urbana, Ill., 1982).

23. Adelman, *Sporting Time,* 31–38. On Stevens's sporting interests, see Rader, *American Sports,* 37–39; John Dizikes, *Sportsmen and Gamesmen* (Boston, 1981), 91–120.

24. Adelman, *Sporting Time,* 38–45, 50–51; Somers, *Sport in New Orleans,* 24–35.

25. Adelman, *Sporting Time,* 77–83; George B. Kirsch, "New Jersey and the Rise of American Sports, 1820–1870," *Journal of Regional Cultures* 4–5 (1984–85): 45; *NYT,* 5 June 1870.

26. Adelman, "Modern Athletics," 149–51, 181–82, 188–93; idem, "Quantification and Sport: The American Jockey Club, 1866–1867, A Collective Biography," in *Sport in America: New Historical Perspectives,* ed. Donald Spivey (Westport, Conn., 1985), 51–65.

27. Adelman, "Modern Athletics," 182, 188, 192–93, 221–23, 234, 236–39; idem, "American Jockey Club," 54, 56–62.

28. Adelman, "Modern Athletics," 494–502; Dizikes, *Sportsmen and Gamesmen,* 105–20; Rader, *American Sports,* 53–54.

29. Thomas Bender, *Towards an Urban Vision: Ideas and Institutions in Nineteenth-Century America* (Lexington, 1975), 21.

30. Chudacoff, *Urban Society,* 41–42, 51, 53–54; Goldfield and Brownell, *Urban America,* 65, 134–65, 172–73.

31. Stephen Hardy and Jack W. Berryman, " 'Public Amusements and Public Morality': Sport and Social Reform in the American City, 1800–1860" (paper presented at the annual meeting of the Organization of American Historians, 2 April 1981, Detroit), 6–8, 10–21; Jack W. Berryman, "Sport, Health, and the Rural-Urban Conflict: Baltimore and John Stuart Skinner's American Farmer, 1819–1829," *Conspectus of History* 1, no. 8 (1982): 47; Paul S. Boyer, *Urban Masses and Moral Order in America, 1820–1920* (Cambridge, 1978); Alice Felt Tyler, *Freedom's Ferment: Phases of American Social History from the Colonial Period to the Outbreak of the Civil War* (1944; rep. New York, 1962); Ronald G. Walters, *American Reformers, 1815–1860* (New York, 1978); John R. Betts, "Mind and Body in Early American Thought," *JAH* 54 (March 1968): 787–805.

32. Betts, "Mind and Body," 797–98, 802, 804–5; John R. Betts, "Public Recreation, Public Parks and Public Health before the Civil War," in *The History of Physical Education and Sports*, ed. Bruce L. Bennett (Chicago, 1972), 45–46. Quote is from *Spirit* 30 (10 March 1860): 54, cited in Adelman, "Modern Athletics," 666.

33. Oliver Wendell Holmes, "The Autocrat of the Breakfast Table," *Atlantic Monthly* 1 (May 1858): 881; Thomas Wentworth Higginson, "Saints and Their Bodies," ibid. 1 (March 1858): 582–95. For other comments comparing Americans unfavorably to their British cousins, see "Thoughts on Manly Education," *Knickerbocker Magazine* 30 (Nov. 1847): 417, quoted in Robert M. Lewis, "Cricket and the Beginnings of Organized Baseball in New York," *IJHS* 4 (Dec. 1987): 320; and A. A. Livermore, "Gymnastics," *North American Review* 81 (1855): 51–52. On Higginson see also John A. Lucas, "Thomas Wentworth Higginson: Early Apostle of Health and Fitness," *JOHPER* 42 (Feb. 1971): 30–33; and Stephen Hardy, *How Boston Played: Sport, Recreation and Community, 1865–1915* (Boston, 1982): 52–53. On the positive influence of sport on the health of urban women, see Betts, "Mind and Body," 798–99; Adelman, "Modern Athletics," 655, 662–63; Lucas and Smith, *Saga of American Sports*, 73–75, 83, 91; Roberta J. Park, " 'Embodied Selves': The Rise and Development of Concern for Physical Education, Active Games and Recreation for American Women, 1776–1865," *JSpH* 5 (Summer 1978): 5–41; and Linda J. Borish, "The Robust Woman and the Muscular Christian: Catharine Beecher, Thomas Higginson, and Their Vision of American Society, Health and Physical Activities," *IJHS* 4 (September 1987): 139–53.

34. Betts, "Public Recreation," 46–48.

35. Adelman, "Modern Athletics," 669. For an excellent discussion of the use of wholesome sport to improve decadent urban society, see Hardy, *How Boston Played*, 45–53.

36. Boyer, *Urban Masses*, 3–120; Hardy, *How Boston Played*, 40–41, 45–49; Rader, *American Sports*, 30–35; Adelman, "Modern Athletics," 581–86, 661.

37. Hardy, *How Boston Played*, 48; Sawyer, *A Plea for Amusements* (New York, 1857), 291, cited in ibid., 50.

38. Hardy, *How Boston Played*, 50–51.

39. Lucas and Smith, *American Sports*, 108–9, 137, 139; Adelman, "Modern Athletics," 674–75; Hardy, *How Boston Played*, 50–51; Charles E. Rosenberg,

"Sexuality, Class and Role in Nineteenth Century America," *AQ* 25 (May 1973): 129; *NYT*, 21 June 1854 (quote), cited in Adelman, "Modern Athletics," 686. See also Benjamin G. Rader, "Muscular Christianity, the Biological Theory of Play, and the Adult-Managed Boys' Sports Movement, 1890–1920" (paper presented at the annual meeting of NASSH, 30 May 1979, Austin, Tex.), 3.

40. On the formation of the urban middle class see Cindy Sondik Aron, *Ladies and Gentlemen of the Civil Service: Middle-Class Workers in Victorian America* (New York, 1987), 1–5; John S. Gilkeson, Jr., *Middle-Class Providence, 1820–1940* (Princeton, 1986); Burton J. Bledstein, *The Culture of Professionalism: The Middle Class and the Development of Higher Education in America* (New York, 1976); and Stuart Blumin, "The Hypothesis of Middle-Class Formation in Nineteenth-Century America: A Critique and Some Proposals," *AHR* 90 (April 1985): 299–338. On middle-class manliness, see E. Anthony Rotundo, "Body and Soul: Changing Ideals of American Middle-Class Manhood, 1770–1920," *JSH* 16 (Fall 1983): 23–38; Peter Stearns, *Be a Man! Males in Modern Society* (New York, 1979); and Joe L. Dubbert, *A Man's Place: Masculinity in Transition* (Englewood Cliffs, N.J., 1979).

41. Faler, "Cultural Aspects of the Industrial Revolution," 381, 383, 393–94; Laurie, *Working People*, 54–60. For a detailed discussion of antebellum working-class sport, see Steven A. Riess, "Working-Class Sports in America, 1820–1920" (paper read at the annual meeting of the American Historical Association, Pacific Coast Branch, 12 Aug. 1982, San Francisco), 1–25.

42. On the impact of the factory system, see Alan Dawley, *Class and Community: The Industrial Revolution in Lynn* (Cambridge, 1977); Paul G. Faler, *Mechanics and Manufacturers in the Early Revolution: Lynn, Massachusetts, 1780–1860* (Albany, 1981); Hirsch, *American Working Class*, esp. 99–100; Gutman, "Work, Culture and Society," 531–88; Chudacoff, *Urban Society*, 55–57. Artisans had dominated the urban labor force in the colonial era, but by 1850 most workers in the largest cities were either unskilled or semiskilled. Goldfield and Brownell, *Urban America*, 150.

43. The traditional historiography is exemplified by Betts, *America's Sporting Heritage*, Lucas and Smith, *Saga of American Sports*, and to a lesser degree, Rader, *American Sports*. The leading revisionist is Adelman, who in *Sporting Time* identified twenty-one leisure sports enjoyed by New Yorkers between 1820 and 1870, including ice skating and croquet, which were popular with the middle classes. See Adelman, *Sporting Time*, 186–87.

44. Melvin L. Adelman, "The First Modern Sport in America: Harness Racing in New York City, 1825–1870," *JSpH* 8 (Spring 1981): 5–32. See also Dizikes, *Sportsmen and Gamesmen*, 237–64; and Dwight Akers, *Drivers Up! The Story of American Harness Racing* (New York, 1938).

45. Adelman, "Harness Racing," 8–9, 19–20; Harlow, *Bowery Days*, 199–201; Akers, *Drivers Up!* 59, 91, 237–38.

46. Adelman, "Harness Racing," 9–10; Akers, *Drivers Up!* 239, 247–48. On the Red House Tavern, see Abram C. Dayton, *Last Days of Knickerbocker Life in New York* (New York, 1897), 335–36.

47. Adelman, "Harness Racing," 20–22.

48. Harlow, *Old Bowery Days*, 75; Adelman, *Sporting Time*, 101–7, 282; Lewis, "Cricket and the Beginnings of Organized Baseball," 323; Kirsch, "American Cricket," 28–29.

49. Berthoff, *British Immigrants*, 149; Adelman, "Modern Athletics," 263, 289, 298–301, 308n26; Kirsch, "American Cricket," 42; idem, "Rise of Modern Sports," 63–66, 76; Walkowitz, *Company Town*, 178n35.

50. Harold Seymour, *Baseball*, vol. 1, *The Early Years* (New York, 1960), 15–23; David Q. Voigt, *American Baseball*, vol. 1, *From Gentleman's Sport to the Commissioner System* (Norman, Okla., 1966), 8; Adelman, "Modern Athletics," 319–25.

51. Adelman, "Modern Athletics," 329–30, 333, 340–42, 349–52; Lewis, "Cricket and the Beginnings of Organized Baseball," 323; Adelman, *Sporting Time*, 127, 129–31, 173.

52. Adelman, "Modern Athletics," 330–32, 356–61, 397–403, 443–51; Stephen Freedman, "The Baseball Fad in Chicago, 1865–1870: An Exploration of the Role of Sport in the Nineteenth-Century City," *JSpH* 5 (Summer 1978): 56; Kirsch, "American Cricket," 32.

53. Seymour, *Baseball*, 1:23, 24; Ted Vincent, *Mudville's Revenge: The Rise and Fall of American Sport* (New York, 1981), 88–95, 101–4; *Brooklyn Eagle*, 10 May 1860, quoted in George B. Kirsch, *The Creation of American Team Sports: Baseball and Cricket, 1838–72* (Urbana, Ill., 1989), 60.

54. Adelman, "Modern Athletics," 329–30 (quote), 378n117, 382; Seymour, *Baseball*, 1:23–24; Vincent, *Mudville's Revenge*, 88–93; Steven Gelber, "Working at Playing: The Culture of the Workplace and the Rise of Baseball," *JSH* 16 (Summer 1982): 3–22.

55. Adelman, *Sporting Time*, 125; Kirsch, "Rise of Modern Sports," 69–70, 74; Bryan D. Palmer, *A Culture in Conflict: Skilled Workers and Industrial Capitalism in Hamilton, Ontario, 1860–1918* (Montreal, 1979), 53–54.

56. Kirsch, "American Cricket," 42; Harry B. Weiss and Grace M. Weiss, *Early Sports and Pastimes in New Jersey* (Trenton, N.J., 1960), 93–97, 139–40; Brian J. Danforth, "Hoboken and the Affluent New Yorker's Search for Recreation, 1820–1860," *New Jersey History* 91 (Autumn 1977): 133–38; *Jersey City Sentinel*, 9 Sept. 1856, quoted in Kirsch, "Rise of Modern Sports," 76.

57. Perry Duis, "Whose City? Public and Private Places in Nineteenth-Century Chicago," *Chicago History* 12 (Spring 1983): 2–27.

58. Neil Harris, *Humbug! The Life of P. T. Barnum* (Boston, 1973); Adelman, *Sporting Time*, 222, 227–28, 232, 241–42.

59. Adelman, *Sporting Time*, 33, 39–45, 49–51; William H. P. Robertson, *The History of Thoroughbred Racing in America* (New York, 1964), 62; "The Great Contest: Fashion v. Peytona," *New York Herald*, 5 May 1845, in *The American Sporting Experience: A Historical Anthology of Sport in America*, ed. Steven A. Riess (West Point, 1984), 91–103. On the intersectional series, see Nancy L. Struna, "The North-South Races: American Thoroughbred Racing in Transition, 1823–1850," *JSpH* 8 (Summer 1981): 5–32; Allan Nevins, ed., *The Diary of Philip Hone* (New York, 1936), 601; Kirsch, "New Jersey and the Rise of American Sports," 44.

60. Somers, *Sports in New Orleans*, 24–35; Dizikes, *Sportsmen and Gentlemen*, 123–57.

61. Adelman, "Harness Racing," 10–14, 20–22; idem, *Sporting Time*, 57–58, 63–64.

62. Rader, *American Sports*, 38–40; Adelman, *Sporting Times*, 212–13; George Moss, "The Long-Distance Runners of Ante-Bellum America," *Journal of Popular Culture* 8 (Fall 1973): 370–82.

63. Adelman, *Sporting Time*, 41–42, 213–15; Cumming, *Runners & Walkers*, 19–28; Rader, *American Sports*, 40; Lucas and Smith, *Saga of American Sports*, 97.

64. Seymour, *Baseball*, 1:25, 48–49; Adelman, *Sporting Time*, 132–34, 148–51, 159–60, 328n45; George B. Kirsch, "Baseball Spectators, 1855–1870," *Baseball History* 3 (Fall 1987): 5–7, 13.

65. Kirsch, "Baseball Spectators," 4, 6, 9, 10, 12, 14–18.

66. David R. Goldfield, *Cotton Fields and Skyscrapers: Southern City and Region, 1607–1980* (Baton Rouge, 1982), 29; Goldfield and Brownell, *Urban America*, 16–17, 185; Hardy, *How Boston Played*, 28, 31; Betts, "Public Recreation," 36–37. Quote is from Samuel Barber, *Boston Common* (Boston, 1916), 188, in ibid., 37.

67. Goldfield and Brownell, *Urban America*, 185–86; Cynthia Zaitzevsky, *Frederick Law Olmsted and the Boston Park System* (Cambridge, 1982), 17; John W. Reps, *The Making of Urban America: A History of City Planning in the United States* (Princeton, 1965), 325–30.

68. Quoted in Betts, "Public Recreation," 47. On banning street games, see, e.g., Click, "Leisure in the Upper South," 193–94. Public demands for municipalities to protect traffic and trade from inconsiderate sportsmen who disrupted commerce or made it dangerous to walk in the street dates back to mid-seventeenth-century Boston. See Nancy Struna, "Puritans and Sport: The Irretrievable Tide of Change," *JSpH* 4 (Spring 1977): 6–14, 17–19; Carl Bridenbaugh, *Cities in the Wilderness: Urban Life in America, 1625–1742* (1938, rep. New York, 1955), 276; Hans-Peter Wagner, *Puritan Attitudes towards Recreation in Early Seventeenth-Century New England, with Particular Consideration of Physical Recreation*, Mainzer Studies zur Amerikanistik, Ban 17 (Frankfort Am Main, 1982), 34–35.

69. *New York Packet*, 15 Aug. 1785, quoted in Ian R. Stewart, "Central Park, 1851–1871: Urban and Environmental Planning in New York City" (Ph.D. diss., Cornell University, 1973), 68; Clarence C. Cook, *A Description of the New York Central Park* (New York, 1869), 13, quoted in Ian R. Stewart, "Politics and the Park: The Fight for Central Park," *New York Historical Society Quarterly* 61 (July/Oct. 1977): 126.

70. Stewart, "Politics and the Park," 125–29, 131–34; Betts, "Public Recreation," 38–41, 43; Andrew Jackson Downing, *Rural Essays* (New York, 1869), 139–42, quoted in Stewart, "Politics and the Park," 132. Brooklyn's foremost park advocate was *Brooklyn Eagle* editor Walt Whitman, who sought a breathing space in East Brooklyn, the most densely populated section of his city, inhabited mainly by "mechanics and artificers." See Donald E. Simon, "The Public Park

Movement in Brooklyn, 1824–1873'' (Ph.D. diss., New York University, 1972), 114, 116, 130, 136–37.

71. Stewart, ''Politics and the Park,'' 132, 134–35, 137–39, 141–42, 146–47; Betts, ''Public Recreation,'' 39, 41, 44–49; Mary V. Frye, ''The History and Development of Municipal Parks in the United States: Concepts and Their Applications'' (Ph.D. diss., University of Illinois, 1964), 34; Adelman, *Sporting Time*, 274–76. Outside of New York, the largest city in the country, securing recognition as a first-class progressive city depended even more on cultural than on economic and demographic development. When Bostonians debated the need for a municipal park, one councilman argued, ''If Boston cannot afford such expenditure . . . it must be because she has entered the ranks of cities like Newburyport and Salem, which have ceased to grow.'' Quoted in Betts, ''Public Recreation,'' 41.

72. Betts, ''Public Recreation,'' 47; Stewart, ''Politics and the Park,'' 134–55.

73. Stewart, ''Central Park,'' 148–50, 155–56, 225–27, 235, 242–43, 255, 324–25; Adelman, ''Modern Athletics,'' 624–25, 627–28; Frye, ''Municipal Parks,'' 55–57, 66; Laura Wood Roper, *FLO: A Biography of Frederick Law Olmsted* (Baltimore, 1973), 131–39; Elizabeth Stevenson, *Park Maker: A Life of Frederick Law Olmsted* (New York, 1977), 174, 175; Frederick Law Olmsted, Jr., and Theodora Kimball, eds., *Frederick Law Olmsted, Landscape Architect, 1822–1903* (1922–28; rep. New York, 1970), 126–27, 131, 139–40, 424; *NYT*, 13 March 1870.

74. Stewart, ''Central Park,'' 347–48; Olmsted and Kimball, *Olmsted*, 90–91; Stevenson, *Park Maker*, 296; Roper, *FLO*, 348–51.

75. Bender, *Urban Vision*, 176; Roy Rosenzweig, *Eight Hours for What We Will: Workers and Leisure in an Industrial City, 1870–1920* (Cambridge, 1983), 128. See also Hardy, *How Boston Played*, 80; Stewart, ''Central Park,'' 214.

76. Betts, ''Public Recreation,'' 41–42; Olmsted and Kimball, *Olmsted*, 223, 239, 276–77, 421–22, 424–25, 427, 430, 526–27; *New York Clipper* 13 (13 May 1865): 34; *Wilkes Spirit of the Times* 12 (8 April 1865): 85, in Kirsch, *Creation of American Team Sports*, 96; Stewart, ''Central Park,'' 239, 303–4, 315–16; Frye, ''Municipal Parks,'' 57. Quote is from Charles E. Beveridge and David Schuyler, eds., *The Papers of Frederick L. Olmsted*, vol. 3, *Creating Central Park, 1857–1861* (Baltimore, 1984), 213. Olmsted believed that if the park commissioners had wanted athletic fields they should have purchased them in sections of the city located closer to the homes of intended users. See Olmsted and Kimball, *Olmsted*, 196–97.

77. Adelman, *Sporting Time*, 257–59; Olmsted and Kimball, *Olmsted*, 424; Stewart, ''Central Park,'' 92, 324–25; Frye, ''Municipal Parks,'' 55–57, 66; Stevenson, *Park Maker*, 174, 175; *NYT*, 29 Nov. 1873.

78. The best option for city folk was to flee to the countryside, ''where the streams and ponds have not been 'fished to death,' '' according to Robert Bonner, publisher of the *New York Ledger*, or else to head for the fresh air of the mountains. But this was impossible for most urbanites in 1860, and instead the *Ledger* recommended astute planning for the future, when cities would become more

congested. Other cities were urged to copy New York and go even further to secure open-air bathing facilities to promote cleanliness. Other papers and magazines echoed these sentiments. See *Ledger*, 26 May, 4 Aug 1860, quoted in Betts, "Public Recreation," 48–49. On the impact of Central Park, see Goldfield and Brownell, *Urban America*, 188; Glen E. Holt, "Private Plans for Public Places: The Origins of Chicago's Park System, 1850–1875," *Chicago History* 8 (Fall 1979): 173–84; Harold M. Mayer and Richard C. Wade, *Chicago: Growth of a Metropolis* (Chicago, 1969), 100–10; Zaitzevsky, *Olmsted*, 28–32.

79. Ralph Wilcox has found rare evidence of municipally sponsored athletics in Boston. In 1826 a public gymnasium was established on a municipally owned site, and then in 1854 the city organized an annual Fourth of July regatta, with purses awarded to the winners. Ralph C. Wilcox, "Sport in Bristol (U.K.) and Boston (U.S.A.): A Cross-National Comparison, 1870–1900" (Ph.D. diss., University of Alberta, 1982), 249, 729.

Chapter Two

1. Thorstein Veblen, *The Theory of the Leisure Class* (1899; rep. New York, 1967), chap. 10. On the historic study of urban elites see E. Digby Baltzell, *Philadelphia Gentlemen: The Making of a National Upper Class* (New York, 1958); Frederick C. Jaher, *The Urban Establishment: Upper Strata in Boston, New York, Charleston, Chicago, and Los Angeles* (Urbana, Ill., 1982).

2. John F. Reiger, *American Sportsmen and the Origins of Conservation* (New York, 1975), 88–91, 118–23.

3. William H. P. Robertson, *The History of Thoroughbred Racing in America* (New York, 1964), 176–80, 225, 260; *National Cyclopedia of American Biography*, s.v., "Belmont, August (II)"; Mark D. Hirsch, William C. Whitney: Modern Warwick (New York, 1948), 585–92; Albert S. Crockett, *Peacocks on Parade: A Narrative of a Unique Period in American Social History and Its Most Colorful Figures* (New York, 1931), 136–41; Harold Zink, *City Bosses in the United States: A Study of Twenty Municipal Bosses* (Durham, 1930), 138–41; *NYT*, 5 Jan., 6 June 1907.

4. A. T. Andreas, *A History of Chicago*, 3 vols (Chicago, 1886), 3:674 (quote); C. B. Parmer, *For Gold and Glory: The History of Thoroughbred Racing in America* (New York, 1939), 124–25, 128; Robertson, *Thoroughbred Racing*, 90–92, 148–51.

5. *NYT*, 9 Dec. 1894, 12, 15, 22 Feb., 1, 22 Mar., 1, 3 Apr., 3, 10 May 1895.

6. John A. Lucas and Ronald A. Smith, *Saga of American Sport* (Philadelphia, 1978), 72, 191–203; Guy M. Lewis, "America's First Intercollegiate Sport: The Regattas from 1852 to 1875," *Research Quarterly* 38 (Dec. 1967): 637–48; idem, "The Beginnings of Organized Collegiate Sport," *AQ* 22 (Summer 1970): 222–29; Joseph R. DeMartini, "Student Culture as a Change Agent in American Higher Education," *JSH* 9 (June 1976): 526–41.

7. John Higham, "The Reorientation of American Culture in the 1890s," in *The Origins of Modern Consciousness*, ed. John Weiss (Detroit, 1965), 25–48; Joseph Doubert, *A Man's Place: Masculinity in Transition* (Englewood Cliffs,

N.J., 1979), 175–82; Lucas and Smith, *Saga of American Sport*, chap. 17; Gerald F. Roberts, "The Strenuous Life: The Cult of Manliness in the Era of Theodore Roosevelt" (Ph.D. diss., Michigan State University, 1970), 84–144; William James, *The Moral Equivalent of War and Other Essays* (New York, 1971), 6–7, 12; Charles K. Adams, "Moral Aspect of College Life," *Forum* 8 (Feb. 1890): 672–74.

8. Guy M. Lewis, "The American Intercollegiate Football Spectacle, 1865–1917" (Ph.D. diss., University of Maryland, 1963), 30–55. The first time that spectators were charged admission to attend a game was in 1873, when 500 spectators paid an entrance fee for the Yale-Rutgers game. Their student athletic associations divided $180 from the gate to defray expenses. Football was originally surpassed as a money-making sport by baseball and crew. In 1888 Yale grossed $2,800 from football and $5,000 from each of the other sports. But in the 1890s football profits reached over $50,000 a year, and in 1903, $106,000—one-eighth of the college's total budget. See, on the commercialization of football, John Hammond Moore, "Football's Ugly Decades, 1893–1913," *Smithsonian Journal of History* 2 (Fall 1967): 49–59; David L. Westby and Allen Sack, "The Commercialization and Functional Rationalization of College Football: Its Origins," *Journal of Higher Education* 47 (Nov./Dec. 1976): 625–47; Clarence Deming, "The Money Power in College Athletics," *Outlook* 80 (July 1905): 570; Smith and Lucas, *Saga of American Sport*, 235–57; Edward S. Jordan, "Buying Football Victories," *Collier's* 36 (2 Dec. 1905): 19, chastised the University of Minnesota for allying with Minneapolis commercial interests to advertise the good name of the city in return for special railroad rates. On the business of football at another major urban university, see Robin D. Lester, "The Rise, Decline and Fall of Intercollegiate Football at the University of Chicago, 1892–1939" (Ph.D. diss., University of Chicago, 1974), 32–46.

9. Lewis, "Intercollegiate Football," 77–78, 90–100; Lucas and Smith, *Saga of American Sport*, 236–39; *NYT*, 28 Nov. 1891.

10. Stephen Hardy, *How Boston Played: Sport, Recreation and Community, 1865–1915* (Boston, 1982), 127–29, 139–41; Benjamin G. Rader, *American Sports: From the Age of Folk Games to the Age of Spectators* (Englewood Cliffs, N.J., 1983), 50–52; Richard G. Wettan and Joe D. Willis, "Effect of New York Athletic Club on America's Athletic Governance," *Research Quarterly* 47 (Oct. 1976): 499–505; idem, "Social Stratification in the New York Athletic Club: A Preliminary Analysis of the Impact of the Club on Amateur Sport in Late Nineteenth-Century America," *Canadian Journal of History of Sport and Physical Education* 7 (May 1976): 41–53; Joe D. Willis and Richard G. Wettan, "Social Stratification in New York's Athletic Clubs, 1865–1915," *JSpH* 3 (Spring 1975): 45–64. On voluntarism, see, e.g., Jack C. Ross, *An Assembly of Good Fellows: Voluntary Association in History* (Westport, Conn., 1976); and Don H. Doyle, "The Social Functions of Voluntary Associations in a Nineteenth Century Town," *Social Science History* 1 (Spring 1977): 333–55.

11. Malcolm W. Ford, "The New York Athletic Club," *Outing* 33 (Dec. 1898): 251; Rader, *American Sports*, 55–56.

12. Rader, *American Sports*, 56–57.

13. Ibid.; Bob Considine and Fred B. Jarvis, *The First Hundred Years: A Portrait of the NYAC* (London, 1969), 18–20, 43.

14. John Cumming, *Runners & Walkers: A Nineteenth-Century Chronicle* (Chicago, 1981), 129–61; Joe D. Willis and Richard G. Wettan, "L. E. Myers, 'World's Greatest Runner,'" *JSpH* 2 (Fall 1975): 93–111; Rader, *American Sports*, 58–61.

15. John A. Lester, ed., *A Century of Philadelphia Cricket* (Philadelphia, 1951), 42–267; Charles Blancke, "Cricket in America," *Harper's Weekly* 35 (26 Sept. 1891): 732; George S. Patterson, "Cricket in the United States," *Lippincott's Magazine* 50 (Nov. 1892): 650; Hardy, *How Boston Played*, 131, 135, 138; *Brooklyn Eagle*, 18 June 1894; *NYT*, 2 May 1893; *Chicago Times*, 24 Nov. 1889. On polo, see Willard Roby, "The Beginnings of American Polo," *Outing* 40 (June 1902): 318–21; Lucas and Smith, *Saga of American Sport*, 165–66; *NYT*, 14, 18 May 1876.

16. Hardy, *How Boston Played*, 140–42, 144–46.

17. Caspar W. Whitney, "Evolution of the Country Club," *Harper's* 90 (Dec. 1894): 16–33; H. W. Wind, "Golfing In and Around Chicago," *Chicago History* 4 (Winter 1975–76): 44–51; Gustave Kobbé, "The Country Club and Its Influence on American Social Life," *Outlook* 68 (1 June 1901): 301–21; Janet Ann Northam, "Sport and Urban Boosterism: Seattle, 1890–1910" (M.S. thesis, University of Washington, 1978), 56–59; Rader, *American Sports*, 65–68.

18. Robert Dunn, "The Country Club: A National Expression," *Outing* 57 (Nov. 1905): 165; Hardy, *How Boston Played*, 139–45; Whitney, "Country Club," 30; Baltzell, *Philadelphia Gentlemen*, 123–24.

19. For a valuable discussion of the social functions of elite athletic clubs, see Hardy, *How Boston Played*, 144–46. On metropolitan men's clubs, see David Hammack, *Power and Society: Greater New York at the Turn of the Century* (New York, 1982), 65–73; and for comparisons of athletic clubs, see Baltzell, *Philadelphia's Gentlemen*, 335–63; Rader, *American Sports*, 56–57; and Willis and Wettan, "New York's Athletic Clubs," 45–64.

20. Martin Kaufman and Herbert J. Kaufman, "Henry Bergh, Kit Burns and the Sportsmen of New York," *New York Folklore Quarterly* 28 (Mar. 1972): 15–29; Anthony Comstock, "Pool Rooms and Pool Selling," *The North American Review* 157 (Nov. 1893): 601–10; Melvin L. Adelman, *A Sporting Time: New York City and the Rise of Modern Athletics, 1820–1870* (Urbana, Ill., 1986), 242–43, 248–49.

White-collar workers had little time during the work week for athletics, but a 1913 survey of 806 New York workers found that on Saturday afternoons 10.9 percent of professionals engaged in athletic pastimes or exercises—nearly double the next occupational category (metal trades). On Sunday professionals were still the most likely (5.1 percent), followed by clerks and metal workers (4.6 percent). On holidays, clerks were the most active. See George Esdras Bevans, *How Workingmen Spend Their Spare Time* (New York, 1913), 51.

21. Lucas and Smith, *Saga of American Sport*, 288–91; Adelman, *Sporting Time*, 281–86; Rader, *American Sports*, 150–51; Dubbert, *Man's Place*, chap. 6; Roberts, "Strenuous Life," 84–140; Stephanie Twin, "Jock and Jill: Aspects of

Women's Sports History in America, 1870–1940'' (Ph.D. diss., Rutgers University), 44–65.

22. Hardy, *How Boston Played*, 142. Adelman points out that in 1869 more middle-income athletes belonged to target-shooting companies than to any other sports organizations. They were popular, in part, because the competition provided a substitute for traditional field sports that urbanization had made more difficult to enjoy. See Adelman, *Sporting Time*, 250–52.

23. Hardy, *How Boston Played*, 81; Mary V. Frye, ''Historical Development of Municipal Parks in the United States: Concepts and Their Applications'' (Ph.D. diss., University of Illinois, 1964), 161; Elizabeth Halsey, *The Development of Public Recreation in Metropolitan Chicago* (Chicago, 1940), 21; Max Robertson, *The Encyclopedia of Tennis* (New York, 1974), 53; Jesse F. Steiner, *Americans at Play: Recent Trends in Recreation and Leisure Time Activities* (1933; rep. New York, 1970), 65–68.

24. *NYT*, 11 Mar. 1900, 13 Apr. 1913, 4 Jan. 1920.

25. Chicago Recreational Commission, *Chicago Recreation Survey, 1937*, vol. 3, *Private Recreation* (Chicago, 1938), 126; Steiner, *Americans at Play*, 70, 73–74; John R. Betts, *America's Sporting Heritage, 1850–1950* (Reading, Mass., 1974), 160–62; Rader, *American Sports*, 224–28.

26. Norman L. Dunham, ''The Bicycle Era in American History'' (Ph.D. diss., Harvard University, 1956), 57–113, 142–46; Hardy, *How Boston Played*, 148–52. For a general survey of cycling history, see Robert A. Smith, *A Social History of the Bicycle* (New York, 1972).

27. Hardy, *How Boston Played*, 153–61; George D. Bushnell, ''When Chicago Was Wheel Crazy,'' *Chicago History* 4 (Fall 1975): 172–73, 175.

28. Betts, *America's Sporting Heritage*, 61; Dunham, ''Bicycle Era,'' 271–97; *Sporting Life* 1 (6 May 1883): 6,1 (28 Nov. 1883): 6; *Sporting and Theatrical Journal* 3 (8 Mar. 1884): 277.

29. Richard Harmond, ''Progress and Flight: An Interpretation of the American Cycle Craze of the 1890s,'' *JSH* 5 (Winter 1971): 238–40; *NYT*, 29 Apr. 1896, quoted in Cary Goodman, *Choosing Sides: Playground and Street Life on the Lower East Side* (New York, 1979), 4–6.

30. Smith, *Bicycle*, 134–37, 144–47; Bushnell, ''When Chicago Was Wheel Crazy,'' 174. Sprint racing enjoyed a vogue at the turn of the century—see Marshall W. ''Major'' Taylor, *The Fastest Bicycle Rider in the World* (1928; rep. Battleboro, Vt., 1972)—but long-distance marathon racing was generally more popular. See *NPG* 69 (26 Dec. 1896): 3, 87 (30 Dec. 1905): 10, 111 (1 Dec. 1917): 6; *Brooklyn Eagle*, 10, 11, Dec. 1897; *NYT*, 16 Dec. 1900, 18 Nov. 1904, 12, 13, 16 Dec. 1912, 27 Nov., 9, 11, 13 Dec. 1920. See also Dunham, ''Bicycle Era,'' 395, 457–59; and Fred Hawthorne, ''Six-Day Bicycle Racing,'' in *Sport's Golden Age: A Close-Up of the Fabulous Twenties*, ed. Allison Danzig and Peter Brandwein (New York, 1948), 294–96.

31. Harmond, ''Progress and Flight,'' 240; Bushnell, ''When Chicago Was Wheel Crazy,'' 172, 174–75; Carter H. Harrison II, *Stormy Years: The Autobiography of Carter H. Harrison, Five Times Mayor of Chicago* (Indianapolis, 1935), 104–6 *et seg.*, photographs.

32. Harmond, "Progress and Flight," 243–44; Hardy, *How Boston Played*, 161–62; Lucas and Smith, *Saga of American Sport*, 258–61.

33. Harmond, "Progress and Flight," 248.

34. Gary Allan Tobin, "The Bicycle Boom of the 1890's: The Development of Private Transportation and the Birth of the Modern Tourist," *Journal of Popular Culture* 7 (Spring 1974): 841–45 (quote on 845).

35. Ibid., 845 (quote); Hardy, *How Boston Played*, 165–67; Harmond, "Progress and Flight," 252; John B. Rae, *The American Automobile: A Brief History* (Chicago, 1965), 6, 7, 9–10, 28.

36. On the pastoral mythology, see Allen Guttmann, *From Ritual to Record: The Nature of Modern Sports* (New York, 1978), 100–106; Bruce Catton, "The Great American Game," *American Heritage* 10 (Apr. 1959): 16–25. On the modernization of the sport, see Adelman, *Sporting Time*, 116, 121, 142, 145, 183; Steven Gelber, "Working at Playing: The Culture of the Workplace and the Rise of Baseball," *JSH* 16 (June 1983): 10.

37. Steven A. Riess, *Touching Base: Professional Baseball and American Culture in the Progressive Era* (Westport, Conn., 1980), 20–27, 221–27; Steven Freedman, "The Baseball Fad in Chicago: An Exploration of the Role of Sport in the Nineteenth-Century City," *JSpH* 5 (Summer 1978): 48.

38. Riess, *Touching Base*, 225–28.

39. Freedman, "Baseball Fad," 53–61; Steven M. Gelber, "Their Hands Are All Out Playing': Business and Amateur Baseball, 1845–1917," *JSpH* 11 (Spring 1984): 5–27; idem, "Working at Playing," 8, 10–12.

40. Riess, *Touching Base*, 31–33, 29.

41. On boosterism, see Daniel Boorstin, *The Americans: The National Experience* (New York, 1965), 113–68. On baseball and civic pride, see Riess, *Touching Base*, 18–23; Harold Seymour, *Baseball*, vol. 1, *The Early Years* (New York, 1960), 355–56.

42. Peter R. Shergold, *Working-Class Life: The "American Standard" in Comparative Perspective, 1889–1913* (Pittsburgh, 1982), 49.

43. Ibid., 225; Alan Trachtenberg, *The Incorporation of America: Culture and Society in the Gilded Age* (New York, 1982), 90–91; Clarence D. Long, *Wages and Earnings in the United States* (Princeton, 1960), 4; Albert Rees, *Real Wages in Manufacturing, 1890–1914* (Princeton, 1961), chap. 3.

44. Riess, *Touching Base*, 121, 140–42, 125–28. On the Social Gospel perspective, see, e.g., *New York Tribune*, 22 Mar. 1898; *NYT*, 10, 17 June 1901. Boys playing in the street were far more likely to be interrupted than wealthy golfers at their private clubs.

45. Gene Tunney, *A Man Must Fight* (Boston, 1932), 33; Ted Vincent, *Mudville's Revenge: The Rise and Fall of American Sport* (New York, 1981), 45–53.

46. Riess, *Touching Base*, 28, 30–37. On racetracks that catered to the working class, see *ChiTrib*, 21 July 1893; *NYT*, 23 Oct. 1893, and above, 213–15.

47. Riess, *Touching Base*, 31–34. On the American Association, see Seymour, *Baseball*, 1: chap. 13; David Q. Voigt, *American Baseball: From Gentleman's Sport to the Commissioner System* (Norman, Okla., 1966), 121–30.

48. Riess, *Touching Base*, 125–37.

49. Seymour, *Baseball*, 1:91, 92, 135, 139; Riess, *Touching Base*, 121–25. Minor-league teams in the Deep South generally did not play on Sundays until the 1910s, and frequently much later. Atlanta did not get Sunday ball until 1934. See ibid., 138–42, 149nn.81, 82.

50. Bernard A. Weisberger, *The American Newspaperman* (Chicago, 1961), 90, 93–100; John R. Betts, "Sporting Journalism in Nineteenth-Century America," *AQ* 5 (Spring 1953): 39–56; idem, *America's Sporting Heritage*, 53–55, 57–61, 63–67, 376–77; William Henry Nugent, "The Sports Section," *The American Mercury* 16 (Mar. 1929): 334–38; Gunther Barth, *City People: The Rise of Modern City Culture in Nineteenth-Century America* (New York, 1980), chap. 3; Rader, *American Sports*, 99–102; Alexander Saxton, "George Wilkes: The Transformation of a Radical Ideology," *AQ* 33 (Fall 1981): 437–58; Norris W. Yates, *William T. Porter and the Spirit of the Times* (Baton Rouge, 1957).

51. Francis G. Couvares, "The Triumph of Commerce: Class Culture and Mass Culture in Pittsburgh," in *Working-Class America: Essays on Labor, Community and American Society*, ed. Michael H. Frisch and Daniel J. Walkowitz (Urbana, Ill., 1983), 131 (quote), 144.

52. David Nasaw, *Children of the City: At Work and at Play* (New York, 1985), 20, 34–35; Goodman, *Choosing Sides*, chap. 1, esp. 4–7; Freedman, "Baseball Fad," 49.

53. Jon Kingsdale, "The 'Poor Man's Club': Social Functions of the Working-Class Saloon," *AQ* 25 (Oct. 1973): 472–89; Mark Haller, "Organized Crime in Urban Society: Chicago in the Twentieth Century," *JSH* 5 (Winter 1971–72): 214–16; Perry R. Duis, *The Saloon: Public Drinking in Chicago and Boston, 1880–1920* (Urbana, Ill., 1983), 247–48; Elliott West, *The Saloon on the Rockey Mountain Mining Frontier* (Lincoln, Neb., 1979), 85–87.

54. Duis, *Saloon*, 72; idem, "The Saloon and the Public City: Chicago and Boston, 1880–1920" (Ph.D. diss., University of Chicago, 1975), 706.

55. Ned Polsky, *Hustlers, Beats and Others* (Chicago, 1967), 35–36; John Grissim, *Billiards: Hustlers & Heroes, Legends & Lies, and the Search for Higher Truth on the Green Felt* (New York, 1979), 64; The Survey Committee of the Cleveland Foundation, *Cleveland Recreation Survey*, vol. 5, *Commercial Recreation* (Cleveland, 1920), 59 (hereafter cited as *Cleveland Recreation*).

56. John A. Phelan, *Pool, Billiards and Bowling Alleys as a Phase of Commercialized Amusements in Toledo, Ohio* (Toledo, 1919), 15, 58, 61; Grissim, *Billiards*, 76–79; Henry C. Alley, "Moral Problems of Modern Pool Rooms," (M.A. thesis, University of Chicago, 1915), 5, 9–10; Albert B. Wolfe, *The Lodging House Problem* (Cambridge, 1913), 29; Jenna W. Joselit, *Our Gang: Jewish Crime and the New York Jewish Community, 1900–1940* (Bloomington, 1983), 151 (quote).

57. Bevans, *How Workingmen Spend Their Spare Time*, 19–21, 23–24, 26–31, 33–35, 37–39, 41–43.

58. Chicago Recreation Commission, *The Chicago Recreation Survey, 1937*, vol. 2, *Commercial Recreation* (Chicago, 1938), 53–54 (hereafter cited as *Chicago Recreation*); *Cleveland Recreation*, 56; Frederick Thrasher, *The Gang: A Study of 1,313 Gangs in Chicago*, abr. ed. (Chicago, 1963), 78, 80, 278.

59. Phelan, *Amusements in Toledo*, 16, 33–34; *Cleveland Recreation*, 53; Grissim, *Billiards*, 67, 69, 71.

60. Eighty-five percent of Cleveland's poolrooms had five or fewer tables; most, just two. *Cleveland Recreation*, 51, 57. On the private businesses that provided pool tables for their clients and the ethnicity of their proprietors, see Phelan, *Amusements in Toledo*, 15, 25.

61. Phelan, *Amusements in Toledo*, 25, 31–32; Alley, "Pool Rooms," 9.

62. The location of poolrooms was taken from the *Chicago City Directory, 1890–1900, 1910* (Chicago, 1890–1910). The very high concentration of poolrooms in the late nineteenth century may have reflected the vigorousness of the city's entertainment district or merely an under accounting of small businesses by the directory. The poolroom business had a very high turnover. On the location of rooms during the Depression, see *Chicago Recreation*, 2:54, 58ff. On the city's neighborhoods, see Louis Wirth and Margaret Furez, eds., *Local Community Fact Book, 1938* (Chicago, 1938).

63. *Chicago Recreation*, 2:54.

64. Ibid.; Polsky, *Hustlers*, 36n42.

65. Herman Weiskopf, *The Perfect Game: The World of Bowling* (Englewood Cliffs, N.J., 1978), 36–37. Data on social origins of bowling alley proprietors is based on biographical sketches in John G. Hemmer and W. J. Kenna, eds., *The Western Bowlers' Journal Bowling Encyclopedia* (Chicago, 1904).

66. *Chicago Recreation*, 2:57; *Chicago City Directory* (Chicago, 1904).

67. *Chicago Recreation*, 2:57.

68. Ibid., 2:61.

69. Ibid., 2:57–58, 60; *Chicago City Directory, 1900, 1910; Recreation Survey of Cincinnati* (Cincinnati, 1913), 29–30.

70. *Chicago Recreation*, 2:66ff.; Casimir J. B. Wronski, "Early Days of Sport among Polish-Americans of Chicagoland," in *Poles of Chicago, 1837–1937* (Chicago, 1937), 146–47.

71. William Foote Whyte, *Street Corner Society: The Social Structure of an Italian Slum* (Chicago, 1943), 14–15, 21, 26–27, 30–31, 37–38, 45–46, 256.

72. Weiskopf, *Perfect Game*, 62–75.

73. Alan Metcalfe, *Working-Class Physical Recreation in Montreal, 1860–1895*, Working Papers in the Sociological Study of Sports and Leisure, 1:22, Sports Studies Research Group, School of Physical and Health Education, Queen's University (Kingston, Ont., 1978), 17–21; Vincent, *Mudville's Revenge*, 31, 40, 54–59, 66, 72, 80; *Spirit* 101 (24 Sept. 1881):211; 114 (1 Oct. 1887):342; 116 (25 Aug. 1888):160; *NYT*, 12 June, 7, 8 Aug. 1880, 10 July 1892; *Sporting Life* 2 (8 Oct. 1883): 7.

74. *Brooklyn Eagle*, 29 Sept. 1891, 10 Aug. 1893, 28 Aug., 4, 27 Sept. 1894; *NYT*, 2 Aug. 1892, 11 Sept. 1900.

75. John T. Cumbler, *Working-Class Community in Industrial America: Work, Leisure, and Struggle in Two Industrial Cities, 1880–1930* (Westport, Conn., 1979), 37, 40–41; *NYT*, 6 Sept. 1891; *Brooklyn Eagle*, 8 Sept. 1891; *Spirit* 121 (12 Sept. 1891): 296–97; *Chicago Times*, 16 Aug. 1886, 27 May 1888, 2 Aug.

1891; *The Carpenter* 3 (Sept. 1883): 2; *Cigar Makers Journal* 9 (July 1884): 1, 9 (Sept. 1884): 12.

76. Bryan D. Palmer, *A Conflict in Culture: Skilled Workers and Industrial Capitalism in Hamilton, Ontario, 1860–1914* (Montreal, 1979), 60, 241; Adelman, *Sporting Time*, 152–53; Metcalfe, "Recreation in Montreal," 42. While pleasure seeking was a major goal of premodern workers, the labor aristocracy which led in the development of a working-class culture had many of the same ascetic goals and values as the middle class. See E. P. Thompson, *The Making of the English Working Class* (New York, 1964); Herbert G. Gutman, *Work, Culture, and Society in Industrializing America: Essays in American Working-Class and Social History* (New York, 1978), esp. chaps. 1, 2; Eric Hobsbawm, *Workers Worlds of Labor* (New York, 1984), 194–272.

77. Daniel T. Rodgers, *The Work Ethic in Industrial America, 1850–1920* (Chicago, 1978), esp. 154–56; Stuart Brandes, *American Welfare Capitalism* (Chicago, 1970), 16, 20; Elmer L. Johnson, *The History of YMCA Physical Education* (Chicago, 1979), 126–27, 228. On the YMCA and middle-class youth, see Cumbler, *Working-Class Community*, 50; David Macleod, "A Live Vaccine: The YMCA and Male Adolescence in the United States and Canada, 1870–1920," *Histoire Sociale/Social History* 11 (May 1978): 5–25.

78. Stanley Buder, *Pullman: An Experiment in Industrial Order and Community Planning, 1880–1930* (New York, 1977); Almont Lindsey, *The Pullman Strike: The Story of a Unique Experiment and of a Great Labor Upheaval* (Chicago, 1964), chaps. 3, 4; idem, "The Town of Pullman as a Social Experiment" (Ph.D. diss., University of Illinois, 1936), 191–93; Wilma Pesavento, "Sport and Recreation in the Pullman Experiment, 1880–1900," *JSpH* 9 (Summer 1982): 38–62; Wilma J. Pesavento and Lisa C. Raymond, "Men Must Play: Men Will Play': Occupations of Pullman Athletes, 1880 to 1900," *JSpH* 11 (Summer 1982): 233–51.

79. Daniel Nelson, *Managers and Workers: Origins of the New Factory System in the United States, 1880–1920* (Madison, 1975), 115–16; Brandes, *Welfare Capitalism*, 76–80; U.S. Department of Labor, Bureau of Labor Standards, *Welfare Work for Employees in Industrial Establishments*, Bulletin #250 (Washington, D.C., 1919), 74–81, 90–93; idem, *Health and Recreational Activities in Industrial Establishments, 1926*, Bulletin #458 (Washington, D.C., 1928), 46, 58; John R. Schleppi, "'It Pays': John H. Patterson and Industrial Recreation at the National Cash Register Company," *JSpH* 6 (Winter 1979): 20–28.

80. Brandes, *Welfare Capitalism*, chap. 8; U.S. Department of Labor, *Welfare Work*, 90–93; idem, *Health and Recreational Activities*, 32, 45–48, 55–58; Tamara Hareven and Randolph Langenbach, *Amokeag: Life and Work in an American Factory-City* (New York, 1979), 179.

81. Tom Bennett, et al., *The NFL's Official Encyclopedic History of Professional Football* (New York, 1977), 14–16, 18, 21; Vincent, *Mudville's Revenge*, 8–10; idem, "Breaking Strikes with Sports Teams" (unpublished paper in author's possession), 2, 42–43, 49–50; Harry A. March, *Pro Football: Its Ups and Downs* (New York, 1934), 65; George Halas with Gwen Moran and Arthur Veysey, *Halas by Halas* (New York, 1979), 53–77.

82. Betts, *America's Sporting Heritage*, 318 (quote), 314; U.S. Department of Labor, *Health and Recreational Activities*, 58.

83. Chicago Recreation Commission, *Chicago Recreation Survey*, vol. 3, *Private Recreation* (Chicago, 1938), 149ff; Betts, *America's Sporting Heritage*, 316; Leonard Diehl and Floyd R. Eastwood, *Industrial Recreation* (Lafayette, Ind., 1940), 1–41.

84. Frederick W. Cozens and Florence S. Stumpf, *Sports in American Life* (Chicago, 1953), 210–14.

85. John A. Lucas, "Pedestrianism and the Struggle for the Sir John Astley Belt, 1878–1879," *Research Quarterly* 39 (Oct. 1968): 58; Cumming, *Runners & Walkers*, 85–94, 100–103; Lucas and Smith, *Saga of American Sports*, 279; Randy Roberts, *Papa Jack: Jack Johnson and the Era of White Hopes* (New York, 1983), 90.

86. Riess, *Touching Base*, 153, 157–60; Adelman, *Sporting Times*, 154–56, 174–82; *The Baseball Encyclopedia* (New York, 1969) for birthplaces.

87. Riess, *Touching Base*, 161–65, 171–80, 237–38. See my review of David A. Porter, ed., *Biographical Dictionary of American Sport*, vol. 1, *Baseball* (Westport, Conn., 1987), in *JHS* 5 (May 1988): 152–53, for a brief discussion of the social origins of star baseball players who are biographied in that reference work.

88. Riess, *Touching Base*, 180–84; *St. Louis Post-Dispatch*, 4 June 1905.

89. Study data consisted of 353 and 243 major leaguers who played in Chicago and New York between 1920 and 1939 and 1940 and 1959, respectively. On the geographic origins of players in the interwar era, see Harvey Lehman, "The Geographic Origin of Professional Baseball Players," *Journal of Educational Research* 34 (Oct. 1940): 131–34.

90. Computed from raw data generously provided by Prof. Rudolph K. Haerle, Jr., based on a 1958 questionnaire sent to 876 former major leaguers (335 responded). See Rudolph K. Haerle, Jr., "Career Patterns and Career Contingencies of Professional Baseball Players: An Occupational Analysis," in *Sport and Social Order: Contributions to the Sociology of Sport*, ed. Donald W. Ball and John W. Loy (Reading, Mass., 1975), 510n4. Data on the social origins of star players was drawn from the biographies in Porter, *Biographical Dictionary*. The sample of players born between 1920 and 1939 included men who played in the 1940s when players were drawn from more modest backgrounds, but separating out the players by race indicated the connection between race and social origins.

91. Players in the early 1900s lasted an average of three years. This is somewhat misleading because so many athletes played less than one season. If we discount players who did not last beyond their rookie year, the average rises to eight years. See Riess, *Touching Base*, 198. In my survey of players active between 1920 and 1939 and 1940 and 1959, the average was slightly over six for both cohorts which included men who played less than one season. A study of recent baseball history places the average tenure at under five years. See David Q. Voigt, *American Baseball*, vol. 3, *From Postwar Expansion to the Electronic Age* (University Park, Penn., 1983), 58. On the occupations of early players, see Riess, *Touching Base*, 157–60.

92. Riess, *Touching Base*, 199–207. The source of occupations of players active in the periods 1920–39 and 1940–59 was the Vertical Files, National Baseball Library, Cooperstown, New York. Disaggregation by place of birth found that urban players did just marginally better than rural athletes. Source of data for the sample of players active in the 1950s was Rich Marazzi and Len Fiorito, *Aaron to Zuverink: A Nostalgic Look at the Baseball Players of the Fifties* (Briarcliff, N.Y., 1982).

93. Riess, *Touching Base*, 206–8.

Chapter Three

1. Raymond A. Mohl, *The New City: Urban America in the Industrial Age, 1860–1920* (Arlington Heights, Ill., 1985), 24. In 1900 nearly half of the foreign born (49.5 percent) lived in cities with over 25,000 inhabitants, including three-fourths of Russians, two-thirds of Irish, Italians, and Poles, and half of Germans. U.S. Census Office, *Twelfth Census of the United States Taken in the Year 1900: Population*, vol. 1, part 1 (Washington, D.C., 1901), clc. Second-generation immigrants were usually about as urban as their parents. Niles Carpenter, *Immigrants and Their Children* (1927; rep. New York, 1969), 21.

2. See, e.g., Maxine Seller, *To Seek America: A History of Ethnic Life in the United States* (Englewood, N.J., 1977), 164–65, 180–88, 278–79; Perry Duis, *The Saloon: Public Drinking in Chicago and Boston, 1880–1920* (Urbana, Ill., 1983), chap. 5; and the essays in Peter d'A. Jones and Melvin G. Holli, eds., *Ethnic Chicago* (Grand Rapids, 1981).

3. Stephen Hardy, *How Boston Played: Sport, Recreation and Community, 1865–1915* (Boston, 1982), 137–38; *New York Clipper* 24 (26 Aug. 1876): 173; *Brooklyn Eagle*, 5 July 1891; *Spirit* 116 (29 Sept. 1888): 376, 116 (6 Oct. 1888): 416–17, 116 (20 Oct. 1888): 492, 116 (27 Oct. 1888): 518, 116 (3 Nov. 1888): 561; *ChiTrib*, 26, 28 Sept. 1892. On the history of the GAA, see W. F. Mandle, "The IRB and the Origins of the Gaelic Athletic Association," *Irish Historical Studies* 20 (Sept. 1977): 418–38; idem, "Sport as Politics: The Gaelic Athletic Association, 1884–1916," in *Sport in History: The Making of Modern Sporting History*, ed. Richard Cashman and Michael McKernan (St. Lucia, Queensland, 1979), 180–204.

4. Hardy, *How Boston Played*, 137–38; Carl Wittke, *The Irish in America* (Baton Rouge, 1956), 264–65; *Brooklyn Eagle*, 24 Sept. 1894; *NYT*, 29 July 1892, 28 Oct. 1901, 30 Oct. 1905; *ChiTrib*, 26, 28 Sept. 1892.

5. Frederick M. Thrasher, *The Gang: A Study of 1,313 Gangs in Chicago*, abr. ed. (Chicago, 1963), 13, 48, 52, 60, 124, 315–18.

6. Ibid., 175, 316 (quote), 318. See also Mike Royko, *Boss: Richard J. Daley of Chicago* (New York, 1971), 37, 38.

7. Thrasher, *Gang*, 318; William M. Tuttle, Jr., *Race Riot: Chicago in the Red Summer of 1919* (New York, 1974), 32–33, 54–55, 156, 199–200 (quote), 236–38; Allan H. Spear, *Black Chicago: The Making of a Negro Ghetto, 1890–1920* (Chicago, 1967), 201, 206, 213, 216; Chicago Commission on Race Relations, *The Negro in Chicago* (Chicago, 1922), 237 (quote). On Italian-American SACs in Chicago in the early 1960s, see Gerald D. Suttles, *The Social Order of*

the Slum: Ethnicity and Territory in the Inner City (Chicago, 1968), 89, 107–12, 142, 147, 226–27.

8. Henry Metzner, A Brief History of the American Turnerbund (Pittsburgh, 1924), 17–24, 29–30; Benjamin G. Rader, "Quest for Subcommunities and the Rise of American Sport," AQ 29 (Fall 1977): 360. Statistics are based on a list of 791, for whom the occupations of 780 were reported. See Hugo Gollmer, Namensliste der Pioniere des Nord-Amerik Turnerbundes der Jahre 1848–62 (St. Louis, 1885). The societies included were apparently the oldest and most prestigious ones and contained a smattering of names from socialist branches. My categorization of occupations is based on Stephen Thernstrom, The Other Bostonians: Poverty and Progress in the American Metropolis, 1880–1970 (Boston, 1973), 290–92.

9. Metzner, American Turnerbund, 17–24, 29–30; study data computed from Gollmer, Namensliste. For the occupations of the Chicago Turngemeinde in 1900, I took a sample of the 409 members listed in Harmonie 2 (1902): 270–71 (copy at the Chicago Historical Society). The sample consisted of the 153 names appearing on the left-hand column of each page. Occupational data was found for 122 men in the Chicago City Directory. None were unskilled and just nine were semiskilled. I am indebted to John Jentz for information on the Aurora Turnverein.

10. Illinois Staats-Zeitung, 26 Aug. 1861, 3 Oct. 1881; Chicago Times, 20 Jan. 1873, in CFLPS.

11. Metzner, American Turnerbund, 23–29, 31–39; Illinois Staats-Zeitung, 21 Mar. 1871, 3 Oct. 1881, 4 Jan. 1890, in CFLPS; Rudolph A. Hofmeister, Germans of Chicago (Champaign, 1976), 176–77; Wilma Pesavento, "A Historical Study of the Development of Physical Education in the Chicago Public Schools, 1860 to 1965" (Ph.D. diss., Northwestern University, 1966), 21–27, 46. On left-wing politics, see Metzner, American Turnerbund, 25–27; Chicago Arbeiter-Zeitung, 5 Jan. 1883, 4 Feb. 1888; Illinois Staats-Zeitung, 5 May 1890, in CFLPS; Carl Wittke, Refugees of Revolution: The German 48ers in America (Philadelphia, 1952), 156–57; Horst Ueberhorst, Turner Unterm Sternenbanner: Der Kampf der Deutsch-Amerikanischen Turner für Einheit, Freiheit und Sociale Gerechtigkeit, 1848 bis 1918 (Munich, 1978), 99–114, 127–35.

12. ChiTrib, 20 Feb. 1891; Illinois Staats-Zeitung, 7 May 1900, CFLPS; New York Call, 6 July 1908. On Milwaukee, see Horst Ueberhorst, "Turner und Sozialdemokraten in Milwaukee: Funf Jahrzehnte der Kooperation (1910–1960)," Gesprachskreis Politik und Wissenschaft (Bonn, 1980). The Turner movement in Chicago flourished even after World War I, with sixteen units as late as 1926. However, by 1938 the number had dropped to six, one of which was mainly Swiss, with a total membership of 1,600. They were in an important bastion of recent arrivals who comprised 30 percent of its membership. Chicago Recreation Commission, Chicago Recreation Survey, 1937, vol. 3, Private Recreation (Chicago, 1938), 135–36 (hereafter cited as Chicago Recreation).

13. Abraham Cahan, Yekl and the Imported Bridegroom and Other Stories of the New York Ghetto (1896; rep. New York, 1970), 6; U.S. Immigration Commission, Reports of the United States Immigration Commission: Immigrants in Industries, Part 2, Iron and Steel, 2 vols., Senate Doc. 633, 66th Cong., 2nd

Sess., Serial 5669 (Washington, D.C., 1911), 1:713, quoted in John Bodner, *Immigration and Industrialization: Ethnicity in an American Mill Town* (Pittsburgh, 1972), 92.

14. Vaclad Vesta, ed., *Panorama: A Historical Review of Czechs and Slovaks in the U.S.A.* (Cicero, Ill., 1970), 22–26, 133–36, 145–46; *Svornost*, 12 Aug., 6 Sept., 25 Nov. 1878, 8 Apr. 1890, CFLPS; Jakub Horak, "The Assimilation of Czechs in Chicago" (Ph.D. diss., University of Chicago, 1920), 92. On the Polish experience, see Arthur L. Waldo, "The Origins and Goals of the Falcons," in *Polish Falcons in America: Sixty Years of District IV, 1904–1964* (Pittsburgh, 1965), 5–7. On the paramilitarism of the sokols, falcons, and the Ukrainian *Sich*—an anti-Communist organization complete with air corps, established to fight the U.S.S.R. in the early 1930s—see *Denni Hlasatel*, 30 Apr., 21 May, 17 June 1917; *Dziennik Zwiazkowy*, 15 Sept. 1915, in CFLPS; Myron B. Kuropas, "Ukrainian Chicago: The Making of a Nationality Group in America," in Jones and Holli, *Ethnic Chicago*, 165–73.

15. *Chicago Times*, 1 June 1887; *Svornost*, 8 Apr. 1890; *Denni Hlasatel*, 2 Apr. 1910, 16 Sept. 1911, in CFLPS; Steven A. Riess, *Touching Base: Professional Baseball and American Culture in the Progressive Era* (Westport, Conn., 1980), 37, 191.

16. Edward A. Ross, *The Old World in the New: The Significance of Past and Present Immigration to the American People* (New York, 1914), 289–90. On German-American attitudes, see Cary Goodman, *Choosing Sides: Playground and Street Life on the Lower East Side* (New York, 1979), 37–40; *Chicago Messenger*, 1 Nov. 1909; Chicago Hebrew Institute, *Observer*, Nov. 1912, Dec. 1913, Jan. 1918, in CFLPS. On German-Jewish sport participation, see *The Jewish Encyclopedia*, s.v. "Sports"; Bernard Postel, Jesse Silver, and Roy Silver, *Encyclopedia of Jews in Sports* (New York, 1965); Riess, *Touching Base*, 87. In his classic *The Ghetto* (Chicago, 1928), 170, sociologist Louis Wirth argues that the gap between German and Russian Jews was better demonstrated by their social clubs than by different religious institutions. On one elite Jewish club in New York, see "The City Athletic Club," *The American Hebrew* 84 (20 Nov. 1908): 75; and for a list of its members, see *City Athletic Club Constitution, By-Laws and House Rules, 1913* (n.p., n.d.).

17. Benjamin Rabinowitz, *The Young Men's Hebrew Association (1856–1913)* (New York, 1948), 11–12, 53, 62, 75, 78.

18. Goodman, *Choosing Sides*, 37–40; Morris J. Frank, "Activity of the Jews in Athletics," *The American Hebrew* 83 (18 Sept. 1908): 477; "The Jewish Athlete," ibid. 83 (12 Oct. 1908): 544; "The Jewish Athlete," ibid. 84 (11 Dec. 1908): 171; Nat Osk, Scrapbooks, Special Collections, 92nd Street Y, New York City. The Educational Alliance required gym classes right from the start. For a statement of its goals, see Educational Alliance, *Fifth Annual Report* (1897) (New York, 1898), 43.

19. John R. Betts, *America's Sporting Heritage, 1850–1950* (Reading, Mass., 1974), 281–82; Ellen Brewer, "Bishop Bernard Sheil and the Formation of the Catholic Youth Organization" (seminar paper, University of Chicago, 1979), 1–2; Roger L. Treat, *Bishop Sheil and the CYO* (New York, 1951).

20. Brewer, "Bishop Sheil," 2–6. See also James W. Sanders, *The Education*

of an Urban Minority: Catholics in Chicago, 1833–1965 (New York, 1977), who focuses on the efforts of the archdiocese to acculturate its youth.

21. Brewer, "Bishop Sheil," 6–9. On the success of the CYO and other adult-organized recreational programs in fighting juvenile delinquency in this era, see Betts, *America's Sporting Heritage*, 331; and Chicago Recreation Commission, *Recreation and Delinquency: A Study of Five Selected Chicago Communities* (Chicago, 1942), 236–44.

22. Brewer, "Bishop Sheil," 9; *Chicago Recreation*, 3:71.

23. Brewer, "Bishop Sheil," 11, 12–18; Sanders, *Urban Minority*, 195–96.

24. Steven A. Riess, *Touching Base: Professional Baseball and American Culture in the Progressive Era* (Westport, Conn., 1980), 33–36; James T. Farrell, *My Baseball Diary* (New York, 1957), 29–30.

25. Riess, *Touching Base*, 185–86.

26. Ibid., 36–37, 184–91; Allon Schoener, ed., *Portal to America: The Lower East Side* (New York, 1967), 67–68; Irving Howe, *World of Our Fathers* (New York, 1976), 182 (quote), 259.

27. P. V. Young, "Jim's Own Story," *The Survey* 49 (15 March 1928): 777, quoted in William Carlson Smith, *Americans in the Making: The Natural History of the Assimilation of Immigrants* (New York, 1939), 312.

28. National Commission on Law Observance and Enforcement, *Report on the Causes of Crime*, vol. 2., no. 13 (Washington, D.C., 1931), 4–5, quoted in ibid., 312.

29. *Dziennik Chicagoski*, 27 June 1919, in CFLPS; Casimir J. B. Wronski, "Early Days of Sport Among Polish Americans of Chicagoland," in *Poles of Chicago, 1837–1937* (Chicago, 1937), 146; Richard Sorrell, "Sports and Franco-Americans in Woonsocket, 1870–1930," *Rhode Island History* 31 (Fall 1972): 117–26.

30. Gary Ross Mormino, "The Playing Fields of St. Louis: Italian Immigrants and Sport, 1925–1941," *JSpH* 9 (Summer 1982): 5–16.

31. Riess, *Touching Base*, 186, 189–90; Tilden G. Edelstein, "Cohen at the Bat," *Commentary* 76 (Nov. 1983): 53–56; William M. Simons, "The Athlete as Jewish Standard Bearer: Media Images of Hank Greenberg," *Jewish Social Studies* 44 (Spring 1982): 95–112. Data on Jewish players' birthplaces based on biographical sketches in Postal, *Jews in Sports.*

32. Riess, *Touching Base*, 191–92.

33. Quoted in Postal, *Jews in Sports*, 92; see also Frank, "Jews in Athletics," 477. On the early history of basketball, see Larry Fox, *Illustrated History of Basketball* (New York, 1974), 9–57; and Albert Applin, "From Muscular Christianity to the Marketplace: The History of Men's and Boy's Basketball in the United States, 1891–1957" (Ph.D. diss., University of Massachusetts, 1982).

34. Frank, "Jews in Athletics," 477; Fox, *Basketball*, 47–48; Ted Vincent, *Mudville's Revenge: The Rise and Fall of American Sport* (New York, 1981), 235–38.

35. John H. Mariano, *The Italian Contribution to American Democracy* (Boston, 1921), 144–48; Vincent, *Mudville's Revenge*, 247–53.

36. Vincent, *Mudville's Revenge*, 247–55.

37. Computed from biographical data in Ronald L. Mendell, *Who's Who in Basketball* (New Rochelle, 1973). Mendell's focus on the more notable players may have skewed the study sample.

38. Frank, "Jews in Athletics," 477; "Jewish Athlete," 544, 171; "Abel Kiviat Interview," *JSpH* 13 (Winter 1986): 235–66.

39. Riess, *Touching Base*, 188–89; Daniel Bell, *The End of Ideology* (Glencoe, Ill., 1960), 127–50; and esp., Steven A. Riess, "The Jewish-American Boxing Experience, 1890–1940," *American Jewish History* 74 (March 1985): 223–54.

40. Computed from the names of champions in Bert R. Sugar, ed., *Ring 1981 Record Book and Boxing Encyclopedia* (New York, 1981). On the elite Irish and Sullivan, see Hardy, *How Boston Played*, 174–75.

41. Hardy, *How Boston Played*, 174; Gene Tunney, *A Man Must Fight* (Boston, 1932), 7, 10, 12–16, 23–30, 33–36; Sugar, *Ring Record Book*. For Sullivan's life, see Michael T. Isenberg, *John L. Sullivan and His America.* (Urbana, Ill., 1988).

42. Thrasher, *Gang*, 133–34, 138; Riess, "Jewish-American Boxing," 225–47; Mark Haller, "Organized Crime in Urban Society: Chicago in the Twentieth Century," *JSH* 5 (Winter 1971–72): 221–27.

43. Champions and their ethnicity drawn from Sugar, *Ring Record Book*. On ethnic succession in prize fighting, see Thomas H. Jenkins, "Changes in Ethnic and Racial Representation among Professional Boxers: A Study in Ethnic Succession" (M.A. thesis, University of Chicago, 1951), esp. 85–89. On Jewish-American prize fighters, see Riess, "Jewish American Boxing," 223–47; William M. Kramer and Norton B. Stern, "San Francisco's Fighting Jew," *California History* 53 (Winter 1974): 333–45; Postal, *Jews in Sports*, 144–80. The east European Jews were building on a boxing tradition that dated back to London's West End ghetto in the late eighteenth century. See John Ford, *Prize-Fighting: The Age of Regency Boximania* (New York, 1972); and Todd Endelman, *The Jews of Georgian England, 1714–1830: Tradition and Change in a Liberal Society* (Philadelphia, 1979). On Italian pugilists, see Frederick G. Lieb, "The Italian in Sport," *Ring* 2 (March 1924): 16–17.

44. See, e.g., *Jewish Daily Forward*, 25 Feb. 1925, quoted in Louis Wirth, *The Ghetto* (1928; rep. Chicago, 1956), 252–53; Barney Ross and Martin Abrahamson, *No Man Stands Alone: The True Story of Barney Ross* (Philadelphia, 1957).

45. Ross and Abrahamson, *No Man Stands Alone*, 141, 159.

46. S. Kirson Weinberg and Henry Arond, "Occupational Culture of the Boxer," *American Journal of Sociology* 57 (Mar. 1952): 460–61, 465, 469; Nathan Hare, "A Study of the Black Fighter," *Black Scholar* 3 (Nov. 1971): 2–8; study data on 154 ex-fighters. Biographical data was gathered from a variety of sources including Jack Lawrence, "The Antiques of Fistiana," *Ring* 8 (June 1930): 31–32; and Bob Burrill, *Who's Who in Boxing* (New Rochelle, N.Y., 1974).

47. David Goldfield and Blaine Brownell, *Urban America: From Downtown to*

No Town (Boston, 1979), 260; Howard Rabinowitz, *Race Relations in the Urban South, 1865–1890* (Urbana, Ill., 1980), 185, 187, 189–90, 389n30, 228–30.

48. Dale A. Somers, *The Rise of Sports in New Orleans, 1850–1900* (Baton Rouge, 1972), 11–12, 29, 87, 96–97, 120–21, 142–44, 199–200, 209, 222–24, 241–42, 286 (quote), 286–90.

49. Ibid., 181.

50. Hardy, *How Boston Played*, 138 (quote), 153; *Brooklyn Eagle*, 5 May 1894; *NYT*, 18 Oct. 1914, 14 Aug. 1917. For a detailed study of sport in one black community, see Rob Ruck, *Sandlot Seasons: Sport in Black Pittsburgh* (Urbana, Ill., 1987).

51. C. Howard Hopkins, *The History of the Y.M.C.A. in North America* (New York, 1951), 213, 472; David M. Katzman, *Before the Ghetto: Black Detroit in the Nineteenth Century* (Urbana, Ill., 1973), 79, 161; W. E. B. Du Bois, *The Philadelphia Negro: A Social Study* (1899; rep. New York, 1967), 232; Kenneth L. Kusmer, *A Ghetto Takes Shape: Black Cleveland, 1870–1930* (Urbana, Ill., 1976), 50–58; Spear, *Black Chicago*, 46–47, 52, 100–101, 162, 174, 227.

52. Chicago Commission on Race Relations, *Negro in Chicago*, 253.

53. See, e.g., Riess, *Touching Base*, 194–96, 217n124; Robert Peterson, *Only the Ball Was White* (Englewood Cliffs, N.J., 1970), chaps. 1, 2; Marshall W. Taylor, *The Fastest Bicycle Rider in the World* (Worcester, Mass., 1928); David K. Wiggins, "Isaac Murphy: Black Hero in Nineteenth-Century American Sport, 1861–1896," *Canadian Journal of History of Sport and Physical Education* 10 (May 1979): 15–32; idem, "Peter Jackson and the Elusive Heavyweight Championship: A Black Athlete's Struggle against the Late-Nineteenth-Century Color-Line," *JSpH* 12 (Summer 1985): 143–68; Randy Roberts, *Papa Jack: Jack Johnson and the Era of White Hopes* (New York, 1983); Al-Tony Gilmore, *Bad Nigger! The National Impact of Jack Johnson* (Port Washington, N.Y., 1975).

54. Elizabeth Pleck, "Black Migration to Boston in the Late Nineteenth Century" (Ph.D. diss., Brandeis University, 1974), 188 (quote). (My thanks to Stephen Hardy for bringing this to my attention.) Roberts, *Papa Jack*, chaps. 5, 7–9; Gilmore, *Bad Nigger!* chaps. 5–6; *NYT*, 6, 9, 10–12, 14, 17 July 1910; "The Prize Fight Moving Pictures," *Outlook* 95 (16 July 1910): 541–42. Mixed bouts were barred in New York from 1912 to 1916. See, e.g., *NYT*, 29 Dec. 1911, 7 Jan. 1912, 6 June 1915, 17 Jan. 1916; 18 Feb. 1916; *NPG* 103 (6 Sept. 1913): 10, 107 (12 Feb. 1916): 10, 108 (1 Apr. 1916): 10; "Smith-Langford Cancelled," *Boxing and Sporting World* 1 (4 Oct. 1913): 4; *New York World*, 17 Jan., 29 June, 7, 8, 11, 12 July, 8 Aug. 1916.

55. On white attitudes toward Louis, see Anthony Edmonds, *Joe Louis* (Grand Rapids, 1972), chaps. 4–6; and Frederick C. Jaher, "White America Views Jack Johnson, Joe Louis and Muhammed Ali," in *Sport in America: New Historical Perspectives*, ed. Donald Spivey (Westport, Conn., 1985), 158–73, 177–82. For black attitudes, see Lawrence W. Levine, *Black Culture and Black Consciousness: Afro-American Folk Thought from Slavery to Freedom* (New York, 1977), 433–38. Quote is from Lena Horne and Richard Schickel, *Lena* (Garden City, L.I., 1965), 75, in ibid., 434.

56. In the late 1940s boxers were typically ex-street fighters, often from broken homes, with unemployed fathers. Weinberg and Arond, "Occupational Culture," 460.

57. Computed from Ronald L. Mendell, *Who's Who in Basketball* (New Rochelle, 1973). See also John F. Rooney, Jr., *A Geography of American Sports: From Cabin Creek to Anaheim* (Reading, Mass., 1974), 154–74. Between 1946 and 1983, two-thirds of all College All-Americans (Division I) came from metropolitan areas with over 500,000 residents at a time when those cities comprised just half (49.5 percent) of the national population. New York produced the most (13.5 percent), followed by Chicago (6.3 percent), Philadelphia, and Los Angeles (3.8 percent each). In 1970 they were the leading procurers of Division I players with ratios approximately equal to their share of the national population. *Chicago Sun-Times*, 13 Dec. 1983.

58. Bob Gibson with Phil Pepe, *From Ghetto to Glory: The Story of Bob Gibson* (Englewood Cliffs, N.J., 1968), 6.

59. Pete Axthelm, *The City Game* (New York, 1970), ix–x, book iii; Rick Telander, *Heaven Is a Playground* (New York, 1976).

60. The standard history of black baseball is Peterson, *Only the Ball Was White*, esp. chaps. 2–3. On black baseball in Chicago, see ibid., 62–66; Spear, *Black Chicago*, 117–18; *Spalding's Official Baseball Guide of Chicago, 1906 . . . 1910* (New York, 1906–10); *Chicago Defender*, 12 Dec. 1908, 23 Apr. 1910, 20 Feb. 1915; *CDN*, 10 Jan. 1910; *New York Age*, 14 Apr., 5 May, 21 July 1910, 5 Jan. 1911. Quote is in Peterson, *Only the Ball Was White*, 66.

61. Riess, *Touching Base*, 38, 196–97; Peterson, *Only the Ball Was White*, 257.

62. Foster's team averaged $85,000 in each of its first six years in the NNL, but other clubs took in as little as $10,000 at the gate. Peterson, *Only the Ball Was White*, 86, 86, 89, 90, 114–15.

63. Donn Rogosin, *Invisible Men: Life in Baseball's Negro Leagues* (New York, 1983), 14–17, 103–8, 213. On the early Crawfords, see Ruck, *Sandlot Seasons*, 46–62.

64. Rogosin, *Invisible Men*, 18–19, 23–24, 105, 107, 110, 209; Peterson, *Only the Ball Was White*, 93, 94, 135–36.

65. Rogosin, *Invisible Men*, 22–23, 93–94.

66. Ibid., 25–26.

67. Jules Tygiel, *Baseball's Great Experiment: Jackie Robinson and His Legacy* (New York, 1983), 40–41, 69 (quote).

68. Rogosin, *Invisible Men*, 218. Quote is from *CDN*, 26 Oct. 1972, cited in Tygiel, *Baseball's Great Experiment*, 196.

69. Tygiel, *Baseball's Great Experiment*, 265–84.

70. Ibid, 305, 311–19, 343–44. On the civil rights movement and recreational facilities in the South, see James F. Murphy, "Egalitarianism and Separatism: A History of Approaches in the Provision of Public Recreation and Leisure Services for Blacks, 1906–1972" (Ph.D. diss., Ohio State University, 1972).

Chapter Four

1. David Nasaw, *Children of the City: At Work and At Play* (New York, 1985), 34–35; quote is from Samuel Chotzinoff, *A Lost Paradise* (New York, 1955), 84, cited in ibid., 34. For a reminiscence of swimming in the mid-1920s by working-class boys in a small city, see Thomas S. Yukic, "Niagara River Playground: The Allen Avenue Gang, 1925–1946 (An Historical Glance at a Boyhood on the Niagara River)," *New York Folklore* 1 (1975): 214–27.

2. George Burns, *The Third Time Around* (New York, 1980), 9–10.

3. Representative positivistic interpretations include John R. Betts, *America's Sporting Heritage, 1850–1950* (Reading, Mass., 1974), 174–76; K. Gerald Marsden, "Philanthropy and the Boston Playground Movement, 1885–1907," *Social Service Review* 35 (Mar. 1961): 48–58. On the social control perspective, see Michael P. McCarthy, "Politics and the Parks: Chicago Businessmen and the Recreation Movement," *Journal of the Illinois State Historical Society* 65 (Summer 1972): 158–72; Joel Spring, "Mass Culture and School Sports," *History of Education Quarterly* 14 (Winter 1974): 483; Cary Goodman, *Choosing Sides: Playground and Street Life on the Lower East Side* (New York, 1979); Galen Cranz, *The Politics of Park Design: A History of Urban Parks in America* (Cambridge, 1982), 236–39. For a more temperate view, see Paul Boyer, *Urban Masses and Moral Order in America, 1820–1920* (Cambridge, 1978), 233–51. These monographs almost exclusively studied the park movement from the top down. For sophisticated studies that recognize the complexity of motivations and the countervailing forces involved in the park movement, see Stephen Hardy, *How Boston Played: Sport, Recreation and Community, 1865–1915* (Boston, 1981), chaps. 4, 5; Roy Rosenzweig, *Eight Hours for What We Will: Workers and Leisure in an Industrial City, 1870–1920* (Cambridge, 1983), chap. 5; and Stephen Hardy and Alan G. Ingham, "Games, Structures and Agency: Historians on the American Play Movement," *JSH* 17 (Winter 1983): 285–302.

4. Graham R. Taylor, "Recent Developments in Chicago Parks," *Annals of the American Academy of Political and Social Sciences* 35 (March 1910): 305–7; Elizabeth Halsey, *The Development of Public Recreation in Metropolitan Chicago* (Chicago, 1940), 10, 19–21, 115; Harold M. Mayer and Richard C. Wade, *Chicago: Growth of a Metropolis* (Chicago, 1969), 100; Glen Holt, "Private Plans for Public Spaces: The Origins of Chicago's Park System, 1850–1875," *Chicago History* 8 (Fall 1979): 181–83.

5. Theodore Hershberg, Harold E. Cox, Dale B. Light, Jr., and Richard R. Greenfield, "The 'Journey-to-Work': An Empirical Investigation of Work, Residence and Transportation, Philadelphia, 1850 and 1880," in *Philadelphia: Work, Space, Family and Group Experience in the 19th Century*, ed. Theodore Hershberg (New York, 1981), 142–43, 146–48. See also Clay McShane, *Technology and Reform: Street Railways and the Growth of Milwaukee, 1887–1900* (Madison, 1974), 36. For a brief overview of urban transportation, see Glen E. Holt, "The Changing Perception of Urban Pathology: An Essay on the Development of Mass Transit in the United States," in *Cities in American History*, ed. Kenneth T. Jackson and Stanley K. Schultz (New York, 1972), 324–55; Howard P. Chuda-

coff, *The Evolution of American Urban Society*, 2nd ed. (Englewood Cliffs, N.J., 1981), 72–80; David A. Goldfield and Blaine Brownell, *Urban America: From Downtown to No Town* (Boston, 1979), 143–45.

6. Hardy, *How Boston Played*, 73–77.

7. Rosenzweig, *Eight Hours*, 135–37.

8. *Spirit* 121 (7 Mar. 1891): 302, 123 (5 March 1892): 273; *NYT*, 21–26, 31 March, 8, 12, 14, 15 Apr. 1892; Robert Muccigrosso, "The City Reform Club," *New York Historical Society Quarterly* 52 (July 1968): 250–51. On Olmsted's opposition to the track, see Frederick Law Olmsted, Jr., and Theodora Kimball, eds., *Frederick Law Olmsted: Landscape Architect, 1822–1903* (1922–28; rep. New York, 1970), 276, 277, 526–27. On the Speedway, see *NYT*, 30 Dec. 1900; *New York Sun*, 1 May 1899.

9. Hardy, *How Boston Played*, 75–77, 79–85. Tennis was permitted in Central Park's north meadow in 1884 at a hay field that was difficult to locate. *Spirit* 106 (10 May 1884): 411. The park commissioners forbade children from freely playing on the grass until 1897, although they permitted elite sports like horseback riding and carriage driving on the roadways. *NYT*, 22 Apr. 1886; Richard Knapp, "Parks and Politics: The Rise of Municipal Responsibility for Playgrounds in New York City, 1887–1905" (M.A. thesis, Duke University, 1968), 31. Not until after 1910 did Central Park have permanent tennis courts and baseball diamonds. See Henry Hope Reed and Sophia Duckworth, *Central Park: A History and a Guide* (New York, 1967), 46.

10. McCarthy, "Politics," 159.

11. Chicago Recreation Commission, *Chicago Recreation Survey*, vol. 1, *Public Recreation* (Chicago, 1937), 22 (hereafter cited as *Chicago Recreation*); Halsey, *Recreation in Metropolitan Chicago*, 145; Jacob Riis, *How the Other Half Lives: Studies among the Tenements of New York* (1890; rep. New York, 1966), 183.

12. Knapp, "Parks and Politics," chap. 3; and Jerry G. Dickason, "The Development of the Playground Movement in the United States: A Historical Survey" (Ph.D. diss., New York University, 1979), emphasize the role of elites. See also n. 3, above. For the contributions of other social groups and individuals, see Hardy, *How Boston Played*, chaps. 4, 5; Rosenzweig, *Eight Hours*, chap. 5; and Daniel M. Bluestone, "Olmsted's Boston and Other Park Places," *Reviews in American History* 11 (Dec. 1983): 532–33. Contemporaries did not clearly distinguish between the terms *playground* and *small park*. A playground usually meant a children's playing area, supplied with special equipment, that was fenced off from the surrounding area. Playgrounds could be free standing or located inside a park.

13. Hardy, *How Boston Played*, 86–88, 91–102; Rosenzweig, *Eight Hours*, 144–48. See also Dominick Cavallo, *Muscles and Morals: Organized Playgrounds and Urban Reform, 1880–1920* (Philadelphia, 1981); Bernard Mergen, "The Discovery of Children's Play," *AQ* 27 (Oct. 1975): 339–420; Mark Kadzielski, "'As a Flower Needs Sunshine': The Origins of Organized Children's Recreation in Philadelphia, 1886–1911," *JSpH* 4 (Summer 1977): 169–88.

14. Knapp, "Parks and Politics," 45–49, 53.

15. Ibid., 28, 52–53.

16. Ibid., 84–100; *NYT*, 17 Nov. 1912, 2 Apr. 1913.

17. Knapp, ''Parks and Politics,'' 100–118.

18. Ibid., 109–10; Jeffrey Gurock, *When Harlem Was Jewish, 1870–1930* (New York, 1981), 35, 42, 161.

19. Knapp, ''Parks and Politics,'' 131; Goodman, *Choosing Sides,* 56.

20. Hardy, *How Boston Played,* 87–88, 99–101; Rosenzweig, *Eight Hours,* chap. 5.

21. Boston, *Reports of Proceedings of the City Council,* 28 Apr. 1873, quoted in Hardy, *How Boston Played,* 90.

22. Hardy, *How Boston Played,* 93–99; Cynthia Zaitzevsky, *Frederick Law Olmsted and the Boston Park System* (Cambridge, 1981), 95–103.

23. Hardy, *How Boston Played,* 88–89, 97–98.

24. Rosenzweig, *Eight Hours,* 132, 135, 144.

25. Hardy, *How Boston Played,* 99–106; Worcester Commission on Shade Trees and Public Grounds, *Annual Report for the Year Ending November 30, 1904* (Worcester, 1905), 14–15; and *Labor News,* 22 June 1907, both quoted in Rosenzweig, *Eight Hours,* 137.

26. Halsey, *Recreation in Metropolitan Chicago,* 26, 145, 163–64, 166; Chicago Recreation, 1:14–15; Clarence Rainwater, *The Play Movement in the United States* (Chicago, 1922), 18–19; McCarthy, ''Politics,'' 159–60; Humbert Nelli, *The Italians in Chicago, 1880–1930, A Study in Social Mobility* (New York, 1970), 96.

27. Halsey, *Recreation in Metropolitan Chicago,* 26, 145, 163–64, 166, Chicago Recreation, 1:14–15; Clarence Rainwater, *The Play Movement in the United States* (Chicago, 1922), 18–19; McCarthy, ''Politics,'' 159–60; Humbert Nelli, *The Italians in Chicago, 1880–1930, A Study in Social Mobility* (New York, 1970), 96.

27. Halsey, *Recreation in Metropolitan Chicago,* 26, 145, 163–64, 166, Chicago Recreation, 1:14–15; Clarence Rainwater, *The Play Movement in the United States* (Chicago, 1922), 18–19; McCarthy, ''Politics,'' 159–60; Humbert Nelli, *The Italians in Chicago, 1880–1930, A Study in Social Mobility* (New York, 1970), 96.

27. Halsey, ''History of the Development of Municipal Parks in the United States: Concepts and Their Applications'' (Ph.D. diss., University of Illinois, 1964), 162–64.

28. Rainwater, *Play Movement,* 92–100; McCarthy, ''Politics,'' 161, 163–64; Frye, ''Municipal Parks,'' 162–64.

29. *Special Committee to Investigate the South Park Commissioners* (Chicago, 1905), 17–18, quoted in McCarthy, ''Politics,'' 166; Allen T. Burns, ''Relation of Playgrounds to Juvenile Delinquency,'' *Charities and the Commons* 21 (3 Oct. 1908): 29.

30. McCarthy, ''Politics,'' 167–70.

31. Ibid., 171–72; Jesse Steiner, *Americans at Play* (1933; rep. New York, 1970), 33.

32. Steiner, *Americans at Play,* 25–29. The creation and operation of municipal recreational facilities was a difficult political task that required special state legislation. Only in 1917 did any state pass enabling laws giving its cities the power to facilitate public recreation and raise taxes to pay for it, but such provisions would be fairly common by 1931. A confusing array of governmental agencies administered public recreation, and there were a lot of overlapping responsibilities. Recreation was usually under a park commission (28.9 percent), playground and recreation commission (25.3 percent), or board of education (21.2 percent), with age being a major variable for dividing up responsibilities. See ibid., 167–70.

33. Per capita expenditures of city recreation departments rose from $0.60 in

1915 to $1.44 in 1928, which was slightly above the average increase for all city agencies. Steiner, *Americans at Play*, 173–74, 179–80, 181–82. On Sabbatarian reform, see above, 69–71; John R. Betts, *America's Sporting Heritage, 1850–1950* (Reading, Mass., 1974), 352–55; Steven A. Riess, *Touching Base: Professional Baseball and American Culture in the Progressive Era* (Westport, Conn., 1980), chap. 5, esp. 137, 140; Blaine A. Brownell, "Birmingham, Alabama: New South City in the 1920s," *Journal of Southern History* 38 (Feb. 1972): 38–39.

34. Steiner, *Americans at Play*, 30–31, 62, 65, 70–73; *New York Herald-Tribune*, 26 Jan. 1934, quoted in Robert A. Caro, *The Power Broker: Robert Moses and the Fall of New York* (New York, 1975), 335.

35. Steiner, *Americans at Play*, 52. On the Burnham Plan, see Mayer and Wade, *Chicago*, 274, 276–80.

36. Steiner, *Americans at Play*, 76–78.

37. Caro, *Power Broker*, 392; Betts, *America's Sporting Heritage*, 286–87; U.S., Federal Works Agency, *Final Report on the WPA Program, 1935–43* (1947; rep. Westport, Conn., 1976), 48–50, 51–52. For an extensive study of federal support for urban recreation during the Depression, see Judith Anne Davidson, "The Federal Government and the Democratization of Public Recreational Sport, New York City, 1933–43" (Ph.D. diss., University of Massachusetts, 1983).

38. Caro, *Power Broker*, 144–45, 331–33, 453.

39. Ibid., 336–38, 344–45.

40. Ibid., 360–78; Barbara Blumberg, *The New Deal and the Unemployed* (Lewisburg, Penn., 1979), 177.

41. "Stadiums," *Playground* 20 (July 1926): 198.

42. James R. Johnson, "Make No Little Plans: Soldier Field and the Plan of Chicago" (unpublished seminar paper, Northeastern Illinois University, 1979); Mayer and Wade, *Chicago*, 276, 294, 298; Perry Duis and Glen Holt, "The Classic Problem of Soldier Field," *Chicago Magazine* 27 (April 1978): 170–73; *NYT*, 21 Nov. 1937.

43. Steven A. Riess, "Power Without Authority: Los Angeles' Elites and the Construction of the Coliseum," *JSpH* 8 (Spring 1981): 52–56, 58–63.

44. Ibid.

45. Benjamin G. Rader, *American Sports: From the Age of Folk Games to the Age of Spectators* (Englewood Cliffs, N.J., 1983), 210–11; Harry Jebsen, Jr., "The Public Acceptance of Sports in Dallas, 1880–1930," *JSpH* 6 (Winter 1979): 16.

46. Gerald D. Suttles, *The Social Order of the Slum: Ethnicity and Territory in the Inner City* (Chicago, 1968), 54.

47. Rosenzweig, *Eight Hours*, 135, 137, 139, 149–50.

48. Suttles, *Slum*, 54–56; Fredrick M. Thrasher, *The Gang: A Study of 1,131 Gangs in Chicago*, abr. ed. (Chicago, 1963), 134–35.

49. Howard Rabinowitz, *Race Relations in the Urban South, 1865–1890* (Urbana, Ill., 1980), 187, 189–90; Dale A. Somers, *The Rise of Sports in New Orleans, 1850–1900* (Baton Rouge, 1972), 282–84; Carl V. Harris, *Political Power in Birmingham, 1871–1921* (Knoxville, 1977), 165–67.

50. Betts, *America's Sporting Heritage*, 338.

51. Allan H. Spear, *Black Chicago: The Making of a Negro Ghetto, 1890–1920* (Chicago, 1967), 205–6; Chicago Commission on Race Relations, *The Negro in Chicago* (Chicago, 1922), 272–80, 288–90, 293, 297.

52. Chicago Commission on Race, *Negro in Chicago*, 272–78, 286, 292; Spear, *Black Chicago*, 212–22; William M. Tuttle, Jr., *Race Riot: Chicago in the Red Summer of 1919* (New York, 1974), chap. 2; Arthur Waskow, *From Race Riot to Sit-In* (New York, 1965), chap. 4.

53. Caro, *Power Broker*, 453, 456–57, 512–14.

54. Suttles, *Slum*, 54–57, chap. 6; Frederick W. Cozens and Florence S. Stumpf, *Sports in American Life* (Chicago, 1953), 253–55; Betts, *America's Sporting Heritage*, 338.

55. Edward F. Haas, *DeLesseps S. Morrison and the Image of Reform: New Orleans Politics, 1946–1961* (Baton Rouge, 1974), 75–76, 305n77; idem, "The Southern Metropolis, 1940–1976," in *The City in Southern History: The Growth of Urban Civilization in the South*, ed. Blaine Brownell and David Goldfield (Port Washington, N.Y., 1977), 163; William H. Chafe, *Civilities and Civil Rights: Greensboro, North Carolina, and the Black Struggle for Freedom* (New York, 1980), 111; Darryl Paulson, "Stay Out, the Water's Fine: Desegregating Municipal Swimming Facilities in St. Petersburg, Florida," *Tampa Bay History* 4 (Fall–Winter 1982): 6–17.

Chapter Five

1. The literature on youth sports and related topics has become quite substantial. See Benjamin G. Rader, *American Sports: From the Age of Folk Games to the Age of Spectators* (Englewood Cliffs, N.J., 1983), chap. 8; Stephen Hardy, *How Boston Played: Sport, Recreation and Community, 1865–1915* (Boston, 1982), chaps. 5, 6; C. Howard Hopkins, *History of the YMCA in North America* (New York, 1951); Paul S. Boyer, *Urban Masses and Moral Order in America, 1820–1920* (Cambridge, 1978), chap. 7; David I. Macleod, *Building Character in the American Boy: The Boy Scouts, YMCA and Their Forerunners, 1870–1920* (Madison, 1983); Cary Goodman, *Choosing Sides: Playground and Street Life on the Lower East Side* (New York, 1979); Dominick Cavallo, *Muscles and Morals: Organized Playgrounds and Urban Reform, 1880–1920* (Philadelphia, 1981); David Nasaw, *Children of the City: At Work and At Play* (New York, 1986); and Lawrence A. Finfer, "Leisure and Social Work in the Urban Community: The Progressive Recreation Movement, 1890–1920" (Ph.D. diss., Michigan State University, 1974). For a summary of the activities of street youth as reported by contemporary recreational surveys in the Progressive era, see Alan Hyvig, "The Commercial Amusement Audience in 20th-Century American Cities," *Journal of American Culture* 5 (Spring 1982): 1–19.

2. Joseph Kett, *Rites of Passage: Adolescence in America, 1790 to the Present* (New York, 1977), 138, 183–89; Jeffrey Miral, "From State Control to Institutional Control of High School Athletics: Three Michigan Cities, 1883–1905," *JSH* 16 (Winter 1982): 84; David Tyack, *The One Best System* (Cambridge, 1981), 183.

3. Hardy, *How Boston Played*, 109–12; *Illinois Staats-Zeitung*, 21 Mar. 1871, in CFLPS; Wilma Pesavento, "A Historical Study of the Development of Physical Education in the Chicago Public Schools, 1860 to 1965" (Ph.D. diss., Northwestern University, 1966), 21–27; John R. Betts, *America's Sporting Heritage, 1850–1950* (Reading, Mass., 1974), 107.

4. Hardy, *How Boston Played*, 111–12; Mirel, "High School Athletics," 84–92.

5. Hardy, *How Boston Played*, 113–16.

6. Ibid., 117–22; Rader, *American Sports*, 161; Mirel, "High School Athletics," 90–93, 95 (quotes).

7. Hardy, *How Boston Played*, 113–14, 120–21, 123; Mirel, "High School Athletics," 95; Rader, *American Sports*, 162–66. For an argument that emphasizes the need to limit adolescent sexuality through sport as part of a program of imposed social control, see Joel Spring, "Mass Culture and School Sports," *History of Education Quarterly* 14 (Winter 1974): 483–95.

8. Timothy O'Hanlon, "School Sports as Social Training: The Case of Athletics and the Crisis of World War I," *JSpH* (Spring 1982): 1–14; Frederick W. Cozens and Florence S. Stumpf, *Sports in American Life* (Chicago, 1953), 83.

9. O'Hanlon, "School Sports," 10–14.

10. The sociological literature on academic attainment and sport is summarized in Emil Bend and Brian M. Petrie, "Sports Participation, Scholastic Success and Social Mobility," *Exercise and Sport Sciences Review* 5 (1977): 1–44. See also Eldon E. Snyder and Elmer A. Spreitzer, *Social Aspects of Sport*, 2nd ed. (Englewood Cliffs, N.J., 1981), chap. 8.

11. See, e.g., W. Lloyd Warner, *The Social System of American Ethnic Groups* (New Haven, 1945), 142; Philip Earl Frohlich, "Sport and the Community: A Study of Social Change in Athens, Ohio" (Ph.D. diss., University of Wisconsin, 1952), 137; Robert S. Lynd and Helen Merrell Lynd, *Middletown: A Study of Modern American Culture* (New York, 1929), 284, 485. On sport and community building after World War II, see Herbert J. Gans, *The Levittowners: Ways of Life and Politics in a New Suburbia* (New York, 1967), 90, 92, 120–23.

12. Lynd and Lynd, *Middletown*, 212–14, 284, 485; idem, *Middletown in Transition: A Study in Cultural Conflicts* (New York, 1937), 218n, 291–92.

13. In 1971–72 Pittsburgh had the highest rate of any major city—2.56 times its share of the national population. Los Angeles was the single most productive county, although its index (1.02) was just above average; Cook County (Chicago and its environs) was second, with an even lower index (0.86). Baltimore, Philadelphia, and St. Louis all had indexes below 0.60. New York's was a dismal 0.13 compared to the surrounding Nassau, Westchester, and Bergen counties, whose ratios ranged from 1.0 to 1.75. See John F. Rooney, Jr., *A Geography of American Sport: From Cabin Creek to Anaheim* (Reading, Mass., 1974), 117–31, 142–45. On the Chicago game, see *Chicago Tribune*, 21 Nov. 1937; *NYT*, 21 Nov. 1937.

14. Harry Edwards, *Sociology of Sport* (Homewood, Ill., 1973), 272; Jack Scott, *The Athletic Revolution* (New York, 1970), 174; Pete Axthelm, *The City Game* (New York, 1970), 125–26.

15. On the nineteenth-century YMCA, see Boyer, *Urban Masses*, 112–13, 115–16; Hardy, *How Boston Played*, 55, 57; Elmer L. Johnson, *The History of YMCA Physical Education* (Chicago, 1979); Hopkins, *YMCA*; Macleod, *Building Character*, chap. 4; Betts, *America's Sporting Heritage*, 107–8; Aaron Abell, *The Urban Impact of American Protestantism, 1865–1890* (Cambridge, 1943), 204–6. On sexuality and the muscular Christian, see Melvin L. Adelman, *A Sporting Time: New York City and the Rise of Modern Athletics, 1820–1870* (Urbana, Ill., 1986), 283–84; Charles E. Rosenberg, "Sexuality, Class, and Role in Nineteenth-Century America," *AQ* 25 (May 1973): 129, 133–34, 139; Rader, *American Sports*, 151.

16. Rader, *American Sports*, 151; Hardy, *How Boston Played*, 55–57. Despite the rhetorical support of the ideology of sport, a poll of 751 Chicago clergymen found that just a handful of churches provided gymnasiums and sports programs. Boyer, *Urban Masses*, 137–40.

17. David I. Macleod, "A Live Vaccine: The YMCA and Male Adolescents in the United States and Canada, 1870–1920," *Histoire Sociale/Social History* 11 (May 1978): 7–11; Betts, *America's Sporting Heritage*, 107–10. Quote is from I. E. Brown, "Association Work among Boys," *Watchman* 11 (1885): 185, in Macleod, "Live Vaccine," 9.

18. *DAB*, s.v. "Gulick, Luther"; Rader, *American Sports*, 152–53.

19. Rader, *American Sports*, 153–54.

20. Hardy, *How Boston Played*, 143; Abell, *Urban Impact*, 45–46. Quote is from *Harper's Weekly* 13 (11 Dec. 1869): 786, in Betts, *America's Sporting Heritage*, 108.

21. Rader, *American Sports*, 155; Cavallo, *Muscles and Morals*, 55.

22. Rader, *American Sports*, 155.

23. Ibid., 154–57; Benjamin G. Rader, "Muscular Christianity, the Biological Theory of Play, and the Adult-Managed Boys' Sport Movement, 1890–1920" (paper read at the annual meeting of the North American Society for Sport History, 30 May 1979, Austin, Texas), 13.

24. Rader, *American Sports*, 155; idem, "Muscular Christianity," 14–16. Quote is from Luther Gulick, *A Philosophy of Play* (New York, 1920), 92, in ibid., 26. For church-sponsored athletics in the early 1900s, see e.g., *NYT*, 18 Feb., 13 June, 11 Dec. 1904, 5 May 1905, 7 Feb. 1913.

25. Luther Gulick, "Athletics for School-Children," *Lippincott's Monthly Magazine* 88 (Aug. 1911): 201, in Rader, *American Sports*, 157; J. Thomas Jable, "The Public Schools Athletic League of New York City: Organized Athletics for City School Children, 1903–1914," in *The American Sporting Experience: A Historical Anthology of Sport in America*, ed. Steven A. Riess (West Point, 1984), 221–22.

26. *NYT*, 29 Nov., 13 Dec. 1903, 14 Apr. 1907; Jable, "Public Schools," 218–19.

27. *NYT*, 29 Nov. 1903.

28. *NYT*, 13 Dec. 1903.

29. Ibid.; Jable, "Public Schools," 223–26.

30. Jable, "Public Schools," 227.

31. Ibid., 227–28.

32. Ibid., 228–30.

33. Ibid., 230–31; *New York World*, 11 Mar. 1916; *NYT*, 5 July 1913, 7 July 1919.

34. *NYT*, 8 Feb., 13 Apr. 1907; PSAL, Girls' Branch, *Official Handbook, 1917–1918* (New York, 1917), 20–24; quotes are from idem, *Official Handbook, 1915–1916* (New York, 1915), 66, 19; Jable, "Public Schools," 231–33.

35. Jable, "Public Schools," 233–35; Rader, *American Sports*, 159; quote from Albert B. Reeve, "The World's Greatest Athletic Organization," *Outing* 57 (Oct. 1910): 110.

36. Jable, "Public Schools," 235.

37. Jane Addams, *The Spirit of Youth and the City Streets* (New York, 1909), 95–96; Lillian D. Wald, "The House on Henry Street, Ch. II: Children and Play," *Atlantic Monthly* 115 (Apr. 1915): 473; Boyer, *Urban Masses*, 222–24; Hardy, *How Boston Played*, 56–57. The standard history of the movement is Allen F. Davis, *Spearheads for Reform: The Social Settlements and the Progressive Movement, 1890–1914* (New York, 1967).

38. Addams, *Spirit of Youth*, 95–96, 127.

39. Davis, *Spearheads for Reform*, 61–62, 88–89; Allen F. Davis, *American Heroine: The Life and Legend of Jane Addams* (New York, 1973), 68–73; Chicago Chronicle, 25 May 1902, in Allen F. Davis and Mary Lynn McCree, *Eighty Years at Hull House* (Chicago, 1969), 77; Jane Addams, *Twenty Years at Hull House* (1910; rep. New York, 1954), 443–44.

40. *NYT*, 22 Mar. 1903; 12 May 1907; Inter-Settlement Athletic Association, *Official Handbook, 1911* (New York, 1911), 3.

41. Humbert S. Nelli, *The Italians in Chicago: A Study in Social Mobility, 1880–1930* (New York, 1970), 96; Thomas C. Campbell, "Sport for Neglected Boys," *The Church Militant* (Dec. 1900): 13, quoted in Jerry G. Dickason, "The Development of the Playground Movement in the United States: A Historical Study" (Ph.D. diss., New York University, 1979), 212.

42. Clarence Rainwater, *The Play Movement in the United States: A Study in Community Recreation* (Chicago, 1922); Cavallo, *Muscles and Morals*; Boyer, *Urban Masses*, chap. 16; Rader, *American Sports*, 159–60.

43. Rainwater, *Play Movement*, 196; Rader, *American Sports*, 159; Goodman, *Choosing Sides*, 56, 97–98; Gunther Barth, *City People: The Rise of Modern City Culture in Nineteenth-Century America* (New York, 1980), 177; *NYT*, 17 Nov. 1912, 2 Apr. 1913, 12 Jan. 1914.

44. Goodman, *Choosing Sides*, 6–7, 13–18; *NYT*, 5 July 1913; Edward C. Devereux, "Backyard Versus Little League Baseball: The Impoverishment of Children's Games," in *Social Problems in Athletics: Essays in the Sociology of Sport*, ed. Daniel M. Landers (Urbana, Ill., 1976), 37–56.

45. Rader, *American Sports*, 160.

46. Rader, "Muscular Christianity," 25–26.

47. Jack Berryman, "From the Cradle to the Playing Field: America's Emphasis on Highly Organized Competitive Sports for Preadolescent Boys," *JSpH* 2 (Fall 1975): 112–31.

Chapter Six

1. Benjamin G. Rader, *American Sports: From the Age of Folk Games to the Age of Spectators* (Englewood Cliffs, N.J., 1983), 99–100; Dale A. Somers, *The Rise of Sports in New Orleans, 1850–1900* (Baton Rouge, 1971), 170.

2. Somers, *Sports in New Orleans*, 159–73; Elliott J. Gorn, *The Manly Art: Bare-Knuckle Prize Fighting in America* (Ithaca, N.Y., 1986), 230–35.

3. Somers, *Sports in New Orleans*, 167–70, 174–75.

4. Ibid., 174–76.

5. Ibid., 177–91.

6. On the start of the New York boxing revival, see *Brooklyn Eagle*, 1 July, 14 Aug. 1892; *NYT*, 21–28 Sept. 1, 2 Oct. 1893; "Arthur Lumley, Veteran Sportswriter, Manager, and Promoter," *Ring* 6 (May 1927): 23; Steven A. Riess, "In the Ring and Out: Professional Boxing in New York, 1896–1920," in *Sport in America*, ed. Donald Spivey (Westport, Conn., 1985), 96–99.

7. Theodore A. Bingham, "The Organized Criminals of New York," *Mc-Clure's* 34 (Nov. 1909): 62–63; George K. Turner, "Tammany's Control of New York by Professional Criminals," ibid. 33 (June 1909): 117–34; Roy Crandall, "Tim Sullivan's Power," *Harper's Weekly* 58 (18 Oct. 1913): 14–15; M. R. Werner, *Tammany Hall* (Garden City, N.Y., 1927), 344, 438–40; Thomas M. Henderson, *Tammany Hall and the New Immigrants: The Progressive Years* (New York, 1976), 1–15; *NPG* 66 (18 May 1895): 11, 66 (1 June 1895): 10, 67 (8 Feb. 1896): 11, 69 (5 Dec. 1896): 11, 76 (9 Sept. 1900): 7; *Brooklyn Eagle*, 24 Oct. 1896; *NYT*, 11 June 1899. On Devery, see Steven A. Riess, *Touching Base: Professional Baseball and American Culture in the Progressive Era* (Westport, Conn., 1980), 87–91. For a detailed discussion of the fight to legalize boxing in New York see Riess, "In the Ring and Out," 95–128.

8. *NPG* 69 (19 Sept., 7, 14 Nov. 1896): 10, 76 (12 May 1900): 10. The first publicly exhibited fight film was made in 1894, and three years later the heavy-weight title bout between Corbett and Fitzsimmons grossed $75,000. Robert Cantwell, *The Real McCoy: The Life and Times of Norman Selby* (Princeton, N.J., 1971), 97–100.

9. *NPG* 73 (18 Feb. 1899): 11, 95 (17 Feb. 1910): 10, 96 (21, 28 Apr. 1910): 10, 76 (5, 12, 19 May 1900): 11, 78 (16 March 1901): 10, 86 (13 May 1905): 6, 86 (2 Sept. 1905): 10, 87 (3, 10 Feb. 1906): 10, 88 (28 Apr. 19, 26 May 1906): 10; *NYT*, 20 June 1899, 19, 25 Jan. 1900, 16 Nov. 1905, 1 June 1906, 2 Apr. 1907, 2 Nov., 18 Dec. 1908; Boxing Scrapbooks, vol. 1, pp. 87, 93, Chicago Historical Society, Chicago, Ill.; *New York Call*, 26 Oct. 1908.

10. *NPG* 85 (21 Jan. 1905): 10, 89 (15 Sept. 1906): 3, 89 (22 Sept. 1906): 10; James Chinello, "The Great Goldfield Foul," *Westways* 68 (Sept. 1976): 27–30, 88; Walton Bean, *Boss Ruef's San Francisco* (Berkeley, 1952), 85–88; *NYT*, 28 Nov., 8 Dec. 1909, 17 Apr., 6, 9, 12 July 1910; Randy Roberts, *Papa Jack: Jack Johnson and the Era of White Hopes* (New York, 1983), chap. 6.

11. *NYT*, 13 Apr., 8, 9, 22 June, 29 Sept., 27 Oct. 1911, 15, 29 Feb., 3 Mar. 1912, 26 Apr. 1913, 4 Jan. 1915; "Prize-Fighting in New York," *Outlook* 99 (9 Sept. 1911): 56–57; William Inglis, "The State and the Boxing Business," *Harp-*

er's Weekly 54 (16 Sept. 1911): 19; E. B. Osborn, "The Revival of Boxing," Nineteenth Century 70 (Oct. 1911): 771–81.

12. NYT, 5, 9 Oct. 1915, 30 Dec. 1916, 30, 31 Jan., 1–3, 5, 6 Feb., 24, 26 Apr., 8, 11 May 1917; New York Herald, 30 Nov. 1915.

13. Guy Lewis, "World War I and the Emergence of Sport for the Masses," The Maryland Historian 4 (Fall 1973): 109–22; NYT, 14, 27 Mar., 11, 12 Apr. 1908, 4, 18, 27 Feb., 13, 20, 27 Mar., 10, 11, 17 Apr. 1919, 23 Feb., 25 Mar., 2, 25 Apr., 25 May 1920; Gene Fowler, Beau James: The Life and Times of Jimmy Walker (New York, 1949), 100–101.

14. NYT, 9, 14, 15, 29 Mar. 1916, 13, 16 Aug., 18 Sept. 1920; New York World, 9, 10, 13, 26, 29 Mar. 1916; Richard J. Butler and Joseph Driscoll, Dock Walloper: The Story of "Big Dick" Butler (New York, 1928), 264; Mrs. Tex Rickard, Everything Happened to Him: The Story of Tex Rickard (New York, 1936), 274–75; Don S. Kirschner, City and Country: Rural Responses to Urbanization in the 1920s (Westport, Conn., 1970), 141–43; Randy Roberts, Jack Dempsey: The Manassa Mauler (Baton Rouge, 1979), 95–99.

15. On underworld influence in prize fighting in the 1920s, see Nat Fleischer, 50 Years at Ringside (New York, 1958), 5, 49–50, 193–94, 208–10; Ruby Goldstein and Frank Graham, Third Man in the Ring (New York, 1959), 31, 34–35; Mickey Walker with Joe Reichler, Mickey Walker, The Toy Bulldog, and His Times (New York, 1961), 52–53, 58–59, 66–68, 71–73, 188–92; Jack "Doc" Kearns and Oscar Fraley, The Million Dollar Gate (New York, 1963), 225–27; Leo Katcher, The Big Bankroll: The Life and Times of Arnold Rothstein (New York, 1958), 117–18.

16. U.S. Cong., Senate, Professional Boxing: Hearings before Subcommittee on Anti-Trust and Monopoly, 86th Cong., 2nd sess., Pursuant to S. Res. 238, Dec. 5–14, 1960 (Washington, D.C., 1961), 105–6, 425–47, 547–58 (hereafter cited as Professional Boxing); Barney Nagler, James Norris and the Decline of Boxing (Indianapolis, 1964), 19–20, 26–32, 90–99; Jeffrey T. Sammons, Beyond the Ring: The Role of Boxing in American Society (Urbana, Ill., 1988), chap. 6; Steven A. Riess, "Only the Ring Was Square: Frankie Carbo and the Underworld Control of American Boxing," IJHS 5 (May 1988): 29–52.

17. Professional Boxing, 664–731.

18. Ibid., 60–63, 71–77, 1433, 1454; Nagler, Decline of Boxing, 100–103; Robert Coughlan, "How the IBC Runs Boxing," Sports Illustrated 1 (17 Jan. 1955): 47; NYT, 23, 31 Mar. 1956; Governor's Committee on the Study of Boxing and Wrestling in California, Report (Sacramento, 1956), 83–84, 111, 115, 117 (hereafter cited as Governor's Committee, Report).

19. Professional Boxing, 7–34; Jake LaMotta, Raging Bull: My Story (Englewood Cliffs, N.J., 1970), 156–63; Nagler, Decline of Boxing, 19–20, 28–29, 32–33, 90–92, 228–30.

20. Governor's Committee, Report, 29, 42–43, 49, 60–61.

21. Robert Coughlan, "Nationwide Look at Boxing's Straw Bosses," Sports Illustrated 1 (31 Jan. 1955): 18–19, 48–53; Coughlan, "How the IBC Runs Boxing," 11–13, 47–50; Martin Kane and James Shepley, "The Case against the

IBC," *Sports Illustrated* 3 (23 Apr. 1956): 26–29, 59; *NYT*, 6 Dec. 1960; *Professional Boxing*, 308–9, 550–51, 875–92; Nagler, *Decline of Boxing*, 17–19, 44–49; interview with Ben Bentley, 7 April 1984, Chicago, Ill.

22. *Professional Boxing*, 875–92; Norris, *Decline in Boxing*, 44–99; Kane and Shepley, "Case against IBC," 26–29, 59; Martin Kane, "IBC Guilty as Charged," *Sports Illustrated* 5 (18 March 1957): 16–17; idem, "James D. Norris Must Get Out," ibid. 6 (1 July 1957): 10–11.

23. *Professional Boxing*, 1075–82, 1450, 1512–28, 1519 (quotes); Nagler, *Decline of Boxing*, 113; *NYT*, 4, 15 Mar., 21 May, 3 Dec. 1961.

24. Somers, *Sports in New Orleans*, 108; David C. Hammack, *Power and Society: Greater New York at the Turn of the Century* (New York, 1982), 101, 103, 111, 342n109, discusses the sporting style of elite politicians. On racing and urban machines see Herman Kogan and Lloyd Wendt, *Lords of the Levee: The Story of Bathhouse John and Hinky Dink* (Indianapolis, 1943), 21, 28–29, 50–54, 109–10; Mark Haller, "Organized Crime in Urban Society: Chicago in the Twentieth Century," *JSH* 5 (Winter 1971–72): 214–16, 218–19, and Steven A. Riess, "The Politics of Horse Racing in Chicago, New York, and New Jersey, 1891–1895" (paper presented at the annual convention of the North American Society for Sport History, Manhattan, Kan., 24 May 1982); *DAB*, s.v., "Croker, Richard," "Sullivan, Timothy."

25. *NYT*, 5 Nov. 1893; Somers, *Sports in New Orleans*, 94–99.

26. *Spirit* 102 (31 Dec. 1881): 607; *NYT*, 115 (4 Feb. 1888): 53, 115 (19 May 1888): 620–21, 115 (9 June 1888): 738; William H. P. Robertson, *The History of Thoroughbred Racing in America* (New York, 1964), 90–92; C. B. Parmer, *For Gold and Glory: The History of Thoroughbred Racing in America* (New York, 1939), 128; Henry Chafetz, *Play the Devil: A History of Gambling in the United States from 1492 to 1955* (New York, 1960), 267.

27. *Spirit* 102 (31 Dec. 1881): 607; *NYT*, 12 Jan. 1884; *Chicago Times*, 23 July 1887; Anthony Comstock, "Pool Rooms and Pool Selling," *The North American Review* 157 (Nov. 1893): 601–10; Parmer, *Gold and Glory*, 124–25; Robertson, *Thoroughbred Racing*, 148–51; Harold C. Syrett, *The City of Brooklyn, 1865–1898* (New York, 1944), 182–86; Oliver R. Pilat, *Sodom by the Sea: An Affectionate History of Coney Island* (Garden City, N.Y., 1941), 66–70.

28. *Spirit* 114 (21 Jan. 1888): 872, 115 (28 Jan. 1888): 16; *Chicago Times*, 8 Feb. 1887, 22 Jan. 1888, 21 Aug. 1889; *NYT*, 1 Oct. 1892, 1 Oct. 1893; *New York World*, 25 Mar. 1916; Robertson, *Thoroughbred Racing*, 90–92; Parmer, *Gold and Glory*, 128; Chafetz, *Play the Devil*, 267.

29. *NYT*, 22 Oct. 5, 26, 29 Nov. 26 Dec. 1893; *Spirit* 127 (10 Feb. 1894): 127, 127 (24 Mar. 1894): 346; William E. Sackett, *Modern Battles of Trenton, Being a History of New Jersey's Politics and Legislation from the Year 1868 to the Year 1894* (Trenton, 1895), 385–88, 440–41, 444–49, 454–61; Samuel T. McSeveney, *The Politics of Depression: Political Behavior in the Northeast, 1893–1896* (New York, 1972), 45–48, 55–56, 62.

30. Bessie Louise Pierce, *A History of Chicago*, 3 vols. (Chicago, 1937–57), 3:477; *CDN*, 11 Oct., 8 Dec. 1884, 28 Jan. 1885; *Chicago Times*, 18, 29 July 1888, 31 Mar. 1889, 4, 8, 13–15, 19, 20 July, 7, 23 Aug. 1891; *NYT*, 21 July, 19

Dec. 1891; *Spirit* 120 (27 July 1890): 381, 121 (24 Jan. 1891): 1, 122 (25 July 1891): 2, 122 (19 Sept. 1891): 329–30, 122 (5 Dec. 1891): 717; Kogan and Wendt, *Lords of the Levee*, 27–30, 49–57, 109–10.

31. *NYT*, 24 Sept., 21 Oct., 9 Nov., 9 Dec. 1894, 12, 15, 22 Feb., 1, 22 Mar., 1, 3 Apr., 3, 10 May 1895.

32. *CDN*, 18 June 1885; *Chicago Times*, 11 May 1888, 20 Apr. 1889; *Spirit* 115 (21 Jan. 1888): 872; *NYT*, 4, 5 Jan. 1890, 15 Sept. 1891; Flavel Scott Mines, "The Study of a Pool-Room," *Harper's Weekly* 36 (17 Dec. 1892): 1210; Comstock, "Pool Rooms," 606–7.

33. John R. Betts, *America's Sporting Heritage, 1850–1950* (Reading, Mass., 1974), 72–74; Alvin Harlow, *Old Wires and New Waves: A History of the Telegraph, Telephone and Wireless* (New York, 1926), 280; *NYT*, 10 Mar. 1900. In one method of reporting results a wire service employee wrote down the race results, placed it into a hollowed-out ball, and threw it over the fence to a waiting confederate. Another technique was to send a female agent to the track with carrier pigeons hidden underneath her dress. After each race she would release a bird with the results pinned to its legs. *NYT*, 29, 30 May 1891.

34. See n. 32 above; *NYT*, Mar.–May, 24–25, 30 June, 2 Oct. 1891, 4 Feb., 14, 15, 18, 25 Mar., 18 Dec. 1893, 25 Dec. 1899, 23 Dec. 1900, 13 Oct., 13, 27 Dec. 1901, 31 Aug., 2 Dec. 1902, 5 Jan. 1907, 11 Feb. 1926; *Brooklyn Eagle*, 1, 22 Mar. 1893, 9 Nov. 1894; Josiah Flynt, "The Men behind the Pool-Rooms," *Cosmopolitan Magazine* 42 (Apr. 1907): 39–48, 46–47 (quote); John P. Quinn, *Gambling and Gambling Devices* (Canton, Ohio, 1912), 275–77, 281; Herbert Asbury, *Sucker's Progress: An Informal History of Gambling in America from the Colonies to Canfield* (New York, 1938), 451–57.

35. *NYT*, 18, 19 May, 20 July 1904; Flynt, "Men behind the Pool Rooms," 45–47; John Landesco, *Organized Crime in Chicago*, part 3 of the *Illinois Crime Survey*, 1929 (1929; rep. Chicago, 1968), 46–48, 50–61.

36. *NYT*, 2, 4, 5 Jan., 9 Apr. 1908; "The Breed of Horses and the Breed of Men," *Independent* 64 (20 Feb. 1908): 428–29; "The Governor's Crusade," ibid. 64 (12 Mar. 1908): 592–93; "Repulsed But Not Beaten," *Outlook* 88 (18 Apr. 1908): 845–56; "The End of Race-Track Gambling," ibid. 89 (20 June 1908): 354–55; Daniel W. McGuire, "Governor Hughes and the Race Track Gambling Issue: The Special Election of 1908," *Niagara Frontier* 18 (Winter 1971): 66–72; Robert F. Wessner, *Charles Evans Hughes: Politics and Reform in New York, 1905–1910* (Ithaca, 1967), 189–208.

37. *NYT*, 3 July, 8, 21 Nov. 1908, 10 Nov. 1909, 14, 21, 22 Apr., 5 May, 4, 16 June 1910, 22 Mar. 1911, 14 Oct. 1912, 22 Feb. 1913; Robertson, *Thoroughbred Racing*, 151.

38. Betts, *America's Sporting Heritage*, 266–67; Kirschner, *City and Country*, 109–11; Robertson, *Thoroughbred Racing*, 275.

39. Betts, *America's Sporting Heritage*, 267; Humbert S. Nelli, *The Business of Crime: Italians in American Syndicate Crime* (New York, 1976), 228–30; Edward C. Devereux, Jr, *Gambling and the Social Structure: A Sociological Study of Lotteries and Horse Racing in Contemporary America* (Salem, N.Y., 1980), 298, 344–45; Thomas B. Littlewood, *Horner of Illinois* (Evanston, 1969),

151–54; Hank Messick, *The Politics of Prosecution: James Thompson, Richard Nixon, Marge Everett, and the Trial of Otto Kerner* (Ottawa, Ill., 1978), 20–21.

40. "Yankee Putsch," *Newsweek* 10 (1 Nov. 1937): 12; Devereux, *Gambling*, 333–37, 345, 346; Lyle W. Dorsett, *The Pendergast Machine* (New York, 1968), 23. For a first-hand account of the political problems of a track operator in the 1960s, see Bill Veeck with Ed Linn, *Thirty Tons a Day* (New York, 1972), esp. chaps. 7, 8, 10.

41. Devereux, *Gambling*, 340–43; Bernard Postal, Jesse Silver, and Roy Silver, *Encyclopedia of Jews in Sports* (New York, 1965), 305–22; Littlewood, *Horner*, 51, 62, 67, 78, 93, 156, 206, 245; Messick, *Politics of Prosecution*, 20–29.

42. Devereux, *Gambling*, 331–33.

43. *NYT*, 15 Mar. 1954; Dwight Akers, *Drivers Up! The Story of American Harness Racing* (New York, 1947), 347–54.

44. *NYT*, 4–6, 14, 15 Mar., 4, 5 May, 12, 22 Oct. 1954. State Senator Dunnigan played a leading role in organizing the Buffalo Trotting Association, and between 1944 and 1954 his family earned $700,000 from stock deals. *NYT*, 6 Mar. 1954.

45. Nelli, *Business of Crime*, 229; U.S. Cong., House Select Committee on Crime, *Organized Crime in Sports (Racing)*, Hearings, 92nd Cong., 2nd sess. (Washington, D.C., 1973), 7 (hereafter cited as *Organized Crime in Sports*); Messick, *Politics of Prosecution*, 71. On the underworld and the harness tracks, see *NYT*, 3, 18, 19, 23, 30 Sept., 2, 3, 5 Oct. 1953; 6 Jan., 2, 13 Mar., 2, 10 Apr., 14 May, 21 Aug., 25 Sept., 13, 14 Oct. 1954, 5 Apr., 14 Aug. 1957.

46. Dan Parker, "Massachusetts Goes to the Dogs," *Saturday Evening Post* 212 (6 Jan. 1940): 16–17, 56–58; Devereux, *Gambling*, 290, 344–45; Richard L. Neuberger, "Oregon Goes to the Dogs," *Nation* 173 (8 Sept. 1951): 189–91.

47. Robertson, *Thoroughbred Racing*, 300; Bryan Field, "Horse Racing," in *Sport's Golden Age: A Close-Up of the Fabulous Twenties*, ed. Allison Danzig and Peter Brandwein (New York, 1948), 94–95; Mark Haller, "Bootleggers and American Gambling, 1920–1950," in *Gambling in America*, App. 1, Commission on the Review of the National Policy towards Gambling (Washington, D.C., 1976), 129–30 (hereafter cited as *Gambling in America*); *Organized Crime in Sports*, 2–3, 5, 7, 16–17, 319, 571, 750, 824, 840–42, 851–52, 857–58, 865–66, 1413, 1461, 1563–65, 1568.

48. Mark Haller, "The Changing Structure of American Gambling in the Twentieth Century," *Journal of Social Issues* 35, no. 3 (1979): 88, 91–92 (quote), 111. On gambling as a rational activity for working-class bettors, see Maureen Kallick et al., "Survey of American Gambling Attitudes and Behavior," in *Gambling in America*, 178–82; and Ross McKibbin, "Working-Class Gambling in Britain, 1880–1939," *Past and Present* 82 (Feb. 1979): 163–66.

49. Haller, "American Gambling," 91–92.

50. Ibid., 98–99; Katcher, *Big Bankroll*, 100–103.

51. Haller, "American Gambling," 101–3; Estes Kefauver, *Crime in America*, ed. Sidney Shalot (Garden City, N.Y., 1951), chap. 3.

52. Very little muckracking was done on the national pastime. See Hugh C.

Weir, "Baseball: The Men and the Dollars Behind It," *World Today* 17 (July 1909): 752–61; Edward Mott Woolley, "The Business of Baseball," *McClure's* 39 (July 1912): 241–56. For a review of the baseball ideology and a laudatory press in the Progressive era, see Riess, *Touching Base*, 17–26. Baseball was not immune to the problem of gambling, and certain seating areas were well known as betting sections, but after the Louisville scandal of 1877, most fans believed that the game was honest, at least until the Black Sox scandal in 1920 severely shook American sensibilities and confidence. See ibid., 62–63; Harold Seymour, *Baseball*, vol. 1, *The Early Years*, vol. 2, *The Golden Years* (New York, 1960–71), 1:87–88, 295, 2:chap. 14; David Q. Voigt, *American Baseball*, vol. 1, *From Gentlemen's Sport to the Commissioner System* (Norman, Okla., 1966), 38–39, 71–73, 82–83.

53. Ted Vincent, *Mudville's Revenge: The Rise and Fall of American Sport* (New York, 1981), 98–110, 125–28, 173–74, 176–77, 206–7, 210–14; Riess, *Touching Base*, 50–54, 66–68, 70–71.

54. Voigt, *American Baseball*, 1: chap. 3; Seymour, *Baseball*, 1:56–57; Adelman, *Sporting Time*, 170–72; Vincent, *Mudville's Revenge*, 127–29; Federal Writers Project, Illinois, *Baseball in Old Chicago* (Chicago, 1938), 11; Stephen Freedman, "The Baseball Fad in Chicago, 1865–1870: An Exploration of the Role of Sport in the Nineteenth Century," *JSpH* 5 (Summer 1978): 5–24. Chicago's success encouraged its commercial rival, St. Louis, to also promote baseball to prove its progressive and forward-looking character. See Gregg Lee Carter, "Baseball in Saint Louis, 1867–1875: An Historical Study of Civic Pride," *Missouri Historical Bulletin* 31 (July 1975): 253–63.

55. Seymour, *Baseball*, 1:59–60, 75–79; Voigt, *American Baseball*, 1:35–39; Vincent, *Mudville's Revenge*, 130–32.

56. Seymour, *Baseball*, 1:chap. 7, 86–89; Voigt, *American Baseball*, 1:chap. 5.

57. Seymour, *Baseball*, 1:139–47; Voigt, *American Baseball*, 1:121–30.

58. U.S. Congress, House Judiciary Committee, *Organized Baseball: Hearings before Subcommittee on Study of Monopoly Power*, 82nd Cong., 1st sess., 1951, ser. 1, pt. 6 (Washington, D.C., 1952), 1394, 1436–37, 1591; Seymour, *Baseball*, 1:104–20, 221–39, 269, 274; Voigt, *American Baseball*, 1:57–58, 232–33, 259, chap. 9; Lee Lowenfish and Tony Lupien, *The Imperfect Diamond: The Story of Baseball's Reserve System and the Men Who Fought to Change It* (New York, 1980), pt. 1; Riess, *Touching Base*, 54.

59. Riess, *Touching Base*, 54–55, 69–70, 76, 82n61, 84n78; Seymour, *Baseball*, 2:68–72; David Quentin Voigt, *American Baseball*, vol. 2, *From the Commissioners to Continental Expansion* (Norman, Okla., 1970), 108–9; U.S. Cong., *Organized Baseball*, 1599–1600, 1615; Wooley, "Business of Baseball," 241–56.

60. Vincent, *Mudville's Revenge*, 99–104, 106–7; Riess, *Touching Base*, 66–68; Seymour, *Baseball*, 1:214, 296–98; *DAB*, s.v., "Freedman, Andrew."

61. Riess, *Touching Base*, 67–73; Seymour, *Baseball*, 2:140. The Black Sox scandal erupted at a time when old-stock Americans were frightened about the future of "their" country and the maintenance of traditional values and beliefs in

a modern urbanized society. If the sport which epitomized the finest American qualities had been corrupted by Jewish gangsters (like Meyer Wolfsheim of F. Scott Fitzgerald's *Great Gatsby*), then the future looked bleak, particularly in the light of red scares, industrial unrest, and police strikes. On the Black Sox, see Eliot Asinof, *Eight Men Out: The Black Sox and the 1919 World Series* (New York, 1963), and Seymour, *Baseball*, 2:294–339; and on their symbolic importance, see Roderick Nash, *The Nervous Generation: American Thought, 1917–1930* (Chicago, 1970), 130–32.

62. Riess, *Touching Base*, 69, 71–73.

63. Ibid., 52, 58–63, 73–75, and 125–36 for the Sunday ball movement in New York.

64. Ibid., 60–61, 73–75.

Chapter Seven

1. Ted Vincent, *Mudville's Revenge: The Rise and Fall of American Sport* (New York, 1981), 45–53; John Cumming, *Runners & Walkers: A Nineteenth-Century Sports Chronicle* (Chicago, 1981), 85–94, 100–103; Fred Hawthorne, "Six-Day Bicycle Racing," in *Sport's Golden Age: A Close-Up of the Fabulous Twenties*, ed. Allison Danzig and Peter Brandwein (New York, 1948), 293–96. On boxing, see, e.g., William H. Adams, "New Orleans as the National Center of Boxing," *Louisiana Historical Quarterly* 39 (Jan. 1956): 92–112; Dale A. Somers, *The Rise of Sports in New Orleans, 1850–1900* (Baton Rouge, 1972), chap. 8; William M. Kramer and Norton B. Stern, "San Francisco's Fighting Jew," *California History* 53 (Winter 1974): 333–44; Steven A. Riess, "In the Ring and Out: Professional Boxing in New York, 1896–1920," in *Sport in America: New Historical Perspectives*, ed. Donald Spivey (Westport, Conn., 1985), 95–128; Thomas M. Croak, "The Professionalization of Prize-Fighting: Pittsburgh at the Turn of the Century," *Western Pennsylvania History Magazine* 62 (Oct. 1979): 333–43; Benjamin G. Rader, *American Sports: From the Age of Folk Games to the Age of Spectators* (Englewood Cliffs, N.J., 1983), 100; Jack Curley, "Boxing around Chicago in Those Good Old Days," *Ring* 5 (July 1926): 7; Charles H. Hermann, *Recollections of Life and Days in Chicago* (Chicago, 1945), 30–38; Elliott J. Gorn, *The Manly Art: Bare-Knuckle Prize Fighting in America* (Ithaca, 1986), 183–84.

2. Joseph Durso, *Madison Square Garden: 100 Years of History* (New York, 1979), 18–19, 41, 49.

3. John A. Lucas, "Pedestrianism and the Struggle for the Sir John Astley Belt, 1878–1879," *Research Quarterly* 39 (Oct. 1968): 587–95; Cumming, *Runners & Walkers*, 104; Daniel Boorstin, *The Americans: The Democratic Experience* (New York, 1974), 532 (quote); John R. Betts, *America's Sporting Heritage, 1850–1950* (Reading, Mass., 1974), 78.

4. Durso, *Madison Square Garden*, 49–50; P. F. Dibble, *John L. Sullivan: An Intimate Narrative* (Boston, 1925), 38, 40–41, 64–67; Gorn, *Manly Art*, 218–19. For accounts of Sullivan's fights at the Garden, see John L. Sullivan, *I Can Lick Any Sonofabitch in the House!* (New York, 1980), 75–76, 83–84, 87, 91–93,

120–27, Michael T. Isenberg, *John L. Sullivan and His America* (Urbana, Ill., 1988), 121–23, 134–38, 172–76, 178–82.

5. Durso, *Madison Square Garden*, 67–69 (quote is from *Harper's Weekly*), 71–73, 77–81; Charles DeKay, "The Madison Square Garden," *Harper's Weekly* 35 (18 July 1891): 542; Barnet Phillips, "The Construction of Great Buildings," ibid. 34 (12 April 1890): 282–83; "Madison Square Garden," ibid. 34 (13 Sept. 1890): 718; M. G. Van Rennsalaer, "The Madison Square Garden," *Century* 47 (Mar. 1894): 734, 740, 746–47; *NYT*, 17 June 1890 for the opening day ceremonies.

6. Durso, *Madison Square Garden*, 78, 82; DeKay, "Madison Square Garden," 542; *NYT*, 28 Feb., 1 Mar. 1900.

7. Riess, "In the Ring and Out," 97–112. See also *Brooklyn Eagle*, 24 Oct. 1896; *NYT*, 11, 20 June 1899, 25 Jan. 1900, 16 Nov. 1905, 1 June 1906, 2 Apr. 1907, 2 Nov., 18 Dec. 1908; *NPG* 69 (19 Sept., 7, 14 Nov. 1896): 10, 73 (18 Feb. 1899): 11, 95 (17 Feb. 1910):10, 96 (28 Apr. 1910): 10; "Prize-Fighting in New York," *Outlook* 99 (9 Sept. 1911): 56–57; William Inglis, "The State and the Boxing Business," *Harper's Weekly* 54 (16 Sept. 1911): 19; E. B. Osborn, "The Revival of Boxing," *Nineteenth Century* 70 (Oct. 1911): 771–81.

8. *NYT*, 9, 14, 15, 29 Mar. 1916, 13, 16 Aug., 18 Sept. 1920; *New York World*, 9, 10, 13, 26, 29 Mar. 1916; Richard J. Butler and Joseph Driscoll, *Dock Walloper: The Story of "Big Dick" Butler* (New York, 1928), 264; Mrs. Tex Rickard, *Everything Happened to Him: The Story of Tex Rickard* (New York, 1936), 274–75; Randy Roberts, *Jack Dempsey: The Manassa Mauler* (Baton Rouge, 1979), 95–99; Durso, *Madison Square Garden*, 115.

9. On the riotous tradition in boxing in mid-century, see, e.g., Gorn, *Manly Art*, 171–77. For examples of subsequent riots, see, e.g., *NPG* 63 (25 Nov. 1893): 10, 85 (10 Dec. 1904): 3; *Brooklyn Eagle*, 11 Mar. 1895; *NYT*, 24 Nov. 1904. Once in a rare while, rival ethnic groups would be won over by the bravery and skills of opponents from competing ethnicities. See, e.g., Steven A. Riess, "A Fighting Chance: The Jewish-American Boxing Experience," *American Jewish History* 74 (Mar. 1985): 230. For riotous behavior at a six-day marathon race, see *New York World*, 4 May 1884. For valuable explanations of riotous sporting crowd behavior, see Allen Guttmann, *Sports Spectators* (New York, 1986), 163–73; and Michael D. Smith, "Sport and Collective Behavior," in *Sport and the Social Order: Contributions to the Sociology of Sport*, ed. Donald W. Ball and John W. Loy (Reading, Mass., 1975), 277–330.

10. *NYT*, 31 Aug., 1, 2, 7, 16 Sept., 21 Dec. 1911, 13 Sept. 1913. For an early riot at Madison Square Garden, caused by overcrowding, see *New York World*, 6 May 1884.

11. Roberts, *Dempsey*, 119–20; Edward S. Jordan, "Buying Football Victories," *Collier's* 36 (2 Dec. 1905): 19; Robin Dale Lester, "The Rise, Decline and Fall of Intercollegiate Football at the University of Chicago, 1892–1939" (Ph.D. diss., University of Chicago, 1974), 32–54, 159, 161–63, 188–90; John A. Lucas and Ronald A. Smith, *Saga of American Sport* (Philadelphia, 1978), 247; Guy M. Lewis, "The American Intercollegiate Football Spectacle, 1875–1917" (Ph.D. diss., University of Maryland, 1963), 30–55.

12. Howard P. Chudacoff, *The Evolution of American Urban Society*, 2nd ed. (Englewood Cliffs, N.J., 1981), 81–84; David R. Goldfield and Blaine A. Brownell, *Urban America: From Downtown to No Town* (Boston, 1979), 205–8. For an excellent comparative account of mass transit in three major cities, see Charles W. Cheape, *Moving the Masses: Urban Transportation in New York, Boston and Philadelphia, 1880–1912* (Cambridge, 1980).

13. W. E. Harrington, "Report of the Committee on Promotion of Traffic," *Street Railway Journal* 30 (26 Oct. 1907): 864; Vincent, *Mudville's Revenge*, 45–49, 177–78; Betts, *America's Sporting Heritage*, 78; Clay McShane, *Technology and Reform: Street Railways and the Growth of Milwaukee, 1887–1900* (Madison, 1974), 32–33.

14. *NYT*, 10, 11 June 1871, 2 June 1872, 30 May 1903; *Brooklyn Eagle*, 20 Mar. 1892, 3, 5, 10 July 1894; *Spirit* 116 (22 Dec. 1888): 776; Francis Trevelyan, "The American Turf: The Race-Course of the East," *Outing* 20 (May 1892): 129–31; Stanley I. Fischler, *Moving Millions: An Inside Look at Mass Transit* (New York, 1979), 31–32; John R. Betts, "Organized Sport in Industrial America" (Ph.D. diss., Columbia University, 1951), 140n72.

15. Harold M. Meyer and Richard C. Wade, *Chicago: The Making of a Metropolis* (Chicago, 1969), 146; *Chicago Times*, 16 July 1888, 31 Mar. 1889, 13, 15, 20 July 1891; *Spirit* 114 (30 June 1888): 836, 119 (27 Sept. 1890): 381, 121 (23 May 1891): 786, 121 (30 May 1891): 840, 122 (19 Sept. 1891): 330.

16. David Black, *The King of Fifth Avenue: The Fortunes of August Belmont* (New York, 1981), 283–84; William H. P. Robertson, *The History of Thoroughbred Racing in America* (Englewood Cliffs, N.J., 1964), 150, 182–83; Charles B. Parmer, *For Gold and Glory: The Story of Thoroughbred Racing in America* (New York, 1939), 133; *Chicago Times*, 21 Aug. 1889, 7 Aug. 1891; *NYT*, 10 June 1871, 2 June 1872, 30 May 1917; *Spirit*, 121 (12 Jan. 1884): 720, 119 (25 Oct. 1890): 542, 121 (23 May 1891): 786, 121 (30 May 1891): 840, 121 (25 July 1891): 2.

17. *NYT*, 2 June 1891, 25 July 1893; *Chicago Times*, 18 July 1888, 3, 7 Aug. 1891; *New York Clipper* 28 (26 June 1880): 107; *New York Herald*, 7 Jan. 1917.

18. On the size of crowds, see e.g., *NYT*, 6 June, 14 Oct. 1870, 7 June 1891, 24 July 1893, 27 May, 17 June, 9 Sept. 1900, 5 May 1901. On the use of lights, see Somers, *Sports in New Orleans*, 100, who dates experimentation with artificial illumination back to 1881; and also *NPG* 44 (23 June 1884): 10; *Brooklyn Eagle*, 12 Sept. 1894; Parmer, *Gold and Glory*, 138.

19. On the perceived composition of crowds, see note 18, above; *Chicago Times*, 23 July 1887, 5 July 1888; *Spirit* 118 (7 June 1890): 865; *Brooklyn Eagle*, 31 Aug. 1892 (quote): *NYT*, 27 May 1900. For instances of disorder among travellers to and from Chicago's plebeian West Side Park, see *CDN*, 20 June 1885; and on disorder resulting from disgruntled bettors, see *NPG* 56 (16 Aug. 1890): 10; *Brooklyn Eagle*, 5 Sept. 1899.

20. Maurine Kallick et al., "Survey of American Gambling Attitudes and Behavior," in Commission on the Review of the National Policy towards Gambling, *Gambling in America*, App. 1 (Washington, D.C., 1976), 300.

21. Steven A. Riess, *Touching Base: Professional Baseball and American*

Culture in the Progressive Era (Westport, Conn., 1980), 101, 112n6, 116n44; Harold Seymour, *Baseball*, vol. 2, *The Golden Years* (New York, 1971), 68–71; Riess, "In the Ring and Out," 113–14, 127n46. Gunther Barth's essay, "Ball Park," in his *City People: The Rise of Modern City Culture in Nineteenth-Century America* (New York, 1980) provides an engaging view of that institution's role in promoting a homogeneous urban culture, but his conclusions, based on dubious assumptions, erroneous inferences, and factual misstatements, are unreliable. See my review in *JSpH* 8 (Summer 1981): 104–7.

22. Vincent, *Mudville's Revenge*, 175–79, 206–7; Harold Seymour, *Baseball*, vol. 1, *The Early Years* (New York, 1960), 214–15, 225–26; Riess, *Touching Base*, 49–52, 88.

23. Seymour, *Baseball*, 1:203, 225–27; Vincent, *Mudville's Revenge*, 177–78; Riess, *Touching Base*, 70–71, 88–89.

24. Riess, *Touching Base*, 85–89, 91–92, 112n8. In 1886 and 1887, the Metropolitans of the American Association played at a Staten Island amusement park owned by Erastus Wiman, who had purchased the club from the syndicate that had owned both the Mets and the Giants. Wiman, a millionaire who operated the ferry from Manhattan to the island, expected to profit from increased traffic. He was negotiating with the B&O R.R., which was going to make Staten Island its New York terminal, for rates for the use of his ferries and other facilities. The rates would be based on ferry traffic over a period of years, and thus Wiman had a big incentive to bolster the use of his ferries. See Seymour, *Baseball*, 1:214–16.

25. Riess, *Touching Base*, 85–87, 111nn2–4, 6; Federal Writers Project, Illinois, *Baseball in Old Chicago* (Chicago, 1938), 11; "The Chicago Base-ball Grounds," *Harper's Weekly* 27 (12 May 1883): 200; *ChiTrib*, 25 June 1884, 25 Feb., 31 May, 7 June 1885; Steven A. Riess, "Professional Baseball and American Culture in the Progressive Era: Myths and Realities, with Special Emphasis on Atlanta, Chicago, and New York" (Ph.D. diss., University of Chicago, 1974), 133–43; Philip J. Lowry, *Green Cathedrals* (Cooperstown, N.Y., 1986), 42. Three of Williamson's teammates also hit twenty or more home runs. One year later, Williamson hit only three homers playing in the more spacious Congress Street Grounds.

26. Riess, *Touching Base*, 86.

27. Ibid., 88, 94–95, 114n23; Seymour, *Baseball*, 2:50–51.

28. Riess, *Touching Base*, 95–96.

29. Ibid., 89–91, 97–98, 102–5, 107–8.

30. Seymour, *Baseball*, 2:49–54; Riess, *Touching Base*, 94–97, 99; David John Kammer, "Take Me Out to the Ballgame: American Cultural Values as Reflected in the Architectural Evolution and Criticism of the Modern Baseball Stadium" (Ph.D. diss., University of New Mexico, 1982), 84; see also Lowry, *Green Cathedrals*, chap. 2.

31. Kammer, "Take Me Out to the Ballgame," 87–89, 227; Riess, *Touching Base*, 95; Bill Shannon and George Kaminsky, *The Ballparks* (New York, 1975); Robert F. Bluthardt, "Fenway Park and the Golden Age of the Baseball Park," *Journal of Popular Culture* 21 (Summer 1987): 46; Philip Bess, "A Model for a New Chicago Ball Park" (paper delivered at the annual meeting of the Society of

American Baseball Researchers, 12 July 1986, Chicago, Ill.) On baseball's competition, see, e.g., Robert Sklar, *Movie-Made America* (New York, 1975), 45–46; Albert F. McLean, *American Vaudeville as Ritual* (Lexington, 1965), 193–210; John F. Kasson, *Amusing the Million: Coney Island at the Turn of the Century* (New York, 1978), 57–86; Lary May, *Screening Out the Past: The Birth of Mass Culture and the Motion Picture Industry* (Chicago, 1980), chaps. 1, 2; Perry Duis, *The Saloon: Public Drinking in Chicago and Boston, 1880–1920* (Urbana, Ill., 1983); Jon M. Kingsdale, "The 'Poor Man's Club': Social Functions of the Urban Working-Class Saloon," *AQ* 25 (Oct. 1973): 472–89.

32. Riess, *Touching Base*, 56–57, 97–99, 110, 118n69.

33. Ibid., 99, 100, 102–8; Ebbets to August Herrmann, 12 May 1912, August Herrmann Papers, National Baseball Library, Hall of Fame, Cooperstown, N.Y.; *NYT*, 7 Apr. 1912, 21 Feb. 1913, 19 Apr. 1925, 11 Feb., 15 Mar., 13 May 1915, 7 Feb. 1921, 19 Apr. 17 May 1923; Kammer, "Take Me Out to the Ball Game," 117–28.

34. Riess, *Touching Base*, 108.

35. Ibid., 97–100, 110; Robert Heuer, "Neighbors: The Cubs and the Community: Seven Decades of Love and Pain," *Chicago Reader* 14 (12 Apr. 1985): 11, 24, 26; Bluthardt, "Fenway Park," 50.

36. Riess, *Touching Base*, 98–100; Bluthardt, "Fenway Park," 50–51; *Sanborn Insurance Map of Chicago: Lakeview* (1894, 1922) (Chicago, 1894–1922); *Rascher Atlas of Chicago* (1891), vol. 9 (Chicago, 1891); *Olcott's Land Values Blue Book of Chicago, 1909–1930* (Chicago, 1909–30); George W. Bromley and Walter S. Bromley, *Atlas of the City of New York, Borough of Manhattan* (Philadelphia, 1905); *Atlas of the Borough of Manhattan* (1912) (New York, 1912); *Manhattan Land Book. City of New York* (1934) (New York, 1934); *Manhattan Land Book of the City of New York* (1955, 1971) (New York, 1955–1971); New York City, City Record Office, *Annual Record of Assessed Valuations of Real Estate in the City of New York: Supplement to the City Record, 1904–1930* (hereafter cited as Assessed Valuations).

37. Riess, *Touching Base*, 103–4; *Miniature Atlas of the Borough of Brooklyn* (1912) (New York, 1912); *Desk Atlas of the Borough of Brooklyn, City of New York* (1920) (New York, 1920); *Desk Atlas, Borough of Brooklyn, City of New York* (1929) (New York, 1929); *Assessed Valuations*, 1910–30.

38. Riess, *Touching Base*, 108–10; *Sporting News*, 7 Feb. 1929; *NYT*, 12 Apr. 1871; *Atlas of the Borough of the Bronx, Sections 9 to 13* (1912, 1928) (New York, 1912–1928); *Atlas of the City of New York, Borough of the Bronx* (1934) (Philadelphia, 1934); *Bronx Land Book of the City of New York* (1960, 1971) (New York, 1960–1971); Edwin Spengler, *Land Values in New York in Relation to Transit Facilities* (New York, 1930), 90–91, 165; *Assessed Valuations*, 1920–30.

39. *St. Louis Post-Dispatch*, 19 May 1883. See also the elite *Boston Evening Transcript*, 22 Sept. 1887, which identified the baseball crowd as comprised of "the merchant and banker, the salesman, clerk and office boy, the contractors and his men and boys on Saturday half-holidays, [and] even women and girls by the hundreds."

40. The Survey Committee of the Cleveland Foundation, *Cleveland Recreation Survey*, vol. 5, *Commercial Recreation* (Cleveland, 1920), 125–29; *Cleveland Plain-Dealer*, 20, 21 Sept. 1914.

41. U.S. Congress, House Judiciary Committee, *Organized Baseball*, Hearings before Subcommittee on Study of Monopoly Power, 82nd Cong., 1st sess., 1951, ser. 1, pt. 6 (Washington, D.C., 1952), 1394, 1436–37, 1591 (hereafter cited as *Organized Baseball*); David Q. Voigt, *American Baseball*, vol. 1, *From Gentleman's Sport to the Commissioner System* (Norman, Okla., 1966), 117, 181, 268–69.

42. *Organized Baseball*, 1394, 1436–37, 1591, 1593, 1616–19.

43. Voigt, *American Baseball*, 1:64–65, 295–96; Riess, *Touching Base*, 27–28, 59–60. This is not to imply the sport has been riot free but that crowds rarely get out of control except under the most unusual circumstances, such as the infamous Beer Night at Cleveland's Municipal Stadium (4 June 1974) when beer was sold for five cents a cup. The game was halted in the last of the ninth in a tied game when drunken fans took over the field. The result was a forfeit. There are also the annual riots of joy when teams win pennants or championships, but in this case the problem is usually outside the ballpark in city streets.

44. Voigt, *American Baseball*, 1:286–88; Seymour, *Baseball*, 1:340–41; *NYT*, 9 Aug. 1884; David Q. Voigt, *American Baseball*, vol. 2, *From the Commissioners to Continental Expansion* (Norman, Okla., 1970), 101.

45. Guttmann, *Sports Spectators*, 106–8, chaps. 7, 8; Smith, "Sport and Collective Violence," 305–6; Janet Lever, *Soccer Madness* (Chicago, 1983), 5, 16, 30, 69, 126–28.

46. Riess, *Touching Base*, 60; *Brooklyn Eagle*, 13 Apr. 1912. A riot occurred on Opening Day 1907 at the Polo Grounds. The reform police commissioner had refused to assign city police to patrol the park, which was private property, and the Giants failed to hire any private security. At the beginning of the ninth inning, many of the 17,000 spectators swarmed onto the playing field and refused to leave. Umpire Bill Klem had to declare the game a forfeit. See *NYT*, 13 Apr. 1907; Seymour, *Baseball*, 2:63; Riess, *Touching Base*, 74. For other instances when special police could not cope with frightening crowds, see newspaper clippings dated 30 May 1907, Henry Chadwick Diaries, Albert G. Spalding Collection, New York Public Library; *Chicago Record-Herald*, 22 May 1907; *NYT*, 23 Apr. 1908, 28 June, 10, 12 Oct. 1911, 16 Aug. 1920; *New York Tribune*, 17 Apr. 1911; *Brooklyn Eagle*, 13 Apr. 1912; *Atlanta Constitution*, 31 Aug. 1919.

Chapter Eight

1. Larry Fox, *Illustrated History of Basketball* (New York, 1974), 46–57; Ted Vincent, *Mudville's Revenge: The Rise and Fall of American Sport* (New York, 1981), 247–54.

2. Glenn Dickey, *The History of Professional Basketball since 1896* (New York, 1982), 25–31; Fox, *Basketball*, 57; Vincent, *Mudville's Revenge*, 281–82, 289–90.

3. Dickey, *Basketball*, 37–42; Vincent, *Mudville's Revenge*, 291–305; James

Quirk and Mohamed El Hodiri, "The Economic Theory of a Professional Sports League," in *Government and the Sports Business*, ed. Roger G. Noll (Washington, D.C., 1974), 49–50.

4. Tom Bennett et al., *The NFL's Official Encyclopedic History of Professional Football* (New York, 1979), 21, 23–25; Quirk and Hodiri, "Professional Sports," 48; Harry A. March, *Pro Football: Its Ups and Downs* (New York, 1934), 98, 99; William Gundelunas and Stephen R. Crouch, "The Stolen Championship of the Pottsville Maroons: A Case Study of the Emergence of Modern Professional Football," *JSptH* 9 (Spring 1982): 53–64.

5. George Halas with Gwen Moran and Arthur Veysey, *Halas by Halas* (New York, 1979), 94; Bernie Parrish, *They Call It a Game* (New York, 1971), 198; Rob Ruck, "Sandlot Seasons: Sport in Black Pittsburgh" (Ph.D. diss., University of Pittsburgh, 1983), 420–30; Ted Vincent, "Breaking Strikes with Sports Teams" (unpublished paper in author's possession), 2, 49–50.

6. Bennett, *NFL*, 55–57.

7. Ibid., 38.

8. Quirk and Hodiri, "Professional Sports," 50–51, 79–80.

9. Bill Veeck with Ed Linn, *The Hustler's Handbook* (New York, 1965), 270–85; U.S. Cong., House Judiciary Committee, *Organized Baseball, Hearings before Subcommittee on Study of Monopoly Power*, 82nd Cong., 1st sess, 1951, ser. 1, pt. 6 (Washington, D.C., 1952), 1616–19 (hereafter cited as *Organized Baseball*); Ira Horowitz, "Sports Broadcasting," in Noll, *Government*, 291.

10. David Quentin Voigt, *American Baseball*, vol. 3, *From Postwar Expansion to the Electronic Age* (University Park, Penn., 1983), xxiv–xxv.

11. Lee Lowenfish, "A Tale of Many Cities: The Westward Expansion of Major League Baseball in the 1950's," *Journal of the West* 17 (July 1978): 74–75.

12. Between 1952 and 1956 the Dodgers averaged $371,800 in profits—about $2,000 more than the Braves. But if we just count the Milwaukee years, then the Braves averaged $478,000 in profits. In 1955 the Braves earned $807,395—nearly double the Dodgers' $427,195, which was the second greatest profit in the major leagues. But in the next season, after the Dodgers had won the World Series, they surpassed all teams with $487,462. Computed from table in U.S. Cong., House Judiciary Committee, *Organized Professional Team Sports, Hearings before the Antitrust Subcommittee of the House Committee on the Judiciary*, 95 Cong., 1st sess. (Washington, D.C., 1958), 353. See also Cary S. Henderson, "Los Angeles and the Dodger War, 1957–1962," *Southern California Quarterly* 62 (Fall 1980): 263. For the most detailed analysis of the Dodgers' migration, see Neil J. Sullivan, *The Dodgers Move West* (New York, 1987). This controversial book argues that O'Malley earnestly tried to stay in Brooklyn but was stymied by an uncooperative municipal leadership. Sullivan then goes on to applaud O'Malley's foresight and vision in moving to virgin territory in Los Angeles. I agree with most historians who found O'Malley's actions far less benign than Sullivan represents them.

13. Lowenfish, "Tale of Many Cities," 73–74; Henderson, "Dodger War," 263–65; Norris Poulson, "The Untold Story of Chavez Ravine," *Los Angeles* 3

(Apr. 1962): 15–16; idem, "Memoirs," Department of Oral History, Research Library, UCLA, Los Angeles, Calif.; U.S. Cong., *Team Sports*, 1853–86.

14. Lowenfish, "Tale of Many Cities," 78–79.

15. Ibid., 79; Henderson, "Dodger War," 267–85; Poulson, "Chavaz Ravine," 16–17, 50; idem, "Memoirs," 337–50, 367–74.

16. Henderson, "Dodger War," 285–86; Thomas S. Hines, "Housing, Baseball, and Creeping Socialism: The Battle of Chavez Ravine, Los Angeles, 1949–1959," *Journal of Urban History* 8 (Feb. 1982): 123–43. On the negative impact on Brooklyn, see, e.g., Lowenfish, "Tale of Many Cities," 80; U.S. Cong., *Team Sports*, 1815–16.

17. Richard Beddoes, Stan Fischler, and Ira Gitler, *Hockey: The Story of the World's Fastest Sport* (New York, 1971), 81–87; Voigt, *American Baseball*, 3:112, 114; Gary Davidson, *Breaking the Game Wide Open* (New York, 1974), 32, 61, 154. Of course such start-up costs may seem like a bargain compared to recent purchases of the Mets for $40 million (and the repurchase in 1986 for $100 million) or the Cowboys for $80 million.

18. Horowitz, "Sports Broadcasting," 289, 298–99.

19. Benjamin A. Okner, "Subsidies of Stadiums and Arenas," in Noll, *Government*, 325–26.

20. *NYT*, 27 Aug. 1971, 24 Mar., 17 Aug. 1972, 17 July 1975; Robert Lipsyte, "A Diamond in the Ashes," *Sports Illustrated* 44 (26 Apr. 1976): 43 (quote). For a critical analysis of stadium subsidies, see Robert A. Baade, *Is There an Economic Rationale for Subsidizing Sports Stadiums?* Heartland Policy Study no. 13 (Chicago, 1987).

21. Ray Kennedy and Nancy Williamson, "Money in Sports, Part 1," *Sports Illustrated* 49 (17 July 1978): 71–72 (quote); Okner, "Subsidies of Stadiums," 328, 344n31, 346; Charles G. Burck, "It's Promoters vs. Taxpayers in the Superstadium Game," *Fortune* 87 (Mar. 1973): 106, 180, 182; Thomas Karnes, "Promises, Promises: Stadium Politics and the Public" (paper delivered at the annual convention of the North American Society for Sport History, 26 May 1979, Banff, Alb.).

22. Burck, "Superstadium Game," 106; Mark S. Rosentraub and Samuel R. Nunn, "Suburban City Investment in Professional Sports; Estimating the Fiscal Returns of the Dallas Cowboys and Texas Rangers to Investor Communities," *American Behavioral Scientist* 21 (Jan./Feb. 1978): 393. In 1987, one-fifth of the NBA (21.7 percent) and the American cities in the NHL (21.4 percent) played in suburban arenas, but just one-eighth (12.5 percent) of the American major league baseball teams played in suburban ballparks. Only four new major league fields have been built in the last fifteen years, and the two new American sites (Seattle's Kingdome and the Humphrey Metrodome in Minneapolis) were located in cities. A far different pattern occurred in professional football, where nearly one-third of the stadiums (32.1 percent) were located in the suburbs, including seven of the thirteen sites built since 1970 (53.8 percent). These facilities are only used for eight regular season games plus exhibitions and playoffs and consequently don't have to be centrally located.

23. *NYT*, 8, 29 Jan. 1984, 26 Apr. 1986, 24 Jan. 1989; "Houses with Holes," *Sports Illustrated* 28 (4 Mar. 1968): 9.

24. Kennedy and Williamson, "Money in Sports," 71–72; Thomas L. Karnes, "Stadiums and Politics" (paper delivered at the fourth annual Canadian Symposium on the History of Sport and Physical Education, 24 June 1979, Vancouver, B.C.), 4–9; Voigt, *American Baseball* 3:119.

25. Burck, "Superstadium," 105–6; "Domed Stadium: Spurt to City's Economy: Houston's Astrodome," *U.S. News & World Report* 59 (11 October 1965): 10; David John Kammer, "Take Me Out to the Ballgame: American Cultural Values as Reflected in the Architectural Evolution and Criticism of the Modern Baseball Stadium" (Ph.D. diss., University of New Mexico, 1982), chap. 5; George Lipsitz, "Sports Stadia and Urban Development: A Tale of Three Cities," *Journal of Sport and Social Issues* 8 (Summer/Fall 1984): 10–13.

26. Burck, "Superstadium," 105–7, 178–82; Kennedy and Williamson, "Money in Sports," 72; Kearns, "Stadiums and Politics," 8–10.

27. Roger G. Noll, "The U.S. Team Sports Industry: An Introduction," in Noll, *Government*, 29–32; Okner, "Subsidies," 335–43.

28. Kennedy and Williamson, "Money in Sports," 71–72.

29. Okner, "Subsidies," 328, 344n31, 345; Karnes, "Promises," 11–13.

30. Rosentraub and Nunn, "Suburban City Investment," 393, 401–12; Donald Chipman, Randolph Campbell, and Robert Cavert, *The Dallas Cowboys and the NFL* (Norman, Okla., 1970), 145–49.

31. *ChiTrib*, 28 Sept. 1985; Karnes, "Promises," 4–5; Lipsyte, "Diamond in the Ashes," 41.

32. *ChiTrib*, 17 Nov. 1985; Lipsitz, "Sports Stadia and Urban Development," 3–7.

33. Noll, "Team Sports Industry," 13, 16–19, 22–29; Roger G. Noll, "Attendance and Price Setting," in Noll, *Government*, 137–38; Benjamin G. Rader, *American Sports: From the Age of Folk Games to the Age of Spectators* (Englewood Cliffs, N.J., 1983), 258.

34. Noll, "Attendance," 115–20, 141–46.

35. Ibid., 126–28, 133–34. In the period 1951–57 the Knickerbockers were the only NBA team to show a profit. The most unprofitable teams in ascending order were Fort Wayne, Minneapolis, Rochester, Syracuse, St. Louis, and Boston. Philadelphia's financial records were not reported. U.S. Cong., *Team Sports*, 2938.

36. Noll, "Attendance," 122–23, 127–28, 139–40, 144–45.

37. Ibid., 123–24.

38. Ibid., 134–36. In 1981, sixteen of twenty-three teams lost money, yet salaries continued to rise, reaching an average of $300,000 in the mid-1980s. But unlike the previous decade, revenues outpaced costs as the sport boomed. Between 1981 and 1984 gross revenues rose from $108 million to $191 million. Consequently, by 1984 fifteen teams made money, and all teams were expected to make money in 1985. On this dramatic turnabout, see Brenton Welling, Jonathan Tasini, and Don Cook, "Basketball: Business Is Booming," *Business Week*, 4 Mar. 1985, 75–76.

39. Noll, "Attendance," 120–22, 124–26, 136–37, 140; Voigt, *American Baseball*, 3:283–84.

40. Noll, "Attendance," 124.

41. Ibid., 128–29, 140.

42. Ibid., 129–30. The fears of white fans attending Comiskey Park, which was adjacent to Chicago's Black Belt, go back to the 1910s. See, e.g., James T. Farrell, *A World I Never Made* (New York, 1936), 12.

43. David Quentin Voigt, *American Baseball*, vol. 2, *From the Commissioners to Continental Expansion* (Norman, Okla., 1971), 230–34; Frederick W. Cozens and Florence S. Stumpf, *Sports in American Life* (Chicago, 1953), 145–46, 151–52; Horowitz, "Sports Broadcasting," 285–86, 290–92, 306–9; Rader, *American Sports*, 254–58.

44. Horowitz, "Sports Broadcasting," 284–85, 287, 296–97; Rader, *American Sports*, 286–87; Voigt, *American Baseball*, 3:108.

45. Horowitz, "Sports Broadcasting," 298–99.

46. Kennedy and Williamson, "Money in Sports," 76.

Index